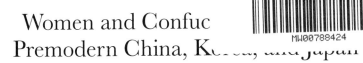

# Women and Confuc
## Premodern China, Korea, and Japan

# Women and Confucian Cultures in Premodern China, Korea, and Japan

EDITED BY

Dorothy Ko,
JaHyun Kim Haboush,
and Joan R. Piggott

UNIVERSITY OF CALIFORNIA PRESS

*Berkeley    Los Angeles    London*

University of California Press
Berkeley and Los Angeles, California

University of California Press, Ltd.
London, England

Library of Congress Cataloging-in-Publication Data

Women and Confucian cultures in premodern China, Korea, and Japan /
edited by Dorothy Ko, JaHyun Kim Haboush, and Joan R. Piggott.
  p. cm.
Includes bibliographical references and index.
  ISBN 0-520-23105-8 (cloth : alk. paper)—ISBN 0-520-23138-4 (pbk. :
alk. paper)
  1. Women—China—History. 2. Women—Japan—History. 3. Women—
Korea—History. 4. Confucianism—Social aspects. I. Ko, Dorothy.
II. Haboush, JaHyun Kim. III. Piggott, Joan R.
HQ1767 .W64 2003
305.4'0951—dc21                                              2003001855

Manufactured in the United States of America

12  11  10  09  08  07  06  05  04  03
10  9  8  7  6  5  4  3  2  1

The paper used in this publication meets the minimum requirements of
ANSI/NISO Z39.48-1992 (R 1997) (Permanence of Paper). ♾

# CONTENTS

# ILLUSTRATIONS AND TABLES

*vii*

MUSIC EXAMPLES

TABLES

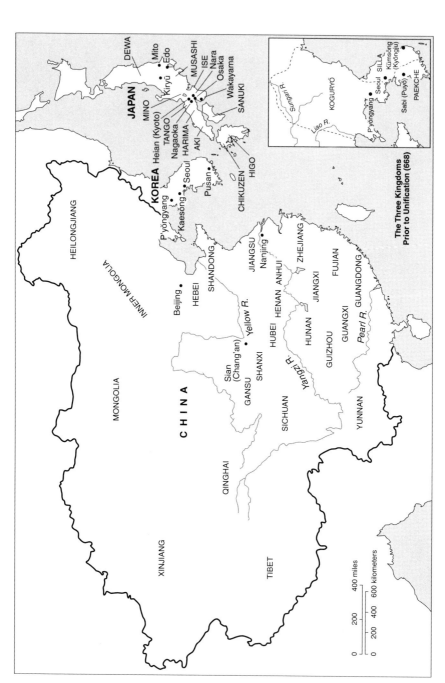

DEWA

Mito
Edo
Kiryū  MUSASHI
MINO  ISE
TANGO  Nara
JAPAN  Nagaoka  Osaka  Wakayama
Heian (Kyoto)  HARIMA  SANUKI
KOREA  AKI

Seoul
P'yŏngyang  Pusan
Kaesŏng  CHIKUZEN  HIGO

HEILONGJIANG

INNER MONGOLIA

Beijing
HEBEI
SHANDONG
JIANGSU
Nanjing
ZHEJIANG
MONGOLIA  ANHUI
HENAN  FUJIAN
Sian  HUBEI  JIANGXI
(Chang'an)  SHANXI  HUNAN
GANSU  Yellow R.  GUANGDONG
C H I N A  Pearl R.
GUIZHOU  GUANGXI
SICHUAN
Yangzi R.
QINGHAI  YUNNAN

XINJIANG

TIBET

The Three Kingdoms
Prior to Unification (668)

Sungari R.
KOGURYŎ  SILLA
Liao R.  Kŭmsŏng  (Kyŏngju)
Seoul
P'yŏngyang  Sabi (Puyŏ)  PAEKCHE

0  200  400 miles
0  200  400  600 kilometers

Premodern East Asia

# PREFACE

This book is the product of collaboration across many boundaries; no individual could have written it alone. It is a companion volume to *Under Confucian Eyes*, a collection of documents on gender in Chinese history also published by the University of California Press and edited by Susan Mann and Yu-Yin Cheng. Both grow out of a long-term project seeking to rethink Confucianism in East Asia by using gender as a category of analysis. Planning began in September 1994, when Susan Mann convened a workshop in Davis, California, funded by the Joint Committee on Chinese Studies of the Social Science Research Council (SSRC) and the American Council of Learned Societies, as well as the SSRC's East Asia Regional Research Working Group. The colleagues who attended the workshop laid the groundwork for the documents collection and began planning an international conference.

In summer 1996 more than thirty invited scholars participated in a three-day conference at the La Jolla campus of the University of California, San Diego (UCSD), where Dorothy Ko was teaching at the time. This conference received support from a host of agencies. From within the University of California system, funding was provided by the Pacific Rim Research Program, the Humanities Research Institute, and the Council for East Asian Studies of UCSD. We are particularly grateful to Patricia O'Brien, Martha Kendall Winnacker, and Joshua Fogel for their personal encouragement. In addition, we acknowledge the generous and timely support from the Social Science Research Council and the Cressant Foundation.

The scholars who gathered in La Jolla came from Britain, China, Hong Kong, Japan, Korea, and the United States. We were relieved to find that language differences did not constitute a barrier. In fact, some non-native speakers of English were the most enthusiastic leaders in discussions. This is in large part due to the excellent simultaneous interpretation provided by a highly competent team during the four days: Madeleine Yue Dong for Chinese and Hiromi Mizuno and Elizabeth Leicester for Japanese. Jenny Heying Zhan helped with informal Chinese interpretation, and Sherri Bayouth provided assistance with Japanese.

The cultural and intellectual assumptions each of us brought to the table posed a bigger challenge. This was not only because a host of disciplines were represented—classics, history, literature, music, and religious studies—but also because of the divergent history and conventions of each discipline in each country. Negotiating these differences became an edifying experience. We hope that the pages that follow convey a sense of the excitement we felt and the intellectual possibilities such conversations opened up.

Many colleagues have contributed to the success of the meetings and the production of this volume. Beverly Bossler, Yu-Yin Cheng, Clara Wing-Chung Ho, Kate Wildman Nakai, Vivian-Lee Nyitray, Reiko Shinno, Hitomi Tonomura, and Anne Walthall presented papers that are not included here. Many also led workshops to facilitate boundary-crossing discussions during the conference. These and other colleagues gave generously of their time and expertise in reading drafts, sending international faxes, and helping with translation and editing. Charlotte Furth, the main discussant at the conference, has been a critical source of inspiration and support.

Graduate students were integral to the project from the start. We are particularly grateful to Yu-Yin Cheng and Reiko Shinno for their leadership roles in the organizing collective. In addition, Mark Eykholt, Michael Chang, and Susan Fernsebner served as rapporteur, gofer, chauffeur, and photographer to ensure the smooth running of the conference. The six invited graduate student fellows in La Jolla, chosen from a national competition, made a difference in numerous ways. They are Neil Katkov, Christine Kim, Beth G. Lyon, Hiromi Maeda, Margaret Mar, Grace May, and Jenny Heying Zhan. Christine Kim and Jenny Zhan sacrificed sleep and holidays retranslating drafts of papers. Other graduate students contributed to the translation of papers at various stages and in different capacities: Sherri Bayouth, Yu-Yin Cheng, Yuki Terazawa, and Hye-June Park. The future belongs to them.

# NOTES ON CONVENTIONS

In this book the personal names of Asian men and women are usually given with family name first, for example, Zang Jian. One exception is that the Asian authors of chapters in this book are listed by given name and then family name, for example, Jian Zang, in the Contents and on the chapter opening pages.

It is customary for scholars of Japan to refer to famous historical and literary figures by their first names. Hence Tsuda Ume is often called Ume. The family name can be ascertained from context.

All references to age in this book are by Asian reckoning, which assumes a person to be one year old at birth.

Chinese names and terms, when cited in the text, appear in the Pinyin system of romanization. We have not, however, changed the names in the Wade-Giles system that appear in published book titles. Hence in the text we may speak of the "Family Instructions of the Yan Clan" compiled by Yan Zhitui. The standard English translation of this text, given in the notes, reads "Family Instructions of the Yen Clan" by Yen Chih-t'ui.

Korean names and terms appear in the McCune-Reischauer system. Exceptions are made for contemporary persons who prefer their names to be romanized in their own personal fashion. Thus Hai-soon Lee instead of Hyesun Yi.

We use a standard list of English titles for the Confucian classics and didactic books across the region. Standardized titles allow the reader to see, for instance, that the *Classic of Filial Piety* was popular in China, Korea, and Japan. It does not automatically mean, however, that the texts translated and published in Korea and Japan are the same as the Chinese classic bearing the same name.

Translations of Chinese official titles follow those in Charles O. Hucker, *A Dictionary of Official Titles in Imperial China* (Stanford: Stanford University Press, 1985). Translations of Korean and Japanese titles follow conventional usage.

|  | CHINA | KOREA | JAPAN |
|---|---|---|---|

Years (top to bottom): 1100, 1000, 900, 800, 700, 600, 500, 400, 300, 200, 100, 0, 100, 200, 300, 400, 500, 600, 700, 800, 900, 1000, 1100, 1200, 1300, 1400, 1500, 1600, 1700, 1800, 1900

**CHINA**
- Zhou Dynasty
- Qin Dynasty
- Han Dynasty
- Three Kingdoms / Six Dynasties
- Sui Dynasty
- Tang Dynasty
- Five Dynasties
- Song Dynasty
- Yuan Dynasty
- Ming Dynasty
- Qing Dynasty

**KOREA**
- Three Kingdoms Period
- Unified Silla Dynasty
- Koryŏ Dynasty
- Chosŏn Dynasty

**JAPAN**
- Nara Period
- Heian Period
- Kamakura Period
- Ashikaga Period
- Tokugawa Period

Comparative Time Chart for China, Korea, and Japan

# Introduction

*Dorothy Ko, JaHyun Kim Haboush, and Joan R. Piggott*

The purpose of this book is to open up a new field and a new way of viewing East Asian societies and histories. The old stereotype construes Asian women as victims of tradition, or Confucian patriarchy. Our premise is that to correct this simplistic picture we need to recognize that neither "woman" nor "Confucian tradition" is a uniform or timeless category. To restore both female subjectivity and historical complexity, the authors of each chapter begin by examining Asian categories and terms of analysis. They then analyze the complex constellations of constraint and opportunity shaping the lives of men and women in China, Korea, and Japan from the seventh to the nineteenth century.

At the heart of this book are women in these premodern societies, illuminated by the cultures that made them and the worlds they made. We strive, with various degrees of success, to understand the concrete processes of female subject formation and to recover textures of female everyday lives in specific historical locations. Neither rebels nor victims, these women appear as agents of negotiations who embraced certain aspects of official norms while resisting others. In other words, our goal is to situate women at center stage and then cast a spotlight on the complex constellations and trajectories of their subjectivities.

## THE CENTRALITY OF GENDER

Many of these women are known by their kinship roles instead of their personal names: marriage partner, mother, daughter, widow. Others are marked by their formal and informal power: female sovereigns in early Japan, seductive musicians in China, queens and princesses of Korea, authors, teachers. Still others are fictional tropes and ideal types, flesh and blood transformed into moral exemplars: the chaste widow, the filial child, the faithful wife. Many are commoner daughters, but it is hardly surprising that those whose lives were preserved in the archives with structure and texture are women from elite families. In avoiding blanket statements about an abstract womanhood, we have taken the caution to heart that women are as divided by class, age, and geography as they are united by shared gender. Yet it is undeniable that what we term here "the Confucian discourse" envisioned a universal and undifferentiated womanhood, defined as the mutually constitutive Other of manhood.

To illuminate both the multiple locations of women and the singularity of womanhood, the contributors to this volume have adopted an array of strategies for analyzing gender. As recent scholars have used "gender" in a confusing variety of ways, we wish to clarify the terms and approaches of our inquiries. First, in focusing on gender, our goal is to return women to the center of historical analysis. In this sense "gender" implies a focus on "women." Because of a long history of neglect, we have yet to command a full picture of even the rudimentary facts about women's locations in history and society. How prevalent were uxorilocal marriages in early Japan? What books did daughters in Chosŏn Korea read? How did the cult of chastity in China change the expectations and behavior of widows?

In correcting this situation by focusing on women, we do not intend to suggest that the contours of their lives can be understood in isolation. Indeed, the second and most prevalent meaning of "gender" used in this book is "male-female relations," on individual and institutional levels. In asking questions about the contexts of women's lives, we see gendered relations as relations of power that were made in processes of negotiation. In this regard, we have found the state—staffed by pragmatic officials intending to centralize power and by idealistic scholars bent on civilizing society—an unusually active agent shaping terms of gender interactions. In propagating laws as well as canonical and didactic texts, the state was instrumental in naming the category "woman" and defining norms of womanhood. In emphasizing this fact, we walk a fine line between highlighting the hegemonic power of structures and emphasizing women's agency. We hope that in our formulation of gender as a product of negotiation, we manage to avoid exaggerating oppression or romanticizing resistance.

To avoid simplification, we find it important to highlight not only the contexts but also the texts of women's lives. In this connection we evoke a third aspect of gender important to some of our authors, that of "female subjectivities." In using the term "subjectivity" we seek to shift analytic focus from external structures to interior motives, identity formation, and perceptions of the world, always a vexing terrain for historians.[1] We face an additional difficulty in that we need other terms than those provided by the modern Euro-American understanding of the gendered self—the dualities of self-other, discipline-freedom, mind-body, and sexual pleasure–procreation, to name a few—in discussing premodern East Asia.[2] We do not have the space to treat this problem in full in this volume. Suffice it to say that it is productive to begin investigation into female subjectivities by locating the female body in space and in practice—in short, by focusing on woman's embodied self and the social processes of embodiment.

Whatever the specific usage of "gender," we hope that the chapters in this volume will open our readers' eyes to the marginality of women in the historical and textual traditions in premodern China, Korea, and Japan. This very marginality renders it difficult yet vital to conduct gender-focused analysis.

## THE PROBLEM OF CONFUCIANISM

A major obstacle to our project of making women visible is the real and alleged power of "Confucianism" to subjugate women, resulting in their erasure from official discourses and records. And yet, however we define it, Confucianism was by no means the only ideological and cultural force that shaped the lives of East Asian women and men. This is obviously true for Korea and Japan, where imported Chinese institutions and texts were superimposed on native social structures. Even in China, the Confucian discourse had to compete with other philosophical and ethical systems with equally universalist claims, often subsumed under the rubrics "Buddhism" and "Daoism."

On the most basic level, what "Confucianism" means is simple: premodern Korean and Japanese scholars viewed it as a cluster of ethical ideals articulated in the Chinese classics as well as the texts themselves. The composition of the classical canon, however, was subject to debate in and out of China. Interpretations of and commentaries on the classics, too, changed through time, as did political and cultural institutions modeled on them. To highlight its dynamic and word-based nature, we often use the term "Confucian discourse." Because our primary goal is not to define the boundaries of Confucianism but to highlight its relevance for gender, we are not concerned with issues of orthodoxy except in passing. Recognizing that the meaning of being Confucian shifts with time, locale, and vantage point, our working assumption is that there is not one but many Confucianisms. All made an indelible impact on women's lives.

Although Confucianism is such an amorphous and ahistorical concept, we opt to adopt it with caution rather than discard it. A major reason is that the term still exercises enormous rhetorical power on scholarly and popular minds. There is a long history of using "Confucianism" as a shorthand for something less amenable to a simplistic narrative: Chinese civilization, secret of Asian economic success, or obstacle to modernization.[3] The historian Lionel Jensen has shown that the Latinized label "Confucianism" and probably even the name "Confucius" itself had no commonly recognized Chinese counterparts. They were manufactured by Jesuit missionaries in sixteenth- and seventeenth-century China, hence imparting coherence to highly complex native systems of thoughts and practice.[4] The Jesuits' positive assessments of Chinese culture notwithstanding, the making of Confucianism into a symbol and Confucius into an icon distorts by simplification. For recent examples of similar distortions one only has to look to the scholarly and journalistic treatises expounding the contributions of Confucianism to the Asian economic miracle in the early 1990s. We were spared only when the bubble burst.[5]

Even more powerful than the Jesuits' vision of sagely philosopher kings is the modern nationalistic image of Confucianism as ossified tradition. The rise of nationalism created an evil twin to the earlier benign image, both equally totalizing. The multiplicities and contradictions within the Confucian tradition were elided; Confucianism became a stand-in for whatever undesirable baggage seemed to impede progress, be it authoritarianism or feudalism.[6] That Confucianism had to be vilified in modern East Asia is in part because the modern nation is an artificial community that is extremely difficult to conceive. In twentieth-century Korea, Japan, and China, this arduous process and its attendant state-building enterprise were facilitated by the identification of two enemies: tradition and colonialism. From this perspective, the "failure" of Confucianism was in fact highly productive. Indeed, it would not be an exaggeration to say that without Confucianism there would be no modern national subject.

To Euro-American and Asian critics alike, the failure of Confucianism was manifested most blatantly in its oppression of women. Confucianism became synonymous with patriarchy, and "victim" became the universal name for East Asian women. In investigating the complicated relationships between Confucianism and women before the nineteenth century, we are performing a delicate balancing act. We find the singular term "Confucianism" simplistic but recognize its rhetorical power to shape perceptions and realities. We object to the nationalist formulation of woman-as-victim, for it denies historical women their agency and precludes explorations of their subjectivities. But we do not overlook the hierarchical structures in political, familial, and textual realms that perpetuated male dominance. We have to first deconstruct before constructing an alternative vision, yet our deconstructive and constructive goals are sometimes at loggerheads. For heuristic purposes, we continue to use the term "Confucianism" even as we acknowledge its limitations and artificiality. The authors of each chapter strive to specify the historical, cultural, and linguistic parameters of the term as they use it.

In sum, returning women to the center stage of history transforms not only our image of the victimized women but also our portraits of Confucian pasts. For this reason, we employ Woman and Confucianism as our twin analytic foci, a coupling reflected in the title of the book. A gendered and comparative analysis provides a convincing way to dispel the immutability of Confucianism. Our woman-centered gaze, in turn, exposes both the power and the limitations of the Confucian persuasion.

## NEGOTIATING THE SHIFTING
## MEANINGS OF CONFUCIANISMS

As our point of departure is to write against the prevailing tendency to view Confucianism and Woman as uniform across time and space, we seek to present multiple viewpoints and analytic perspectives in this book without imposing a unifying vision. The contributors adopt working definitions of Confucianism in ways that make the most sense in light of their academic traditions, historical materials, and personal convictions. Some view "Confucianism" as a discursive process in order to stress its contested and contingent nature. Others focus on the variety of Confucian institutional structures that most directly impinged on people's lives and behavior. The most salient examples of these structures are kinship and kingship, more commonly represented in premodern East Asia as family and state. Analogous realms bound by a metaphorical relationship, kinship and kingship provided the concrete contexts in which such Confucian virtues as filiality and loyalty were to be realized. By examining such diverse texts as primers, edicts, canonization lists, and private writings, the contributors illuminate the multiple forms that kinship and kingship could take and the myriad historical meanings of so-called Confucian virtues.

The label "Confucian" proves to be most problematic to historians of Japan, where the influence of the Confucian discourse was most limited in scope and impact. Sekiguchi Hiroko sees limited utility in the term "Confucianism," referring specifically to the "patriarchal family paradigm" embedded in the Chinese bureaucratic structures and law codes introduced to Japan from the fifth to eighth centuries. Focusing on the realm of kingship in the eighth century instead of law and society, Joan Piggott analyzes the impact of the Chinese "male script" of monarchy, or the advancing consensus that the occupant of the throne should be male at the later eighth-century Nara court. Hesitating to label this male script "Confucian"—she notes that no term can be readily found in her texts that refers specifically to what is now considered Confucianism—she speaks of advancing acculturation of "the classical discourse of Chinese civilization." Sugano Noriko, in turn, uses "Confucian ethics" only once to refer to the virtue of filial piety promoted by the Tokugawa shogunate in the seventeenth and eighteenth centuries. Martha Tocco situates her study of Tokugawa women's education in the intellectual context of the official sponsorship of Neo-Confucian thought but revises the conventional view in showing that many Confucian scholars in Tokugawa Japan were champions of women's learning.

Both Sugano and Tocco suggest that the Tokugawa shogunate adopted certain tenets of Neo-Confucian thought as its ruling ideology and sought to promulgate such virtues as filiality among the commoners. Only in this circumscribed sense might Tokugawa Japan be dubbed "Confucian" but with important caveats: national learning (*kokugaku*) rivaled Neo-Confucian learning at the shogun's court, and the larger society remained largely untouched by rigidly patriarchal and patrilineal paradigms. The concept of Confucianism is thus of marginal utility to all four Japan specialists who contributed to this book. Ironically, this fact makes the inclusion of Japan in our comparative framework all the more essential. Allowing us an outsider's perspective, Japan exposes the rhetorical and geographic limits of the universalist claims and self-image of the Confucian discourse.

Scholars of Korea are eager to distinguish between "Chinese" and "Confucian," but they find the latter a more prevalent and visible force in Korean history. In her chapter on the twelfth-century Korean scholar Kim Pusik, Lee Hai-soon treats Confucianism as a complex intellectual movement comprising different schools whose practitioners were embroiled in political struggles at court. Martina Deuchler speaks of a pervasive process of "Confucian transformation" of society initiated by Chosŏn legislators in the fourteenth century. For elite women, the most salient element of Confucianism was the introduction of the patrilineal family paradigm.

Yet "Confucianism" in Korean eyes was quite different from how it was viewed by the Japanese or Chinese. Elite men of the Chosŏn era viewed Confucianism as a universal system of truth available to all civilized people regardless of geography, and they often claimed to be more faithful transmitters of Confucian orthodoxy than were the Chinese themselves. After the fall of the Ming dynasty to the Manchus in 1644, Korean scholars considered themselves the sole guardians of Confucian civilization.[7] Chosŏn women, in turn, believed that the relevance of Confucian culture transcended gender boundaries and that they too embodied Confucian virtues. As JaHyun Kim Haboush shows, it was this conviction that allowed the maligned Queen Inhyŏn (1667–1701) to claim moral autonomy and power in the face of adversities.

Our comparative perspective points to a paradox: in the eyes of Japanese and Korean statesmen who introduced selective Chinese elements of rulership to strengthen their own positions, the meaning of Confucianism was at once circumscribed and diffuse. When scholars in Korea and Japan spoke of the way of China, they had in mind a complex of elements, of which "Confucianism" was but one component not easily separated from others. Once we shift from a China-centered view of the region to one that takes the periphery as its focus, "Confucianism" does not seem so immutable or monolithic.

Scholars of China are less inclined to treat Confucianism in a transnational and comparative context. Yet even in regard to China, the status and utility of the term "Confucianism" are open to question. Zang Jian echoes the prevalent view of modern Chinese historiography in construing Confucianism as an orthodoxy that oppressed women, but she argues for a dynamic process through which popular mentalities influenced Confucian normative structures. Suzanne Cahill, shying away from a rigid bifurcation of a Confucian "big tradition" and the "small traditions" of Daoist and folk religions prevalent in previous scholarship, analyzes how all these elements came to bear on the bodily practices of Tang women. Du Fangqin and Susan Mann have no trouble identifying the virtue of wifely fidelity as a key Confucian value. They emphasize the instability of its meaning, however, by documenting the range of conflicting behaviors that came to be subsumed under the virtue.

In short, our strategy is to dispel the monolithic category of Confucianism by placing it in specific historical and cultural locations. In so doing, we demonstrate its power in the realms of social and textual practice. Although we offer no coherent view of Confucianism, all the contributors agree that Confucian institutions and practices pose a challenge to certain conventions of Western thought. For example, the modern Western dichotomy between "private" and "public" spheres has no meaning in a Confucian discourse. The boundaries between kinship and kingship in all Confucianized societies were blurred: the inner and the outer interpenetrated, and social bodies merged with the body politic. And yet an important presupposition of the discourse is the separation of official (C: *gong;* K: *kong;* J: *ko*) from unofficial (C: *si;* K: *sa;* J: *shi*). In seventh- and eighth-century Japan, for example, courtier-scholars quoted Chinese texts to admonish officials to separate official duties from their personal or private affairs. In prescription, the official was preeminent.

In many contemporary English accounts, this official-unofficial distinction, more circumscribed in implication, is rendered the equivalent of the public-private distinction in the modern Western sense. Adding to the confusion is the facile equation of the domestic realm with the private, a view now common in scholarly and popular discourses. In her efforts to develop a female-centered reading strategy, JaHyun Kim Haboush has discussed the public-private distinction as alternatively referring to spheres of activity, signifier of morality, and social spaces. Its very theoretical flexibility allows women to conduct negotiations with forces of domination. This issue of interconnected spheres is taken up in individual chapters. Suffice it to say here that we reject the misleading image of Confucian women as cloistered beings who had no access to public spheres, regardless of prescriptive texts urging such isolation. If the meaning of Confucianism cannot be fixed, neither can the location of women be frozen in a space that exists outside of history. Both are enlivened only as we fix our analytic gaze on the processes of negotiation between the two.

### DEFINING *RU*: CONFUCIAN DISCOURSES IN CHINA

It is easier to say what Confucianism is not than what it is. One commonly held view is that the epoch spanning the Han (202 B.C.E.–220 C.E.) and Tang (618–907) dynasties constituted a "first great age of Confucianism."[8] It witnessed the codification of fundamental texts often termed "Confucian classics" and the structures of imperial state government those classics underpinned. The texts and structures elaborated ideals associated with Confucius's own age as well as precedents from Han and post-Han imperial governance such as the official ritual program, school and exam systems designed to reproduce officialdom, patronage of scholarly literary and historical projects, and expanding technical expertise from the fields of provincial administration, criminal law, calendrical science, *yin-yang* theory, and astrology. All can be said to constitute the substance of official Confucian learning.

Although accurate to an extent, the idea of a Han-to-Tang synthesis presents an image of Chinese Confucian culture that is too monolithic. The Chinese term for "Confucian," *Ru*, was at once more specific and diffuse. In the formative Han times, *Ru* could denote the school of Confucius, a classicist, a government official,

or simply an adherent of the way of being human (*ren*) according to the five relations.[9] The Han dynasty can be said to be Confucian to the extent that *Ru* masters
were recruited to serve in government, where they applied precepts associated with
the Master and his followers to everyday problems of administrative rule. But *Ru*
thought and its canon of five classics—the *Book of Changes*, the *Book of History*, the
*Book of Rites*, the *Book of Odes*, and the *Spring and Autumn Annuals*—remained diverse
and volatile, and their interpretation was subject to constant debate.[10]

While various official mandates canonized different clusters of classics and their
commentaries, over time Chinese scholar-officials themselves fashioned complicated intellectual stances that defied the facile label "Confucian." One telling example was that of the scholar Yan Zhitui (531–91). In his famous *Family Instructions
for the Yan Clan* (Yanshi jiaxun), Yan emphasized strict child rearing and education
of heirs in the canonical classics and official histories. The objective was office holding, which required sobriety, sincerity, fulfillment of duties, and the sacrifice of self.[11]
At the same time, however, Yan emphasized the saving power of the Buddha. For
Yan, learning and living according to the ideals of the classics and the precepts of
Buddhism were both desirable, which is why one biographer of Yan has characterized him as a "Buddho-Confucian."[12] Yan's work and his broad intellectual outlook struck a sympathetic chord among Japanese courtiers in Nara two centuries
later.

Although the *Ru* or "Confucian" discourse in China underwent significant shifts
through the centuries, by Tang times broad agreement on its general substance had
emerged. It comprised a body of classical texts and scholarship as sources of political and moral authority; ideal practices such as ritual, righteousness, and filial
piety—including gender hierarchy—prescribed for all levels of social hierarchy; a
comingling of state and family; the alliance of state and scholars in ruling the realm;
and the cosmic notion that virtuous rule by the Son of Heaven linked heaven, man,
and earth.[13] All were prominent elements adopted by societies on China's periphery for their own "civilizing" projects. What resulted in varying locales—the degree and nature of acculturation—differs significantly.

## CONFUCIANIZATION AS A CIVILIZING PROCESS

If we shift from a China-centered to a multicentered regional perspective, the Confucian discourse can appear in a different light. Therefore, we now turn to survey
the transmission of elements of the Confucian discourse among China, Korea, and
Japan, with a focus on implications for women in various social and historical locations. To do so we find it productive to speak of a "Confucianizing process"
whereby canonical books, didactic texts, norms of behavior, and paradigms of familial organization crossed geographic and social boundaries over a *longue durée*. Active promotion by reform-minded state builders and officials often provided the political and institutional impetus. But the "Confucianization" of society was first and
foremost a cultural process. In the eyes of many promoters, Confucianization was

a civilizing process that promised to humanize social mores and practices by transforming morality. Of course, it had a political facet as well: it gave power to monarchs, courts, and associated elites.

Norbert Elias's classic on the history of manners provides insights for our use of the concept of a civilizing process.[14] First of all, it is useful to think of a two-step process involving external or institutional promotion followed by internalization (acculturation) on the individual level. In Europe as in Asia, the civilizing process—the diffusion of courtly culture—was unleashed in periods of political centralization to create a new political subject. The promulgation of law codes and didactic texts from above was swift and relatively easy to identify, but the process of individual internalization at various levels of society certainly took centuries and is less amenable to historical detection. To a large extent, all of the contributors seek to analyze the realm of institutional and textual practices to gain entry into the more elusive realm of broader gender relations and female subjectivities. Negotiating the space between structures of domination and human agency, we show how the civilizing process could empower certain women at the same time that it diminished their inheritance rights or choice of marital partners.

In mapping the civilizing processes in China, Korea, and Japan, the chapters in this book do not offer comprehensive coverage of premodern history in the China Sea sphere. They are grouped into four parts according to themes instead of chronology and cluster around three periods: seventh to tenth centuries; twelfth to thirteenth centuries; sixteenth to nineteenth centuries. We have chosen these periods because we want to situate women in times of change while avoiding presentation of an image of an immobile and reified tradition. Especially in China and Korea, these are times when Confucian paradigms made inroads into society and produced significant changes in the contexts of women's lives, in large part because of state promotion. We present women as agents who actively remade tradition and society through their actions, as evinced by their embodiment of virtues as well as their roles as rulers, teachers, and authors of didactic texts. Nonetheless, there is no denying that women generally did not initiate the legislative and bureaucratic changes in the political domain.

## *Korea and the Confucian Civilizing Process*

Traffic in scribes, books, and ideas was brisk and multidirectional in the northeastern inland and China Sea sphere from the late centuries B.C.E. and throughout premodern history. It reached new heights during the seventh and eighth centuries, giving birth to what we can call the "East Asian region." On the continent the establishment of the Sui (581–619) and Tang (618–907) dynasties reversed a century-long process of disunity. Centralizing polities were also formed on the Korean peninsula and the Japanese archipelago. Significantly, all were outward-looking in political as in cultural matters. The volume of traffic in the China Sea sphere grew dramatically: not only scribes but also students, craftsmen, monks, and merchants traversed seas and mountains. The result was a geographic region in which the political entities shared a degree of compatibility in written language, institutions, law, religions, and aesthetics. Confucian texts, along with Buddhist sutras, gave elites a common vocabulary that transcended ethnic and national boundaries. It is important to note, however, that as one of the most cosmopolitan premodern regions, East Asia was anything but monolithic in worldviews and tastes. In due time, as travelers found their way to India and beyond, consciousness of the world beyond East Asia expanded as well.

Korean scribes and monks played a key role in fostering the cosmopolitan identities of East Asia. The civilizing process on the Korean peninsula began with a confluence of politics and culture: the early Korean state emerged in contradistinction to the outposts that the Chinese established in what would become Korean territory, yet under the influence of the Chinese concept of a bureaucratic state. Although the exact dates of their beginnings are in dispute, by the fourth century the three peninsular states of Koguryŏ, Silla, and Paekche vied to appropriate aspects of Chinese political, intellectual, and religious systems they deemed useful. In the ensuing centuries, when a unified "Korean" identity had yet to be formed and China itself was in disarray, the three states maintained multidirectional traffic in scribes, books, and artifacts among themselves as well as with Chinese and Japanese polities. Finally in the seventh century, Silla integrated the peninsula into one kingdom and negotiated a peaceful albeit ambiguous relationship with Tang China.

The Silla state adopted certain laws based on the Tang code and established such Chinese-style institutions as the Confucian temple at the royal university in the capital. But classical Chinese discourse did not predominate; at the same time craftsmen were sent to Japan and Buddhist clergy went on pilgrimages to India. The civilizing process also led to multilayered interactions in the realms of kinship and kingship in Silla. The rigidity of the native status society characterized by its bone-rank system retained its hold, obstructing the advance of gender hierarchy. Furthermore, an individual's status continued to be determined bilaterally, taking into account the status of both father and mother, instead of patrilineally. Although political loyalty and filiality, the twin linchpins of Confucian ethics, were introduced to Korea, the former virtue received greater emphasis on the peninsula than in China.

Kingship in Sillan Korea was the site of contestations between Chinese and native discourses, between ideology and practice, and between class and gender. Although the Confucian ideal of benevolent rulership was introduced, succession was determined not by the Chinese patrilineal principle but by nonlinear descent. Even as a demarcation of the official-male and domestic-female spheres slowly advanced, gender considerations remained secondary to those of class and status in kingly succession. Therefore, two female rulers ascended the throne, Queen Sŏndŏk (r. 632–47) and Queen Chindŏk (r. 647–54), because they were of the highest status, that known as the holy bone rank. Notably, however, they were the last representatives of that status, and after the latter's death the throne was assumed by a male ruler of the next highest bone rank. But because still another female sovereign, Queen Chinsŏng (r. 887–97), ruled in the waning years of the Silla state, we may surmise that as late as the ninth century gender was merely one of the elements for consideration in the transfer of power; it never constituted the unconditional grounds for exclusion.

The complicated ways in which Chinese and native discourses interacted in the domains of kinship and kingship persisted in Koryŏ Korea (918–1392). Although kingship continued to be a locus of competing ideologies and practices, Confucian appurtenances pertaining to the official sphere began to take sturdier root in the tenth century with the concept of the Mandate of Heaven, the civil service examination, and the bureaucracy. In the twelfth-century *Record of the Three Kingdoms* (Samguk sagi), the earliest extant Confucian historiography, we find convincing textual evidence that Korean scholars had begun to internalize a Confucian worldview. At the center of its evaluative scheme, for example, was the binary of the civilized and the barbarous. The *Record* nonetheless exhibits different degrees of conviction concerning this worldview as it moves from the official to the unofficial sphere.

The civilizing process during the Chosŏn period (1392–1910) has been extensively discussed elsewhere; briefly, the Confucianizing process—conceived and launched by state officials—aimed at transforming society and state in accordance with a Neo-Confucian moral vision.[15] As such, it evolved along a different trajectory than did earlier efforts. The domestic sphere was now seen to be just as crucial as the public sphere as the target of civilizing influence. The establishment of patrilineal descent groups and the ascendancy of such virtues as filiality and wifely loyalty indicate that kinship as much as kingship became the locus of attention. The scholarly consensus is that the sixteenth century witnessed the internalization of this moral vision in the political sphere, whereas the seventeenth century saw associated structures fashioned for the social and domestic spheres. Divorce and remarriage of women all but disappeared, and daughters' inheritance, which had been equal to that of their brothers, shrank. Although this took place mostly in the more visible strata—educated and elite families—nonelite segments of the population were also steadily drawn into the orbit of Confucian civility.

In discussing the process of the Confucian civilizing of Korea, it is tempting to chart, if only for heuristic purposes, its progression through different spheres, classes, and genders, but one should remember that this was by no means a linear process. Each sphere displayed its own pattern of negotiation between Chinese and native discourses and between ideology and practice. Furthermore, negotiations in any one sphere were not made in isolation but in interaction with those in other spheres. The result is a collage wrought of sedimentary layers that defies linear narratives of progression or change.

The well-known story of the filial daughter Sim Ch'ŏng, who threw herself into the sea so that her blind father could see again, illustrates the complicated negotiations whereby the Confucian virtue of filiality blended with a native sentiment that viewed daughters as important members of the family. One may argue that the popularity of this story in many genres in the eighteenth century testifies to the ascendancy of filiality, the Confucian virtue associated with kinship, in all sectors of Korean society. But curiously the emblem of this virtue is represented by a daughter instead of a son, a fact that contravenes the basic tenets of Confucian patriarchy and patrilineality while harking back to the native kinship structure in which daughters were highly valued.[16] Coincidentally, the filial daughter did not drown but was rescued by the Dragon King of Buddhist *Lotus Sutra* fame. Happily, Sim Ch'ŏng subsequently became an empress of China and Mr. Sim was so overjoyed by the voice of his daughter that he regained his eyesight.

### *The Japan-China Dialectic: The Civilizing Process in Japan*

On the Japanese islands, the diffusion of courtly culture, including Buddhist, Daoist, Legalist, and Confucian elements, took place in a dynamic environment, and the results were as complicated as in Korea. By the Nara period (710–84), a mélange of continental structures and customs had reached Japan. The literary scholar David Pollack has characterized the comingling of Japanese meanings and Chinese forms over time as a Japan-China (Wakan) dialectic.[17] While previous historiography has tended to see the eighth century in relatively static terms—as a time of constant borrowing and emulating things Chinese—the reality is more nuanced.

At least three stages in the dialectic can be identified: one early in the century, when Chinese-style law codes were first promulgated; another datable to the 730s, when new texts and know-how significantly expanded knowledge of Tang ways in Nara; and a third beginning in the 750s, characterized by dynamic emulation and institutionalization of Tang ways in government and at court. The latter stage continued into Heian (794–1185) times, when the court was moved to the new capital at Heiankyō, present-day Kyoto.

During the first stage in the early 700s, elite literacy among the Nara courtiers and provincial elites grew, as did familiarity with Chinese classics, called "illuminating classics" (*myōkyō*) in the Taihō Ritsuryō Code of 701. In that text the chapter concerning education of officials provided for operation of a royal university where study of a long series of nine of the classics was mandated: the *Book of Rites*, the *Zuo Commentary*, the *Book of Odes*, the *Rites of Zhou*, the *Book of Etiquette and Ceremonial*, the *Book of Changes*, the *Book of History*, the *Analects*, and the *Classic of Filial Piety*.[18] Meanwhile, from the late seventh century onward writing preserved on wooden documents (*mokkan*) evidences intense study of Chinese dictionaries and encyclopedias by elites in the capital and in the provinces.[19] In 704 Chinese scholarship was expanded by the return of an embassy from Tang China with a large trove of Chinese primers, dictionaries, and medical works.[20] The poet Yamanoue Okura was a member of that embassy, and his familiarity with Sui and Tang texts made him the leading China scholar of his generation. Use of *man'yōgana*—Chinese characters used to represent Japanese sounds—in eighth-century histories and poetry anthologies evidences increasing facility in Chinese on the part of Nara elites.[21]

In emulation of Chinese Sons of Heaven, Nara's own Heavenly Sovereigns (*tennō*) took patronage of scholarship very seriously. In an edict of 721 the female monarch Genshō (r. 715–24) proclaimed the study of medicine, divination, astronomy, and *yin-yang* geomancy critical for governance. She exhorted her scholar-officials, both civilian and military, to devote themselves to virtues prescribed by the illuminating classics: they were to serve the commonweal (*kō*) loyally (*chū*), all the while shunning self-interest (*watakushi*). Accepting a fundamental premise from the *Analects* and *Mencius* that virtuous service must be nurtured by the ruler's remuneration, the *tennō* ordered the granting of rewards to her premier classicists, administrators, litterateurs, accountants, yin-yang specialists, physicians, musicians, and military strategists.[22]

It was in 735 that the Buddhist monk Gembō and the scholar-official Kibi Makibi returned from study in Tang China with great numbers of Chinese texts. Their arrival marked the beginning of the second stage in the transmission of Chinese texts and growing comprehension concerning practical application. While Gembō reportedly brought back five thousand mostly Buddhist manuscripts, Kibi returned from a prolonged stay of nineteen years with an array of materials concerning such governmental matters as calendar making, music, ritual, and history. In addition to an iron-measuring apparatus, musical instruments, and military technology such as bows and arrows, he presented the sitting monarch Shōmu Tennō (r. 724–49) with the recently compiled compendium of Tang court ritual known as the *Tang Code of Rituals of the Kaiyuan Era*.[23] Based on three classics on ritual, the code outlined one hundred fifty rites and became a handbook for court ceremonies in Nara. Another influential text probably introduced by Kibi and much admired by courtiers was the Chinese Buddho-Confucian scholar Yan Zhitui's *Family Instructions for the Yan Clan*, which Kibi himself would later imitate in his *Collected Family Instructions* for his heirs.[24]

Recognizing that Kibi possessed rare expertise concerning the state of education in contemporary Tang China, Shōmu Tennō sent him to the royal university to update the curriculum. Kibi's reformed curriculum focused on five of the illuminating classics, three official histories, law, accounting, music, composition, and calligraphy.[25] Whereas the classics presented students with the ideal, the histories presented them with narratives of actual rulership, ideal and otherwise. Later Kibi moved on to the household of Shōmu's crown princess, Abe. At this point Nara elite women were reading and writing Chinese; calligraphy by Shōmu's queen consort, Kōmyō, Princess Abe's mother, is still extant, as is a letter-writing handbook she used.[26] Moreover, an inventory of newly copied texts produced by the queen's private scriptorium lists 126 Buddhist texts, termed "inner texts" (*naiten*), and 43 non-Buddhist texts, termed "outer texts" (*gaiten*).[27] Division of newly imported knowledge of the day into these two categories suggests a perceived distinction between an interior (personal) Buddhist realm and an official (public) realm where learning from the "illuminating" classics held sway. Also notable is the preponderance of Buddhist texts prepared by the scriptorium.

The 750s ushered in the third stage in the Japan-China dialectic, as deeper acculturation of Confucian values and political circumstances led to institutionalization of Tang ways at the Nara court.[28] During each decade from 752 until 779, at least two embassies regularly left for China. Production of both the *Manyōshū* Japanese verse anthology and the *Fond Recollections of Poetry* (Kaifūsō), an anthology of Chinese poetry written by Japanese courtiers, reflected the court's embrace of the Sinic notion that royal patronage of literary arts facilitated virtuous government. Verses and headnotes in the anthologies demonstrate how Nara courtiers looked back to both the sixth-century Chinese anthology *Selections of Refined Literature* (Wenxuan) and the early Tang court poetry for inspiration. It is no surprise that the *Fond Recollections* provides our earliest extant evidence that the Chinese concept of "Heavenly" universal monarchy legitimized by the Mandate of Heaven and signified by the use of characters such as *tei* (C: *di*) and *kō* (C: *huang*) had been in vogue at later seventh-century courts where Chinese verse was first composed in Japan.[29] And that late-eighth-century pedants kept a close eye on continental developments is evidenced by the fact that in 769 the curriculum at the royal university was once again adjusted to reflect ongoing developments in Tang education: five classics and five histories were then made the basis of the program.[30] About this same time, the Nara royal residence (*dairi*) came to be a venue for royal banquets, also following Tang practice.[31] Meanwhile, Queen Dowager Kōmyō and her daughter, who was on the verge of retiring as *tennō*, may well have been dressing according to Tang fashion, as seen in the full-figured images of Tang beauties adorning folding screens from Shōmu's household collection (Figure I.1).

How did official enthusiasm for Tang ways affect individual courtiers' lives? Acculturation of prescriptions from the classics, but with a syncretist bent, is evidenced in the mid-eighth-century biography of Fujiwara Fuhito's son and Queen Kōmyō's brother, Fujiwara Muchimaro (680–737). Consider this extract:

> He [Muchimaro] mourned his mother when he was young—with tears of blood he destroyed his health, he refused to eat even rice gruel and threatened to waste away.... As he grew older ... [h]e did not take a single step without propriety, and he accepted nothing in which there was no honor. He preferred remaining calm and kept himself distant from noise and commotion.... He made loyalty and faithfulness his principles and always made humanity and honor his precepts.... He was pure and clean, upright and honest in all respects.[32]

That the minister Muchimaro is depicted here cultivating filiality, propriety, sincerity, scholarship, sobriety, and loyalty shows how virtues from the classics were being idealized at the midcentury Nara court. But note that Muchimaro mourned his mother rather than the father he probably did not know well (he had doubtless been raised uxorilocally, according to current practice, at his mother's home).[33]

Figure I.1. Tang Lady on a Folding Screen in Shōmu Tennō's
Private Collection. Courtesy of the Shōsō-in Treasure House,
Nara, Japan.

Muchimaro's biography also records emerging scholarly specialization. We hear
therein about experts in *Ru* (Confucian) texts, elegant writing, divination, study of
directional taboos, *yin-yang*, calendrical arts, and theurgy. And although Muchimaro
was steeped in the illuminating classics, his tastes were eclectic and he particularly
favored Buddhist texts:

> He studied the different theories of scholars and the three philosophies [of Confu-
> cius, Laozi, and Buddha]. He rated the teachings of Buddha highest and was also
> partial to the teachings of immortality. He respected those who knew the way and
> revered the virtuous. He gave alms to the poor and had pity for the lonely. Every
> year in the summer, in the third month, he invited ten learned monks to lecture on
> the *Lotus Sutra* and thus learned its inner teachings.[34]

Additional indications of acculturation come from Japan's earliest extant familial precepts, the *Collected Family Instructions* (Shikyō ruijū), written by the royal tutor Kibi Makibi in the 760s or 770s. Kibi's *Instructions* were almost certainly inspired by Yan Zhitui's sixth-century *Family Instructions*, which Kibi may have brought back to Nara.[35] For Kibi as for Yan Zhitui two centuries earlier, Buddhist precepts and Confucian virtues were to be practiced in tandem; he exhorted heirs to practice "both the inner [Buddhism] and the outer [Confucian]." Like Yan, Kibi urged dedication to scholarship, filiality, loyalty, bodily discipline, probity, uprightness, and restraint. Arts useful to officials such as divining, healing, calligraphy, accounting, and archery were to be mastered, while dabbling in alchemy, faking oracles and omens, drunkenness, careless behavior including gambling, and disregard for taboos were forbidden. Kibi also cautioned, "Do not take two wives." This was curious given that most high-ranking ministers at the Nara court had several consorts. Doubtless Kibi was hoping his heirs could avoid the disharmony plaguing discussions of succession and inheritance in households where no clear hierarchy of wives and consorts existed.

To summarize, dynamic acculturation of Tang ways was integral to the court-led "civilizing process" in Nara times. By midcentury the Chinese classics and histories were widely studied, although just as in China different groups of texts were mandated for study at different moments. Promulgation of law codes based on Sui and Tang models meant that practices and structures idealized in the illuminating classics were enshrined in government and courtly protocol. Particularly emphasized were themes such as filiality, patrilineality, ministerial loyalty, and Heaven's mandate. Nonetheless, no term that might be properly translated as "Confucianism" appears frequently associated with such texts. Instead we hear only of the "illuminating classics" and "outer texts" from which Japanese Heavenly Sovereigns learned every ruler's duty to oversee the civilizing process of All Under Heaven (*tenka*). So did Nara *tennō* preside over the royal university and a host of scholarly projects, just like Chinese Sons of Heaven. And so did Shōmu Tennō's daughter and successor, Kōken-Shōtoku Tennō, make the virtues of filiality and loyalty emphatic qualifications for those who might succeed her.

Along with their dedication to the illuminating classics, Nara elites demonstrated strong belief in Buddhism, not unlike the Chinese official Yan Zhitui in the sixth century. As the scholar Isonokami Yakatsugu (729–81) put it in describing his book-collecting practices in the 770s, "To aid and supplement Buddhist texts, I collect secular texts as well."[36] Joan R. Piggott's chapter demonstrates the dual emphasis on both Heaven and the Buddha as protectors of realm and throne in edicts issued by Kōken-Shōtoku Tennō during her two reigns in the late eighth century. For all its gridlike streets and elegant ladies, Nara was not merely a "little Tang," as has too often been supposed. The disposition toward "Buddho-Confucian" syncretism by Nara thinkers contrasts dramatically with the purges and repressive campaigns launched against Buddhism by Tang Sons of Heaven and their officials. Such a contrast is also the background against which the monk Kūkai's *Indications of the Goals of the Three Teachings* (Sangō shiiki), composed in 797, is to be viewed. After broad study of Confucian, Daoist, and Buddhist teachings, Kūkai—arguably one of the best educated and most productive intellectuals of his day—agreed with Isonokami. He too found Buddhism superior. And while Buddhism would gradually disappear as an official cult embraced by Chinese Sons of Heaven, it would remain central to Japanese Heavenly kingship right through the dawn of the modern era in 1868.

The civilizing process based on imported structures—the Japan-China dialectic—had ambivalent gender implications, just as it did in Korea. The promulgation of a set of penal and administrative codes (*ritsuryō*) modeled on Tang law ushered in the *ritsuryō* process of realmwide integration, as discussed in Sekiguchi Hiroko's chapter. New structures established by the codes prescribed the separation of official from unofficial spheres as well as gender hierarchy in the realms of kinship and kingship. Prescriptions for patrilineal stem descent and male-dominant marital units, which characterized the patriarchal family paradigm, were promoted; but their social impact advanced more gradually than has previously been acknowledged.

Nonetheless, as Piggott argues, in the realm of royal succession a slowly advancing gender hierarchy is evident. Although there had been a long tradition of female rule extending back to the Wa leader Himiko in the third century, by the late eighth century there was a growing sense at court based on the illuminating classics and *ritsuryō* law that women should not rule. And since the law codes established ideals of court culture as exemplary for officials and ultimately all civilized persons in the realm, the notions that configured kingship and court diffused to influence gender relations far beyond the Nara capital.

The consolidation of a male-centered political sphere is evinced by other aspects of court life from the eighth into the ninth century. It is no coincidence that in the Heian period women generally ceased writing *kanji*, the Chinese script that signified erudition and political power. The patrilineal ideal embedded in the eighth-century codes worked its way slowly to alter the bilineal organization and associated practices of elite families.[37] Between the tenth and twelfth centuries the transition to a more male-dominant form of marriage and household structure, with strengthened rights for fathers and husbands and a specialized housewife (*shufu*) role, is noticeable in various strata, from courtiers downward.[38] And although the early Heian court maintained a rhetorical emphasis on gender complementarity, stressing differentiation between the functions of male and female courtiers, women's roles in courtier and provincial official families became increasingly subordinate as official prerogatives and perquisites of the male sex were privileged. In the course of the Heian period what one historian has termed "the barometer of patriarchy" rose steadily if gradually as women's status and freedom in society slid downward when both political and economic potential as well as agency were constrained.[39]

And yet in terms of kinship and marital practices the results of acculturating the classical Chinese discourse in Japan remained far from full-fledged develop-

ment of Chinese-style patriarchal family organization, with its male-centered marriage and inheritance patterns.[40] Divorce by choice of either mate, a variety of marital residence practices, and partible inheritance continued well into medieval
times.[41] Filiality to both parents was emphasized, and women enjoyed a degree of
social freedom that surprised European visitors in the sixteenth century.[42] Furthermore, the gap between Confucian ideals and actual social practices persisted
into the early modern Tokugawa period (1600–1868). As Sugano Noriko's chapter
describes, shogunal officials propagated ideals of filial piety to all classes of the populace in the eighteenth century in an effort to shore up the patriarchal family. Yet
family life in Japan remained significantly different from both Chinese norm and
practice. There was, for example, greater choice for female affiliation, multiplicity
of marital residence, and recognition that both sexes could serve their households—
consisting of parents and sibs—as virtuous family members. One millennium after the formal introduction of the patriarchal family paradigm by the eighth-
century codes, the overarching concern in Japanese kinship remained less status
and gender hierarchy than assuring the practical needs of the household, which
men and women were seen to serve in largely complementary fashion.

## THEMES AND ORGANIZATION

This book is divided into four parts, each featuring a dominant actor or sphere of
action: the male scholar or courtier, the civilizing state, society, and the female subject. Part 1, "Scripts of Male Dominance," maps the parameters of female life and
outlines the rules of the worlds where women found themselves.[43] An exploration
into the attributes of male agency, or rather the agency of elite educated men, it
highlights the male-centered nature of the Confucian discourse. The chapters show
how Confucian norms and values were embedded in a variety of institutional and
textual traditions: law codes (Sekiguchi), kingship (Piggott), official historiography
(Lee's *Record of the Three Kingdoms*), and the classics (Lam's *Record of Music* and its
commentaries). These constitute the building blocks of the official hegemonic tradition, through which Chinese canonical values—values typically associated with
Confucianism—were codified and transmitted.

In using the term "male script," we call attention to the conflation of word and
power so central to the Confucian persuasion and the perpetuation of male dominance within it. This word-power nexus places culture, writing, and civility—encapsulated in one word (C: *wen;* K: *mun;* J: *bun*)—in the same realm.[44] That is to say,
production of the word, moral authority, education, and office holding were con-
joined, all construed as the reason and reward for male privilege. Although it is
tempting to seek the origins of the script of male privilege, we cannot answer that
question in this volume. Suffice it to say that by the time the classics were codified
from Han to Tang times in China, male domination was such an entrenched assumption that the female perspective was almost completely expunged. Joseph
Lam's chapter in this part, which tells the story of the erasure of the bodies and

voices of female musicians from the classics, provides a rarely seen visualization of this process.

In a world organized around male scripts, women were either erased from the canons, relegated to marginal positions, or assigned phantasmic existences, as the chapters in part 1 demonstrate. This is not to say that women were entirely absent in the visions of male scholars, lawmakers, and historians. But the presence of woman seems contingent if not tropelike; she exists mainly to tell—or complement—male stories and perspectives. In an extreme case, Lee Hai-soon argues that the female exemplars in Korea's first official female biographies can be seen as metaphors for male scholars' ideal images of themselves. Even Kōken-Shōtoku, Japan's last female sovereign in the classical age, who can hardly be said to have been absent from history, has been written under the shadow of her monk-lieutenant Dōkyō in conventional historiography.

Parts 2 and 3 trace the trajectories of the Confucian civilizing process through time and space, with a focus on their gender implications. Part 2, "Propagating Confucian Virtues," sketches in broad strokes the institutional and structural frameworks that were crucial to the transformation of social customs and mores. The main actor here is the state, staffed by Confucian scholar-officials of various persuasions and controlling a repertoire of resources, cultural and political. One of the important channels of indoctrination was the publication of didactic texts for women. Martina Deuchler's chapter surveys the transmission and reception of the most popular Chinese didactic texts in Chosŏn Korea. Drawing from the writings of male officials, Deuchler details the eagerness with which women took to their education, leading to their exemplary comportment as wives, daughters, and mothers.

A second official channel for civilizing society in Korea and China was the civil service examination. In China it was the sole gateway to officialdom from the Song dynasty to 1905, serving as a key venue for the shaping and contesting of cultural norms. It also acquired rather exclusive prestige in Korea, but despite its continued practice from the tenth to nineteenth centuries, it functioned more within the confines of the elite population. Curiously, the examination system never took root in Japan, where ascription, status, and cliency relations remained key. Zang Jian's chapter in part 2 analyzes this important institution in China, offering a provocative argument that it not only served to spread Confucian values to the lower levels of society but also became a conduit for transforming official culture by transmitting popular mores from the bottom up. The same two-way traffic between state and society is witnessed in Sugano Noriko's chapter, which focuses on a third source of evidence concerning the civilizing of society: canonization of filial sons and daughters in Tokugawa Japan. As the Chinese and Korean states also used canonization of filial people and chaste women to effect social changes, the insights provided by the Japanese case have wide applicability.

Whereas part 2 focuses on three official channels of indoctrination, part 3, "Female Education in Practice," offers fine textual studies tracing the transmission and reception of specific virtues and norms. If the agent of change in part 2 is the state, in part 3 it is men and women as social actors. Here we analyze the education and canonization processes not as structures but as fields of negotiation. Du Fangqin and Susan Mann, in a revisionist reading of the cult of chastity in late imperial China, document both an intensification of the moral demands on Chinese women from all classes and the internal inconsistencies of these normative demands. In showing these inconsistencies, they are able to penetrate official rhetoric and locate agency in the bodies of the virtuous women. Martha Tocco adopts a similar revisionist woman-centered approach in her study of the theory and practice of female education in Tokugawa Japan. Resisting the conventional view that the Confucianization of Tokugawa society represented heightened oppression for women, Tocco argues instead that the broadened channels of education allowed more women to realize their moral worth.

The two chapters in part 3 lead us to depart from the Confucian discourse, its self-representation, and its visions of the world. We begin to enter a world in which the labels "Confucian" and "non-Confucian" mattered little, in which norms were internalized through processes of negotiation, and in which women assumed moral agency by enacting and embodying abstract norms. We realize that as important as the written tradition—or the word-power nexus—may be, the transformative power of Confucian ethics hinges on the process of human embodiment. The marginality of woman to the written tradition contrasts sharply with her centrality in the realm of social and corporeal practice.

Part 4 takes us farther from the self-representations and terms of the Confucian discourse. The two chapters by Suzanne Cahill and JaHyun Kim Haboush, although diverse in time and themes, have much in common. Both place women at the center, examine female-authored texts, and ask the objects and subjects of writing to instruct us about their subjectivities. Cahill, who investigates the corporeal practices of medieval Chinese holy women, suggests that the body was a necessary vehicle of transcendence. In examining both male-authored hagiography and female-authored poetry, she conveys the volition of these women by focusing on what is most important to them: the physicality of the body expressed in terms of food and sex. The hagiographers considered these women "Daoist," but Cahill eschews a world neatly demarcated by Confucian-Daoist sensitivities.

The chapter by Haboush, in defiance of the male script, considers reading and writing as a woman's vocation. To recover a woman's perspective and construct a woman-centered reading strategy, she conducts an intertextual reading of three stories of a suffering wife, two of them written by men, one by a woman. The portrayal of Queen Inhyŏn in the latter provides a fitting image of the female heroine in a Confucian world: dignified in the face of accusations; serene and free in the face of strictures. The word, like the body, is at once an instrument of indoctrination and a vehicle for expressing female subjectivities. The label shifts with one's position and perspective.

It gives us pleasure to begin the book with an understanding of male dominance and the subordination of women in official traditions and then to end it with the portrait of a woman in the center of her world, speaking, acting, and creating her own version of the world and her own reality. It might as well end this way: what begins as a project defining the meanings of Confucianism across East Asian time and space ends up reframing the question by shifting the subject of our gaze.

NOTES

1. Having distilled these three aspects of "gender" from our authors' usage, we recognize that they bear a remarkable resemblance to the ones discussed by Joan Wallach Scott in her essay "Gender: A Useful Category of Historical Analysis," in *Gender and the Politics of History* (New York: Columbia University Press, 1988). Originally published in 1986, this famous essay has had an indelible impact on the fields of Asian women's history, as chapters of this book attest.

2. David L. Hall and Roger T. Ames have pondered the philosophical issues involved in conceptualizing premodern and non-Western selves. See especially their *Thinking from the Han: Self, Truth, and Transcendence in Chinese and Western Culture* (Albany: State University of New York Press, 1998).

3. See, for instance, the recent and very useful overview by Xinzhong Yao, *An Introduction to Confucianism* (Cambridge: Cambridge University Press, 2000).

4. Lionel Jensen, *Manufacturing Confucianism: Chinese Traditions and Universal Civilization* (Durham: Duke University Press, 1997). The Chinese "Kong Fuzi" was often cited as the original for Confucius. Yet Jensen has found no reference to it in the literature of antiquity, fictive genealogical texts, and court ritual manuals. It appeared to have come into common use only in the sixteenth century, the time of the Jesuit translation projects (pp. 83–84).

5. For an argument against these distortions that also reaffirms the relevance of Confucianism to modern Asia, see Wm. Theodore de Bary and Tu Weiming, eds., *Confucianism and Human Rights* (New York: Columbia University Press, 1998).

6. According to Stefan Tanaka, in the Meiji period Confucianism was "the principal artifact that enabled Japanese intellectuals to claim both their orientalness and their distinctiveness [from China]." *Japan's Orient: Rendering Pasts into History* (Berkeley: University of California Press, 1993), p. 19. For colonial and postcolonial discourses on Confucianism in Korea, see Michael Robinson, "Perceptions of Confucianism in Twentieth-Century Korea," in *The East Asian Region: Confucian Heritage and Its Modern Adaptation*, ed. Gilbert Rozman (Princeton: Princeton University Press, 1991).

7. JaHyun Kim Haboush, "Constructing the Center," in *Culture and the State in Late Chosŏn Korea*, ed. Haboush and Martina Deuchler (Cambridge, Mass.: Harvard University, Council on East Asian Studies, 1999).

8. David McMullen, *State and Scholars in T'ang China* (Cambridge: Cambridge University Press, 1988), pp. 1–2.

9. See Michael Nylan, "A Problematic Model: The Han 'Orthodox Synthesis,' Then and Now," in *Imagining Boundaries: Changing Confucian Doctrines, Texts & Hermeneutics*, ed. Kaiwing Chow et al. (Albany: State University of New York Press, 1999), esp. pp. 18–19, 33. See also Howard Wechsler, "The Confucian Impact on Early T'ang Decision-Making," *T'oung Pao* 66, nos. 1–3 (1980): 1–40 passim.

10. The office of "Erudite of Five Classics" (*Wujing boshi*) was established during the Han dynasty to staff the National University. For a checklist of key texts considered components

of the classics repertoire by Tang times, see Sun-ming Wong, "Confucian Ideal and Reality: Transformation of the Institution of Marriage in Tang China" (Ph.D. dissertation, University of Washington, Seattle, 1979), pp. 6–7.

11. For an English translation of Yan's precepts, written circa 589, see Ssu-yu Teng, trans., *Family Instructions for the Yen Clan* (Leiden: Brill, 1968).

12. Albert E. Dien, "Yen Chih-t'ui (531–91): A Buddho-Confucian," in *Confucian Personalities*, ed. A. D. T. Wright (Stanford: Stanford University Press, 1962).

13. See Joan Piggott, *The Emergence of Japanese Kingship* (Stanford: Stanford University Press, 1997), pp. 172–73, for elements of Chinese-style rulership abstracted from the classics.

14. Norbert Elias, *The Civilizing Process: The History of Manners and State Formation and Civilization*, trans. Edmund Jephcott (Oxford: Blackwell, 1994).

15. Martina Deuchler, *The Confucian Transformation of Korea* (Cambridge, Mass.: Council on East Asian Studies, Harvard University, 1992). For a brief survey, see JaHyun Kim Haboush, "The Confucianization of Korean Society," in Rozman, *East Asian Region*.

16. JaHyun Kim Haboush, "Filial Emotions and Filial Values: Changing Patterns in the Discourse of Filiality in Late Chosŏn Korea," *Harvard Journal of Asiatic Studies* 55, no. 1 (1995): 154–77.

17. David Pollack, *The Fracture of Meaning* (Princeton: Princeton University Press, 1986), p. 48. And for a detailed history of Chinese books and scholarship imported into Japan, see Ōba Osamu, *Kanseki yunyū no bunkashi* (Tokyo: Kyūbun shuppan, 1997).

18. Piggott, *Emergence*, p. 170. Study of many of the same commentaries required in mid-seventh-century Tang China was also mandated by the Japanese codes. See also Inoue Mitsusada, *Ritsuryō* (Tokyo: Iwanami shoten, 1976), p. 263. And for details, see McMullen, *State and Scholars in T'ang China*, pp. 71–79.

19. In Japanese, see Hirakawa Minami, *Yomigaeru kodai monjo* (Tokyo: Iwanami shoten, 1994); and Kaneko Hiroyuki, *Mokkan wa kataru* (Tokyo: Kōdansha, 1996).

20. In the *Nihonkoku genzai sho mokuroku*, a Heian-period catalog of Chinese books in Japanese collections in 891, these three categories still contain the greatest number of volumes.

21. Yamanoue was particularly interested in alchemical and medical texts. The most recent study of his thought and writing is Masuo Shin'ichirō, *Man'yō kajin to Chūgoku shisō* (Tokyo: Yoshikawa kōbunkan, 1997).

22. *Shoku nihongi* 721 01/27. The *Shoku nihongi* is the compilation of official court annals recording events from the reigns of nine sovereigns who ruled from 697 through 791. The text was completed in 797, but compilation was done in several stages. The first twenty of forty volumes are thought to have been finished before 757 but then edited again before 797. See Piggott, *Emergence*, pp. 290–92. A good annotated edition is Aoki Kazuo et al., eds., *Shoku Nihongi*, 5 vols. (Tokyo: Iwanami shoten, 1989–98). For this entry dated 721, see Aoki's vol. 2, pp. 85–87. Henceforth *Shoku nihongi* entries are cited with their references in Aoki, including volume and page numbers.

23. Miyata Toshihiko, *Kibi Makibi* (Tokyo: Yoshikawa kōbunkan, 1961), pp. 33–45. On this *Great Tang Ritual Code of the Kaiyuan Era*, in English see Oliver Moore, "The Ceremony of Gratitude," in *State and Court Ritual in China*, ed. J. P. McDermott (Cambridge: Cambridge University Press, 1999); David McMullen, "Bureaucrats and Cosmology," in *Rituals of Royalty*, ed. D. Cannadine and S. Prince (Cambridge: Cambridge University Press, 1987), esp. pp. 199–210; and Howard Wechsler, *Offerings of Jade and Silk* (New Haven: Yale University Press, 1985).

24. The *Family Instructions for the Yan Clan* is thought to have been brought to Nara by Kibi when he returned from Tang China in 735. See Takikawa Masajirō, "*Shikyō ruijū* no kōsei to sono shisō," *Shigaku zasshi* 41, no. 6 (1961): 53–98, esp. pp. 53–72.

25. The five classics were the *Book of Changes*, the *Book of History*, the *Book of Odes*, the *Book of Rites*, and the *Zuo Commentary*. The three histories were Sima Qian's *Records of the Grand Historian*, the *History of the Former Han Dynasty*, and the *History of the Later Han Dynasty*. See Momo Hiroyuki, *Jōdai gakusei no kenkyū* (Kyoto: Shibunkaku shuppan, 1994), pp. 37–39.

26. On Kōmyō, see Hayashi Rokurō, *Kōmyō kōgō* (Tokyo: Yoshikawa kōbunkan, 1961).

27. The list, which is fragmentary, is entitled the *Shashōsōmokuroku*. See Dai Nihon komonjo, *Shōsōin monjo* (Tokyo: Tokyo Daigaku shuppankai, 1901–40), vol. 3, pp. 84–90. For Chinese texts imported to Nara at this time, see Ōba Osamu, "Nihon ni okeru Chūgoku tenseki no demma to eikyō," in *Nichū bunka kōryūshi sōsho: Tenseki* (Tokyo: Taishūkan shoten, 1996), esp. pp. 15–24.

28. See, for instance, Furuse Natsuko, *Nihon kodai ōken to gishiki* (Tokyo: Yoshikawa kōbunkan, 1998), pp. 132–33.

29. Piggott, *Emergence*, pp. 118–22, 299.

30. The classics newly mandated for study were specified in the edict. They included the *Book of Changes*, the *Book of History*, the *Book of Odes*, the *Book of Rites*, and the *Spring and Autumn Annals*. The five histories were the *Historical Annals*, *History of the Former Han Dynasty*, *History of the Later Han Dynasty*, *History of the Three Kingdoms*, and *History of the Jin Dynasty*. By this time the school system included not only the royal university in Nara but also a school at the distant Dazaifu headquarters in Kyūshū.

31. Furuse Natsuko, *Nihon kodai ōken to gishiki*, pp. 132–33 passim; and Furuse Natsuko, "Heian jidai no gishiki to tennō," *Rekishigaku kenkyū* 560 (1986): 36–45.

32. Muchimaro's is one of three biographies in a compendium called the *Kaden*. Here I have translated the text based on that annotated by Ōsone Shōsuke in Yamagishi Tokuhei et al., *Kodai seiji shakai shisō* (Tokyo: Iwanami shoten, 1979), pp. 25–38. A newly annotated Japanese edition has just appeared, Okimori Takuya et al., *Fuji-shi kaden* (Tokyo: Yoshikawa kōbunkan, 1999).

33. The annotator, Ōsone, suspects particular influence from the *Analects, Mencius, Laozi, Zhuangzi*, and the *Book of Changes* in Muchimaro's biography.

34. Ōsone glosses this as a reference to the official *History of the Wei Dynasty*. It seems to refer to Muchimaro's memorializing the throne. In his preference for Buddhism among the three ways, Muchimaro anticipates the monk founder of the Shingon school, Kūkai, who wrote similarly in early Heian times.

35. Takikawa, "*Shikyō ruijū* no kōsei," pp. 58–59, quoting the abstract in the Kamakura-period dictionary, *Jūkaishō* ("Kyōkaibu"). Remnants and references to the precepts are also found in the late-Heian-period documentary compilation, *Seiji yōryaku* (an accessible text can be found in the Shintei zōhō Kokushi taikei series of historical sources).

36. Kimoto Yoshinobu, "Isonokami Yakatsugu to Fujiwara Shikike," *Seiji keizai shigaku* 287 (1990): 61–87. The citation comes from Yakatsugu's posthumous biography in the *Shoku nihongi*, dated Ten'ō 1 (781) 06/.

37. Yoshie Akiko, *Nihon kodai no uji no kōzō* (Tokyo: Yoshikawa kōbunkan, 1986), p. 18.

38. In contrast to Sekiguchi, Fukutō objects to calling this form of marriage "monogamy." The term she correctly uses is "polygyny" (*ippu tasai*), one husband with many wives. Fukutō calls the new male-dominated household "an emergent *ie*," that is, a medieval house structure. See Fukutō Sanae, *Heianchō no haha to ko*, p. 62.

39. Fukutō Sanae, *Heianchō no haha to ko*, p. 62.

40. Patricia Ebrey has argued that since the Han dynasty, the normative Han Chinese family has been distinguished by three characteristics: patrilineality, filial piety, and patriarchy. See her "Women, Marriage and the Family in Chinese History," in *Heritage of China: Contemporary Perspectives on Chinese Civilization*, ed. Paul Ropp (Berkeley: University of California Press, 1990). She has also suggested that the preference among upper-class families of the Song (960–1279) for more substantial dowries worked to further strengthen the patrilineal principle. "Shifts in Marriage Finance from the Sixth to the Thirteenth Century," in *Marriage and Inequality in Chinese Society*, ed. Rubie S. Watson and Patricia Buckley Ebrey (Berkeley: University of California Press, 1991).

41. A particularly interesting case of this can be seen in a set of documents translated by Jeffrey Mass in his *Development of Kamakura Rule, 1180–1250* (Stanford: Stanford University Press, 1979). We see there the difficulty bystanders had even knowing whether a woman had remarried, given the still unregularized nature of marital residence.

42. Fukutō Sanae, *Heianchō no haha to ko*, p. 7.

43. The phrase "scripts of male dominance" is adopted from Peggy Sanday. Used in contrast to "scripts of female power," it refers to such attributes as courage or crisis-management abilities. See her cross-cultural study, *Female Power and Male Dominance* (Cambridge: Cambridge University Press, 1981). Our use of the term, as explained in this section, is somewhat different from hers.

44. For an analysis of the transformations of *wen* culture shared by the Chinese educated elites from the seventh to twelfth centuries, see Peter K. Bol, *"This Culture of Ours": Intellectual Transitions in T'ang and Sung China* (Stanford: Stanford University Press, 1992).

# PART ONE

# Scripts of Male Dominance

# CHAPTER ONE

# The Patriarchal Family Paradigm in Eighth-Century Japan

*Hiroko Sekiguchi*

As it developed in early China, "Confucianism" can best be characterized as an ethical system built on hierarchies of human relationships known as the "three bonds" (*sankō*) and "five relations" (*gorin*). The three bonds distinguish primary functional pairings—those between ruler and minister, father and son, and husband and wife. The five relations, as they were articulated by the classical philosopher Mencius (ca. 372–289 B.C.E.), cover a broader spectrum of relationships: filiality between father and son, loyalty between ruler and minister, differential harmony between husband and wife, precedence between elder and younger sibs, and trust between friends.[1]

In China, from the Han dynasty reign of Emperor Wu (141–87 B.C.E.) onward, canonical texts articulating rites and ethics of virtuous propriety based on these hierarchies were promulgated by successive dynasties. To the extent that the father-husband was the head of both family and state, we may refer to this system of ethical values and priorities as the "patriarchal family paradigm." As I make clear below, the ideal family thus prescribed is marked by gender hierarchy, patrilineal descent, and virilocal residence. By the time of the Tang dynasty (618–907), lawmakers were eager to nurture this paradigm with legislation, as evidenced by the Tang penal and administrative codes. Beyond Tang times, this paradigm as the ethical core of the Chinese state was adopted to varying degrees by states along Tang China's borders. Early Japan was one example.

## THE RECEPTION OF THE PATRIARCHAL FAMILY PARADIGM IN EARLY JAPAN

Transmission of classical Chinese texts and ideas was under way on the Japanese archipelago by the late fifth century. Hierarchical protocols for courtly behavior drawn from Chinese texts were evident, for example, in Prince Shōtoku's

Seventeen Articles of 604, Japan's first statement of the ethical foundation of courtly government.[2] Dicta governing gender relations also found their way into Japan. Yamanoue Okura's (660–ca. 733) poems in the eighth-century poetry anthology the *Ten Thousand Leaves* (Man'yōshū),[3] for example, cited the "thrice following" (*sanjū*) and the "four virtues" (*shitoku*) to be performed by a virtuous woman. Also mentioned were the "three bonds" and the "five teachings," or five relations, that constituted the core of Confucian propriety. "Thrice following" refers to the three responsibilities of a virtuous female, as cited in the canonical *Etiquette and Ceremonial:* to follow her father at home, her husband when she married, and her sons if widowed. The *Book of Rites*, in turn, explains the "four virtues": womanly work, womanly deportment, womanly virtues, and womanly words. Together they define the prescriptive core for womanhood in China. Later, in the early-ninth-century collection, *Miraculous Stories of Japan* (Nihon ryōiki), there are also didactic stories lauding filial treatment of parents, respectful subordination before teachers and superiors, and honorable behavior by virtuous women.[4]

By far the most important indicators of Chinese influence were the penal and administrative codes (*ritsuryō*) of the eighth century. So central were these codes to the administrative and legal structures thus established—Japan's first state formation—that some historians refer to the entire polity as the *ritsuryō* state. The codes took Tang law articulating canonical ideals as their inspiration and often incorporated the Tang codes in toto.[5] Thus they played a key role in transmitting what are termed Confucian principles in early Japan.

The penal and administrative codes sought to establish a polity headed by a figure of supposed centralized authority, the *tennō* (Heavenly Sovereign), whose authority was articulated in terms of a familial metaphor—as the subject's parent. Hence a sovereign's proclamation late in the century that "I am the father and mother of the people."[6] One aspect of this project was the establishment of courtly rituals on which the moral prestige of the Heavenly Sovereign's rule was based. This chapter focuses on another change occurring at the foundation of society, the introduction of the patriarchal paradigm into familial organization, and evaluates its impact. For this purpose I examine the articles relevant to family and marital relations in the Yōrō Ritsuryō Code, composed in 720 during the Yōrō era, supplemented by household registers, official histories, and literary sources from the eighth and ninth centuries.[7]

To state the conclusion in advance, my argument is that while *ritsuryō* lawmakers hoped to organize household units in their realm according to Chinese-style patriarchal principles so as to centralize taxation and stabilize the polity, there was a significant gap between legal prescriptions derived from Tang law and actual kinship practices in Japan. Because social and economic conditions in China were not replicated on the archipelago, marital practices and familial organization in eighth-century Japanese society rarely matched those mandated by the law.

## THE COMINGLING OF FAMILY AND STATE
### IN CONFUCIAN ETHICS

Education was a central tenet of the Confucian civilizing project, in China as in Japan. The *ritsuryō* codes stipulated the establishment of a royal university, in addition to provincial academies, as the training facility for officials. Rites memorializing Confucius were mandated. In addition, teachers were to ensure that all students were thoroughly versed in the Confucian canon, among which the prescribed texts included the *Book of Changes*, the *Book of Documents*, the *Rites of Zhou*, and the *Book of Etiquette and Ceremonial*. Of all the books in the curriculum, the most important were the *Analects* (of Confucius) and the *Classic of Filial Piety*.[8] The import of filial piety to the public and social orders was evinced by the inclusion of the classics among the required texts. The norms that governed familial behavior were integral to the ideology of rule in the *ritsuryō* state.[9]

Other sections of the codes established the institutional framework for local officials to promote the virtue of filial piety within their jurisdictions. For instance, the head of the Ministry of Popular Affairs was enjoined to exempt filial children and grandchildren, as well as virtuous husbands and wives, from taxation.[10] Fostering the five relations was designated a responsibility of administrators charged with popular governance, including the head of the Office of the Left Division of the Capital, the head of the Office for Settsu, and heads of provincial offices.[11] Even more explicitly, every provincial governor was commanded to tour his jurisdiction annually and to spread the five teachings by rewarding filial children and loyal family members, recommending the virtuous for official posts, and punishing offenses against filiality and public order.[12]

Thus the law code made duty to parents and the state the concern of officials connected with the Ministry of Popular Affairs and mandated that people be taught the Confucian virtues. Article 17 of the Administrative Code (*ryō*) Law on Tax and Labor stipulates how this was to be carried out: "When provincial officials hear of the existence of filial children, obedient grandchildren, righteous husbands and virtuous wives, let them be reported to the Council of State in memorials, and let plaques be hung before their gates. Furthermore, let members of their residence units be exempted from taxation."[13]

Two aspects of Confucian ethics are revealed in these admonitions. First, the foundation is the patriarchal family; and second, when filiality in the family is extended to the public realm, it becomes loyalty, the basis of public morality. Loyalty to the family patriarch is thus the foundation of state rule. In this light, the patriarchal family paradigm as reflected in the text of the code was the expression of a very real expectation for political and social transformation. Eventually the *ritsuryō* monarchs sought to legitimate their claim to rule the whole land by presenting themselves as the parents of the people and as patriarchs of the family state. The Japanese historian Ishimoda Shō has contended that the rule of the Chinese emperor ("Son of Heaven") derived from propriety in the family and that family ethics were "an indispensable part of the public, official order."[14] This fusion of family and state in Confucian ethics was useful to the early Japanese rulers in their efforts to establish a centralized polity, at least on paper.

### THE PATRIARCHAL FAMILY PARADIGM IN RITSURYŌ LAW

In addition to emphasizing the virtue of filial piety, Japanese penal law (*ritsu*) enforced the Tang codal maxim that "the wife considers her husband to be heaven."[15] The General Principles of Penal Law (Myōrei ritsu), for instance, defines murder of a husband's parents as one of eight seditious offenses (*hachigyaku*).[16] Crimes such as slandering the parents of one's husband, charging them with a crime, or plotting harm against them are considered in the same category of heinous offenses.[17] Likewise, failing to mourn a husband publicly was considered a serious offense; and any offense by a wife against her husband's parents was treated more harshly than a similar transgression by the husband against his wife's parents.[18] And while a husband's assault on his wife's parents automatically terminated a marriage, there is no provision condemning a husband for causing bodily injury short of death to his wife. While the murder of a wife was viewed as a grave offense, neither slander of the wife's parents nor accusing them of crimes was designated a serious transgression. The privileging of the husband's status is similarly apparent in the Penal Law on Official Crimes (Shikisei ritsu) and the Penal Law on Violence and Robbery (Zokutō ritsu).

The Yōrō Law on Official Residence Units also prescribes forms of familial propriety that privilege the husband as patriarch, together with his legally designated heir (*chakushi*). There we find the head (*koshu*) of the residence unit (*ko*) empowered as head of house (*kachō*), while his legal wife (*chaku, chakusai*) and her offspring are privileged as inheritors of the first order.[19] Grounds for mandatory divorce (*gizetsu*) include a wife maligning the husband's parents or grandparents, or her attempt to injure them. We find stipulations against a wife's adultery and provisions for a husband-to-be wishing to terminate his engagement or for a husband wishing to divorce a wife. No parallel clauses permit initiation of divorce by the wife. Other provisions privileging male roles include using a male "marriage-master" (*shukon*) and the seven grounds for husbandly repudiation of his wife (*shichishutsu*).[20] Such provisions all are derived from Tang law.

### FROM IDEALS TO PRACTICE: THE CENSUS REGISTERS

Having seen how the Chinese patriarchal family paradigm served as an underlying principle of Japanese law, we must now ask how such injunctions influenced eighth-century society. First, let us look to census records—residence unit registers (*koseki*)—for clues to what was happening in the countryside. The codes represent lawmakers' desire to stabilize a fluid society by organizing all people into residence units (*ko*), subject to the heads of those units. The unit was meant to function as the final link in the administrative chain that integrated the *ritsuryō* polity according to the model of the Chinese bureaucratic state: from court to province, province to district, district to hamlet, and hamlet to residence unit. As conceived in China, one objective of this organization was to inculcate Confucian notions of propriety—familial virtues—in the household to strengthen these vital units as the foundation of public administration.[21]

In Japan the bureaucratic organization was established in part for the purpose of taxation. Under the *ritsuryō* state, all of the rice land in the realm was to be held by the ruler, who in turn allotted specific portions to each adult at regular intervals. Taxes were levied in return, and the residence unit was to be the basic unit of taxation. Codal law and subsequent supplementary legislation prescribed differential treatment of taxable and nontaxable members in the unit; male as well as female adults paid various kinds of taxes. The law also included detailed instructions concerning the formation of new units as well as the maintenance of registers. Fortunately, some of these records are extant. Two examples will serve to suggest how the registers reflect recorders' desires to impose Chinese patriarchal and patrilineal ideals from the top down. Underneath the use of Chinese terminology, however, lies a complex field of social relations that requires a different frame of understanding.[22]

Consider first a register of the residence unit headed by Mononobe Hoso, who resided in Kawanobe hamlet of Shima district in Kyushu's Chikuzen Province.[23] The record is dated 702 and lists twenty-three individuals: the head, his wife and a concubine, plus all their offspring, forming what appears to be an extended patrilineal family group (see Chart 1.1). Here, just as the Tang and Japanese codes mandated, married sons were included in the register along with their wives and children, with wives distinguished from concubines. However, a second register from the same locale and time that was headed by Mononobe Hirabu suggests other principles of familial organization (Chart 1.2).[24] Here, just as in Hoso's register, the presence of two sons—one age 28 and one 24—with their wives and children provide the appearance of a patrilineal extended family. But if we look very closely, we notice curious omissions: there was a 34-year-old son—the senior heir—who was without wife and children, a 30-year-old son with three children but no wife, and a 26-year-old daughter with a daughter but no husband. Where were their spouses?

We could explain the absences away by surmising that the heir, his brother, and his sister were either widowed or divorced. But similar instances of single parents with children are quite common in eighth-century registers. That fact, taken with an abundance of written records from Nara (645–794) and Heian (794–1185) times that depict uxorilocal and "visiting" marital relationships, suggests another explanation. Takamure Itsue (1894–1964), a pioneer feminist historian, long contended that the prevailing marital customs of the time were anything but patrilineal. The husband either "visited" the wife's home or moved in with her uxorilocally. These

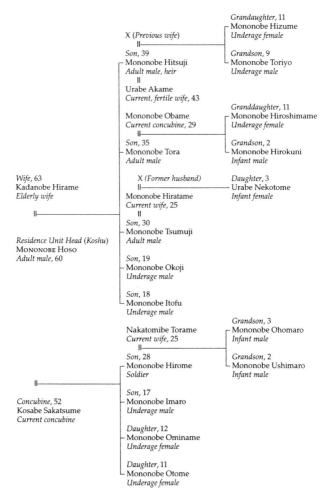

Chart 1.1. The Taxable Residence Unit (*ko*) Headed by
Mononobe Hoso, Residing in Kawanobe Township, Shima
District, Chikuzen Province

marital practices were rooted in a kinship system radically different from that of
Tang China. The uniform format of the census registers, with the name of the residence unit head appearing at the top, creates the illusion of an organized and neatly
differentiated patrilineal household. Takamure argued, however, that these registers
represent attempts to gloss a matrilineal family with imported patrilineal principles.[25]
Indeed, I have argued in detail elsewhere that families in eighth-century Japan were
predominantly matrilineal rather than patrilineal and virilocal.[26]

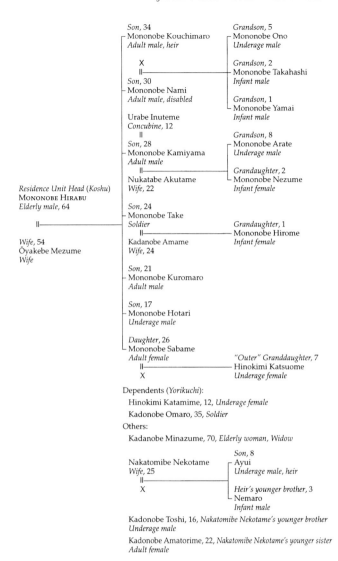

Chart 1.2. The Taxable Residence Unit (*ko*) Headed by Mononobe Hirabu, Residing in Kawanobe Township, Shima District, Chikuzen Province

A curious incongruity between the registers and commentaries to the codes further confirms the alienness of the patriarchal family paradigm. Ninth-century legal commentaries often conflate the residence unit head with his heir, which suggests the lack of a clear concept of a family head. *The Commentary on the Administrative*

*Code* (Ryō no gige, 833), for example, explains Article 5 of the Law on Residence Units ("in general, the head of the residence unit will be the family head") with an additional comment: "The family head is the senior heir [*chakushi*]." The *Ana setsu* cited in the *Collected Commentaries on the Administrative Code* (Ryō no shūge, 859–76) also interprets the article as "the heir is to be made the family head."[27] The jurists passed up the opportunity to discourse on the difference between "family head"— the man in charge of family affairs—and "residence unit head," the family's sole representative in the eyes of the *ritsuryō* authorities. This is likely because there was neither legal nor customary consensus on the exact meaning of "family head," an understandable problem if the family itself was constituted in a fluid manner. In this context, the legal categories of headship and heirdom were at best dimly reflected in social practice. Likewise, both administrative and penal codes stipulated differentiation between wife and concubine, as well as between the children of same.[28] But as I have demonstrated elsewhere, it is doubtful that these distinctions were being followed in eighth-century Japan to any great extent.[29]

The orderly residence units that appear in the census registers are more prescriptions than descriptions. So why were such administrative and legal fictions perpetuated? The adoption by the *ritsuryō* state of patrilineal descent as a principle of social organization may have been connected to changes under way within the dominant social strata. Chiefly lineages in various regions of Japan were adopting patrilineal succession for family headship, a practice that privileged the heir and suggested transition to a patrilineal family system.[30] The Tang-style *ritsuryō* registration system represents an attempt to extend such changes broadly among the population.

PUBLIC COMMENDATION
OF FAMILIAL VIRTUES

The most notable state policy used by eighth-century officials to promote the patriarchal family paradigm was that of commending virtuous behavior. We have seen that the Law on Tax and Labor stipulated that filial children, obedient grandchildren, righteous husbands, and virtuous wives should receive public recognition and that the fusion of familial and public morality was a hallmark of Confucian ethics. Here I explore evidence that this was more than mere legal prescription. There exist many references to such adulation and rewards in the eighth-century court record known as *Chronicle of Japan, Continued* (Shoku nihongi), and in subsequent official histories. In rewarding righteous behavior, officials put emphasis on wives in general and chaste widows in particular; the latter were praised for refraining from remarriage and for maintaining their husbands' graves. Instances in which wives were acclaimed for virtuous behavior continued to appear in the historical record until near the end of the ninth century.[31]

A well-known example of royal commendation occurred in 715, when the female sovereign known as Genshō ascended the throne. In that year a propitious omen led to the change of the era name, a general amnesty was granted, and "filial children, obedient grandchildren, righteous husbands, and virtuous wives" received commendations. All were to enjoy tax-exempt status for the remainder of their lives.[32] Such treatment, accompanying propitious signs in the heavens and the start of a new reign, evidences the correlation between familial virtues and harmony in the realm.

A royal edict issued by Heavenly Sovereign Kōken (r. 749–58) in 757, when she proclaimed Prince Ōi her crown prince and successor, states in no uncertain terms the importance of filial piety for rulership: "From of old, ruling the people and bringing peace to the realm has been accomplished through filiality. Now a propitious sign has expressed the bounteous aid of high heaven and the acclaim of the deities. So should every house acquire a copy of the *Classic of Filial Piety* for frequent reading and study. Furthermore, let those who follow the path of filiality be recognized, and let those who lack filiality and respect, or those who are not faithful friends and obedient grandchildren, be exiled to stockades on the distant frontier."[33]

So was filiality conflated with loyalty to the throne, and heaven's accord legitimated both. As we saw earlier, the *Classic of Filial Piety* served as one of the required texts for students at the royal university. Kōken's edict suggests that the *Classic* was not intended for bureaucrats alone but for the populace in general. It is worth noting that the edict may have been modeled on an amnesty issued by the Tang emperor Xuanzong in 744, more than a decade earlier. Later in this volume Sugano Noriko analyzes how a millennium later the Tokugawa government would apply these same principles in a nationwide campaign to shore up popular morality.

By now we have surveyed three venues in which rulers and lawmakers sought to promote the patriarchal family paradigm: *ritsuryō* law, census registers, and state policy. Yet these efforts were relatively unproductive. To fully understand the reasons, a closer examination of the structures of familial authority, property ownership, and patterns of marital residence is in order.

## WOMEN CONTROLLING PROPERTY

In his well-known theory of the evolution of monogamy founded on private property holding, Engels contended that before the emergence of concepts of private property and the patriarch's domination over wife and household, members of a collective group possessed land and other goods in common. He argued further that marital relations within such collectivities, which he termed "pairing marriage" (following Lewis Henry Morgan), were informal and impermanent.[34] That is to say, the birth of private ownership led to a change in family structure—from nonpatriarchal to patriarchal—and in the form of marriage—from pairing marriage to male-dominant monogamy. Engels envisioned that all parts of the world underwent similar stages of development (see Table 1.1).[35]

TABLE 1.1 Developmental Structure of Property Ownership, Family, and Marriage

| Developmental Stage of History | Form of Property Ownership | Family Structure | Relationship between Male and Female | Relationship between Individual and Collective |
|---|---|---|---|---|
| Savagery | Common ownership by collective or clan | Collective, clan | Parity (plural marriage in the group) | Individual subsumed in collective |
| Barbarism | Ownership by the collective; rights to access by individuals | Incipient family under collective (non-patriarchal) | Parity (pairing marriage) | Individual began to be separated from the collective |
| Civilization | Private ownership by individual | Patriarchal family | Domination of female by male (polygynous monogamy) | Establishment of the individual |

In eighth-century Japan land rights took the form of individual rights among men and women to land held in joint possession.[36] The family structure in that stage, which could be called "Barbarism," in Engels's terms, would have been non-patriarchal, as was indeed the case. Examples from historical and literary sources show that male-female relationships in personal and financial affairs were marked by parity.

That gender hierarchy was little advanced in the arena of property ownership is confirmed by tales archived in the early-ninth-century *Miraculous Stories.* Consider the story of a daughter of a wealthy provincial. Tanaka-no-mahito Hiromushime of Sanuki Province is depicted as "the wealthy holder of many treasures, including horses and cattle, slaves, coin and rice, and both dry and wet fields."[37] All were productive resources needed for successful agricultural operations. And in Mino Province's Katagata District, a census register records that the wife of a provincial chieftain possessed more slaves than did her husband and that another female reportedly purchased a substantial piece of property.[38] Other records verify that women bought and sold both land and slaves. The story of Hiromushime indicates that some women were able to use their possessions as loan capital to increase their wealth. In other words, women were not only possessors of assets in name but were de facto managers as well. Like men, women held debtor's and creditor's rights, as indicated by records of women acting as borrowers and lenders of money in business and private transactions.[39]

Such conditions contrasted significantly with those idealized by Tang law, which prescribed that goods should be held corporately by the patriarch-led household and that women should be excluded from inheritance. Whereas in China such exclusion produced the Chinese patriarchal family paradigm and its associated ethics of filiality, in Japan, where property was held individually both by women and by men, there was no patriarch who possessed or managed all property. In other words, gender parity in property holding prevented the establishment of the patriarchal family system. This gendered difference in property rights between Tang China and ancient Japan lies at the root of the divergent policies in land allotment. In Japan the Administrative Code Law on Rice Fields (Taryō, Article 3) mandated distribution of rice fields to both men and women, including wives and daughters. But under Tang law, women could receive official allotments only as widows, that is, as proxies for their deceased husbands.

The absence of a patriarch as formal family head in the eighth-century Japanese family can be attested through contemporary sources. In the *Miraculous Stories* collection, many instances appear in which the family representative in large-scale agricultural management was the husband *and* wife team. Elites of the time managed their land by running their agricultural businesses jointly.[40] Family management was conducted by the husband and wife as a pair, and the fact that both were representatives of the family means that neither the patriarchal family nor the patriarch had yet come into existence.

This type of property-holding pattern and what Morgan would call a "pairing" form of marriage gave rise to a form of "family" that was at best fluid. As will be further elaborated later, eighth-century marriages were one-on-one relationships between wife and husband that endured only as long as the partners wished. Under such circumstances, the separate possessions of husband and wife were not yet combined as corporate holdings of a permanent marital household. The family constituted by pairing marriage was not yet an institutionalized unit, and it lacked any real socioeconomic status to be passed on from generation to generation. Such a family had no use for a designated heir and hence no reason to differentiate between children born of the wife and children born of a concubine. The formidable gap between Chinese canonical ideals and Japanese practice was thus rooted in economic conditions and marital relations.

## PATTERNS OF MARITAL RESIDENCE

The instability of the family founded on pairing marriage was in part a result of transitory residence patterns. In the *Miraculous Stories* only 3 of the 116 stories mention virilocality—the marital residence mode assumed by Tang law. Instead we glimpse the wide variety of arrangements possible in the eighth century. In the course of a marriage, the couple's place of residence could shift. After an initial period of the husband "visiting" at the wife's home, the couple might choose to progress to a uxorilocal and then to a neolocal pattern. Or they might move from "visiting" straight to neolocal residence.[41] To complicate matters further, within one family there could be diverse patterns at any given time. One daughter might take in a husband at her natal home to live uxorilocally—what I call Type A marital relations.

Other daughters might reside with their mates neolocally (Type A1). Or multiple daughters might take in husbands and live with them uxorilocally (Type B).

What sort of family units were created by these arrangements? In Type A relations, the couple and their children lived with the wife's unmarried sibs to form a matrilineal unit. In Type A1 relations, a nuclear family was established. And in Type B, an aggregate matrilineal household was the result. An example of a Type A marriage during Heian times is that of the court leader Fujiwara no Michinaga (966–1028). In 987 he married Minamoto no Rinshi, daughter of the powerful Minamoto no Masanobu, and moved to his wife's residence, the Tsuchimikado Palace. The following year a daughter was born there. Michinaga and his wife lived with his wife's parents and her unmarried brothers and sisters. The Tsuchimikado Palace remained Michinaga's official residence throughout his life, as his father-in-law eventually passed it to Michinaga and his wife and moved with his family to a site nearby.[42]

These types of residence and family units are best seen as descriptions of different stages in a cycle rather than as fixed structures. In the written record there are cases in which a married couple living uxorilocally eventually left the bride's natal home to reside neolocally, forming a new nuclear family.[43] After a couple had raised its children to adulthood, a similar pattern was no doubt replicated. When relations were so fluid, it made sense for each family member to control his or her own wealth instead of relying on the family as a property-owning corporate unit. A family that thrives on instability and flexibility has no need to establish an heir or a clear line of descent. Ultimately, it is this fluidity that accounts for the divergence of the Japanese family as it existed from the patriarchal paradigm in the *ritsuryō* code.

## SEXUALITY: THE IRRELEVANCE
## OF CHASTITY AND ADULTERY

According to Morgan and Engels, impermanence is a hallmark of pairing marriage. Pairing marriage has a superficial resemblance to monogamy, in that both are formed by the union of one man and one woman. But they depend on different economic foundations. In pairing marriage, before the development of private property, the union does not result in the husband's possession of the wife's property and sexuality. Thus a pairing marriage can be dissolved at will by either party. Furthermore, because marriage does not involve exclusive sexual service of either party, there is no concept of chastity. Fidelity can result as a matter of personal choice, but it is not a categorical moral obligation.[44]

Let us adopt the vantage point of a woman in this situation and imagine what life would be like. She would be free, in mutual consent with the man, to decide if she is willing to engage in a sexual or marital relationship (and indeed the line between the two was blurry.) Just as freely she can opt to dissolve such ties.[45] In modern terms, she enjoys full rights to pursue sexual love, marriage, and divorce. Naturally she also has the right to initiate courtship or propose marriage. We might assume that in a relationship based on mutual affection and agreement there is no danger of sexual coercion because she has the authority to say no.

There is substantial evidence that women in the eighth century were free to choose to participate in or terminate mating unions. In eighth-century texts such as the *Chronicle of Ancient Matters* (Kojiki), myths archived in the section "Age of Gods" include stories of female deities who freely chose their mates. The goddess Yagamihime, for instance, chose to wed Ōnamuchinokami while refusing proposals from his brother, telling the latter: "I will not accept your offers."[46] Similarly, in a remnant from the eighth-century *Tango Gazetteer* (Tango fudoki) a woman proposed to her chosen mate with the words, "My heart is firmly and forever yours."[47] Still other written sources depict women making decisions about terminating relationships, even when they were living neolocally or virilocally with their spouses. In the ninth-century *Tales of Yamato* (Yamato monogatari), a collection of poems with prose introductions, a wife pondered, "Where will I go if I leave my man?"[48] And in the poetry anthology *Ten Thousand Leaves* (Man'yōshū), a woman actually barred the door of her home against her lover, who begged in verse: "Last night, that pitch-black night, you sent me back. Do not send me back this evening too, back on the distant road."[49]

In such a society a woman was well-placed to decide whether to engage in sexual relations. In the *Harima Gazetteer* (Harima fudoki) we find the story of Hikamitome:

> Of old, the deity Sanukinohiko proposed marriage to Princess Hikamitome, but she rejected him. Thereupon the male deity tried to compel her compliance. She grew angry and retorted, "Why are you trying to force me?" They fought and he was defeated. As he departed the scene, he bemoaned his weakness.[50]

The historical record contains many similar instances in which the man's proposal was refused by the woman and he was left with no recourse but to comply. As the passage from the *Ten Thousand Leaves* tells us, a woman in a pairing marriage could refuse the sexual advances of even her husband.[51]

Because pairing marriages were not exclusive, the sexuality of the wife was not considered the exclusive property of her husband. Therefore, neither "chastity" nor "adultery" were relevant concepts. In this regard, consider a tale from *Miraculous Stories* in which "a wicked man," suspecting his wife of having a sexual relationship with a monk, said to the monk, "You vile priest, you have seduced my wife. You deserve to have your head smashed in!"[52] When the same tale was recounted three centuries later, in the early-twelfth-century *Tales of Times Now Past* (Konjaku monogatarishū), the husband calls the monk a "thief."[53] This and other retold stories suggest that by the later Heian period the idea of a husband owning his wife's sexuality had made its way into the countryside. In the ninth century, although a moral rebuke of the monk is implied by the adjective "vile," he was not condemned as an adulterer. But by the tenth century a new term for a perpetrator of adulterous relations—"secret man" (*misoka otoko*)—and legal sanctions against the deed begin to appear in the courtly world of the capital. Therefore, we can say that between the ninth and twelfth centuries the sexuality of a courtier's wife became the exclusive possession of her husband. The linguistic term for such an idea, "adultery" (*kantsū*), had in fact developed by the late twelfth century.[54]

This transition to the "monogamy" mode of male-dominated marriage in the ninth century affected the situation of Heian-period women appreciably, beginning with the aristocracy and diffusing outward. From the tenth century on, the prerogative of a noble woman to initiate or terminate a marital union was transferred to her father.[55] Moreover, if a wife felt that she had lost her capacity to attract her husband sexually, it came to be thought of as refined behavior for her to separate from him before he could divorce her. Numerous examples of rape can also be found in the *Tales of Times Now Past*, and accounts of female prostitution became common after the beginning of the tenth century. By mid-Heian times, women were suffering a significant loss of agency in marital, sexual, and familial matters.

CONCLUSION

Provisions in the eighth-century *ritsuryō* codes—including those prescribing differentiated roles for the residence unit head, heir, wife, and concubines, as well as those delineating distinctions between the offspring of same, rites of betrothal or marriage, repudiation, and mandatory divorce—began the process of acculturating elements of the Chinese patriarchal paradigm in Japanese society. The motive force for the propagation of this paradigm was political. The early Japanese polity was a secondary construction: its structures and concepts were borrowed from China and then promulgated in a society at a different stage of development. Given the preeminence of China in the China Sea sphere during the seventh century, Japanese leaders were strongly disposed to adopt Chinese ways.[56] Considering the dangers Japan found itself in by 660, when its policy of assisting the Paekche kingdom on the Korean peninsula failed and the Paekche capital fell to the united forces of Tang China and Silla, it is not hard to understand why court strategists consciously adopted a more complete Chinese framework of state formation and began a concerted attempt to unify the archipelago against possible attack from the continent.[57]

Yet the social foundations in Japan were those of an earlier stage of development, "Barbarism" in Engels's terminology. Written sources depict both husbands and wives holding and managing capital resources as well as informal and unstable marital relations. The type of union constituted by pairing marriage mitigated against the development of a patriarchal family system.

This gap between prescriptive law and actual social conditions accounts for the rapid decline of the *ritsuryō* polity and, to a large extent, for the demise of the Chinese classics and their influence as well. In the latter half of the ninth century, the Confucian canon ceased to be the mainstay of the curriculum at the royal university. It was not until the period of the Tokugawa shoguns (1603–1867) that Neo-Confucian mores came to exert greater impact on Japanese society. But even then, there remained key differences between the practice of kinship and gender relations in Japan and China, as the chapters that follow show.

*Translated by Gaynor Sekimori*
*Edited by Dorothy Ko and Reiko Shinno*

NOTES

*Editors' Note:* The late Professor Sekiguchi was one of a handful of senior women historians in Japan. This chapter is a brief summary of the thesis of her magnum opus, *Nihon kodai kon'inshi no kenkyū* (A study of the history of marriage in ancient Japan), published in 1993. Through analyses of laws, their application, and consequences, Professor Sekiguchi furthered our understanding of the ancient Japanese social, especially marital, structure that resisted the framework of imported Chinese patriarchal ideals.

The historian Takamure Itsue (1894–1964) published her *Shōseikon no kenkyū* (A study of matrilocal marriage) in 1953. It laid the foundation for what would later develop as the field of women's history in Japan. Like Takamure's, Sekiguchi's research is guided by theoretical insights obtained from Lewis Henry Morgan's *Ancient Society* and Friedrich Engels's *The Origin of the Family, Private Property and the State*, both of which illuminate the correlations between family system and stages of political and economic development. We regret that Professor Sekiguchi passed away in April 2002, before this book went to press.

1. *Mencius* 3A:4. For an English translation, see D. C. Lau, *Mencius* (New York: Penguin Books, 1970).

2. Hisaki Yukio, "Jukyō" (Confucianism), in *Kokushi daijiten* (Dictionary of Japanese history), vol. 7 (Tokyo: Yoshikawa kōbunkan, 1986). See the English translation of the Seventeen Articles in Wm. Theodore de Bary, ed., *Sources of Japanese Tradition*, vol. 1 (New York: Columbia University Press, 1964), pp. 47–51; also in David Lu, ed., *Japan: A Documentary History* (Armonk, N.Y.: M. E. Sharpe, 1997), pp. 23–26.

3. *Man'yōshū*, in Nihon koten bungaku taikei, vols. 4–7 (Tokyo: Iwanami shoten, 1957–62). Partially translated as *The Man'yōshu* (Nippon Gakujutsu Shinkōkai). Reissue New York: Columbia University Press, 1965. Also, *The Ten Thousand Leaves*, partially translated by Ian Hideo Levy (Princeton: Princeton University Press, 1981).

4. *Nihon ryōiki*, Kyōkai, ca. 804. Nakada Norio, *Nihon ryōiki*, in Nihon koten bungaku zenshū (Tokyo: Shōgakukan, 1975–76). Translated by Kyoko Motomichi Nakamura as *Miraculous Stories from the Japanese Buddhist Tradition* (Cambridge, Mass.: Harvard University Press, 1973). The episodes cited are "On an Evil Man Who Was Negligent in Filial Piety to His Mother and Gained an Immediate Penalty of Violent Death" (I, 23); "On an Evil Daughter Who Was Negligent in Filial Piety to Her Mother and Gained an Immediate Penalty of Violent Death" (I, 24); "On Taking Others' Possessions Unrighteously, Causing Evil, and Gaining a Penalty Showing an Extraordinary Event" (I, 30); "On the Miraculous Survival of a Buddha's Picture Offered by a Widow Who Made a Vow to Have It Painted for Her Dead Husband" (I, 33).

5. My premise is that the clauses of the Japanese *ritsuryō* are consistent with their counterparts in the Tang code, unless otherwise noted. The Law on Residence Units of the Yōrō Ritsuryō Codes was translated into English by George B. Sansom, "Early Japanese Law and Administration, Parts I and II," *Transactions of the Asiatic Society of Japan*, 2d ser., vol. 9 (1932); and vol. 11 (1934). Parts of Sansom's abstract can be found in Lu, *Japan*, pp. 33–36. For a translation of the Tang penal code, see Wallace Johnson, *The Tʻang Code* (Princeton: Princeton University Press, 1979), and *The Tʻang Code II: Specific Articles* (Princeton: Princeton University Press, 1997).

6. *Shoku nihongi* (compiled 797), Enryaku 1 (782) 7.25. Similar expressions can be found in entries dated Jinki 3 (726) 6.14 and Tenʼō 1 (781) 7.5. This source is partially translated by J. B. Snellen as "*Shoku nihongi:* Chronicles of Japan, Continued, from 697–791 A.D.," *Transactions of the Asiatic Society of Japan*, 2d ser., vol. 11 (1934).

7. I will not deal with those articles concerning ethical government by the sovereign, such as the giving of alms and interpretation of good omens, in the following: Administrative Code: Law on Residence Units, Article 45; Law on Decorum, Article 45. Nor will I analyze here the introduction of a system of protocol based on *li* (propriety), such as funerary regulations.

8. The Law on Scholarship (Gakuryō). Regarding the rites to Confucius, see note 3 of the same in *Ritsuryō*, ed. Inoue Mitsusada (Tokyo: Iwanami shoten, 1976), p. 595.

9. Administrative Code: Law on Scholarship, Articles 1, 3, 5.

10. Administrative Code: Law on Official Postings (Shokuinryō), Article 21.

11. Administrative Code: Law on Official Postings, Articles 66, 68, 70, respectively.

12. According to the *Ryō no shūge* (Koremune no Naomoto, compiled 859–84), these "five teachings" were based on the commentary on the *Book of Documents* (Shangshu) by the Han Confucian scholar Kong Anguo, who noted "the teachings of the five constants (*wuzhang*), that is, the five relationships: a father's righteousness, a mother's compassion, an elder brother's amity, a younger brother's respect, and a child's filial respect" (*Ritsuryō*, pp. 262–68). An accessible text of the *Ryō no shūge* can be found in Kokushi taikei henshūkai, ed., *Ryō no shūge* in *Shintei zōhō kokushi taikei* (Tokyo: Yoshikawa kōbunkan, 1978).

13. Administrative Code: Law on Residence Units, Article 33. According to Niida Noboru's reconstruction of Tang law, the articles in the Law on Residence Units in the Japanese and Tang codes closely match each other. See his *Tōryō shūi* (Remnants of the Tang Code compiled) (Tokyo: Tōkyō Daigaku shuppankai, 1964), p. 257. The articles in the Law on Tax and Labor are likewise very similar (p. 683).

14. Ishimoda Shō, "Kodaihōshi" (A history of ancient law), in *Nihon kodai kokkaron* (A discussion of the ancient Japanese state), pt. 1 (Tokyo: Iwanami shoten, 1973), pp. 198–99.

15. For the Tang provision, see Johnson, *Tʻang Code I*, p. 88. It should be noted, however, that the Tang penal code also emphasized the full partnership of husband and wife. For instance, the subcommentary for Article 177 states, "According to ritual, the Sun appears in the east and the moon in the west. They are like the meaning of husband and wife. She is equal to him, such is her importance!" And Article 189 reads, "The way of husband and wife is to expect to be in the same grave. Once joined, they do not change during their lifetimes." See all in Johnson, *Tʻang Code I*, pp. 154, 167. Still, if we accept the universality of the heavenly metaphor of the Tang Code's Article 120, it would appear that marriage could never be an equal partnership.

16. See Johnson, *Tʻang Code I*, esp. pp. 42–43.

17. See Johnson, *Tʻang Code I*, n. 176.

18. For the Tang provision, see Johnson, *Tang Code II*, p. 88.

19. Clauses 1, 5, 7, 13, 16, 19, 22, and 25 of the Law on Residence Units (Koryō) seem particularly faithful in their transmission of Tang law. For the Japanese texts, see *Ritsuryō*, pp. 225–39. Meanwhile, designation of the husband as house head and stipulation of a legal wife with clear status differentiation between her issue and those of lower-ranking concubines was also a concern of the Penal Law on Households and Marriage (Kokonritsu), which has been only partly reconstructed. See *Ritsuryō*, pp. 562–63. In a note there, the editors indicate that remnants from the Kokonritsu can be found in the Heian-period legal compendium, *Ryō no shūge*.

20. On mandatory divorce (C: *yi-jue*, J: *gizetsu*), see Johnson, *Tang Code II*, p. 168, and *Tang Code I*, p. 297. See also Hikaku kazoku shigakkai, ed., *Jiten: Kazoku* (Tokyo: Jōbundō, 1966), p. 259; and Yen-hui Tai, "Divorce in Traditional Chinese Law," in *Chinese Family Law and Social Change*, ed. D. C. Buxbaum (Seattle: University of Washington Press, 1978). For the Japanese provision, see *Ritsuryō*, p. 235. The "marriage-master" (*shukon*) was, according to Wallace Johnson, "the person actually responsible for the marriage arrangements." See Johnson, *Tang Code I*, p. 76; and *Tang Code II*, pp. 158–59. For the Law on Residence Units provision, see *Ritsuryō*, p. 233. The seven grounds for husbandly repudiation of the wife (*shichishutsu*) were not having any children, immoral behavior, not serving parents-in-law, loquacity, committing robbery, jealousy, and incurable disease. See *Tang Code II*, p. 167. See also the Law on Residence Units in *Ritsuryō*, p. 234.

21. The articles designed to restructure the population and nurture the patriarchal norm include Article 1 (50 residence units make up one township); Article 5 (the family head is to be the residence unit head, the person with legal responsibility for the residence unit, differentiating between those with and without taxation liabilities); Article 13 (creating new residence units); Article 19 (instructions for making residence unit registers); and Article 22 (specifying how long the registers were to be kept). Because Article 19 requires the register to be drawn up "according to the *shiki*," it is clear that detailed requirements for making registers were included in subsequent rules elaborating the code. Their existence is verified by a reference, dated 721, to the "*Sekishiki*" (elaboration of rules regarding registers) in the commentary *Koryō ōbunjō shūge koki* (Ancient records of interpretations of the articles of the Household Code).

22. Japanese protocols for drawing up registers were adopted almost word for word from the Tang code. Article 1 of the Japanese Law on Residence Units is virtually the same as Article 1 of the Tang Household Code, as are Articles 5 and 7, 13 and 16, 19 and 23, and 22 and 25 respectively.

23. Tokyo Daigaku shiryō hensanjo, ed., *Dai Nihon komonjo: Shōsōin monjo*, vol. 1 (Tokyo: Tokyo Daigaku shuppankai, 1901–40), p. 107 ff.; Takeuchi Rizō, ed., *Nara ibun* (Tokyo: Tōkyōdo shuppan, 1962), vol. 1, p. 100 ff.

24. *Dai Nihon komonjo*, p. 139 ff.; *Nara ibun*, vol. 1, p. 103 ff.

25. Takamure Itsue, *Shōseikon no kenkyū* (A study of matrilocal marriage) (Tokyo: Rironsha, 1966), p. 236 ff. If we follow this argument, the 34-year-old son would have registered singly because his wife and children lived at the wife's home and would not have appeared on his register. Similarly, the 30-year-old son might have registered only his children, and the 26-year-old daughter, with her husband living elsewhere, would have been registered together with her child with her birth family.

26. Sekiguchi Hiroko, "Nihon kodai kazoku no kiteiteki chien jūtai ni tsuite," in *Kodaishi ronsō*, vol. 2, ed. Inoue Mitsusada Hakushi kanreki kinenkai (Tokyo: Yoshikawa kōbunkan, 1978).

27. Concerning the lack of a concept of heir, see Sekiguchi Hiroko, "Ritsuryō kokka ni okeru chakushoshi ni tsuite" (Heirs and status differentiation among sons in the *ritsuryō* state), *Nihonshi kenkyū* 105 (1969): 3–38.

28. On wife and concubine, see Penal Code: Law on Residence Units and Marriage (Articles 9, 29); Administrative Code: Law on Residence Units (Articles 23, 27). On children of wife and concubine, see Penal Code: Law on Residence Units and Marriage (Article 9); Administrative Code: Law on Succession (Keishiryō, Articles 2, 3).

29. For the absence of any distinction between wives and concubines, see my "Ritsuryō kokka ni okeru chakusai shōsei ni tsuite" (Wives and concubines in the *ritsuryō* state), *Shigaku zasshi* 81, no. 1 (1972): 1–31.

30. Yoshida Takashi, *Ritsuryō kokka to kodai no shakai* (The *ritsuryō* state and ancient society) (Tokyo: Iwanami shoten, 1983), p. 124. See also Sekiguchi, *Nihon kodai kon'inshi*, vol. 1, pp. 12–14, for a discussion of Yoshida's views.

31. For emphasis on wives and chaste widows, see the commentaries in the *Ryō no shūge*. On this issue, see Sugawara Ikuko, "Seppukō" (Concerning virtuous wives), *Nihon rekishi* 349 (1977): 19–33; Takeda Sachiko, "Ritsuryō kokka ni okeru jukyōteki kazoku dōtoku kihan no dōnyū" (The introduction of the pattern of Confucian family ethics in the *ritsuryō* state), in *Kodai tennōsei to shakai kōzō* (The ancient *tenno* system and social structure), ed. Takeuchi Rizō (Tokyo: Azekura shobō, 1980).

32. Aoki Kazuo et al., *Shoku nihongi* (Tokyo: Iwanami shoten, 1989), p. 715. The Japanese text of Genshō's edict is in *Shoku nihongi*, Reiki 1 (715) 9.2.

33. *Shoku nihongi*, Shin Nihon koten bungaku taikei, 3 (Tokyo: Iwanami shoten, 1992), p. 182, n. 14. The character used here for "house" (*ke*) may refer to district offices as it did in an earlier edict mandating the worship of Buddhism by district chieftains in Temmu's time. For Kōken's edict in Japanese, see *Shoku nihongi*, Tempyō-hōji 1 (757) 4.4.

34. Frederick Engels, *Origin of the Family, Private Property, and the State* (New York: New World Publications, 1972). See also Lewis Henry Morgan, *Ancient Society* (Tucson: University of Arizona Press, 1985). For my reading of the relative theoretical merits of Morgan and Engels as applied to Japan, see *Nihon kodai kon'inshi*, vol. 1, pp. 49–102.

35. See Sekiguchi, *Nihon kodai kon'inshi*, vol. 1, p. 45 et seq.

36. For a study of ownership in ancient Japan, see Sekiguchi Hiroko, "Kodai ni okeru Nihon to Chūgoku no shoyū, kazoku keitai no sōi ni tsuite" (Differences between ancient Japan and China regarding ownership and family morphology), in Joseishi sōgō kenkyūkai, ed., *Nihon joseishi*, vol. 1 (History of women in Japan) (Tokyo: Tōkyō Daigaku shuppankai, 1982).

37. *Miraculous Stories*, III, 26, pp. 257–59. Nakada, *Nihon ryōiki*, pp. 326–30.

38. The Mino man was named Ōniwa; the woman who purchased land was called Nakajima-no-muraji Ōtojiko. Tokyo Daigaku shiryō hensanjo, *Dai Nihon komonjo*, vol. 1, pp. 42–44.

39. Sekiguchi, "Kodai ni okeru Nihon to Chūgoku no shoyū," pp. 245–90.

40. For management by the husband (*kachō*) and the wife (*kashitsu*), see Takamure, *Shōseikon no kenkyū*, vol. 2, p. 8 et seq.

41. Sekiguchi, *Nihon kodai kon'inshi*, vol. 2, pp. 371–418. "Visiting"-type marriage was widespread in the eighth century but rare after the tenth century. For three examples of virilocality, see *Nihon ryōiki*, I, 2; and II, 20 and 27 (*Miraculous Stories*, pp. 104–5, 187–88, 197–99).

42. Takamure, *Shōseikon no kenkyū*, pp. 405, 691. Also, *Heian Kamakura Muromachi kazoku no kenkyū* (A study of the family in the Heian, Kamakura, and Muromachi periods) (Tokyo: Kokusho shuppanka, 1986), pp. 28, 47. This example is unfortunately the only sure evidence we have of a matrilineal family of the time. Because of the lack of extant documents, it is difficult to reconstruct how people lived together in the same residence during this period.

43. See *Nihon kazokushi*.

44. See Sekiguchi, *Nihon kodai kon'inshi*, vol. 1, p. 49 ff.

45. Her and his freedom to dissolve a sexual or marital relationship was subject to communal restraints. *Nihon kodai kon'inshi*, vol. 1, p. 337 ff. For the slippage between sexual love and marriage, see vol. 2, p. 298 ff.

46. *Kojiki*, trans. Donald L. Philippi (Tokyo: University of Tokyo Press, 1968), bk. 1, chap. 21, pp. 93–95. This is a story of the marriage of a deity, but the story is based on regional legends and is thought to reflect marriage customs of the time.

47. For the *Tango fudoki* remnant, see Akimoto Kichirō, ed., *Fudoki* (Tokyo: Iwanami shoten, 1987), p. 470. For an English translation, see Aoki Michiko, *Records of Wind and Earth* (Ann Arbor: Association for Asian Studies, 1997). The corollary of this female ability to refuse a man is that a man may violate her free choice. This suggests that logically a concept of rape within marriage did exist in classical Japan. There are, however, no extant examples in the documents. See Sekiguchi, *Nihon kodai kon'inshi*, vol. 1, pp. 345, 347.

48. *Yamato monogatari*, sec. 148. For an English translation, see Mildred Tahara, *Tales of Yamato: A Tenth-Century Poem Tale* (Honolulu: University of Hawaii Press, 1980).

49. *Man'yōshū*, Poem 781. The translation is Ian Levy's. See Levy, *Ten Thousand Leaves*, p. 337.

50. *Harima fudoki* in Akimoto, *Fudoki*. The episode is contained in the description of Tsuma in Takuga District. For an English translation, see Michiko Aoki, *Records of Wind and Earth*.

51. I have argued that the absence of prostitution can be surmised from the fact that there is no documentary mention of it and that the price of female slaves, the usual source of commercial sex, was lower than that of males. This is a complicated issue the full exploration of which lies outside the scope of this chapter. See Sekiguchi, *Nihon kodai kon'inshi*, vol. 1, pp. 362–87.

52. *Miraculous Stories*, II, 11, pp. 175–76.

53. *Konjaku monogatari shū*, Scroll 16, tale 38. The text can be found in the Nihon koten bungaku taikei edition, vol. 3, p. 498.

54. Sekiguchi, *Nihon kodai kon'inshi*, vol. 1, pp. 362–87; vol. 2, pp. 112–15, 125–66.

55. Monogamous marriages decided on by the father could take place against the wishes of the woman. I consider these arrangements a form of "rape" when they violated the daughter's self-determination in sexual matters. For the disappearance of female rights regarding marriage, proposal and separation, the occurrence of rape, the growth of prostitution, and the appearance of the concept of adultery, see Sekiguchi, *Nihon kodai kon'inshi*, vol. 2, p. 83 ff.

56. The import of Chinese characters for writing best illustrates the cultural preeminence of China. According to Engels, writing moves a culture from the stage of "Barbarism" to that of "Civilization" (*Origin of the Family*). Before Japan developed her own writing system, Chinese characters were adopted to express Japanese sounds. Indigenous scripts based on Chinese characters were not developed until the tenth century. See Hiroko Sekiguchi,

"Heian jidai no danjo ni yoru moji (buntai) tsukaiwake no rekishiteki zentei" (Historical premises for differentiation in the use of scripts by men and women in the Heian Period), in *Nihon ritsuryōsei ronshū* (Collected essays on the *ritsuryō* system in Japan), vol. 2 (Tokyo: Yoshikawa kōbunkan, 1993).

57. Steps toward the formation of the *ritsuryō* state were first taken with reforms during the reign of Tenji (662–71) and then with the completion of the Kiyomihara Code during the reigns of Temmu (673–86) and Jitō (690–97).

# CHAPTER TWO

# The Last Classical Female Sovereign

## Kōken-Shōtoku Tennō

*Joan R. Piggott*

Our task in this volume is to investigate the influence of the classical discourse of Chinese civilization, loosely termed "Confucian," on women's lives across geography, class, and time in premodern East Asia. My focus is on the latter days of female kingship at Japan's Nara-period court (710–84). Using the framework of the Japan-China dialectic discussed in the introduction, I explore facets of the dialectic at work as it redefined kingship as a fully gendered male script during the era of Shōmu Tennō's daughter and successor, Kōken-Shōtoku Tennō (r. 749–58, 764–70).

Historians of Japan writing in English—including James Murdoch, George Sansom, and John Whitney Hall—have argued that Kōken-Shōtoku Tennō discredited female rulership by her "scandalous" partnership with the monk Dōkyō, who is generally portrayed as plotting to seize throne and state. The fact is, however, that such scenarios ignore the crisis that faced Kōken-Shōtoku's reign as a female Heavenly Sovereign (*tennō*). Eighth-century Japanese attempts to institutionalize the Chinese practice of royal patrilineal succession resulted in female sovereignty, but at the same time deepening acculturation of Sinic ideals of male rulership was steadily delegitimizing female monarchs.

Some prefatory remarks on what can be termed the male script of Chinese rulership are needed before I proceed. The doctrine of rulership developed in Han China (third century B.C.E. to early third century C.E.) was a cosmological vision that privileged the male in politics and society. Han *Ru* discourse established the cosmological significance of the Son of Heaven (*tenshi*) as the linchpin linking the three realms of heaven, earth, and human society. This vision of political and social order elided the spheres of state and family and glorified the virtue of filiality shown to both fathers and rulers, as Sekiguchi Hiroko shows elsewhere in this volume. Filial piety was the virtue that legitimized the familial and the state hierarchy, and it gave precedence to males, whether rulers, fathers, or elder brothers. As a Han chronicler put it in the "Treatise on the Five Phases" in the *History of the Former Han Dynasty,* "Where a hen announces the dawn, the master will not prosper. Where women conduct government, peace will not reign."[1]

So was the male-dominant patriarchal family paradigm implicit at the levels of both family and broader society over which the Chinese imperial state presided. By privileging fathers and husbands, the compilers of Tang codes made law out of gender hierarchical prescriptions from canonical texts such as the *Great Learning,* the *Book of Rites,* and the *Classic of Filial Piety.*[2] The *Book of Rites* urges, "the man takes the initiative, not the woman"; "faithfulness is the virtue of a wife"; and "the wife is to be the rank of her husband; by herself, she has no rank."[3] While support for gender complementarity can be found in both the classics and the Chinese law codes in the notion of an ideal partnership between husband and wife, male dominance remains the primary thrust. As Article 120 of the Tang penal code proclaims, "The wife considers her husband to be heaven, and her mourning for him is like that for her parents."[4] And Article 190 adds, "The wife follows the husband and does not determine her own way."[5]

On the Japanese archipelago, from the late seventh century onward Japanese *tennō* and their advisers looked to this Chinese classical ("Confucian") discourse for guidance on ideological, legal, and ritual matters as they sought to consolidate their rule. Nevertheless, finding clues as to how ideas from the classics and law codes were actually read and acculturated at the Nara court is difficult. An inscribed folding screen that numbered among the intimate personal effects of Shōmu Tennō (r. 724–49) provides insights. It urges viewers,

> When the seed is good and the field fertile, as a matter of course the crop is abundant. When the ruler is wise and the ministers good, prosperity results. Flattering words produce much joy and suit the feelings. Honest words trouble the heart and are harsh to the ear. Nonetheless, if you make honesty your principle, the gods will aid you. Fortune or misfortune enter as one beckons. Moreover, as parents do not love unfilial children, enlightened rulers do not employ useless ministers. Purity and poverty bring enduring pleasure while impure wealth brings constant worry. As filial piety invariably makes its best effort, loyalty always sacrifices itself. When lords and ministers mistrust each other, the state is unstable. When fathers and sons mistrust each other, the household lacks harmony.[6]

The linking of agriculture with governance, parenthood with rulership, and filiality with ministerial loyalty recalls the synchronization of kinship and kingship in both the *Classic of Filial Piety* and the more contemporary text on Tang rulership, *Plan for a Universal Monarch* (Difan), authored by the early Tang emperor Taizong in about 648. In fact, historians surmise that the latter was brought back to Nara by one of many returning diplomatic embassies after the mid-seventh century.[7] Coming as it did in the early eighth century, Shōmu Tennō's rule as a Chinese-style Heavenly Sovereign was still quite new and vulnerable. Indeed, Shōmu was reportedly the first Japanese monarch to don full Chinese ceremonial garb, includ-

Figure 2.1. The Chinese-style *Benkan*, Crown of the
Heavenly Sovereign

ing the crown of streaming jewels, in the New Year court assembly of 732 (see Figure 2.1).[8] It is hardly surprising that Shōmu and his advisers would have eagerly looked to Chinese texts, old and contemporary, for inspiration.

While the reign of Shōmu and the construction of the Tōdaiji Great Buddha represented a high point in the development of Chinese-style monarchy in Nara, regular diplomatic missions sent abroad in the second half of the eighth century resulted in ongoing "Tangification."[9] On one occasion, for instance, Shōmu's daughter and successor, Kōken Tennō, ordered copying and distribution of a newly imported edition of the *Classic of Filial Piety* for provincial elites across her realm in 757. She was likely emulating the Tang emperor Xuanzong (r. 712–56), who had composed his own commentary on the *Classic* and distributed it on the continent just fourteen years earlier.[10] Then in 758 Kōken's successor, Junnin Tennō, ordered that all Japanese court ministries be renamed according to their Tang counterparts and that Tang policies should be widely emulated.[11] He also mandated widespread study of rubrics for sage rulership compiled in the era of Wu Zetian (690–705). Wu, originally a Tang empress, had established her own Zhou dynasty and ruled as monarch for fifteen years. Junnin's preference for a female ruler's prescriptions may well reflect the bond with Wu Zetian felt by Nara's own powerful women, Kōken Tennō and her mother, Queen Kōmyō.[12] I explore the historical context of these developments in detail later in this chapter.

While eighth-century courtiers were acculturating structures of Chinese monarchy as the century progressed, the process was made more complex by the Sinic view that only males should rule. As Sekiguchi has noted, the Chinese patriarchal family paradigm contradicted local practices characterized by gender complementarity, bilineality, and shared social leadership by men and women.[13] Most telling, six female monarchs presided over the court between 583 and 770, even during a time when Sinic practices such as patrilineal inheritance and primogeniture were being promulgated by the *ritsuryō* codes. Nonetheless, as I show here, by the later eighth century reign by a female monarch was coming to be seen as inappropriate. Analysis of the process by which Nara kingship was redefined as a male script serves as an informing case study of the gradual and partial advance of the Japan-China dialectic over the course of the eighth century. Specifically, I argue that three vectors delegitimized female rule and ultimately made it impossible for Shōmu's daughter to preserve the throne either for her own lineal heirs or for future female sovereigns. First, ongoing exposure to Chinese patriarchal structures embedded in the *ritsuryō* codes and in the expanding archive of Chinese texts read by Nara courtiers effectively propagated the ideal of male-dominant gender hierarchy. Second, as the realm was further integrated by the ongoing *ritsuryō* process, the privileging of male scripts penetrated society far beyond the capital, rendering female leadership at court increasingly suspect.[14] Third, the need of court and dynasty to regularize royal succession suggested the need to narrow the candidate pool, an objective that could be served by disinheriting female royals as claimants to the throne. The story that follows demonstrates how all three vectors reached a crisis point during the era of Shōmu's daughter, who became Japan's last classical female sovereign.

### "EVEN THOUGH A WOMAN": PRINCESS ABE AS ROYAL HEIR

Shōmu Tennō's daughter, known as Princess Abe, was born to Crown Prince Obito, the future Heavenly Sovereign, and a Fujiwara consort named Asukahime in 718 (see Chart 2.1). Since the time of Fujiwara Kamatari in the mid-seventh century, Asukahime's family had served as advisers to the throne, and by the turn of the century under Fujiwara Fuhito (659–720), family members gained increasing influence at court as ministers and royal affines. Abe's birth was followed by that of a brother, Prince Motoi, in 727. As by then Shōmu had taken the throne, Motoi was quickly named crown prince. This made excellent sense according to *ritsuryō* law: following the Chinese patrilineal stem ideal, the Law on Succession in the Taihō Ritsuryō Code of 701 prescribed that an aristocrat's senior heir be his eldest son by his senior consort. The throne was expected to follow these same rubrics. But

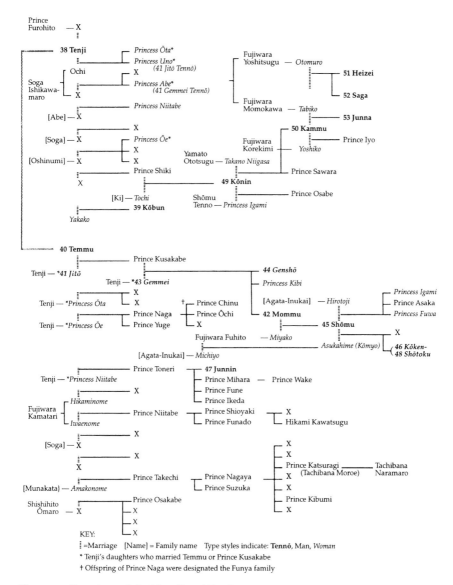

Chart 2.1. Genealogy of the Nara Royal Family

some at court were vexed by these events: the idea of a crown prince was itself an innovation based on Chinese practice, and there had never been an infant heir designate to the throne.[15] Moreover, in Motoi's case the baby's appointment and eventual succession was sure to enhance the prestige of his maternal grandfather, Fujiwara Fuhito. Other aristocratic families at court, already outnumbered by the Fujiwara on the Council of State (Daijōkan), which coordinated the activities of officialdom, feared any increase in Fuhito's power. The immediate crisis was forestalled when Motoi died only months after birth, but the debate over who would succeed Shōmu and how it would affect the power of the Fujiwara became ever more contentious.

After Prince Motoi's death it became apparent that Shōmu—surrounded by his Fujiwara uncles, affines, and ministers—was determined that Asukahime's issue should succeed him and that Fujiwara preeminence continue. Politics turned nasty when a rival potential heir to the throne, Prince Nagaya, was implicated in a coup and his whole family was destroyed.[16] In the wake of that episode, Shōmu proclaimed Asukahime his queen consort (kōgō). That appointment, like Prince Motoi's as crown prince, was unprecedented. Never before had a woman from outside the royal kin held the queenly status of kōgō, which status would privilege her offspring for future succession.[17] An extralegal agency staffed by hundreds, the Queen Consort's Household Agency, was established to see to the new queen's needs while also providing hundreds of lucrative posts for relatives and clients. All this meant that even after Motoi's death, Shōmu's court was increasingly dominated by the queen's supporters.

Counter to Shōmu's hopes, however, no additional children were born to him and his queen, now known by her Buddhist sobriquet Kōmyō, meaning "bright and clear." Circumstances looked even bleaker in 736 and 737 when a plague killed all four of the queen's brothers (see Chart 2.2). It was at this time of crisis for both the court and the Fujiwara that Shōmu Tennō announced his appointment of his twenty-one-year-old daughter, Abe, as heir apparent in 738. In a much later edict Abe recalled her appointment this way: "My mother revealed that the royal stem line of the Oka-no-miya sovereign [Prince Kusakabe, the monarch Temmu's heir] would end. To prevent that, it was necessary that I succeed, even though a woman."[18]

"Even though a woman": were these words of regret or pride? We can only speculate on the feelings behind these words. There is no doubt, however, that the Chinese ideal of patrilineal stem succession—succession by the eldest son of a monarch's designated senior wife—had proven difficult to actualize at the Nara court. One obstacle was, as Sekiguchi has pointed out, that the practice of ranking consorts and their offspring was not yet standard. And there were other obstacles to smooth royal successions. At the beginning of the century the female ruler Jitō (r. 690–97) had taken the throne because her son by Temmu Tennō (r. 673–86), Prince Kusakabe, had died and left only an infant heir, the future Heavenly Sovereign Mommu (r. 697–707). Because kingship in Japan had never been held by a

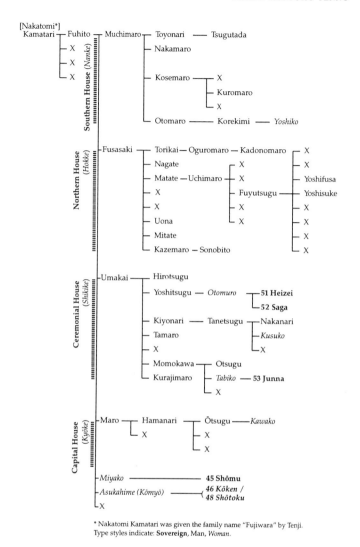

* Nakatomi Kamatari was given the family name "Fujiwara" by Tenji.
Type styles indicate: **Sovereign**, Man, *Woman*.

Chart 2.2. Selected Genealogy of the Fujiwara

child, the grandmother took the throne for seven years until Mommu Tennō came of age and could succeed. Later Jitō also served as senior (retired) *tennō* (*daijōtennō*) to train and protect the young Mommu after he ascended the throne. And after Mommu's early death when his own heir was an infant, first Mommu's mother and then his sister ruled as Gemmei Tennō (r. 707–15) and Genshō Tennō (r. 715–24), holding the throne for more than seventeen years until the heir, Shōmu Tennō, was ready to rule.[19] These female monarchs (*jotei*) of the early eighth century were con-

sidered place-holders, female royals whose past roles as queen consorts gave them
sufficient status in the ruling line to hold the throne until the designated male heir
could take over rulership. Their intermediacy was critical for patrilineal stem succession as the founders of *tennō*-centered governance had envisioned it.[20] But here
was Shōmu in 738 naming Abe as his senior heir (*chakushi*) "even though a woman"
and without a designated male heir, something neither Chinese practice nor the
Japanese *ritsuryō* codes nor precedent countenanced. Similarly foreboding for future succession, the unmarried crown princess was unlikely to produce an heir:
according to the code she could marry only a prince, after which according to the
patrilineal assumptions of codal law, her offspring would represent her husband's
line rather than her father's.

Given this history, Crown Princess Abe's circumstances were truly exceptional
and divisive.[21] Entries in the Nara court annal, the *Shoku nihongi*, or *Annals of Japan,
Continued,* suggest that non-Fujiwara advisers were encouraging Shōmu to name his
one living son, Prince Asaka, as heir. But he was loath to do so: the kin of Asaka's
mother, unlike Abe's Fujiwara kin, had little wealth or influence, and they could
not serve him as Kōmyō's family did. So when Asaka died under mysterious circumstances in 744, despite considerable unrest at court, Princess Abe was left in
place as Shōmu's heir.[22]

Princess Abe was educated for rulership by an exceptional tutor, Kibi Makibi.
According to the *Shoku nihongi*, the princess learned to read Chinese classics such
as the *Book of Rites* and the *History of the Former Han Dynasty* from this veteran of
study abroad in Tang China. It was probably Kibi who, convinced of the centrality of court ritual at the Tang court, suggested that the crown princess perform
the filial *Gosechi* dance before both Shōmu Tennō and Genshō Daijōtennō in early
spring 743. Shōmu's edict on that occasion evoked the name of his ancestor, Great
King Temmu, "who ruled the whole realm from the palace of Asuka Kiyomihara,
whose very name brings forth awe." Shōmu, like his ancestor Temmu, was proclaimed on this occasion to believe "that ceremonial and music were two necessary
means by which peace and harmony were maintained under Heaven, and that by
these would the proper functioning of the hierarchy ordering those above and below be assured."[23] Furthermore, by dancing before a pair of co-rulers, one female
and one male, Abe also signaled that as her father's filial daughter she would serve
as her soon-to-retire father's partner in gender-paired rulership, just as had countless female deities and chieftains whose stories filled court myth histories like the
*Kojiki* and the *Nihon shoki.* Confirming that, it was a few years later, in an edict issued before his retirement in 749, when Shōmu Tennō again reminded his courtiers
of the principle of gender complementarity in terms of service to the throne:

> As for offspring of my ministers, let sons be promoted according to their service. As
> for daughters, [normally] they could not be promoted. But reflecting upon the fact
> that only sons carry on the father's name, should daughters go unrewarded? It is fit-
> ting that both serve together.[24]

In contrast with Chinese practice prescribed in the Taihō Code—the norm by which daughters could not be promoted save in a few offices in the back palace (*kōkyū*)—Shōmu called for service from and rewards for sisters, wives, and daughters alongside brothers, husbands, and sons.[25] Such gender complementarity was a particularly important argument for Shōmu to reinitiate just before his own daughter acceded to his throne.

### THE SUN-LINE CHARTER AT MIDCENTURY

Crown Princess Abe at last ascended the throne in 749. An exchange of royal proclamations between her father as retiring *tennō* and the new monarch plus an introduction by the prime minister as head of officialdom included various images of rulership and legitimacy.

> *Prime Minister Tachibana Moroe:* Hear the royal command of the monarch [Shōmu] of Yamato, who rules by command of the heavenly deities that dwell in High Heaven, and who through the royal grandchild and distant ancestors inherited the realm over which he rules as a numinous being (*kamunagara*).

> *Shōmu:* The Tennō [Genshō] who ruled at Nara spoke thus: "According to the unchanging rubric proclaimed by the Sovereign [Tenji] of the Ōtsu palace—I tremble to speak his name—this office of the Sun-line heir is mine [to bestow]. Succeed me now and rule." While trembling I have followed her command and ruled the realm. But the manifold prerogatives of my royal office have continued to increase and my body can no longer endure. According to law let this office be transmitted to my heir. You princes of the royal line, great ministers and officials, and all my subjects, hear my command!

> *Kōken:* He [Shōmu] whose name I tremble to speak commands that I assume his office as *tennō* and serve. While unable to advance or retreat and with reticence and humility I accept his command. Let all hear my words! Attending to his order, however unworthy I may be, princes, ministers, and others are to oversee affairs of governance in the *tennō*-centered realm. Serve me without error, with clear and pure hearts, and All Under Heaven shall be blessed with peace and prosperity. Such is my will as a numinous being. Let all attend to my command.[26]

Here in the prime minister's preface and then in Shōmu's resignation we find a clear elaboration of the "Sun-line" (*hitsugi*) royal charter that had been reconfirmed in every accession rite since the late seventh century: how heavenly male and female deities had dispatched a heavenly grandson to rule the earth; how from generation to generation royal ancestors linked lineally by blood had carried on that Heavenly mandate; and how from the reign of Tenji (r. 668–71) onward royal ancestors had passed on the *tennō*'s throne according to an "unchanging rubric" (*fuhen jōten*) of patrilineal succession until Shōmu's own time. This emphasis on the patrilineal transmission of Sun-line kingship reflects strong Chinese influence, while the premise of divine kingship—both Shōmu and his daughter identify themselves as "numinous beings"—is rooted in island traditions of sacral rulership. Meanwhile, frequent references to female deities and female rulers of the past served to legitimate Abe's inheritance of her father's office. These edicts of 749 can be read as artifacts from an era when notions of gender complementarity and male-scripted rulership were both salient.

## FILIALITY AND KŌKEN'S REIGN

Despite the optimism of these accession statements, once enthroned, Kōken Tennō's lack of an heir proved an ongoing source of instability for court and government, which is why on his deathbed seven years later Shōmu finally broke the "unchanging rubric" of patrilineal succession to proclaim a male cousin, Prince Funado, his daughter's heir designate.[27] But the change of mind did not resolve the situation. The new crown prince was kin of the Fujiwara by neither blood nor marriage, and thus Kōken Tennō repudiated Funado shortly after her father's death. The terms of that repudiation are particularly striking because, when compared with the proclamations of 749, they evidence marked changes in the charter of Heavenly Sovereignty, especially in their emphasis on the classical "Confucian" virtues of filiality and propriety.

Specifically, in an edict proclaimed on the fourth day of the fourth month in 757, Kōken Tennō justified Funado's removal for breaches of filiality and ritual propriety:

> The lord is master of the realm. The crown prince provides assistance. In accord with the previous sovereign's final testament, Prince Funado was elevated to the office of crown prince. But during the mourning period, when rites were not yet finished and grass did not yet cover the royal tomb, the prince [Funado] secretly carried on with a servant and failed to show proper respect for the deceased sovereign. His demeanor during mourning demonstrated no signs of grief. . . . I prayed to the Three Jewels and to the gods to judge the merits and demerits of my rule and to provide a sign. On the twentieth day of last month the characters "Peace in the realm" were clearly seen on a palace curtain. So do the gods make manifest high Heaven's aid for my rule. . . . The Three Jewels make manifest that the realm will be peaceful while the gods of heaven and earth signal the enduring stability of the realm. . . . The child who is unfilial cannot become a merciful father, nor can the vassal lacking propriety become a sage lord. Following Heaven's sign, let him [Prince Funado] be set aside.[28]

Here behavior emphasized in the Chinese classics as meriting Heaven's mandate—filiality, propriety, and loyalty—replace the patrilineal and sacral foci of the earlier Sun-line charter. Confirming the new emphasis on Chinese virtues, this edict of 757 went on to order that copies of the *Classic of Filial Piety* be distributed to district chieftains in the provinces, which deed literally emulated a Tang precedent.[29] Historians see a new eara of "Tangification" under way at this time.

That Kōken chose to highlight filiality in dismissing Funado is not surprising. When her denigrators complained about her sex and inability to produce an heir, she responded by emphasizing her filial relationship with her father and the prerogatives that ensued therefrom, including her right to expect subordination from similarly filial ministers and subjects in the realm. At the same time, Kōken signaled the importance of the Three Jewels of Buddhism in addition to Japan's own geo-local deities as intermediaries with Heaven. Her father, self-proclaimed "servant of the Buddha" who constructed Tōdaiji's Great Buddha while also honoring deities across the realm, had propitiated both. His filial daughter did so as well, and in return propitious signs signaled Heaven's mandate. Kōken's edict of 757 reflects a new synthesis of the Sun-line myth, strong belief in Buddhist realm protection, and emphasis on the Chinese classical discourse.

Kōken's critics responded violently to her new claims and dismissal of Prince Funado in the seventh month of 757. Tachibana Naramaro, son of the retired prime minister Tachibana Moroe, led a stunning coup that reportedly involved nearly four hundred fifty individuals, a huge percentage of court society.[30] Had the main protector of both Kōken and Queen Kōmyō, Fujiwara Nakamaro, not succeeded in marshaling the necessary military manpower, the plotters would have won the day. In the wake of the grisly violence that led to not a few deaths by execution, Kōken Tennō passed her throne to her newly chosen heir, Prince Ōi, another of Temmu's grandsons, in 758. Ōi, known by the reign name Junnin Tennō, had long been close to Queen Kōmyō and her favorite nephew, Nakamaro.[31] In fact, Ōi was Nakamaro's son-in-law and had long resided in Nakamaro's home. Given the bilineal organization of Nara elite society and this uxorilocal marital residency, he even called Nakamaro "father" in one edict. Junnin's accession meant that a trio of royal voices presided over the court: Kōken as senior *tennō*, Junnin as sitting *tennō*, and Kōmyo as the deceased Shōmu's queen and Kōken's mother. Poised at their side as chief adviser was Nakamaro, who became leader of the Council of State as Minister of the Right and Grand Protector (Taiho).[32] Nakamaro championed ongoing adoption of Tang ways to provide a more complete body of structures and precedents for Heavenly Sovereignty at a time when the crisis of succession still gripped the court.

### THE RETIRED *TENNŌ* REASSERTS HER AUTHORITY

Not surprisingly there were tensions and disagreements among these court leaders, and they accelerated after Kōmyō's death in mid-760. By that time the retired Senior Tennō Kōken lay sick in a detached palace on the shores of Lake Biwa, where the court had been moved by Nakamaro while repairs were proceeding at the Nara palace. There Kōken was treated by a healer-monk named Dōkyō. Apparently cured by that monk's theurgistic ministrations, in the fifth month Kōken returned to Nara, where she shaved her head and donned nuns' robes. Thereupon in the sixth month she issued an unprecedented edict castigating Junnin Tennō for serious breaches of filiality and loyalty and announced that she was dividing the powers of the throne between herself and Junnin. Her words were, "As for government, the sitting monarch will handle small matters. Matters of importance—punishments and rewards—will be mine to command."[33]

There had been retired monarchs in Japan since Jitō's day at the turn of the eighth century, and there may have been occasional disagreements between sitting monarchs and their seniors. But Kōken's proclamation of 762 was unprecedented. Where could she have gotten the idea of splitting the powers of the monarchy? It seems likely that Kōken was inspired by a Chinese precedent from half a century earlier: in 712 the Tang emperor Ruizong passed his throne to his heir, Xuanzong, after dividing responsibility for "matters great and small" between them.[34] Kibi Makibi brought texts on the early history of the Tang dynasty back with him in 735, and some report of that event may well have been included.

After their return to Nara the retired monarch and the sitting monarch with their respective followings continued feuding. By late 762 Junnin Tennō had promoted three of Nakamaro's sons to seats on the Council of State.[35] And in 763 the struggle moved to the Buddhist sphere when Kōken had an ally of Nakamaro removed from the Prelates Office (Sōgōsho), to be replaced by her monk-healer, Dōkyō. Not only was such termination of a venerable cleric irregular; Dōkyō also jumped over several less prestigious offices to be named Lesser Secondary Prelate (Shōsōzu), third of five in the Prelates Office.[36] Then in the subsequent New Year appointments of 764, Junnin made Nakamaro's sons governors of Mino and Echizen, rich provinces bordering Ōmi that Nakamaro already controlled. Nakamaro himself was put in command of provincial militias near the capital. Finally, perhaps to bring their fight to a head, in the ninth month Kōken sent her emissary to take possession of the royal seal, needed for promulgating important state documents, from Junnin's residential palace. Violence resulted when the emissary was killed, but the incident convinced Nakamaro to flee Nara, taking the post-station bells needed for official travel, the royal seal, the seal of the Council of State, and a Temmu-line prince named Shioyaki. Notably, Junnin refused to accompany his chief minister in rebellion, who needed an enthronable prince at his side for any hope to later legitimize his authority. Kōken decreed Nakamaro a traitor and promised rewards to all who would fight for her.

The record in the *Shoku nihongi* annal suggests that Nakamaro and his following underestimated their opponents' organizational and strategic abilities, especially those of Kibi Makibi. Kibi, the *tennō*'s onetime tutor who had once brought military paraphernalia back from Tang China as a gift for Shōmu Tennō, now showed himself an able commander. He assembled a cavalry force from the palace guard, organized control of ports on Lake Biwa and provincial forces in Ōmi, and set up a special guard to protect the senior monarch.[37] Also rallied against Nakamaro were Fujiwara scions from lineages other than Nakamaro's Southern House, many of whose fortunes had not fared well under Nakamaro. The descendants of Fujiwara Umakai, known as the Capital House Fujiwara because of their service in the Capital Office (Kyō-shiki), were particularly active among Kōken's supporters in the fight against Nakamaro.

On the run in Ōmi Province, Nakamaro declared his companion prince "acting sovereign," but when agents at various barriers refused to honor the putative ruler's edicts Nakamaro's force was defeated and its commander killed. In Nara, although Junnin had refused to join Nakamaro, he was dethroned and sent into exile. Thereupon Kōken ended her retirement and retook the throne. Defending that decision—critics said a shaved-headed nun could not represent the Sun-line—she made public her father's admonishment to deal firmly with anyone who obstructed her royal will. Shōmu had told her, she remembered:

> If the princes try to make you their servant, if they claim that you are their agent, do as you will. As for your successor, if he lacks respect and propriety, he should not sit on the throne. The proper path for ministers is to serve you with upright and pure hearts. [Only] then can you rule as Heavenly Sovereign.[38]

Shōmu's words as his daughter recalled them leave no doubt that in Kōken's mind she possessed the full prerogatives and perquisites of the Heavenly Sovereign's office. Given that, any royal heir designate to her throne was mandated to demonstrate filiality and loyalty to her, or face dismissal. Such notions had Tang precedents: the emperor Taizong removed his first heir apparent, installed his ninth son as a second heir apparent (the patrilineal stem ideal was not always adhered to in China either), and then came close to changing his mind a third time.[39] Shōmu and his daughter were insistent that decisions about royal succession belonged to the lineal descendant and holder of the throne, not to princes or ministers of the court.

For the young *tennō*-centered polity, the costs of such visible friction at the center were high. Even when victory against Nakamaro was proclaimed as a sign of Heaven's favor for her, fighting between two Heavenly Sovereigns and their ministers could not help but weaken both the legitimacy and the continuity of governance over the realm. So did Kōken reascend the throne in 764 in desperate need of an heir who could help her unify the court while assuring the continuity of Heavenly Sovereignty into the future. But where was such a candidate to be found? Her frequent edicts demonstrate that Shōmu's daughter placed her greatest faith in Heaven, with the gods and buddhas as intermediaries. Historians have usually described her as an exclusively Buddhist monarch, but in fact a close reading of the records of both her reigns shows that Kōken-Shōtoku should be characterized as a "Buddho-Confucian" for whom the ways of Heavenly rulership exemplified by Tang monarchs, especially the exemplary female sovereign Wu Zetian, were focal.

## SHŌTOKU TENNŌ AND HER MONASTIC LIEUTENANT

After retaking the throne in 764, Shōtoku Tennō reorganized her court to establish two lines of command, one to be overseen by her Council of State and one to be directed by her monk-lieutenant, Dōkyō. In other words, those responsible for both non-Buddhist (outer) affairs and Buddhist (inner) affairs were formally integrated at her court for the first time. Fujiwara Toyonari of the Fujiwara's Southern House was made Minister of the Right and leader of the Council of State, and

Nagate of the Fujiwara's Northern House, Kibi Makibi, and several royal princes were also seated on the council.[40] On the Buddhist side, the prelate Dōkyō was given a new title, Healer-Monk cum Grand Minister (*daijin-zenshi*). Shōtoku justified that unprecedented honor to a monk by reminding critics that for a bodhisattva ruler, a monk-minister was appropriate:

> Although my head is shaved and I wear Buddhist robes, I still must govern the realm. As the Buddha declared in the [Bommō] *Sutra*, "Kings, you who ascend the throne receive the ordination of a bodhisattva!" Such words show that there can be no objection to rule by one who has taken orders. Furthermore, since the reigning monarch has taken the precepts, it is fitting that the grand minister (*daijin*) should also be a monk.[41]

Her father Shōmu had been counseled by loyal monks, and some 127 healer-monks had been invited into the palace to cure him during his final days.[42] But monk advisers to the throne had never before been given court ranks or bureaucratic posts. In appointing Dōkyō to a seat on her Council of State, Heavenly Sovereign Shōtoku went beyond precedent to fully integrate Buddhist prelacy into officialdom. The model for this new organization may well have come from Tang's Wu Zetian. She had made Buddhist affairs the purview of her Ministry of Rites in 694. Shōtoku Tennō continued her reforms in 766 by establishing parallel hierarchies of Buddhist prelates and secular ministers to advise her. It was at that time when she proclaimed Dōkyō Prince of the Law (Hō'ō).[43]

Scholars have long debated whether Dōkyō's mandate as Prince of the Law actually made him court leader or superintendent of Buddhist affairs only.[44] The documentary evidence for the debate is circumstantial and fragmentary. It seems clear that inspiration for his title came primarily from Buddhist texts such as the *Saishō'ō Sutra* and *Kegon Sutra*, wherein the "Prince of the Law" is represented as a righteous bodhisattva ("Buddha-becoming") ruler whose good works protect the realm from all evils.[45] As we can piece the record together from entries in the *Shoku nihongi* and documents in the Shōsōin archive, his activities were primarily in the Buddhist sphere. He held sole authority to authorize penitential services used to purify monastic celebrants prior to sutra readings; he dominated the certification process for applicants to the monkhood; and he controlled the official seals of the Prelates Office and official temples.[46] At provincial temples (*kokubunji*) he initiated new penitential rituals addressed to Kichijōten, a female deity of prosperity deriving ultimately from India whose image on painted banners used for the ceremony may have evoked that of the female sovereign herself (see Figure 2.2).[47] In addition, the sutra-copying division of the Tōdaiji Construction Agency seems to have been mobilized as a royal copying center under his purview, while oversight of construction efforts at Saidaiji, a new official temple dedicated to the realm-protecting cult of the four protector kings (*shiten'ō*), gave him considerable influence vis-à-vis the large and powerful agency.[48] Dōkyō also superintended construction of shrine temples near major regional shrines, such as the royal ancestral

Figure 2.2. Kichijōten, a Female Deity of Prosperity

shrine at Ise, after Shōtoku initiated the new era of "Tempyō Jingo," meaning "peace under Heaven—protected by the deities," in 765.[49]

An even more ambitious plan for realm protection undertaken by Shōtoku with Dōkyō's assistance was the carving of one million stupas (*hyakumantō*) out of wood, each one to encase a sheet of paper block-printed with one of four prayers (*dharani*) from the *Mukujōkōdarani Sutra*.[50] These prayers celebrated the power of Buddhism to assure long life, prosperity, and freedom from evil or misfortune for the realm of a Buddhist monarch. Just as Shōmu had eagerly embraced the challenge of building Tōdaiji's Great Buddha, now his daughter Shōtoku committed her power and wealth to this alternative means of saving the realm. Work got under way in 764 and, with the help of a staff of 157 workers, was completed in early 770. Each of ten official temples in or around Nara reportedly received one hundred thousand of the stupas—Hōryūji near Nara still has some of its stupas and prayers today.[51] With Dōkyō managing the Buddhist arm of her bifurcate government, Shōtoku intended to make her own contribution to her father's project as a bodhisattva monarch.

Although Japanese historians have revised the earlier common wisdom that Dōkyō was the real ruler in Kōken-Shōtoku's second term, the English historiography has continued to ignore Shōtoku's agency in presiding over her court.[52] I view Dōkyō as Shōtoku's primary lieutenant, in a role replicating that occupied by Nakamaro earlier, although the monk Dōkyō was much more dependent on his monarch than Fujiwara Nakamaro, scion of a ministerial family, had been. Kōken-Shōtoku's oral edicts portray a strong personality insistent on full exercise of her sovereign will. She was not a passive woman: the daughter of Shōmu and Queen Kōmyō was a willful ruler who would not tolerate lèse majesté. Take, for instance, her edict of late 764, when she cautioned courtiers against meddling in her decisions concerning the future succession:

> Those who serve me—whether of high, middle, or low rank—often say, "To stabilize the realm, decide upon a crown prince and everyone will be tranquil and harmonious." However, I have not appointed anyone as yet because the one who people call worthy is not always so.[53] If someone that Heaven will not accept is named, he will not succeed and will be destroyed. As I reflect on it, this office is not something to be decided by a human. Neither is it attainable by violence or coercion. I alone am Heaven's heir, and I will decide about a successor. As I ponder appointing an heir, I believe that Heaven will send the right person. I shall not make my decision for a time. . . . You must not secretly plot, stirring up the people to seize the throne by force, or thinking to set someone up as *tennō* for your own benefit and according to your own views. If you do so, your houses will be destroyed and your heirs will perish. From now on, keep your hearts straight. Do not waver! Serve as I command.[54]

These were not the formal words of royalspeak or myth. The personal voice of the monarch is too strong to ignore in such phrases as "as I reflect on it," "I will decide," and "as I ponder." Whoever prepared this edict—it would normally have been someone in her Ministry of Palace Affairs (Nakatsukasashō)—the sentiments are those of Kōken-Shōtoku Tennō herself, and they hardly reflect the weak and victimized woman portrayed by many historians.

## DENOUEMENT: THE ORACLE EPISODE

Even these forceful warnings did not halt the "secret plotting" that was dividing the court and threatening *tennō*-centered governance. There were coup attempts by rival prince-led factions in 765 and 769, and in the latter incident palace women who were Shōtoku's close relatives were accused of trying to curse her.[55] Into this tense environment word of an oracle from the Usa Hachiman deity of distant Kyūshū arrived at the Nara palace in 769. The oracle was said to have urged that Prince of the Law Dōkyō be enthroned as Heavenly Sovereign to assure peace and prosperity in the realm.[56] Advised of the oracle, Shōtoku sent an emissary, Wake Kiyomaro, to the distant shrine to substantiate the deity's words. The *Shoku nihongi* abstracts these events as follows:

> For reasons of his own, Suge no Aso Maro, the chief shrine official at the Dazaifu, fawningly served Dōkyō. He lied, and saying it was an oracle from the Usa Hachiman deity, he proclaimed, "If Dōkyō is made *tennō,* there will great peace in the realm." When Dōkyō heard this, he was deeply pleased and confident. The Tennō beckoned [Wake] Kiyomaro close to her throne and said, "In my dream last night a messenger from Hachiman appeared and said, 'The deity has something to say to Your Majesty and wishes to transmit it via the nun Hōkin.'" But the Tennō ordered Kiyomaro, "Go in Hōkin's place and hear the deity's oracle." As Wake prepared to leave, Dōkyō said to him, "Perhaps the reason the deity has requested that a messenger be sent is to let it be known that I should be enthroned. [If so] I will be greatly empowered and will see to your rank and post." Kiyomaro proceeded to Usa Hachiman Shrine where the deity's oracle proclaimed, "Our realm has always had a monarch and ministers. Let a Heavenly heir take the throne. The pretender should be ousted without delay!" Kiyomaro returned to the capital and delivered the deity's oracle thus. Dōkyō was enraged. He terminated Kiyomaro's post and sent him far away from court as supernumerary second-in-command at Inaba provincial headquarters. But even before Kiyomaro reached his new posting there was another royal order: "You are exiled without rank and post to Ōsumi." His sister, Hōkin, was laicized and she too was exiled to Bingo Province.[57]

Historians have long been puzzled by these events. Besides the unprecedented nature of the oracle—no such oracle had ever influenced a royal succession—the notion that the healer-monk Dōkyō, scion of a provincial elite family, could succeed to the Sun-line throne would have contradicted the patrilineal and divine charter of kingship that had legitimized Heavenly Sovereignty for nearly a century. The historian Inoue Mitsusada tried to explain this difficulty away by arguing that Nara society at the time must have been "seized by religious ecstasy."[58] While the idea of Heaven's immanence was strong in both Tang China and Nara Japan, in my view that could not have overcome the importance of the Sun-line charter for Heavenly Sovereignty. The idea that Dōkyō or his supporters thought that the monk could easily accede to the throne remains difficult to accept. We must also remember that reports of this whole affair in the *Shoku nihongi* annal are suspect. They were written later, by compilers hostile to both Kōken-Shōtoku and her monk adviser, at a time when Kammu Tennō (r. 781–806) was eager to enhance his own legitimacy by denying that of the royal heirs of Temmu, which he and his father had replaced.[59]

My reading is that the debate has overlooked the fact that all extant reports agree on one point, that the chief ritualist at Usa spread the idea of the faked oracle "for reasons of his own."[60] Dōkyō was not seen as initiator of the hoax. Beyond that the issue remains, was the Usa ritualist's intent simply to gain Dōkyō's favor as the annal suggests, or were there deeper forces at work? Some historians have posited that Shōtoku Tennō herself concocted the oracle scenario to provide herself with a desperately needed heir, but that seems doubtful both in light of her dispatch of Wake to Kyūshū and because she of all persons would have known the importance of Sun-line descent as the basic qualification for becoming *tennō*. It has always seemed more plausible to me that Dōkyō himself was the target of a plot designed to shake the monarch's faith in him. There were numerous courtiers and rival monks eager to be rid of Dōkyō's influence, his domination of the Prelates Office and Nara temples, and his unceasing spending on religious rites and projects. High on the list of Dōkyō's rivals must have been Northern Fujiwara Nagate, then sitting leader of the Council of State.

If Dōkyō was the target the plot failed, perhaps because Shōtoku suspected the plan. The affair was nonetheless the beginning of Shōtoku Tennō's end and the end of Temmu-line rulership as well. Shōtoku survived these events by only months. She became ill in the third month of 770 and died five months later. After her death Fujiwara Nagate claimed the dying monarch had left him final instructions concerning the succession. Following those instructions, the throne went to Prince Shirakabe, a great-grandson of the seventh-century ruler Tenji (r. 668–71). Husband to one of Shōtoku's half sisters, Princess Igami, Shirakabe had also served as a minister on the Council of State. He subsequently ruled for eleven years as Kōnin Tennō. Initially Nagate and others may have hoped that Shirakabe's son with Igami would become the next *tennō,* thereby reuniting the royal lines of Tenji and Temmu and creating a new consensus to unify the court. Had that hope been realized, it would have meant that the limits on a royal daughter's ability to marry and produce her own heir had been overcome and that either a son or a daughter could be the vehicle of patriline succession. But that is not what happened. In 772 Queen Igami was accused of performing secret rites to curse her royal husband; and another prince, Yamabe, who was the son of Kōnin and a Capital House Fujiwara mother (Otomuro), was named crown prince. Igami and her son were eventually killed, and Prince Yamabe acceded to the throne to rule as Kammu Tennō. The Capital House Fujiwara then played an important role as court leaders and royal affines during Kammu's reign. It was Kammu Tennō and his Capital House affines who moved the capital from Nara, long the metropole of Temmu-line monarchs, to a new capital at Nagaoka in 784.

So did Kammu's enthronement end the royal line of heirs to Temmu and Jitō. Over the following decades, the new royal lineage descended from Tenji through Kōnin and Kammu avoided recourse to female monarchs by alternating patrilineal with fraternal succession for several generations. And after the mid-ninth century, Fujiwara regents from the Northern House ensconced themselves as court leaders and king makers by depending on affinal relations between *tennō* and their

Fujiwara sisters and daughters. Thus Shōtoku Tennō proved to be the last female sovereign to reign and rule in classical Japan.[61]

## CONCLUSION

In the English historiography the end of female sovereignty has been explained by Shōtoku's relationship with Dōkyō and Dōkyō's purported determination to usurp the throne. But that is not the conclusion one reaches after careful study of the historical record. Enthronement of female sovereigns ended in late Nara times for two main reasons. First, growing familiarity with the Chinese classics and *ritsuryō* prescriptions resulted in broader acceptance of male-dominant gender hierarchy, patriarchy, and patrilineality. Although these values characterizing the patriarchal family paradigm may have had less impact on general kinship practices, in the realm of kingship female rulers were delegitimized. Second, the historical experience of Kōken-Shōtoku's two unstable reigns led court leaders to the conclusion that female succession resulted in problems for court and throne that were best avoided.

At the turn of the eighth century and beyond, the ideal of patrilineal stem succession imported from China had curiously resulted in the practice of placing female sovereigns on the throne until a young male heir was ready to accede. In China, the young prince himself took the throne to be subsequently aided by his mother as regent. But in Japan, where Heavenly Sovereignty was still new, no such practice was attempted. Instead a royal woman of the ruling line took the throne to await the prince's majority. When Shōmu Tennō had no Fujiwara-related male issue to succeed him at midcentury, he used this precedent but went far beyond it by making a daughter his heir. His logic was that of the bilineal society in which he lived: Princess Abe was her father's offspring, "even though a woman." But the result of her enthronement was a crisis of succession that lasted two decades, with high costs to fledgling *tennō*-centered government: dissension at court and repeated coups.

By the late eighth century some at court had come to understand that narrowing the candidate pool would help to achieve a more regularized and less destabilizing system of royal succession. Although royal polygamy and the relative lack of hierarchy among leading royal consorts were legacies of history that were difficult to change, excluding princesses as royal successors proved easy at a time when familiarity with the classics and admiration for Tang ways was advancing male-dominant gender hierarchy. In addition, the long tradition of strategic alliances between princes aiming for the throne and their affines—an "affinal strategy" visible as far back as the historical record goes—gave powerful families little reason to support princesses as royal heirs.[62] Princesses could be sacrificed because unlike princes, who frequently married the daughters of powerful ministers, female royals were forbidden from marrying outside the royal kin. No powerful affines with an interest in preventing their disinheritance came forward to defend the interests of princesses.

And yet proponents of enthroning another princess emerged during discussions concerning succession in Kōnin Tennō's reign. Kōnin himself reportedly proposed enthroning Princess Sakahito, his daughter with his discredited queen Igami, but his proposal did not prevail. And presumably to guarantee that any offspring she might have would be his own, Kammu Tennō subsequently took his half sister Sakahito as a consort.[63] "Even though a woman," Sakahito might have succeeded to the throne, but after the troubles of the era of Kōken-Shōtoku, courtiers feared the outcome of enthroning another female *tennō*.

Kōken-Shōtoku's reign as the last classical female sovereign was but one aspect of a broader decline in the status and agency of women at the *tennō*'s court. Queen consorts and female officials in the royal residence lost autonomy and stature as well. We know, for instance, that during the reign of Kōnin Tennō the queen consort took up residence in the royal domicile for the first time. Kōnin's second queen, of the Fujiwara Capital House, came from much less wealthy circumstances than had Queen Kōmyō earlier. That facilitated integration of the queen's household into the back palace. When the capital was moved from Nara to Nagaoka in 784 and then on to Heian in 794, an increasingly complex architectural formation housing royal consorts developed behind the *tennō*'s own residential palace.[64] The result was virilocal residence for queens and royal consorts. Furthermore, by the early 800s autonomous functions of the queen consort's household—sewing clothes, making ceramic ware and sake, providing potable water—came to be reassigned to offices in the Ministry of the Royal Household (Kunaishō).[65] Such changes made the throne less dependent on its highest-ranking affines while the queen consort became more dependent on the *tennō*'s staff. Around this same time Kammu Tennō was consciously expanding his role as "husband of the realm" (it is recorded that he took thirty-two consorts in hypergamous relations that bound elite families from across the realm to him while preventing any one affinal group from dominating his court after the death of his Capital House Fujiwara queen Otomuro in 790). This strategy cuts a sharp contrast with Shōmu Tennō's strong dependence on Queen Kōmyō's Fujiwara kin earlier in Nara times.

As for the status of female officials, during Shōmu's Tempyō era (729–67), female staff in the palace had joined male colleagues for celebratory rites on the seventh day of each new year, and men and women received their promotions at the same assemblies. During Kammu's reign, however, separate occasions were instituted for male and female promotions, with far fewer promotions going to women.[66] While high-ranking female officials in the back palace had made their way up to high ranks by means of talent and familial connections in earlier Nara times, by Kōnin Tennō's era female officials in the *tennō*'s residential palace were generally consorts of Council of State ministers.[67] Palace staff came to be distinguished from officials, while ministerial wives serving in the back palace were seen to represent their husbands. Sekiguchi has determined that at the same time there was an increasing tendency for women to avoid writing in Chinese characters, as Chinese was considered a male script, an official language deemed appropriate for those in official service. The emphasis on the binary opposition official-man/unofficial-woman further excluded women from public life and ultimately subordinated women at court and in larger society.[68]

Such were the results of the steady advance of the *ritsuryō* process by which codal law and its practices configured and integrated the *tennō*'s realm from the seventh century onward. Through Nara and into Heian times, the *ritsuryō* process privileged males because the codes gave most offices to men. While we occasionally hear of female district chieftains in Nara and early Heian times, by the mid-Heian period the prerogatives of officeholding were fully male gendered.[69] For instance, in the mid-tenth-century fictional world depicted in the *Tales of Utsubo* (Utsubō monogatari), the character Kannabi Shigematsu's role as husband and head of house (*kachō*, alt. *ie no osa*) was taken for granted—even though his wife had some wealth of her own, she was economically, politically, and socially her husband's inferior.[70] The key factor in the transformation from complementary paired executors in eighth-century households to dominion by a male patriarch in mid-Heian times was therefore political. In Kannabi's case, his official post as local tax collector and factotum for the provincial headquarters privileged him over his wife.

This political privileging of men and male scripts had other economic effects as well. The historian Fukutō Sanae has noted that while there is extensive evidence of women buying and selling land during the ninth century, the written record thereafter evidences fewer instances of females with extensive landholdings.[71] By the tenth century, just when Sekiguchi argues that male-dominated monogamous marriage led to a new concept of adultery among the Heian nobility, the prerogative of an aristocratic woman to choose to participate in marital relations was taken over by her father. Thereafter a woman could neither pick a mate nor divorce one, and only with her husband's permission could she take Buddhist vows.[72] In the early-eleventh-century courtly novel the *Tale of Genji* (Genji monogatari), we find numerous hypergamous relations in which a husband like Prince Genji assumed responsibility for lower-ranking consorts' material concerns. And by this time a noble woman who lost the protection of father or husband could well face penury.

At court, as structures and procedures of *tennō*-centered government became more regularized in late Nara times and beyond, ministers from the Council of State came to play an ever greater role in the government, the locus of which had become the *tennō*'s own residence. As intimates of the Heavenly Sovereign, ministers and their aides replaced the female staff that had predominated in earlier palaces.[73] Female chamberlains in the back palace, known as *naishi*, began to lose some of their prerogatives to male staff in the Office of the Chamberlain, or Kurō-dodokoro, established by a son of Kammu, Saga Tennō (r. 809–23), in 810. By the tenth century transmission of royal orders once seen to by *naishi* was completely dominated by the Chamberlain's staff, which also superintended provisioning of the royal residence by the mid-ninth century.[74]

The loss of status and autonomous agency by queens, royal consorts, and female officials as well as the disappearance of female sovereigns reflected the gradual acculturation of the Chinese ideal of male-dominant gender hierarchy in the course of the ongoing *ritsuryō* process. Like the Japan-China dialectic described earlier, the *ritsuryō* process progressed gradually and was affected by both domestic and international events. Although Sekiguchi argues that at the level of family organization and marital relations the acceptance of Chinese kinship ideals was glacial, at the level of kingship Chinese notions of male-dominant gender hierarchy and male-only rulership transmitted by the classics and *ritsuryō* law became normative by the end of the eighth century.

## NOTES

1. For more detail concerning gender relations in marriage during Han times, see Jack I. Dull, "Marriage and Divorce in Han China: A Glimpse at 'Preconfucian' Society," in *Chinese Family Law and Social Change*, ed. C. D. Buxbaum (Seattle: University of Washington Press, 1978). For a discussion of gender hierarchy in the classics, see Richard Guisso, "Thunder Over the Lake: The Five Classics and the Perception of Women in Early China," in *Women in China: Current Directions in Historical Scholarship*, ed. Richard Guisso and Stanley Johannesen (Youngstown, N.Y.: Philo Press, 1981).

2. See Wang Sun-ming, "Confucian Ideal and Reality: Transformation of the Institution of Marriage in Tang China" (Ph.D. dissertation, University of Washington, 1979), pp. 6–7; and Dull's "Marriage and Divorce."

3. Ch'u Chai and Winberg Chai, eds., *Li Chi*, trans. James Legge, 2 vols. (New Hyde Park, N.Y.: University Books, 1967), pp. 439–41.

4. Wallace Johnson, *The T'ang Codes* (Princeton: Princeton University Press, 1979), vol. 2, p. 88.

5. Ibid., p. 169.

6. The text appears in Takikawa Masajirō, "'Shikyōruijū' no kōsei to sono shisō," *Shigaku zasshi* 41.6 (1961): 85. The screen, known as the *Torige tensho byōbu*, was among the personal effects of Shōmu Tennō presented to Tōdaiji after the monarch's death, according to a record in the Shōsōin archives. See *Dai Nihon komonjo Shōsōin monjo*, ed. Tōkyō daigaku Shiryō Hensanjo (Tokyo: Tōkyō daigaku shuppankai, 1901–40), vol. 4, p. 162. Henceforth cited as *Shōsōin monjo*. The screen remains in the Shōsōin royal storehouse. See the catalog from the *Exhibition of Shōsōin Treasures, Shōsōinten* (Nara: Nara kokuritsu hakubutsukan, 1991), p. 67; and the frontispiece of Kimura Hōkō, *Shōsōin no chōdō* [*Nihon no bijutsu*, vol. 294] (Kyoto: Shibundō, 1990).

7. For an excellent introduction and annotated translation, see Denis Twitchett, "How to Be an Emperor," *Asia Major* 9.1–2 (1996): 1–103. Note that I gloss *ti* (Jap. *tei*) in *Tifan* as "universal monarch" or "Heavenly monarch" rather than as "emperor." I am inclined to agree with Yoshimura Tadasuke and Watanabe Shin'ichirō concerning the problematic usage of "emperor" and "imperial" in the Chinese as well as in the Japanese contexts. See Yoshimura's "'Teikoku' to iu gainen ni tsuite," *Shigaku zasshi* 108.3 (1999.3): 38–61; and his *Kodai Ro-ma teikoku* (Tokyo: Iwanami shinsho, 1997); and Watanabe's "Tenka no ideorogi-kōzō," *Nihonshi kenkyū* 440 (1999): 36–49.

8. Aoki Kazuo et al., eds., *Shoku nihongi*, 5 vols. (Tokyo: Yoshikawa kōbunkan, 1961), vol. 2, p. 255, 732 01/01. For more detail, see Joan Piggott, *The Emergence of Japanese Kingship* (Stanford: Stanford University Press, 1962), pp. 250–51.

9. See especially Furuse Natsuko, *Nihon kodai ōken to gishiki* (Tokyo: Yoshikawa kōbunkan, 1998), passim. On diplomatic missions to Tang China, known as Kentōshi, see Tsuchida Naoshige, *Kentōshi to Shōsōin* (Tokyo: Gyōsei, 1986).

10. *Shoku nihongi* Tempyō Hōji 1 (757) 04/04 (Aoki, vol. 3, p. 183). And see Hirakawa Minami, *Yomigaeru kodai monjo* (Tokyo: Iwanami shoten, 1994), pp. 53–63.

11. *Shoku nihongi* Tempyō Hōji 2 (758) 08/25 (Aoki, vol. 3, pp. 283–87).

12. As Junnin's edict put: "I have found the monarch's *Admonishments* useful as a handbook of rulership and personal discipline. So too should the penal codes, administrative codes, and supplementary legislation be studied by all officials, since they set out the fundamental aspects of duty. Let officials exert themselves for the transformation of all subjects." *Shoku nihongi* Tempyō Hōji 3 (759) 06/22 (Aoki, vol. 3, pp. 321–25). Rewards were to be given to members of officialdom and to monastic teachers as well. The royal command was subsequently promulgated, and it appears in *Ruijū sandai kyaku* dated 759 06/27. In 757 Kōken Tennō had also proclaimed specific texts for mastery by professors of seven courses of study—classics, histories, medicine, acupuncture, astronomy, *yin-yang*, and accounting—presumably replicating contemporary Tang practice. See *Shoku nihongi* Tempyō Hōji 1 (757) 11/09 (Aoki, vol. 3, pp. 235–37).

Wu's *Admonishments* (Weicheng dianxun) are not extant, but scholars surmise that each chapter abstracted key points from the classics on good governance for study by the royal heir. The title recalls a story from the *Book of Odes* in which the royal heir and officials were educated in good governance. See Shima Zenkō, "Ijō tenkun kō." *Kodai bunka* 258 (1980): 420–22. The text was brought to Nara sometime before 748, when it was copied. On Wu's "proto-feminism," see Chen Jo-shui, "Empress Wu and Proto-Feminist Sentiments in T'ang China," in *Imperial Rulership and Cultural Change in Traditional China*, ed. Frederick Brandauer and Chun-chieh Huang (Seattle: University of Washington Press, 1994).

13. See Joan Piggott, "Chieftain Pairs and Corulers," in *Women and Class in Japanese History*, ed. H. Tonomura, A. Walthall, and H. Wakita (Ann Arbor: University of Michigan Center for Japanese Studies, 1998).

14. Piggott, *Emergence*, p. 168.

15. Araki Toshio, *Nihon kodai no kōtaishi* (Tokyo: Yoshikawa kōbunkan, 1985), pp. 224–303.

16. For Nagaya's story, see my *"Mokkan:* Wooden Documents from the Nara Period," *Monumenta Nipponica* 45.4 (1990): 449–70.

17. See Kishi Toshio, "Kōmyō rikkō no shiteki igi," in *Nihon kodai seijishi kenkyū* (Tokyo: Hanawa shobō, 1966), pp. 213–56.

18. *Shoku nihongi* Tempyō Hōji 6 (762) 06/03 (Aoki, vol. 3, pp. 9–11).

19. Piggott, *Emergence*, esp. pp. 226–35, 239–41.

20. See Tanaka Shō, "Nakatsusumeramikoto wo meguru shomondai," *Nihon gakushī'in kiyō* 9.2 (1951): 143–64; Hora Tomio, "Nisei nichō, nakatsu tennō, shōsei, kōshin seiji," *Nihon rekishi* 377 (1979): 1–14; Narikiyo Hirokazu, "Jotei shokō" and "Nihon kodai ōikeishō hō shiron," in *Nihon kodai no ōi keishō to shinzoku* (Tokyo: Iwata shoin, 1999).

21. Indeed, according to a later entry in the *Shoku nihongi*, plotting to remove her began as early as 742. The leader of the dissidents was apparently Tachibana Naramaro, son of the former prime minister, Tachibana Moroe. He and his co-conspirators wanted to see

Prince Kibumi, a son of Prince Nagaya, take the throne. See *Shoku nihongi* Tempyō Hōji 1 (757) 07/04 (Aoki, vol. 3, p. 207).

22. See Yokota Ken'ichi, "Asaka Shinnō no shi to sono zengo," *Nanto bukkyō* 6 (1959): 17–37. That her Fujiwara blood was the key to Abe's nomination is made clear by the fact that while he had no other male children, Shōmu had two other daughters, sisters of Asaka. They were never considered for the throne, for the same reason that Asaka was not: their mother lacked sufficiently powerful relatives.

23. *Shoku nihongi* Tempyō 15 (743 05/05) (Aoki, vol. 2, pp. 419–21). An excellent discussion of the significance of Abe's *Gosechi* dance on this occasion is Fukutō Sanae, "Gosechimaihime no seiritsu to henyō," *Rekishigaku kenkyū* 667 (1995): 1–16.

24. *Shoku nihongi* Tempyō Shōhō 1 (749) 04/01 (Aoki, vol. 2, p. 71).

25. In Chinese patriarchal fashion, most posts described in the codes were reserved for males. The only posts prescribed for women were in back palace (*gokū*) offices meant to serve the *tennō* in his everyday life. However Kōmyō's extracodal Queen Consort's Household Agency, which replicated the back palace in its organization, also had a large complement of female officials. Yoshikawa Shinji argues persuasively that the Nara back palace was indeed a place where female officials exercised substantial authority. See Yoshikawa Shinji, "Ritsuryō kokka no jokan," in *Nihon josei seikatsushi*, ed. Josei sōgō kenkyūkai, vol. 1 (Tokyo: Tōkyō daigaku shuppankai, 1990).

26. *Shoku nihongi* Tempyō Shōhō 1 (749) 07/02 (Aoki, vol. 2, pp. 83–85).

27. *Shoku nihongi* Tempyō Hōji 1 (757) 07/04 and *Shoku nihongi* Tempyō Hōji 3 (759) 06/16 (Aoki, vol. 3, pp. 203, 315–19).

28. *Shoku nihongi* Tempyō Hōji 1 (757) 04/04 (Aoki, vol. 3, pp. 179–85).

29. The text could have been brought back to Nara in 753 by a returning embassy whose members included Kibi Makibi. There were also numerous embassies from the Manchurian kingdom of Pohai coming and going from Nara during these years. See David McMullen, *State and Scholars in T'ang China* (Cambridge: Cambridge University Press, 1988), p. 88. In the first month of 757, Kōken also ordered realmwide distribution of the *Bommō Sutra*, so in a sense there were two classics being championed at this time, one Buddhist (inner) and one non-Buddhist (outer). See *Shoku nihongi* Tempyō Hōji 1 (757) 01/05 (Aoki, vol. 3, p. 175).

30. *Shoku nihongi* Tempyō Hōji 1 (757) 07/04 (Aoki, vol. 3, pp. 203–11). A good overview in Japanese is Taira Ayumi, "Kibumi no Ō tei'i keishō kibō to Tachibana Naramaro no hen," *Seiji keizaishigaku* 287 (1990): 1–12.

31. *Shoku nihongi* Tempyō Hōji 2 (758) 08/01 (Aoki, vol. 3, p. 261). Nakamaro's political patronage was critical to the prince, prompting the uxorilocality of the prince's marriage with Nakamaro's daughter[-in-law]. And the prince's royal blood made him enthronable, rendering him valuable to Nakamaro. Given his relationship with Prince Ōi, Nakamaro might well be termed the first "Fujiwara regent," but the mode of regency was certainly different from that of mid-Heian times.

32. The extralegal post of Taiho was the Tang equivalent of Minister of the Right (Udaijin). Shaughnessy has traced it back to Zhou origins and notes its connection with assuring royal succession. That would explain Nakamaro's use of it. See Edward Shaughnessy, *Before Confucius* (Albany: State University of New York Press, 1998), p. 148. For terms of Nakamaro's appointment as Grand Protector, see *Shoku nihongi* Tempyō Hōji 2 (758) 08/25 (Aoki, vol. 3, pp. 283–85). From 758 through 764 the register of membership for the Council of State, *Kugyō bunin*, shows Nakamaro as the highest ranking member, with few other ministers having been appointed. See *Shintei zōhō Kokushi taikei Kugyō bunin* (Tokyo: Yoshikawa

kōbunkan, 1986), vol. 1, pp. 38–45. That is why historians often term Nakamaro's tenure as court leader "Nakamaro *seiken*," the age of [despotic] rule by Nakamaro. On Nakamaro's court leadership, see Kimoto Yoshinobu, "Fujiwara Nakamaro no chihō seisaku," *Kodai bunka* 34.4 (1982): 27–30; Kimoto Yoshinobu, *Fujiwara Nakamaro seiken no kisoteki kōsatsu* (Tokyo: Takashina shoten, 1993); Takinami Sadako, *Nihon kodai kyūtei shakai no kenkyū* (Kyoto: Shibunkaku, 1991); Sonoda Kōyū, "Shōden: Fujiwara Nakamaro," in *Nihon kodai no kizoku to chihō gōzoku* (Tokyo: Hanawa shobō, 1992); and Sonoda Kōyū, "Emi-ke shijo denkō," in *Nihon kodai no kizoku to chihō gōzoku* (Tokyo: Hanawa shobō, 1992).

33.  *Shoku nihongi* Tempyō Hōji 6 (762) 06/03 (Aoki, vol. 3, pp. 409–11).

34.  An excellent comparative study of the retired monarch's office in China and Japan is Haruna Hiroaki's "Daijōtennōsei no seiritsu," *Shigaku zasshi* 99.2 (1990): 1–38. The first Chinese sovereign to retire was Qin Shi Huangdi, and the practice was used occasionally up to Tang times when it reached "institutional maturity," according to Haruna. There were four Tang monarchs who retired, including the founder of the dynasty. The *Old Tang History*, compiled in about 950, records Ruizong's words in its entry dated 712 07/. See Haruna, "Daijōtennōsei no seiritsu," p. 9. In English, Ruizong's retirement is mentioned in Dennis Twitchett's "Hsuan-tsung," in *Cambridge History of China*, vol. 3: *Sui and T'ang China, 589–906*, ed. Denis Twitchett (Cambridge: Cambridge University Press, 1979), p. 344. In his study of Tang didactic texts on governance, Twitchett also notes that after the coup of 626, in which the future Taizong dispatched rivals for the throne and secured his own succession as heir apparent, the future Taizong could issue commands (*rei*) concerning everyday affairs while his father, Gaozong, still dealt with matters of gravity. See Twitchett, "How to Be an Emperor," p. 12. On the retired monarchs in Nara times, see Nitō Atsushi, "Daijōtennōsei no tenkai," *Rekishigaku kenkyū* 681 (1996): 2–15. Haruna and Nitō agree that senior (retired) monarchs were considered preeminent, their authority surpassing that of younger and less experienced sitting monarchs. But in Nara times such relations were not explained in the codes or regularized by protocols.

35.  *Shoku nihongi* Tempyō Hōji 6 (762) 01/, 12/ (Aoki, vol. 3, pp. 401, 415–17). All three were third-ranking advisers (*sangi*), according to the subsequently compiled ministerial register *Kugyō bunin* I (in *Shintei zōhō Kokushi Taikei* [Tokyo: Yoshikawa kōbunkan, 1986], pp. 40–42). The *Kugyō bunin* is thought to have been begun in the mid-tenth century.

36.  This is what the prelates' register, *Sōgō bunin*, indicates. See it in the first Kōfukuji volume from the compendium of Buddhist documentary materials, the *Dai Nihon bukkyō zensho*. The *Sōgō bunin* was, however, not begun until the late Heian period.

37.  *Shoku nihongi* Hōki 6 (775) 10/02 (Aoki, vol. 4, pp. 459–61). On Nakamaro's rebellion, see Sonoda Kōyū, *Nihon kodai no kizoku to chihō gōzoku* (Tokyo: Hanawa shobō, 1992), pp. 13–27; and Tsunoda Bun'ei, "Emi Oshikatsu no ran," *Kodai bunka* 6.6 (1961): 111–33.

38.  *Shoku nihongi* Tempyō Hōji 8 (764) 10/09 (Aoki, vol. 4, p. 43).

39.  See Twitchett, "How to Be an Emperor," p. 34.

40.  See *Kugyō bunin*, vol. 1, pp. 46–47; and my "Tōdaiji and the Nara Imperium" (Ph.D. dissertation, Stanford University, 1987), esp. p. 51.

41.  *Shoku nihongi* Tempyō Hōji 8 (764) 09/20 (Aoki, vol. 4, p. 33). For another English translation, see Ryusaku Tsunoda, *Sources of Japanese Tradition*, 2 vols. (New York: Columbia University Press, 1958), vol. 1, pp. 107–8.

42.  Piggott, *Emergence*, pp. 236–39; and Piggott, "Tōdaiji," pp. 75–77.

43.  *Shoku nihongi* Tempyō Jingo 2 (766) 10/23 (Aoki, vol. 4, p. 141).

44.  In 1970 Yoneda Yūsuke questioned Dōkyō's authority outside the Buddhist sphere. See his "Chokujishō to Dōkyō," *Kodaigaku* 12.1 (1970): 55–66, esp. p. 65. Most scholars in

Japan now agree that Dōkyō presided over the Buddhist sphere. For instance, Narikiyo Hirokazu and Katsuura Noriko have argued that Shōmu's daughter was a woman of strong will who dominated the court especially during her second reign. See their work cited above.

45. Katsuura Noriko argues persuasively that the scriptural basis for Dōkyō's Prince of the Law office was the *Saishō'ō Sutra*, the most fundamental source for Buddhist realm-protecting ideas. See Katsuura Noriko, "Kodai no ie to sōni," *Nihonshi kenkyū* 416 (1997): 88–89.

46. *Shoku nihongi* Tempyō Hōji 8 (764) 09/29; Hōki 1 (771) 08/26, 10/28 (Aoki, vol. 4, pp. 37–39, 301, 321). Also see *Shōsōin monjo*, vol. 5, p. 446. For an analysis of changes in the Prelates Office during Dōkyō's time, see Ushiyama Yoshiyuki, "Dōkyō seikenka no sōgōsei ni tsuite," in *Ronshū Nihon bukkyōshi* (Tokyo: Yūzankaku, 1986), vol. 2, pp. 109–32.

47. Horiike Shumpō, "Dōkyō shikō," in *Nanto bukkyōshi no kenkyū*, 2 vols. (Kyōto: Hōsōkan, 1980), vol. 2, pp. 381–402.

48. Concerning Dōkyō's activities, see evidence from the Shōsōin archives in *Shōsōin monjo*, vol. 5, pp. 238, 402, 433, 434, 441, 446, 447, 449, 451, 456, 498, 513, 522, 528; vol. 16, pp. 414, 459, 451; and vol. 17, p. 1.

49. *Shoku nihongi* Tempyō Jingo 1 (765) 01/07 (Aoki, vol. 4, pp. 61–63). Ross Bender argued that great tension arose between Buddhist and shrine ritualists, but I have found little evidence of that tension in the historical record. There was surely increasing competition between large official establishments, temple or shrine, for royal patronage. See Ross Bender, "The Hachiman Cult and the Dōkyō Incident," *Monumenta Nipponica* 34.2 (1979): 125–53. In Japanese, see Kumatani Yasunori, "Dōkyō seikenka no jingi," *Seiji keizai shigaku* 182 (1981): 1–17.

50. Because such prayers were used by healing monks for thaumaturgic rites like those used to treat Kōken in 762 and because a copy of the sutra was made for Dōkyō by the royal scriptorium in 763, Horiike Shumpō has posited that Dōkyō proposed the project. See Horiike Shumpō, "Emi Oshikatsu no ran to Saidaiji Shōtō'in no zōei," in *Nihon rekishi kōkogaku ronsō*, ed. Nihon rekishi kōkogakkai, 1966 [rpt. in *Nanto bukkyōshi no kenkyū* (Kyoto: Hōsōkan, 1982), vol. 2, pp. 198–224]. On the *Hyakumantō* project in English, see David Chibbett, *History of Japanese Printing* (Tokyo: Kodansha, 1977), pp. 29–32; Peter Kornicki, "Hyakumantō darani," in *The Book in Japan: A Cultural History* (Leiden: Brill, 1998), pp. 114–17; Mimi Hall Yiengpruksawan, "One Millionth of a Buddha: The Hyakumantō Darani in the Scheide Library," *Princeton University Library Chronicle* 48.3 (1987): 225–38; and Miyeko Murase, "Hyakuman-tō," in *Jewel River: The Burke Collection* (Richmond: Art Museum of Richmond, Virginia, 1975), pp. 8–11. Whether the prayers were block printed with wood or metal type, and in what manner (stamped or rubbed), is debated. In Japanese an excellent account of extant artifacts is Hōryūji Shōwa shizaichō henshū iinkai, ed., *Hōryūji no shihō*, vol. 5: *Hyakumantō, Daranikyō* (Tokyo: Shōgakukan, 1991). Printed prayers like those used for the *Hyakumantō* were being made in contemporary Tang China and Silla Korea, signifying that the culture of Buddhist printing was international.

51. Kitō Kiyoaki, "Hyakumantō darani wo chōsa shite," in *Kokushi daijiten* (Tokyo: Yoshikawa kōbunkan, 1990), vol. 11; and Kitō Kiyoaki, "Daranikyō," in *Hōryūji no shihō*, vol. 5.

52. George Sansom, *A History of Japan to 1334* (Stanford: Stanford University Press, 1958), p. 89; John Whitney Hall, *Government and Local Power in Japan, 500 to 1700* (Princeton: Princeton University Press, 1966). In Japanese, see Maekawa Akihisa, "Dōkyō to Kichijōten keka," *Shoku nihongi kenkyū* 150 (1970): 1–14; and Takinami Sadako, *Saigo no jotei* (Tokyo: Yoshikawa kōbunkan, 1998). Araki Toshio has recently published a comparative study of female monarchy across East Asia entitled *Kanōsei toshite no jotei* (Tokyo: Aoki shoten, 1999).

53. This line echoes one of Tang Taizong's own comments on the importance of good officials. See Twitchett's translation of Taizong's *Golden Mirror*, written in 628, in "How to Be an Emperor," p. 26.

54. *Shoku nihongi* Tempyō Hōji 8 (764) 10/14 (Aoki, vol. 4, p. 47).

55. Concerning these coups, see Nakagawa Osamu, "Fujiwara Yoshitsugu no hen," *Shoku nihongi kenkyū* 7.2–7.3 (1960): 1–14; Nakagawa Osamu, "Tempyō Jingō Gannen ni okeru Wake no Ō no muhon," *Nihon rekishi* 179 (1963): 7–16; and Nomura Tadao, "Fujiwara Capital House no seijiteki shinshutsu," *Seiji keizai shigaku* 228 (1985): 1–11.

56. Twitchett points out, however, that early Tang China saw many instances of "prophecies, prognostication, and magical techniques to legitimize the claims of rebels or to predict political change." See Twitchett, "How to Be an Emperor," p. 12.

57. *Shoku nihongi* Jingo Keiun 3 (769) 09/25 (Aoki, vol. 4, pp. 255–57). A slightly different version of the story occurs in the posthumous biography of Wake Kiyomaro in the early Heian court annal, *Nihon kōki*, in the entry dated Enryaku 18 (799) 02/21. See *Shintei zōhō Kokushi Taikei Nihon kōki* (Tokyo: Yoshikawa kōbunkan, 1970), pp. 17–18.

58. See Inoue Mitsusada, "Kodai no kōtaishi," in *Inoue Mitsusada chosakushū*, vol. 1 (Tokyo: Iwanami shoten, 1985), pp. 179–222, esp. p. 220.

59. The *Shoku nihongi* was compiled during the reign of Kammu Tennō (r. 781–806), when Kammu's queen consort (Otomuro) and the people who put him on the throne were Capital House Fujiwara. Concerning the *Shoku nihongi* compilers' stance on the affair, see Nakanishi Yasuhiro, "*Shoku nihongi* to Dōkyō jikken," *Nihonshi kenkyū* 369 (1993): 1–24.

60. *Shoku nihongi* Hōki 3 (772) 04/06 (Aoki, vol. 4, pp. 375–77). Yokota Ken'ichi evaluates various scenarios in *Dōkyō* (Tokyo: Yoshikawa kōbunkan, 1959), pp. 188–200.

61. Two female sovereigns took the throne during the Tokugawa period. By that time, however, *tennō* and court had a very different role in Japanese polity and society, under the leadership of the Tokugawa shoguns.

62. For just such reasons Yoshimura Takehiko argues that male kingship and exogamous royal marriages were normative in the history of Japanese kingship. See "Kodai ōken ni okeru danjo kankei shiron," *Rekishigaku kenkyū* 542 (1985): 2–15.

63. A medieval historical narrative, the *Mizu kagami*, reports that in 772 Kōnin Tennō advocated having his daughter by Queen Igami, Princess Sakahito, succeed him. Since Kōnin was Tenji's grandson and Igami was Shōmu's daughter, Sakahito would have represented both the lines of Tenji and Temmu (or alternatively, those of Shōmu and Kōnin). But Queen Igami had already been dismissed in the third month of that year because of allegations that she had tried to put a curse on the throne. Meanwhile, Capital House Fujiwara members on the Council of State naturally supported Kōnin's Prince Yamabe, who had a Capital House Fujiwara consort. Yamabe eventually took the throne.

64. See my article on changes in the structure of the early Heian palace, forthcoming in *The Kyōto Historical Atlas*, to be published by UNESCO in Paris. Much of the analysis of archaeological reports has been done by Hashimoto Yoshinori. See "Tennōkyū, daijōtennōkyū, kōgōkyū," in *Yamato ōken to kōryū no shosō*, ed. Araki Toshio (Tokyo: Meichō shuppan, 1992); and " 'Gokū' no seiritsu: Kōgō no hembō to gokū no saihen," in *Kuge to buke: sono hikakuteki bummeishiteki kōsatsu*, ed. Murai Yasuhiko (Kyōto: Shibunkaku, 1995).

65. To trace this development, see four orders from the Council of State dating from 815 and 816 in *Ruijū sandai kyaku*: Kōnin 6 (815) 08/07, Kōnin 6 (815) 10/13, Kōnin 7 (816) 06/08, and Kōnin 7 (816) 09/23. For analysis, see Hashimoto, "Tennōkyū, daijōtennōkyū, kōgōkyū," pp. 84–86.

66. See Okamura Sachiko, "Onna joi ni kansuru kisoteki kōsatsu," *Nihon rekishi* 541 (1993): 20–34, esp. p. 20; and Yoshikawa, "Ritsuryō kokka no jokan," p. 120. By the Jōwa era (834–48), male promotions (*dansei joi*) were announced on the seventh day of each new year, while those for women (*onna joi*) were announced on the eighth day. Concerning the women and politics of Kammu's back palace, see Nomura Tadao, *Kōkyū to nyokan* (Tokyo: Kyōikusha, 1978), pp. 197–227; and Hayashi Rokurō, "Kammu-chō kōkyū no kōsei to sono tokuchō," in *Kammu-chō ron* (Tokyo: Yūzankaku, 1994).

67. Okamura, "Onna joi ni kansuru kisoteki kōsatsu," p. 25; and Nomura, *Kōkyū to nyokan*, pp. 171–96.

68. Sekiguchi Hiroko, "Heian jidai no danjo ni yoru moji (buntai) tsukaiwake no rekishiteki zentei," in *Nihon ritsuryōsei ronshū*, ed. Sasayama Haruo Sensei kokikinenkai, 2 vols. (Tokyo: Yoshikawa kōbunkan, 1993), vol. 2.

69. Fukutō Sanae, "Heian jidai no sōzoku ni tsuite: toku ni joshi sōzokuken o chūshin toshite," *Kazokushi kenkyū* 2 (1980): 157–83, esp. pp. 182–83. Fukutō concludes,

> I have analyzed documents from *Heian ibun*, separating those concerning the inheritance of property in circumstances relating to provincial local lordship as opposed to those relating to private land holding in the Kinai and environs. In the eighth and ninth centuries the class of local magnates (*fugōsō*) developed and acquired increased wealth as the ranks of cultivators receiving official fields continued to stratify. In the eleventh century, descendents of those magnates developed as local land openers and domain lords (*zaichi ryōshu*). As powerful local elites, they were able to assemble the surplus labor of local cultivators and use it to open new fields as their own private holdings. During the ninth and tenth centuries, they divided such holdings and transmitted them by partible inheritance to their sons and daughters fairly equally.... Women continued to inherit property even in the late Heian period, but there was change. Whereas in the early and mid-Heian eras, *shiryō* or privately held property was more or less equally inherited by both sexes, in the later Heian era inheritance by women in the class of local land openers decreased even if female inheritance of privately held domain remained constant. It was in the ranks of local lordship during the eleventh century and beyond that the concepts of "house holdings" administered by the patriarch as head-of-house took form.

See also Fukutō's "Heian jidai no josei zaisanken," *Josei bunka shiryōkan hō* 2 (1980): 45–59, esp. p. 47; and for a good overview of Heian women, see her *Heianchō no haha to ko* (Tokyo: Chūkō shinsho, 1991).

70. See Sekiguchi Hiroko, *Nihon kodai kon'inshi*, vol. 2, p. 16, for a discussion of this example.

71. Fukutō Sanae, "Heian jidai no sōzoku ni tsuite," *Kazokushi kenkyū* 2 (1980): 157–83.

72. See one example in *Ise Monogatari*, Section 16. Also see the analysis in Katsuura Noriko, "Kikon josei no shukke to kon'in kankei," in *Kazoku to josei no rekishi*, ed. Zenkindai joseishi kenkyūkai (Tokyo: Yoshikawa kōbunkan, 1989). According to the *Nihon kokugo daijiten* (vol. 9, p. 1290), the term for a male adulterer, *misoka otoko*, appears in such tenth-century texts as the *Gosen wakashū* and the *Utsubo monogatari*. See Sekiguchi, *Nihon kodai kon'ishi*, vol. 2, pp. 112–15, 125–66.

73. Yoshikawa, "Ritsuryō kokka no jokan," pp. 135–37.

74. Ibid., p. 120; and Kakehi Toshio, "Kodai ōken to ritsuryō kokka kikō no saihen: kurō-dodokoro seiritsu no igi to zentei," *Nihon rekishi* 344 (1991): 1–26, esp. p. 14. The Chamberlain's Office functioned as a royal chancellery and household agency, and its staff frequently served concurrently on the Council of State or in the council's secretariat, the Board of Controllers.

# CHAPTER THREE

# Representation of Females in Twelfth-Century Korean Historiography

*Hai-soon Lee*

The *Samguk sagi* (History of the Three Kingdoms), the oldest extant history of Korea, was compiled in 1145 under the general editorship of Kim Pusik (1075–1151), a renowned scholar and statesman. The "three kingdoms" are Koguryŏ, Paekche, and Silla, which were contending for hegemony on the Korean peninsula from the fourth to seventh centuries. As the first history of Korea written in the Confucian historio-graphical tradition,[1] the *Samguk sagi* became a model in form and content for later offi-cial history writing. It was the first historical text that constructed and presented con-cepts of the Korean state, its kingship, ethnicity, and civilization, and the relationships among these entities. Moreover, the terms in which these elements were presented in the *Samguk sagi* served as a point of departure for later discourses on Korean identity.

The lofty concepts of civilization and civility were often expressed in concrete per-sonal terms by way of biographies. Biography occupied a special place in Confucian historiography in China, which construed individuals as moral archetypes of virtue and vice against which later individuals were measured. The men and women profiled in the biographical sections of the *Samguk sagi*, too, acquired immortality as heroes, heroines, or villains in the popular imagination that has continued to the present day. This chapter offers an analysis of some of the women who appeared in the section "Biographies" in the *Samguk sagi*. My thesis, stated briefly, is that the representation of these women played a key role in Kim's construction of an idealized Confucian world.

## THE MEANING OF "CONFUCIAN"
## IN TWELFTH-CENTURY KOREA

Although the historical vision represented in the *Samguk sagi* is identifiably Confu-cian, one should note that Confucianism had not yet acquired hegemony in twelfth-century Korea. The book was written during a volatile period in Koryŏ history (918–1392), when a number of intellectual and political forces contested one another. One conflict was that between literati who privileged belles lettres, especially poetry, and Confucians who valued the Confucian classics. Although the institution of the royal lecture on the Chinese classics was instituted in 1116[2] and lectures were frequently conducted during the reigns of King Yejong (r. 1105–22) and Injong (r. 1122–46), it was still the *sihoe*, gatherings for reciting poetry, attended by the king and his noble officials, that remained the intellectual locus of aristocratic society.[3]

Shaped by this dynamic environment, the "Confucianism" of this period was the combined result of three intellectual trends in court: a continuation of the tradition of studying Confucian classics established in the Three Kingdoms period (313–668 C.E.), the recent influence of Neo-Confucianism and the literary culture of the Northern Song dynasty in China, and marked interest among Korean scholars in the Confucian classic *Doctrine of the Mean* (Zhongyong).

Intellectual developments were embroiled in political conflicts in the volatile twelfth century. At court there were rivalries between the bureaucracy and royal affines, the powerful in-laws of the royal family, although their interests often converged. But perhaps the most serious conflict was that between Buddhist "nativists" and Confucian cosmopolites over diplomatic and military policies. This was a period when China was under constant military threat from the seminomadic peoples of the great northeastern plains. One of these peoples were the Jurchens, who established a contending Jin dynasty (1115–1234) in the north. Song China, a less formidable military power than the Tang or Han, conceded all of northern China to the Jurchens in 1127 and retreated to the south. Subjected to continuous demands from each of these feuding entities on the continent, the peninsula state of Koryŏ required a workable national security policy. The intellectual and political community was divided into two camps that espoused opposing measures. The nativist Buddhist camp insisted that Koryŏ proclaim its equality to the Southern Song and the Jurchen Jin at the risk of war, whereas the Confucian camp endorsed peace and diplomacy even if it meant serving as a tributary state to the Jurchen Jin.

This argument stemmed from radically different worldviews and opposing visions of Korea. The nativists aspired to a Koryŏ distinguished by military prowess and political independence. They regarded themselves as heirs to the Koguryŏ, a state that had repeatedly repelled the Chinese army until it was vanquished by the allied forces of Silla, a contending Korean state, and Tang China in 668. In contrast, the Confucians, a majority of whom were descendants of Silla aristocrats, embraced a vision of a civilized world that transcended national boundaries but was organized by hierarchical relationships. Unable to resolve their differences, the two sides soon came to a confrontation.[4]

## KIM PUSIK AND THE *SAMGUK SAGI*

Kim Pusik was involved in most of these conflicts, consistently taking positions that cast him as the quintessential Confucian scholar-official. He confessed, for example, that his preference had shifted from poetry in his youth to the teachings of Confucius in his maturity.[5] His lectures to the throne, his exposure to Northern Song learning during three visits to China as an envoy, and the fact that his writing was mostly historical rather than poetic bespeak his expertise in and commitment to the classics. Kim's political career, especially in later life, was punctuated by confrontations with opposing camps. He vigorously campaigned to curtail the power and prestige of royal in-laws. When, on two separate occasions, King Injong raised the issue of offering special treatment to Yi Chagyŏm, who was both the king's maternal grandfather and father-in-law, Kim opposed it. He cited a classic Confucian argument, that the public relationship between the two men was that of lord and minister. Propriety required that this public relationship take precedence over whatever private ties they happened to share.

Kim is probably best remembered as a strong opponent of the nativist movement that gained momentum in the early twelfth century. In 1134 Myoch'ŏng and Chŏng Chisang, the nativist leaders, memorialized the throne with measures that would establish Koryŏ equality with the Song and the Jin. They proposed that the Koryŏ monarchy be renamed, that the Koryŏ king designate his own reign name to replace that of the Chinese emperor, and that the capital be moved from Kaesŏng to P'yŏngyang, the sacred capital of ancient Koguryŏ. When Myoch'ŏng subsequently realized that he could not persuade the Koryŏ establishment to take these measures, he proclaimed a separate state and occupied P'yŏngyang, and it was Kim who led the counterinsurgency troops. In 1136, after almost eighteen months, he succeeded in retaking the city.

Later scholars stigmatized Kim as an antinationalist toady for his role in this event. Most hostile to Kim among modern historians was Sin Ch'aeho, the influential nationalist historian of the early twentieth century. Sin, viewing the twelfth-century nativist movement as an early expression of nationalist sentiment, termed Myoch'ŏng's short-lived occupation of the ancient capital "the most significant event in a thousand years." He branded Kim the archvillain of Korean history who extinguished the nationalistic spirit and ushered in the toadyism (*sadae chuŭi*) that characterized later Korean foreign policy. The *Samguk sagi*, completed when Kim was seventy years old, was thus construed as an embodiment of his antinationalistic vision.[6]

It is difficult to deny that Kim's worldview was defined by culturalism, not nationalism. Even a sympathetic modern scholar has described him as committed to "the reform of Koryŏ society according to the cultural ideal of Confucianism by importing the advanced civilization of China."[7] What, then, were the constitutive elements of Kim's Confucian vision, and in what way did Kim interpret Confucianism in the context of the society of his time? He clearly deployed Confucian concepts to criticize contemporary society in the *Samguk sagi*. His view of women represented in the biographical sections of the history permits us to see how he used such concepts.[8]

## BIOGRAPHIES OF WOMEN IN THE *SAMGUK SAGI*

Biographies constitute the most common narrative structure in Korean history. Although the format in official histories does not provide much opportunity for literary embellishment, in comparison to other sections of the *Samguk sagi*, such as the historic annals (*pon'gi*) or treatises (*chi*), compiled according to the rigors of official historiography,[9] biographies contain elements of legend and fiction. Biographies also provide more room for the author to express his personal views. Indeed, the three biographies chosen for in-depth analysis in this chapter—"The Biography of Tomi," "The Biography of Ondal," and "The Biography of Sŏlssinyŏ"— seem to be shaped less by generic conventions than by the author's views and popular imagination.[10] They thus provide a fruitful site to analyze Kim's views of women and Confucianism.

In the analysis below, I pay attention to the taxonomy of these texts by examining the selection and inclusion of factual and nonfactual elements.[11] One salient issue is cross-gender representation of women. That is to say, these biographies are presented in male voices purporting to speak for (and as) women. Is there a reading strategy that will allow us to see these women in their own light? Another issue involves the delineation of the meaning of "Confucian" and its changes through time. If Korea in the twelfth century was not yet completely Confucian, are the representations of women in the *Samguk sagi* different from those in the later centuries of the Chosŏn dynasty (1392–1910), when intellectual life was more fully committed to a Confucian worldview?

At first glance, Kim Pusik appears to have internalized what Joan Piggott, in chapter 2, has called "the male script" of Chinese kingship. Kim criticized the practice of permitting women to accede to the throne during the Three Kingdoms and the Unified Silla periods, stating that this was improper because "men are superior to women (*namjon yŏbi*)."[12] Kim's male-centered view of the world is further evinced by the fact that only two among the numerous biographies are named after their female protagonists, Sŏlssinyŏ and the filial daughter Chiŭn.[13] Kim apparently viewed women as secondary characters in his narration about men.

However, if we consider all the female characters who appear in the biographies either in central or supporting roles, we will see that women played a far greater role in Kim's historiographical vision than his professed view may imply. This chapter examines, in addition to the two women with their own biographies, biographies of the wives of Tomi, Ondal, Sŏk Uno, Sona, Mulgyeja, P'ipsil, and Pak Chesang and those of the mothers of Chiŭn, Ondal, and Wŏnsullang. As their stories unfold within the confines of the domestic sphere, I discuss female consciousness, role, and function by classifying the biographical subjects according to their kinship positions as daughters, wives, and mothers.

## SŎLSSINYŎ, ONDAL'S WIFE, AND CHIŬN: THE PROBLEMS OF FILIAL DAUGHTERS

It is no accident that both women who appear as central figures in the *Samguk sagi* occupy the subject position of daughter; it may not be too far-fetched to deduce that a woman's individuality was best recognized as a daughter. A daughter had to confront two central problems in her life—to choose a husband and to provide for her parents. The biographies tend to focus on the former. In the preface to the biography of Sŏlssinyŏ, she is described as "a daughter of a commoner in Yulli" who, "despite being from an impoverished and humble family[,] was attractive in appearance and upright in behavior."

Kim Pusik frequently availed himself of this construction, making use of "despite" in the biographies of virtuous women to call attention to such class distinctions as commoner versus upper class. His narratives evolve around individuals divided by class instead of gender and often contain a sharp admonition to the upper class. Although Kim was a proponent of the Confucian dictum of "rectification of names" (*chŏngmyŏng*), which often connoted a heightened consciousness of status difference, in his biographies upright moral behavior and resolute will amid poverty was constrasted with depravity and fecklessness in the upper classes. Hence he construed ethical behavior as connected to class differences. His negligence of gender distinctions means, in effect, that men and women from the lower classes were equally likely to be paragons of virtue.

Kim described filial daughter Sŏlssinyŏ's worthiness in these terms: "All who saw her admired her, yet none dared harass her." The young man Kasil adored her, yet was "unable to say a word." Thus Kim illustrated how a woman could fend for herself and be irreproachable by upright behavior. In depicting Sŏlssinyŏ's concern for her elderly father who had been conscripted, Kim obliquely compared her to other filial daughters in Chinese history—Mulan, who took her father's place in the army by disguising herself as a man, and Tiyong, who appealed to the Han emperor to clear her father of false charges.

In Sŏlssinyŏ's case, to save her father the only recourse available is to marry and have her husband take her father's place. But when the lovelorn Kasil makes such a proposition, she is in no position to offer herself as compensation for his goodwill. Instead, the father has to offer his daughter's hand as reward. The biography portrays patriarchal power in no uncertain terms: he "forced her to make a promise to Kasil." Elated by the prospect of marriage, Kasil wants to set a wedding date. Sŏlssinyŏ refuses, saying, "[M]arriage, being a matter of great importance in human affairs, should not be embarked upon lightly; as I have promised myself to you, I would not change my mind even in fear of death." She insisted that the wedding be postponed for three years.

How can we interpret her postponement of the wedding, an act that defies both her father's wish and Kasil's? My interpretation is that her insistence is motivated by prudence and self-respect. Although circumstances render her marriage to Kasil inevitable, the wait allows her to prepare for marriage on her own terms. With her insistence, marriage no longer appears as an unconditional sacrifice on behalf of and forced by her father but rather a decision made according to her own wishes, albeit in circumscribed conditions.

Years have passed, however, and Kasil has not returned from the battlefield. Sŏlssinyŏ's father, concerned that his daughter might grow old alone, pressures

her to marry another. She resists and makes plans to flee home. She does not refuse on the Confucian grounds that a virtuous woman cannot serve two husbands.
Rather, her sense of fairness does not allow her to "betray her trust and go back
on her promise" while Kasil is risking his life "amidst hunger and cold" on her behalf. That is, filial piety is not seen as a virtue so compelling that it can be made to
transcend humanity.

Meanwhile, Sŏlssinyŏ finds herself stranded in a stable, unable to go any farther. She cries in frustration but does not contemplate a drastic measure such as
suicide. It seems safe to assume that had Kasil not returned in time, Sŏlssinyŏ would
have had to obey her father and marry another man. Here, we glimpse Kim's tacit
disapproval of extreme measures to safeguard a woman's integrity. In chapter 9 of
this volume, Du Fangqin and Susan Mann describe how martyrdom was to become the ultimate morality test for Chinese women in similar predicaments.

The conflict between King P'yŏnggang and his daughter in "The Biography of
Ondal" expresses a similar relativist instead of absolutist view on filial piety. As a
child, the princess would often cry to have her way; each time, her father threatened to marry her off to the town fool, Ondal. When she comes of age, King
P'yŏnggang wishes to marry her to a nobleman, but she rebukes him, saying, "How
can Your Majesty break his promise [to marry me to Ondal], when even a common man dares not do so? It is said that the worthy ruler does not jest. What Your
Majesty has just said [that he did not intend to marry her off to Ondal] must be
wrong." The king responds with rage to this perceived disobedience and expels
the princess from the palace.[14]

It appears that the princess understands her relationship to the king as a dual
one: they are father and daughter as well as ruler and subject. In emphasizing the
importance of differentiating between public and private roles, the princess's words
contrasting a common man with the ruler echoes Kim Pusik's own displeasure with
King Injong, who confused his private relations with Yi Chagyŏm for public ones.
The father-daughter conflict is embedded in their differing perspectives—a father
who equates filial piety to absolute obedience and a daughter who considers it her
right to refuse her parent's wishes if they are wrong. At the same time, the king
values his private role (as father) above his public role (as ruler) to the extent that
he fails to realize that his daughter is also his subject to whom a statement, even
one made in jest, is a public proclamation. Although his daughter leaves home as
ordered by her father, it does not signify entry into the public sphere, and so it does
not contradict Kim Pusik's view that women should be confined to the domestic
sphere.

Beyond selection of a spouse, an ethical concern for daughters was the problem of supporting parents. Sŏlssinyŏ, as we have seen, was responsible for her widowed father. In a third biography, the filial daughter Chiŭn had to take care of her
mother. Because the elderly woman was blind, Chiŭn alone bore the responsibility of eking out a living. To support the assertion that Chiŭn possessed "an extremely filial nature," we are told that she had provided for her mother since she

was a child and that she had remained unmarried to the age of thirty-two. For a time, she supported her mother by working for hire and begging. But finally, unbeknown to her mother, she sold herself into indentured servitude for ten bags of rice. After working at her master's house all day, she would return home each evening to serve her mother the hard-earned rice. When her mother remarked that despite the higher quality of her food she found herself without appetite and felt as though her heart were being cut out, the daughter confessed. Appalled by the revelation that she had driven her daughter into servitude, the mother wailed that she would be better off dead.

How can we interpret this confession by Chiŭn? It serves a major function in plot development: because of it mother and daughter wailed together; a passing *hwarang*, or aristocratic warrior, heard them and set in motion events that changed their fate. The scene prompts one to wonder whether truer filial piety might not have been served by a lie, highlighting Kim's ambivalent view of the personal and social significance of filial piety, as we shall see.

## TOMI'S WIFE: THE PARAGON OF FIDELITY

Although filial daughters receive central attention, in the biographies most women appear as wives. This is hardly surprising, for Confucian ethics placed special emphasis on the husband-wife bond as the root of the five relations.[15] Wifely acts meriting inclusion in the virtuous biographies can be divided into several categories: preserving fidelity, guiding one's husband to success, understanding one's husband, and avenging one's husband.

The biography of Tomi's wife presents an archetype of preserving fidelity. It is a story of a couple who remain faithful under the most serious threats and trials. Their nemesis is King Kaeru who, on hearing of the beauty of the wife and the couple's mutual devotion, determines to test them. So challenged, Tomi proves unshakable in his trust of his wife. Summoned to the royal presence, Tomi's wife deceives the king, managing to run away from him to reach the shore. When the forlorn woman cries up to heaven, a boat appears by which she escapes to a neighboring state, rescuing her husband who had been blinded by the king on the way. They live in exile (see Figure 3.1).

To understand Kim Pusik's views on gender relations and emotions expressed here, we may consider why the narrative is called "The Biography of Tomi," despite the wife's more prominent role. Kim's choice of the title reveals his valuation of conjugal trust, not his slighting of women. By making Tomi the central character, the tale highlights his struggles with King Kaeru. In this context the faithfulness of Tomi's wife signifies vindication of Tomi's commitments. King Kaeru is of the opinion that although women might aspire to fidelity, they inevitably succumb to temptation eventually. King Kaeru thus views women in categorical terms—as weak and emotional beings. In contrast, Tomi acknowledges the existence of both proper and improper feelings in human life, male and female alike.

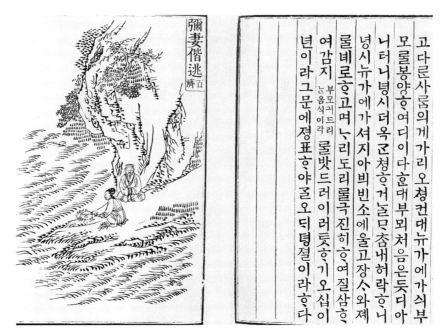

Figure 3.1. Tomi and His Wife in Exile. Courtesy of Kyujanggak Archives, Seoul National University.

He concedes that desire stems from improper feelings but views it not as a womanly vice but as a universal human predicament.

Tomi remains steadfast in his trust of his wife's emotions and moral integrity. His conviction that his wife would not succumb to the king's seduction and threats even in the face of death is based on his personal knowledge of her behavior. We may interpret the narrative focus on Tomi as an expression of the author's own strong faith in women. What Kim valued the most seems to be trust between husband and wife, particularly a husband's unwavering faith in his wife. In making Tomi the protagonist, Kim placed more narrative emphasis on husbandly trust than on wifely fidelity. In this way the story of Tomi and his wife differs from tales of wifely exemplars in Chosŏn didactic literature, as discussed by Martina Deuchler in chapter 6.

We should note that although Kim placed more narrative focus on the man than on his wife, it is her deed that earns the blessing of heaven and that enables their escape. Not only is Tomi's wife unswerving in her primary loyalty to her husband, she is also able to remain faithful to her principles because she exercises good sense. In one story after another, the reader encounters the same admiration with which Kim Pusik wrote of the women's wisdom and their capacity for action in the face of danger. Chiŭn, Sŏlssinyŏ, and Ondal's wife are all wise and prudent; they also show an uncanny ability to be agents of their own fate.

## THE PRINCESS WHO MARRIED A FOOL
### AND GUIDED HIM TO SUCCESS

Ondal's wife—the princess who admonished her father not to jest—represents the wifely virtue of guiding one's husband to success. Her first encounter with Ondal is anything but propitious. He takes her for a fox in disguise, and Ondal's mother suspects she left the palace because she was duped. The princess is even forced to spend a night by the brushwood gates. She perseveres and on marrying Ondal, sets out to transform him. Although she proves to be crucial to his later success, there is an underlying sense that Ondal's own disposition also contributes. Though physically unappealing, Ondal is kindhearted and generous. That he does not resist being called "Ondal, the fool," hardly a happy name, confirms his patience. His initial response to the princess suggests his reasonable personality: he seeks to avoid her on their first encounter on the grounds that "such matters should not be handled by a young woman." He hesitates to accept her desperate marriage proposals on their second encounter and lets her spend a night outside. That it is his mother who decides on the marriage reflects Ondal's filiality.

Nevertheless, Ondal's transformation into a great warrior owes much to his wife. Though the success of a marriage is based on love and trust rather than on material comfort, the princess emerges as a woman of keen judgment. She brings all her jewelry with her when she leaves the palace. Possibly she chose Ondal instead of a life of royal wealth because she foresaw his potential. Her prescience is illustrated by her choice of a horse, and although the narrative tells us little, we can imagine her busily remaking her husband into a warrior. Ondal eventually gains recognition from King P'yŏnggang as a son-in-law. Consequently, the princess enables the king to keep his word as a ruler. Eventually, she vanishes from the narrative as Ondal rises to prominence, not to reappear until after his death. At Ondal's funeral, his coffin cannot be interred until his wife's arrival. Only when she arrives and says, "Life and death have been decided; please depart from this life," does it move. Through this scene not only did Kim convey Ondal's deep affection and gratitude to his wife, he also highlighted the princess's serenity, philosophical disposition, and her courage that was vindicated in the end.

The princess is an exceptional character, and yet in this biography her role is limited to that of a wise wife who brings recognition to her husband's family. As the narrative unfolds, it becomes evident that the main character is Ondal, not the princess. After he is recognized as the king's son-in-law, Ondal comes to enjoy unrivaled power and the king's trust. Were Ondal content with his good fortunes, the story would have focused on the prescience of Ondal's wife. But when King P'yŏnggang, the princess's father, dies and King Yanggang ascends the throne,[16] Ondal expresses a desire to reclaim the territory that Koguryŏ has lost to Silla, and he is permitted to lead the campaign. With this, Ondal becomes something more than an exemplary son-in-law; he acts on his own initiative with no input from his wife and so pursues independent achievements. Although Ondal is ultimately unsuccessful in his quest, his loyalty is held up as a model for future generations and he is equated to other loyal ministers of renown in Korean history such as ŭlp'aso, Pak Chesang, and Kwi San.

"The Biography of Ondal" appears under a unique heading, "the worthy king does not offer words in jest." This focus on the princess's father indicates that Kim Pusik emphasized the loyalty between lord and minister rather than the union between man and wife. In this scheme of things, the princess may appear a secondary character; yet the narrative also illustrates Kim's view of women, namely, that a loyal minister is made by a wise wife. Furthermore, Ondal's transformation establishes the importance of education, not birth, to a man's success. But this story expands the notion that education is a parent-to-child or teacher-to-student activity; it is made to include wifely counsel and assistance (*naejo*).

### WIVES WHO MAGNIFIED AND AVENGED THEIR HUSBANDS

The wives of Sona, Mulgyeja, and P'ipsil represent the wifely virtue of understanding one's husband and publicizing his little noticed accomplishments. They all acquiesce to and even encourage decisions that take their husbands away from home. After losing two brothers in a battle against Paekche and facing an invasion from Koguryŏ, P'ipsil says to his wife: "My brothers have given their names to posterity by dying for the country. Though I am but a humble man, how can I live in dishonor for fear of death? My departure from you today will be our final farewell." By talking about P'ipsil's loyalty, his wife makes his devotion to his country known. The wife of another soldier, Mulgyeja, plays a similar role. It was she who reports his bravery in battle, bravery that went twice unrewarded but won him a place in the *Samguk sagi*.[17]

The wife of another soldier, Sona, spoke in public of her husband's loyalty. She addresses a crowd of mourners gathered to convey condolences for the loss of her husband, dead in battle for his country: "My husband always said, 'A man should die on the battlefield; how can I die in bed, while being cared for by my family?' His death now is as he always wished." Thus she not only accepts her husband's decision to fight to the death but also approves of it and admires him for it. In this way Kim Pusik portrayed women as partaking in their husbands' commitment to public duty and loyalty, not merely as hapless wives who could only follow and obey.

Sŏk Uno's wife, the only woman in the biographies who avenges her husband, bespeaks how active a wife can be. A brave general who successfully repelled a Japanese invasion, Sŏk Uno is also a considerate leader whose concern for his soldiers won their admiration and loyalty. A thoughtless joke to a Japanese envoy, that he wished to capture the Japanese king and queen and enslave them, elicits an invasion by the Japanese. Sŏk Uno assumes responsibility for this careless statement and travels to Japan to offer his apologies, but the incensed Japanese burn him to death. Subsequently, a Japanese envoy arrives to resolve the diplomatic tension. Pretending to offer hospitality, Sŏk Uno's wife invites him to her home. She plies him with drink, lures him into her garden, and sets him aflame.

Kim Pusik offers a commentary on the tale of Sŏk Uno—a good means of expressing his editorial opinion.[18] Kim underscores, as he has already done in "The Biography of Ondal," the weight of words spoken by a ruler or member of the ruling class. Further, Kim criticizes the action's of Sŏk's wife as "perverse and wrong (*pyŏn i pijŏng*)." He disapproves of the extreme manner in which she seeks revenge and ultimately condemns her for it. If her action were to result in additional diplomatic difficulties, it would have opposed her husband's efforts at peacemaking. In Kim's view, she acted to satisfy a personal grievance at the expense of public good.

A similar editorial stance censoring extreme actions in women and sanctioning self-control also characterizes Kim's depiction of the wife of another soldier, Pak Chesang. A comparison of two versions of the life of Pak Chesang in the *Samguk sagi* and a later work, *Samguk yusa* (Memorabilia of the Three Kingdoms), provides an interesting contrast. It demonstrates how Kim edited fictional elements to construct an image of an ideal woman. In contrast to the former as official history, the *Samguk yusa*, written in the thirteenth century by the monk Iryŏn, represents nativist folk tradition. There, Pak's wife pines away when duty takes him to Japan: "Although she tried to catch his boat, she was unable to reach it in time, whereupon she 'laid down on the ground and wailed for a long time.' After much time had lapsed, she was still unable to overcome her longing for him and she died looking in the direction of Japan, lamenting."[19] In the *Samguk sagi*, Pak's wife merely "looked out at the ship sailing away, crying," to bid her husband farewell. Other than a postscript in which the couple's second daughter marries one of the survivors of the expedition, there is no other mention of the bereavement.

### EXEMPLARY MOTHERS AND THE ISSUE OF CLASS

Although none of the biographies in the *Samguk sagi* focuses exclusively on a mother, several tales present a mother figure in a secondary role. They include the mothers of Chiŭn and Ondal, who as we have seen are lower-class women who won a place in the chronicles because of their filial children. A third mother is the aristocratic Lady Chiso, General Kim Yusin's wife. Lady Chiso is unable to forgive her son, Wŏnsullang, for the cowardly act of fleeing battle and returning home. Reasoning that in betraying his country Wŏnsullang has also been unfilial to *her husband*, Lady Chiso maintains that she can no longer recognize him as her son.[20] This provides a glimpse of aristocratic ethics: at least in this idealized depiction Lady Chiso construes the wife-husband relationship as taking precedence over mother-son ties, as dictated by Confucian ethics.

In general, the child depicted in tales of filial children in the *Samguk sagi* serves as a vehicle to convey the virtue of filial piety while simultaneously and conversely exposing the shortcomings of parents, especially fathers, who subject their children to trials and tribulations. For instance, the filial nature of Sŏlssinyŏ is contrasted with her father's breach of faith just as the loyalty of the daughter of King P'yŏng-gang is highlighted by her father's broken promise. Narratives of the practice of filial piety among commoners differ, however. Chiŭn's mother, despite her blindness, is thoughtful enough to sense a change in her daughter's physical well-being after the latter sold herself into servitude; the old woman also expresses great remorse for the burden she has imposed. If Chiŭn's mother can be described as kind-hearted, Ondal's mother is intelligent and level-headed. Despite the poverty of Ondal's household, which forces him to eke out an existence by begging and scraping off tree bark, his mother—with a blind person's intuition—is able to detect the noble stature of the princess and even to show concern that the princess was duped into coming to their humble house. When Ondal is too confused to respond to the princess's marriage proposal, his mother is level-headed and rational, refusing the match on the basis of their lowly station. She allows her son's marriage to the noblewoman only after the princess has persuaded her that poverty is not an obstacle. In the humble families of Chiŭn and Ondal, there is a conspicuous absence of conflicts between the filial child and his or her mother. These mothers are depicted not as authority figures but as purveyors of Confucian virtues.

### THE FLEXIBLE AND RECIPROCAL DEMANDS OF VIRTUES

Compared to Confucian writers who came after him, Kim Pusik displayed remarkable flexibility in interpreting the virtues of filial piety and loyalty as applied to women. He recognized, for example, that conflicting moral demands could open up a space of action for the women. Conflicts arose for women when they chose to resist, rather than mechanically follow, the demands of their fathers or sovereigns in the context of a patriarchal society. In praising these women, Kim focuses his critical gaze on those in authority. In the cases of Sŏlssinyŏ and the daughter of King P'yŏnggang, problems with their fathers arise when they fail to honor their own words. Trust signifies accord between words and action (*ŏnhaeng ilch'i*). Unlike the father of Sŏlssinyŏ, King P'yŏnggang never directly promised his daughter to Ondal. Nevertheless, because of his lofty position, he was held to the most stringent standard of trustworthiness. In both cases, daughters either ran away or attempted to run away when their fathers failed to meet this standard; in so doing, the daughters were able to keep their own commitments. The daughters became filial exemplars through their active intervention that caused a change in circumstances, enabling the fathers to remain true to their promises.

While these tales depict the tensions between filial piety and trust, the story of Chiŭn is propelled by a conflict between filial piety and honesty. If the character of Chiŭn was strong enough to withstand the hardships of selling herself into indentured servitude, she ought to have been able to bear the burden of a white lie to spare her mother pain and humiliation. Chiŭn's subsequent lament is the culmination of several poignant emotions: desperation, self-recrimination, and regret for not having protected her mother from the truth. In fact, the version of this story in the *Samguk yusa* devotes a large section to Chiŭn's remorse whereas the *Samguk sagi* focuses on the social merits of filial piety and the magnanimity of the aristocratic warrior who comes to their aid. In structuring his narrative, Kim Pusik chose to illuminate the social function of filial piety rather than the individual moral dilemma posed by the conflicting demands of filiality and honesty.

Defining the concept of filial piety, which is often viewed as the cornerstone of Confucian ethics, is no easy task. As seen in the *Samguk sagi*, its most basic expression was to remain with one's parents, offering them respect, support, and a peaceful environment. One's own welfare plays little if any part. Problems arose, however, when parents engaged in or demanded erroneous behavior. It is wrong to condone the mistakes, but it is also unfilial to resort to extreme measures when one's parents persist in error.[21] Kim Pusik seems to have prescribed a fine balancing act for the filial son and daughter: sincere filial piety required preventing one's parents from committing improper acts, but it was undesirable to resort to extreme measures even in desperate circumstances.[22] It is significant that Kim equated filial piety with self-realization,[23] and he adopted a flexible interpretation of filial piety that emphasized its social function. In this sense, Kim's view differs from later Neo-Confucian notions of filial piety, which placed greater emphasis on self-sacrifice and according to which extreme acts of devotion were prized with an almost religious fervor.

It is also significant that Kim Pusik construed loyalty as reciprocal, not unilateral or absolute. In the biographies, although the burden of loyalty generally falls to the ruled, it is only when the ruler is upright in behavior that it can be realized.[24] In "The Biography of Ondal," King P'yŏnggang's broken promise and his jestful words represent a discord between words and deeds. "The Biography of Tomi" features a king who, instead of rewarding the faithfulness of a subject, seeks to destroy a household. Kim included other episodes that render rulers in an unfavorable light. King P'yŏnggang's foolishness is illustrated by his inability to recognize a prize horse and by extension a loyal subject; King Kaeru is presented as having committed an evil act in the "Annals" section of the *Samguk sagi*.[25] Their deficiencies are highlighted to suggest that only when the ruler maintains a political climate in which loyalty is valued can the ideal kingly way of government be established.

A question remains, however, about just how a ministerial admonition should be understood. According to Confucian logic, admonition from an official or subject is essential to the health of kingship and the state.[26] King P'yŏnggang's daughter is thus morally correct in confronting her father. Tomi's wife, however, defends herself by tricking the king rather than by admonishing him directly. Her action could have been seen as clever but not exactly right. Critics in subsequent ages have rallied in her defense, arguing that her indirect approach saved the king from debauchery.[27] According to this prevalent view, the result rather than the method of admonition is the major criterion of rectitude. The filial daughter is thus allowed some room to maneuver.

In these biographies conflict between filial piety and loyalty arises in connection with problems of trust between a man and a woman. In the traditional Confucian ethos trust as applied to women was interpreted as either chastity or fidelity. However, Sŏlssinyŏ's insistence on keeping her promise to Kasil is based on kindness and sympathy rather than fidelity. Similarly, it is difficult to construe Tomi's wife's faithfulness as an act of blind adherence to the adage that a good wife is to "serve only one husband." Her rejection of the king's advances and her pursuit of her husband to a foreign land, where they live out their lives in hardship, are better explained as a woman responding with love and sacrifice to a husband who has placed his faith in her and suffered as a consequence.

In the later Chosŏn period, when women's chastity and fidelity were particularly emphasized, the concept of trust was replaced by an emphasis on unilateral adherence to virtue. The "virtuous women" of subsequent generations were generally those who committed suicide to follow their husbands in death, or to avoid being violated by other men. By contrast, in Kim's biographies, when escape failed, Sŏlssinyŏ gave up her efforts; Ondal's wife did not follow her husband into death; and, twice evading the king's advances, Tomi's wife sought to survive. Although each of these women succeeded in preserving her virtue, it was a result of interaction with their husbands rather than by unilateral action.

### RE-CREATING KOREAN WOMANHOOD

Kim Pusik's flexible interpretation of Confucian virtues is all the more striking when his stories are read against those in the Chinese classic *Biographies of Women* (Lienü zhuan; ca. 16 B.C.E.) by the Han scholar Liu Xiang.[28] One of the stories, "Baichi daihuo," conveys the resolve of Baichi, wife of Duke Gong of the Song who elected to burn rather than flee the scene of a fire, stating, "As a wife, I would rather die with my virtue intact, instead of saving my life by leaving the room without my parents' permission." Similarly, "Zhenjiang liutai" recorded that when the wife of King Zhao of Chu, Zhenjiang, was confronted by a flood, she chose to drown rather than follow an envoy who, though dispatched to save her life, bore no credentials from the king. Since Baichi is the only woman praised in the *Spring and Autumn Annals* (Chunqiu),[29] the model for Confucian historiography in China, Kim Pusik's broader conceptualization of female virtue is remarkable.

Kim's emphasis on the social function of women represents another departure from the Chinese model of the Confucian ethos. In the Chinese case, self-cultivation is seen as the beginning of governance, hence has been traditionally regarded as a male prerogative. According to Confucian logic, the cultivation of self leads to order in the household, the country, and eventually to all affairs under heaven. This logic implicitly or explicitly relegates women's roles to indirect social participation, through supporting their husbands or sons. Kim Pusik, however, stressed the social meaning of women's domestic roles. That a good half of his biography of the filial daughter Chiŭn is devoted to how she was memorialized in the Tang court highlights his obsession with the social and public significance of her virtues. What Kim valued above the filial act itself was that it signified the civilized status of Silla and that female virtues elevated Silla's international standing in the eyes of its more powerful neighbor.[30] A similar emphasis on the social functions of mothers also characterizes his portrayals of the mothers of Wŏnsullang, Chiŭn, and Ondal.[31]

The importance that Kim Pusik attached to the social roles of women implied its converse, recognition of the negative impact women might have on public life. The "Hwawang kye" (Strategy of King Hwa) described in the biography of Sŏl Ch'ŏng illustrates female influence on state governance. Here, King Hwa is required to choose between a righteous man named Paek Tuong and a beautiful woman named Chang Mi. When the king appears to be leaning toward Chang Mi, Paek criticizes him for a lack of intelligence, righteousness, and discernment. A similar admonition to recognize righteous subjects is found in "The Biography of Ondal." Presenting Chang Mi as deceptive and immoral, Kim stressed the importance of womanly virtue by showing the consequences of its absence.

### SUBSEQUENT TRANSFORMATION OF WOMEN'S VIRTUES

Kim Pusik's belief that "men are superior to women" and that women's actions should be confined to the domestic sphere and his negative view of political activity by women were embedded in the Confucian ideology of the rectification of names. Kim nevertheless recognized women's subjectivity, valued their capacity for self-realization, and gave weight to the influence they exerted on society. He did not evaluate women exclusively according to the demands of ritual ($ye$) or the moral code ($ŭi$), nor did he insist on death to safeguard chastity or fidelity. Rather, he proposed overcoming obstacles with wisdom. In his view, women were rational beings, capable of solving the problems and crises they encountered through reason. According to Kim, what women valued most was trust; loyalty and filial piety were meaningful only when they were based on trust. It appears that by taking trust as the central human principle—be it in relations among men or between man and woman—Kim placed the fulfillment of trust for women at the core of their ethical worth. This took precedence over any evaluation on the basis of narrow social conventions.

The distinctiveness of Kim's views becomes all the more apparent when they are compared to those of narratives in the *Illustrated Guide to the Three Bonds* (Samgang haengsilto), an influential didactic text published in the first half of the fifteenth century.[32] The first moral instruction book published in the Korean vernacular under government auspices, it embodies the state commitment to popularizing Confucian virtues to a wide public that included women and the lower classes. In addition to featuring characters from the Chinese *Biographies of Women and Female Exemplars from Past and Present* (Gujin lienü zhuan), it contains biographies dating from the Three Kingdoms period to the early part of the Chosŏn period. Overlapping with the *Samguk sagi* are narratives concerning Tomi's wife and Sŏlssinyŏ.

The tale of Tomi's wife in the *Illustrated Guide to the Three Bonds* reverses the gender of the protagonist: it casts her as the heroine who, rather than lead a life of luxury as a palace woman, chooses to eke out a miserable living by following her husband. There is no mention of her husband's character or class status. This editorial decision emphasizes chastity and fidelity as unconditional and absolute virtues. Similarly, the *Illustrated Guide* omits Sŏlssinyŏ's failure to run away when Kasil does not return after six years and her father tries to marry her off to someone else. In this later version, wifely fidelity takes clear precedence over filial piety.[33]

Similarly, the story "Yŏyŏng Takes Revenge" (Yŏyŏng pogu) describes changing views of women who avenge their husbands' murders.[34] When her husband is killed by a thief, Yŏyŏng requests that she be permitted to decapitate the arrested criminal to avenge her husband. Captured by another thief, she dies in the ensuing struggle to preserve her virtue. In that scene, the sky darkens with thunder and lightning, wind, and hail. The thieves, sensing heaven's displeasure, beg forgiveness and give her a proper burial. The epilogue contains a poem eulogizing her virtuous deeds. The *Illustrated Guide* views the decapitation with approval and implies that the heavenly signs are a response not only to her untimely death but also to her courage in avenging her husband.

Such different treatments of women's virtues are related to changes through the centuries in the ways aristocrats and scholar-officials were situated in relation to the royal house, as well as to a general transformation of the Confucian ethos. During the twelfth century, the aristocracy and the royal house were mutually reliant, and coexistence was a necessity. This expressed itself in numerous marital ties between them. In this situation the critical bonding substance was trust, not control or obedience. In a sense the principle of trust that is emphasized in Kim Pusik's biographies of virtuous women, with their tone of admonition of immoral or lax aristocratic behavior, echoes the ideal relationship between sovereign and subject. A poem entitled "A Spontaneous Song in the Military Tent" (Kunmak uŭm), written by Kim on the eve of an attack on Myoch'ŏng, refers specifically to this trust. Having been subjected to severe criticism for recapturing the western capital of P'yŏngyang, Kim's only hope lay with the king's absolute trust in him. This sentiment is echoed by Tomi, who completely trusts his wife.

The issue of women's chastity emerged later in the fourteenth century when Chosŏn Korea was repeatedly invaded by foreign forces, including Japanese pirates, the remains of the Mongol army, and the Red Turbans who spilled into Korea from Northeast China after defeat by the Ming army. It is not far-fetched to assume that there is a correlation between these events and the appearance of a large number of biographies of Korean women who gave up their lives to preserve their honor. These biographies were written by a new group of scholar-officials who turned to Neo-

Confucianism as a way of overcoming the confusion and disorder of the time. They constructed a new society based on the moral vision provided by the philosophy.

According to Neo-Confucian precepts that developed in Song China, moral principle (*i*) preexisted human relationships; hence the virtues of loyalty, filial piety, and chastity and fidelity were seen as unilateral and absolute. Given the enormous number of narratives about women's suicides or murders as they struggled to safeguard their honor in the Chosŏn period,[35] it would seem that literati's concern for women in this period focused on that issue. In contrast to those in Kim's biographies, these biographies upheld as exemplars women who resorted to extreme measures, signifying a change in the intellectual ethos. The new Neo-Confucian ruling elite were intent on establishing a new set of normative precepts. The trend continued in the "Virtuous Women" section of the *The Survey of Human Geography of Korea, Enlarged* (Sinjŭng tongguk yŏji sŭngnam), published in the mid-sixteenth century.

By the seventeenth and eighteenth centuries, however, progressive scholars emerged who, perhaps reflecting the spirit of a new era, criticized ritualistic constraints on women and advocated their pursuit of self-fulfillment. The *sirhak* (Practical Learning) scholar Chŏng Yagyong, in his "Treatise on Virtuous Wives," criticized social conventions that resulted in praise for women who followed their husbands to death. His attack was based on a new philosophy of humanism that valued individual human lives apart from a social system that ritualistically sacrificed women. Others construed this attack on conventional notions of women's virtue as an attack on the prevailing social order. A substantial increase in the number of biographies of virtuous women resulted during this period as well.

From the late Koryŏ onward, members of the literati class often used literary narratives of female marital fidelity as metaphoric representations of their own loyalty to the king. In the "Song of Longing for the Loved One" (Samiin kok) by Chŏng Ch'ŏl (1536–93), the author assumed a feminine persona in poetry, be it *hansi* (Korean poems in classical Chinese), *sijo* (three-line regulated verse in Korean), or *kasa* (prose poems). This poetic convention grew in popularity and was generally understood to be a vehicle for expressing devotion to the sovereign. As the phrase "The loyal minister does not serve two kings; the virtuous wife does not serve two husbands" attests, the two relationships were frequently invoked in tandem, the latter serving as the most effective mechanism for demonstrating a subject's loyalty. In an earlier essay, I have argued that there is a correlation between an accent on the hierarchical relationship of husband and wife—a relationship in which a model wife blames herself for any marital disharmony—and subsequent changes in women's consciousness.[36] In the earlier *Samguk sagi*, however, Kim presented women as subjects with their own identities and not in servitude to men; women appear as living beings and not as martyrs to the demands of hierarchical ritual.

Kim's ultimate concern lay not in portraying women per se but in using women as metaphors for men. They offered opportunities to present a vision of kingship, stressing the weight of the ruler's words, his discernment of talented men, and the import of trust in ruler-subject relations. In this respect one detects in Kim a class interest; he wished to strengthen the power of the scholar-official class. Conversely, though women's subjectivity was suppressed and their humanity sacrificed for ritual demands in the biographies of women that appeared in the fourteenth and fifteenth centuries, the literati class itself emphasized loyalty. Thus in biographies of virtuous women the concept of womanhood is formed in the context of the prevailing power structure and men's perceptions of their times. It is no surprise to find that men's conceptions of women were projections of the way in which they perceived themselves.

*Translated by Christine Kim*
*Edited by JaHyun Kim Haboush*

## NOTES

An earlier version of this essay, "Kim Pusik's View of Women and Confucianism: An Analytic Study of the Lives of Women in *Samguk sagi*," appeared in *Seoul Journal of Korean Studies* 10 (1997): 45–64.

1. Sima Qian's *Shiji* is regarded as the first written in this tradition. See A. F. P. Hulsewé, "Notes on the Historiography of the Han Period," in *Historians of China and Japan*, ed. W. G. Beasley and E. G. Pulleyblank (Oxford: Oxford University Press, 1961).

2. JaHyun Kim Haboush, *The Confucian Kingship in Korea: Yŏngjo and the Politics of Sagacity* (New York: Columbia University Press, 2001), p. 63.

3. Lee Hai-soon, "Aristocratic Culture and Hansi (Korean Poetry in Classical Chinese) in Early Koryŏ," *Han'guk Hanmunhak yŏn'gu* 15 (1992): 60. On the other hand, there was considerable opposition to the disproportionate respect accorded to Chinese poetry. Ch'oe Yak, a descendant of Ch'oe Ch'ung, was among the chief opponents. Ch'oe Cha, *Pohanchip*, vol. 1.

4. Michael Rogers, "Medieval National Consciousness in Korea: The Impact of Liao and Chin in Koryŏ," in *China among Equals*, ed. Morris Rossabi (Berkeley: University of California Press, 1983).

5. Kim Pusik, "Chungni pongbu," *Tongmunsŏn*, vol. 1, *pu*.

6. Sin Ch'aeho, *Chosŏn sa yŏn'guch'o*, in *Tanjae Sin Ch'aeho chŏnjip*, 5 vols. (Seoul: Hyŏngsŏl ch'ulp'ansa, 1977), vol. 2.

7. Yi Chongmun, "Early Koryŏ Literary Culture and the Literature of Kim Pusik," *Hanmunhak yŏn'gu* 2 (1984): 29.

8. In view of the fact that the narrative subject of the *Samguk sagi* is the Three Kingdoms period and that this history was a collaborative work with contributions from numerous historians, not every opinion can be attributed to Kim. Nevertheless, it is safe to assume that the work reflects his mentality and consciousness in its overall structure, basic arguments, and narrative flow. Ko Pyong-ik, "Historical Narration of the *Samguk sagi*," in *Han'guk ŭi yŏksa insik* (Historic reconnaisance of Korea), ed. Yi Wusŏng and Kang Man'gil (Seoul: Ch'angjak kwa pip'yŏngsa, 1976), vol. 1, pp. 37–38.

9. Pei-yi Wu, *The Confucian's Progress: Autobiographical Writings in Traditional China* (Princeton: Princeton University Press, 1990), pp. 3–14.

10. I have attempted to reconstruct the historians' intentions by listing "The Tale of Chang Poko" in the Biographies section, rather than the Annals. See my "Aspects of Descriptive Literature in the Silla Biographies—Focusing on the Biography of Chang Pogo," in *Kyŏngsan Sa Chaedong paksa hoegap kinyŏm nonch'ong Han'guk sŏsa munhaksa ŭi yŏn'gu* (Commemorative volume on the study of descriptive literature in Korea, compiled on the occasion of Professor Sa Chaedong's sixtiethth birthday) (Taejŏn: Chungang munhwasa, 1995).

11. Women played an important role either directly or indirectly in the two events that marked his political career. Hence one may conjecture that his Confucian outlook is expressed in his depiction of women. Yi Chagyŏm, who was Injong's maternal grandfather, also married his third and fourth daughters to Injong. Given Kim Pusik's criticisms of marriages among fellow clansmen as practiced in Silla (see "Silla pon'gi," No. 3 in Kim Pusik, *Samguk sagi*, 2 vols., ed. Yi Pyŏngdo [Seoul: ŭryu munhwasa, 1977], vol. 2, p. 25), he was not uncritical of this arrangement in which two sisters became mother-in-law and daughter-in-law. However, as he wrote in the introduction to the *Samguk sagi*, Kim maintained that each dynasty was entitled to its own customs, even presumably to sanctioning the practice of marriages among close relatives that was common in the early Koryŏ royal house. Ch'oe Yŏngsŏng, *Koryŏ yuhak sasangsa—Kodae, Koryŏ p'yŏn* (The history of Confucian thought in Koryŏ) (Seoul: Asea munhwasa, 1994), p. 302. The issue Kim Pusik raised was not the complicated unethical marriages in royal families but the idea that the relationship between king and subject should not be spoiled by a private one. The ruin of Kaegyŏng by the rebellion of Yi Chagyŏm and King Injong's nervousness are the background for Myoch'ŏng's proposal to move the capital to P'yŏngyang, to call the king an emperor, and to establish Koryŏ reign titles. Although maternal relatives monopolized political power through these marriages between the royal family and aristocratic families, it was Yi Chagyŏm's fourth daughter who prevented his attempt to poison the king. It is probable that this incident caused Kim to consider more seriously the social function or role of women. Their biographies in the *Samguk sagi* reflect his view on women to some extent.

12. *Samguk sagi*, vol. 5, Silla pon'gi 5, Sŏndŏk Yŏwang cho.

13. The number of characters in *Samguk sagi* biographies varies by scholar. Sin Hyŏngsik considers the number of eponymous biographies to be fifty, but he puts the number of persons appearing in the Biographies at sixty-nine. Sin Hyŏngsik, *Samguk sagi yŏn'gu* (Studies of the *Samguk sagi*) (Seoul: Ilchogak, 1981), p. 336.

14. Yi Kibaek conjectures that this narrative element rationalizes the unlikely union across class division lines. He suggests that the king in fact had wished that his daughter marry Ondal but was unable to transgress the prevailing social order. When the king was unable to keep his word, the princess accused him of *breaking* his word. This illustrates that "The Tale of Ondal" provides a source for understanding "mixed marriages" in a caste society and their role in unraveling the social order. Yi Kibaek, "An Examination of 'The Tale of Ondal': An Examination of Caste Order in the Aristocratic Society of Kokuryŏ," in *Samguk sagi non sŏnjip* (Seoul: Paeksan hakhwoe, 1985). Regardless of whether "The Tale of Ondal" combines elements of narrative and history, it is often approached as literature, that is, as an independent entity with an organic structure of its own.

15. It is said in the *Doctrine of the Mean*, "The way of a man of virtue begins from the relation of husband and wife," and in the *Book of Changes*, "After there being heaven and earth, all things exist; after there are all things, men and women exist; after there are men and women, husbands and wives exist; after there are husbands and wives, fathers and sons exist; after there are fathers and sons, kings and subjects exist; after there are kings and sub-

jects, highs and lows exist; after there are highs and lows, customs arrive." Placing husbands and wives before kings and subjects emphasizes the way that husbands and wives comprise the beginning of the five relations.

16. The *Samguk sagi* differs from "The Tale of Ondal" in that it records Koguryŏ's twenty-fourth king as King Yangwŏn (or King Yanggangsangho), who is succeeded by his eldest son, King P'yŏngwŏn (or King P'yŏnggangsangho). The twenty-sixth king, P'yŏngwŏn's eldest son, is King Yŏngyang (or P'yŏngyang). Although Yi Kibaek considers "Yanggang" an incorrect recording of "Yŏngyang," my view is that that the tale of Ondal and the daughter of King P'yŏnggang is a product of the popular imagination. Kim Pusik and other historians have tried to preserve what was handed down to them, and therefore the name is not in error. This is a consequence of the more purely literary nature of "The Tale of Ondal."

17. In the first instance, it was a result of his disagreement with a grandchild of the king.

18. Only twelve other biographies in the *Samguk sagi* appear with commentaries, those of Kim Yusin, ŭlchi Mundŏk, Chang Poko, Chŏng Nyŏn, Sŏk Uno, Kim Hŭmun, Hyangdŏk, Sŏnggak, Yŏn Kaesomun, Namsaeng, Kung'ye, and Kyŏn Hwŏn.

19. *Samguk yusa*, vol. 1, "Kiyi," Biography, No. 1.

20. *Samguk sagi*, vol. 43, Biography, No. 3, chapter on Kim Yusin.

21. Confucius considered the emperor Shun a greatly filial son for having escaped from his father when he sought to kill him, thereby preventing his father from committing an unrighteous act. Zengzi, on the other hand, played the zither on regaining consciousness after a severe beating by his father, to spare his father from experiencing remorse. Confucius criticized Zengzi, saying that his father would have committed an unrighteous act had Zengzi died from his beating. *Kongzi jiayu*, vol. 4, "Liuben," No. 15. "In serving one's parent, one should address them politely. Even if one might disagree with his parents, he must accord them respect without contradicting them, and will not fault them even when they are trying" (from *Lunyu*, "Liren"). "Should one's parents be mistaken, one should advise them but not contradict them" (from *Liji*, "Jiyi").

22. That Kim Pusik did not praise "serving one's parents the flesh cut out of one's thigh" by the filial sons Hyangdŏk and Sŏnggak expresses his disdain for extreme measures in the name of virtuous conduct. *Samguk sagi*, vol. 48, Biography, No. 8.

23. "Self-realization" here does not refer to one's attainment of success in a social context but rather the fulfillment of one's personal or private aspirations, as in a woman's self-fulfillment in marriage. Several marriages across class lines are recorded in the *Samguk sagi* (e.g., Kim Yusin's mother, Lady Manmyŏng; his younger sister, Munhŭi; and the illicit union of Kangsu and the ironsmith's daughter), each of which at times employs fictional elements to rationalize their existence. Kim Pusik depicts Sŏlssinyŏ and the daughter of King P'yŏnggang as pursuing their own hearts, even in defiance of their parents' orders, and characterizes their acts as wise and self-fulfilling.

24. That loyalty was not considered an absolute ideology does not mean it embodied relative characteristics that demanded compensation. Kim Pusik declared his intention of editing the *Samguk sagi* "to provide lessons for all ages through the correct deeds and wrong doings of kings and lords; the loyalty and perfidy of subjects; the state in peace and chaos; the way and disorder of the people," and similarly, the country and people are not composed and governed by subjects' unilateral loyalty. Without establishing the kingly way, loyalty cannot be the basis of social relations.

25. *Samguk sagi*, vol. 23, "Annals of Paekche," No. 1, King Kaeru, chap. 38.

26.  According to Confucius, "If a country has a subject willing to battle against the king's errors, then the king cannot do any wrong and the country will not be in danger; if a father should have a son to advise against committing errors, the father will not overstep the bounds of propriety" (*Kongzi jiayu*, vol. 2, "Sanshu"). He also said, "If a king does not have a subject who ventures to advise him, he will lose the uprightness" (vol. 5, "Zilu chujian").

27.  This point was illustrated in a poem entitled "Chaech'ŏngch'ŏ" by Sim Kwangse, a seventeenth-century poet, who praised her actions for allowing the king to avoid ridicule in subsequent generations. *Haedong akbu* (Hanmun akbu, sa charyojip 1) (Seoul: Kyemyŏng munhwasa, 1988), p. 348.

28.  It is not known in what year the *Lienü zhuan* (Yŏllyŏjŏn) was received in Korea. One possible explanation is that it was included among other writings by Liu Xiang, during the reign of Sŏnjong (r. 1084–94) in the Koryŏ dynasty. Wu K'oejae, "An Examination of the Yŏllyŏjŏn's Reception as Instructional Text," in *Tagok Yi Subong sŏnsaeng hoegap kinyŏm nonch'ong: Ko sosŏl yŏn'gu nonch'ong* (Studies on classical novels in celebration of the sixtieth birthday of Professor Yi Subong) (Taejŏn: Cheil munhwasa, 1988), p. 438. However, considering that the characters that appear in the *Lienü zhuan* had been introduced earlier in the classics and in historical records, Kim Pusik was probably familiar with earlier praise and criticism of the women.

29.  "Guliang zhuan," 5th month of 30th year of the Duke of Xiang.

30.  The tale appears in the *Samguk yusa* as "Pinnyŏ yangmo" (The impoverished daughter provides for her mother) (vol. 5, Hyosŏn No. 9). In this version the fact that a memorial was submitted to Tang China and Hyojongnang became King Hŏn'gang's son-in-law is omitted. Conversely, self-recrimination by Chiŭn for not having performed her duties of filial piety is recorded, as is the fact that a temple was erected. The contrast between the versions corresponds to the two authors' different views. Kim's version emphasizes the social function of filial virtue, whereas Iryŏn's is an attempt to elevate filial piety to a religious level.

31.  Kim was no doubt familiar with the Koryŏ custom of recognizing worthy mothers with generous rewards. One instance was the awarding of thirty sacks of rice to mothers whose sons had passed the civil service examination. In the case of Kim Pusik's family, he and his three brothers earned an additional ten sacks by collectively performing well. Though entitled to an annual stipend as a Great Lady (*tae puin*) for her meritorious efforts in raising these accomplished sons, Kim's mother declined it, causing us to conclude that she was indeed a thoughtful individual. *Koryŏsa* (History of Koryŏ), vol. 97, Biography, No. 10, chapter on Kim Pusik, *pu-i*.

32.  The *Samgang haengsilto* consists of three parts: "Filial Sons," "Loyal Minister," and "Virtuous Women." Although the editors of this publication are not known, it is assumed that the scholars of the Chiphyŏnjŏn (Hall of Worthies) played a critical role. Various appendixes to the volume were authored by court officials or scholars who had accepted Neo-Confucianism.

33.  They appear in stories entitled "Mich'ŏ tamch'o" (Tomi's wife living on grass) and "Sŏlssi bun'gyŏng" (Sŏlssi divides the mirror [with Kasil]).

34.  This piece is not included in the *Lienü zhuan* but in the *Gujin Lienü zhuan* and is entitled "O Hŏsŭng ch'ŏ."

35.  Among the sixteen stories recorded in the "yŏllyŏ p'yŏn" in *Samgang haengsilto*, which correspond to Liu Xiang's *Lienü zhuan*, nine stories concern chastity or fidelity; three, motherhood; two, integrity; one, wisdom; and another, contrivance. The *Samgang haengsilto* thus

favored chastity or fidelity. As for women's chaste or faithful behavior, among the one hundred ten stories of the "yŏllyŏ" section, seventy-four are about dying to preserve virtue; forty-five cases on suicide and twenty-nine on murder. They overwhelmingly exceed the number of cases (fifteen) on maintaining chastity or fidelity. Thus the ideology of chastity or fidelity was strongly reinforced after Chosŏn Korea was founded.

36. Lee Hai-soon, "Studies on *hansi* Written in the Female Voice," in *Han'guk Hanmunhak chŏn'guk haksul taehoe palp'yo nonmun yojijip* (Abstracts from the national conference on the study of Korean and Chinese literature) (Seoul: Han'guk Hanmunhak yŏn'guhoe, April 28, 1995).

# CHAPTER FOUR

# The Presence and Absence of Female Musicians and Music in China

*Joseph S. C. Lam*

*Follow the calendar of the Xia, ride in the carriage of the Yin, and wear the ceremonial cap of the Zhou, but, as for music, adopt the Shao and the Wu. Banish the tunes of Zheng and keep plausible men at a distance. The tunes of Zheng are wanton and plausible men are dangerous.*
CONFUCIUS

*The men of Qi made a present of singing and dancing girls. Jihuanzi [of the Lu state] accepted them and stayed away from court for three days. Confucius departed.*
CONFUCIUS

These quotations from the *Analects*, a collection of Confucius's words and deeds, encapsulate the Confucian view of music: promote proper music (*yayue*) and banish vernacular music (*suyue*).[1] Represented by the "Shao" and "Wu," two legendary works of songs, dances, and instrumental music attributed to the mythical sage-king Shun and King Wu of the Zhou dynasty (1099–256 B.C.E.), proper music is deemed essential to governance and self-cultivation alike. In contrast, vernacular music, represented by the wanton tunes of the Zheng state, corrupts men's hearts and impedes fulfillment of their social and moral obligations. Among diverse kinds of vernacular music, music made by women is singled out by Confucian scholars as particularly corruptive because it seduces not only with sound but also with the physical presence of female performers.

Given such a non grata status of female musicians and the music they made, it is no surprise that females are largely absent from the Confucian canon. And yet if one looks elsewhere in the cultural and textual records, an entirely different picture emerges. The reality is that the Chinese have valorized quite a number of female musicians: Cai Yan (177–?), a *qin*-zither player, and Wang Zhaojun (fl. ca. 40–30 B.C.E.), a *pipa*-lute player, are but two of the many examples. This gap between official disdain and popular embrace opens up many historical and historiographical questions.[2] Is the historical presence of female musicians and music knowable today? Why and how did the illusion of their absence manage to operate for so long? What does the contrast between illusion and reality tell us about gender relations? And what does it say about the history of Chinese music?

This chapter represents a preliminary attempt to address these questions. One of its two purposes is to expound on the Confucian theory and practice of proper music as gleaned from two canonical texts: the early imperial *Record of Music* (Yueji) and the sixteenth-century *Collected Works of Music Theory* (Yuelü quanshu). The former established the official theory of music in early China whereas the latter testified to the vibrancy of these tenets some fifteen hundred years later.

The second purpose of this chapter is to retrieve traces of female musicians and their performance by reading between the lines and outside the Confucian classics. Preliminary remarks are also made about the concept and location of the "musical female" in the history of Chinese music. The analysis focuses on two periods: the formative Han dynasty (140 B.C.E.–220 C.E.) and the late-Ming period, roughly the last century of the Ming dynasty (1368–1644). The vexing relationship between the Confucian discourse of music and the expressive cultures of musical females in the vast historical terrain between these two periods will have to await future research.

In short, this chapter seeks to illuminate the theory and practice of "Confucian music" by delineating what it is and is not in the eyes of its practitioners; what they included in the canon and what they left out. The thesis advanced is that the "absence" of female musicians and music in China is an illusion created by a deliberate Confucian strategy of banishment and retreat. For male scholars who thought of themselves as Confucian, this strategy resolved an intellectual and practical dilemma as well as a conflict in male desires. The very presence of female music and musicians was the root of that conflict.

### MUSIC AND SEPARATION BETWEEN THE TWO SEXES

For a glimpse of the illusory absence of female musicians and music in early imperial China, there is no better choice than the *Record of Music*, a classic of Confucian aesthetics about ritual and music. The edition extant today is found in the classic *Book of Rites*, a ritualist's anthology compiled from ancient sources; a slightly different version also appears in a later work, Sima Qian's (ca. 145–86 B.C.E.) *Records of the Grand Historian.*[3] According to the *History of the Han Dynasty*, an imperial clansman, Liu De (fl. 155–130 B.C.E.), assembled the text from relevant passages in the *Offices of Zhou* (Zhouguan) and various treatises of ancient philosophers.[4] Little is known about Liu other than that he promoted proper music during the reign of the Han emperor Wu (140–87 B.C.E.). Another source, the *History of the Sui Dynasty*, contended that the author was Gongsun Nizi, a philosopher of the Warring States period (475–221 B.C.E.) about whom little is known.[5]

In eleven short chapters, the *Record of Music* describes a wide range of historical facts and theoretical concerns about ancient Chinese music, illustrating how proper music functions as a means of governance and moral cultivation. It discusses, for example, the physical and cosmological attributes of music and how they correspond with human and supernatural elements; the institution of ritual and music in imperial courts; the social and political functions of ritual and music; histories of music and music making in the Warring States period and earlier; classi-fications of music, with paradigms ranging from rhythm to geographic origins to moral values; and singing techniques and patterns of melodies.

Despite this comprehensive coverage, the text includes only five indirect refer-ences to female musicians and music. Reiterating a key Confucian norm of gen-der separation, for example, the chapter on the nature of music states that the mu-sic and rituals performed at weddings and capping ceremonies should serve to differentiate the male and the female.[6] Indeed, ritual and musical separation of the two sexes is a recurrent theme in the text. The chapter on imperial state sacrifices warns that disorder would ensue if the sexes were not differentiated.[7] The chapter on the meanings of music articulates the correlation between music and social re-lations: "When musical pitches are appropriately presented as high and low tones, and when musical phrases are arranged as beginnings and endings, music can be used to represent human affairs and activities, revealing principles behind intimate and remote relationships, high and low status, old and young ages, and males and females. Thus, there is a saying that music shows what is deep inside societies."[8]

For this reason, the difference between good music and bad is more than a mat-ter of taste. The chapter comparing ancient and contemporary music warns: "New music of nowadays shows irregular movements of advance and retreat. Not know-ing how to stop, its wicked sounds are excessive. Its performers are dwarfs, men, and women who act like monkeys, paying no heed to distinctions between fathers and sons. When performances of this kind of music end, the audience is left speech-less, having nothing to say that relates to the way of ancient sages. This is why mu-sic (*yue*) and mere musical notes (*yin*) are related, but there is a world of difference between them."[9]

Warnings in the same chapter are clear and specific: "The excessive tunes of the Zheng state lead to improper thoughts; the entertaining tunes of the Song state and their female performers dull people's consciousness; the rushed tunes of the Wei state disturb people's minds, and the strange music of the Qi state makes people eccen-tric. This is why these four kinds of music are licentious and harmful to the practice of virtues. They cannot be performed at the time of sacrifices."[10] Although there are many improper sounds, those made by women seem particularly disruptive.

## FEMALE MUSICIANS IN EARLY IMPERIAL CHINA

Beyond such formal discourse on music, however, female musicians and music were not as invisible. Most striking are the images of male and female commoners cel-ebrating their lives with music and dance presented in the *Book of Odes* (ca. 1000–600 B.C.E.). The *Odes* is an exceptional text in the Confucian canon: the unabashed tone and amorous scenes in some of the 305 poems have taxed many commenta-tors. The poem entitled "Fallen Leaves" (Tuoxi), for example, depicts a festival in which males and females sang together, and the poem "The Cock Has Crowed" (Nüyue jiming) describes a couple making music with the *qin*- and *se*-zithers.[11] On a different note, the early history the *Zuo Commentary* (Zuo zhuan) recorded transfers of female musicians as gifts between heads of state. There was also the story of the virtuous Lady Wen, who rejected her brother-in-law's attempt to seduce her with a military dance.[12]

Many more instances of women making music are recorded in *The Spring and Autumn of Master Lü* (Lüshi chunqiu), a third-century-B.C.E. compilation. Its text condemns musical females with a cutting analogy: beautiful females and their licentious music are like an ax that cut short the lives of men and nations.[13] The reader was warned of two grave examples: the state of Zhongshan collapsed because its men and women socialized together, indulging in singing and becoming emotionally charged; and the Duke of Rong accepted a gift of singing girls, indulged himself with merry-making and drinking, hence allowing his court to descend into chaos.[14] Female music *is* the femme fatale.

Yet this same historical text credits three women as creators of regional repertories of music.[15] One was the maid of the wife of Xia Yu, the mythical founder of the Xia dynasty, who composed a song about waiting for her master south of Tu Mountain. The song became the earliest example of southern folk songs that were subsequently collected by Zhou officials and sung as the songs of "Zhounan" and "Zhaonan" at the court. These songs were preserved as sections in the *Book of Odes*. Another two girls of the northern Yourong clan sang about the departure of a magical sparrow they desired; their song subsequently became the first example of northern folk songs. Be they mythical or actual personalities, these nameless girls bespeak the popularity, even respectability, of the voices of female singers in early China.

A Daoist classic, *The Book of Liezi* (Liezi) and the second-century compendium of Han cults and beliefs, *Fengsu tongyi*, provides images of female musicians from the popular imagination that are much more pervasive and sanguine than those in the canonical *Record of Music*. Han E, a native of the state of Han, was an itinerant singer who sustained herself on her skills. Her art impressed whole communities and inspired regional singing traditions.[16] Another skilled musician was the wife of Baili Xi. Separated from her husband during the fall of the Yu state, she drifted to Qin where she supported herself as a washing woman. One day, she learned that her husband, now a Qin official, was holding a party. She offered to sing, played the zither as accompaniment, and improvised a song to remind Baili Xi of his lost wife. He was touched and so were they reunited.[17]

If women could be heard singing on streets and in official homes, even more common were palace ladies who entertained emperors and kings, as evinced by the *Records of the Grand Historian* and other Han sources. Most famous was the military strongman Xiang Yu's (232–202 B.C.E.) Concubine Yu, valorized in the modern Peking opera, *Farewell to My Concubine*. Concubine Yu was virtuous *and* musical: In one of the most enduring scenes in Chinese theater, Xiang chanted his swan song in the face of his imminent defeat. The concubine sang along. She then killed herself to facilitate Xiang's escape.[18] Less well known in lore but more enduring in innovation was Lady Tangshan, who participated in the creation of a special kind of ritual court music at the beginning of the Han dynasty.[19] Music also served as a currency for international diplomacy. During Emperor Xuan's reign (73–49 B.C.E.), the nation of Wusun sent a princess to the Han capital to learn to play the zither. On her way back, she married a king of the Qiuzi. She later returned to the Han as a Qiuzi delegate and adopted the use of processional music like a Han court lady.[20]

There is no question that music and dance were the centerpieces of entertainment in early imperial court life. Lady Qi, a concubine of Emperor Gaozu (r. 206–195 B.C.E.) who founded the Han dynasty, was a skilled musician and dancer. Often, when she played the zither the emperor would sing along. Her songs were learned by many palace women, and the ladies' chorus could be heard from afar.[21] An even more renowned zither player was Madame Shen, who lived during Emperor Wen's reign (180–157 B.C.E.) Once the emperor summoned her to perform the instrument and accompanied her playing with his own singing. The music was said to be suffused with an elegiac (*bei*) pathos.[22]

Music in the Han court was not insulated from the sounds of the pleasure quarters. Lady Li, who served in Emperor Wu's court, and the empress Zhao of Emperor Cheng (r. 32–7 B.C.E.) were both skilled in song and dance because they were born and raised in families of entertainers.[23] Indeed, the Confucian scholars were not wrong in associating wanton music with the decadent and the exotic. Even improper music made by men was too alluring to be left alone. One has only to remember the famous Han widow Zhuo Wenjun who eloped with the scholar-poet Sima Xiangru (d. 118 B.C.E.) after he serenaded her with his zither.[24]

### THE GOODNESS OF MUSIC: CONFUCIAN DISCOURSES OF MUSIC AND CULTURE

The preceding discussion sought to reconstruct the presence of female musicians in court and society in the same period as the compilation of the *Record of Music*, admittedly from fragmentary evidence. This section seeks to establish that their dubious reputation was rooted in the very definition of music formulated by Confucius and a deliberate strategy of banishment and retreat that resulted.

As a constituent element of ritual, music is supposed to be practiced by all Confucians if not all humans, regardless of their sex. It is performed and heard not only as a means of governance and self-cultivation but also as a genuine expression of hearts and minds. As such, music is integral if not synonymous with culture (*wen*), a fact that Confucius taught with words and actions. He regularly listened to, practiced, and discussed music throughout his life, leaving many unambiguous examples of what he found musically desirable and undesirable. Stating that a person can be "perfected by music" (*cheng yu yue*) and asking the rhetorical question of what people without benevolence (*ren*) have to do with music, Confucius established the notion that music and cultivation of virtues are inseparable.[25]

Music, then, is also inseparable from politics. According to one text, Confucius practiced a piece of seven-string *qin*-zither music until he understood it as "King Wen's

Tune" (Wenwang cao) and grasped how the music projected the identity and virtues of King Wen, a cultural hero and sage ruler of the Zhou dynasty.[26] Composing the piece "Lone Orchid" to lament that no government in his time adopted his idealistic policies, Confucius showed that music expresses what is deep in people's hearts and mind. As such, music is an indispensable instrument for rulership.

Confucius's valorization of "Shao" and "Wu" as ideal music thus stemmed from an extremely high estimation of the power of music. "Shao" was "perfectly beautiful and good" music because it taught the sage-king Shun's willing abdication to Yu, a peaceful means of dynastic succession and a harbinger of civilized society. In comparison, "Wu," although still laudable, was not perfectly good because it embodied the militancy with which the Zhou king Wu ushered in a peaceful society.[27] Confucius insisted that proper music implies not only harmonious and unified sounds but also appropriate performers and venues, as evinced by his critique of the Ji clan's performance of imperial music in their court.[28]

It is thus clear that Confucius detested vernacular music because its excessive sounds and wanton performers disrupted the harmony of proper music and the ideal sociopolitical order it engendered.[29] His reaction of banishing and retreating from licentious sounds, to use the words of the *Analects*, was not directed against women per se. In light of his overarching goal of constructing an orderly world of benevolent inhabitants, Confucius's views of music should be construed as neither misogynous nor sexist in intent.

As his followers interpreted and expanded on his teachings, a system of thought and institutions gradually took shape during the Han dynasty that produced a dominant discourse of Confucian music in imperial China. This official discourse placed music in a comprehensive cosmological and social scheme wrought of correlative hierarchies. Music thus became gender-specific, and the conflict between proper and vernacular music intensified. The *Record of Music* documents the tenets of this official discourse and its inherent contradictions, as we shall see.[30]

Of fundamental import to the official discourse in the *Record of Music* is the distinction between music and sound. Music arises from people's internal responses to the outside world; by definition, it cannot be dishonest or inauthentic. Music is the direct embodiment of people's emotions in the form of distinctive sounds. This is why governments should, on the one hand, observe commoners' music to learn about their lives and, on the other, institute ritual and music as models to teach them the proper way of living. By touching people's hearts and minds and by teaching them social hierarchies and duties, music unites different strata of people into an orderly society. The *Record of Music* declares: "Ritual and music manifest the will of Heaven and Earth, demonstrate virtues of the divine and perspicacious, coordinate hierarchies and movements of the deities, concretize myriad things and affairs, and regulate the interactions between fathers and sons as well as between rulers and officials."[31]

As such, music is a microcosm of the hierarchical order that structures the cosmological and human worlds. The order of the Five Tones (*wusheng*)—*gong, shang, jue, zhi, yu*—is as immutable as that which regulates the interactions among rulers, officials, people, events, and things. As the hierarchical and sequential pitches are sung and performed on musical instruments such as bell-chimes and stone-chimes, their rhythm and structural patterns reflect dynamics of cosmic elements. As music (*yue*) manifests and cultivates inner virtues, it transcends mere sounds (*sheng*)—products of people's reaction to external things—and tones, which are sounds organized according to specific patterns.

In a nutshell, the message from the *Record of Music* is that only virtuous people can make proper music, and all proper music is virtuous. In theory, men are just as capable of producing disruptive sounds as are women, but somehow the voice of the female seems particularly foreboding.

### BANISHMENT AND RETREAT: AMBIGUITY OF MALE DESIRES

Confucius's call to promote proper music and banish vernacular music cannot be more straightforward, but its implementation was fraught with ambiguities. First, rejection of music made by women contradicts the premise of the Confucian theory of music—music as an expression of natural emotions and a means of ordering society. Second, given the Confucian insistence on gender segregation as the hallmark of an orderly society, females are recognized to occupy specific roles in family and society and have unique experiences. Is it not natural to expect them to express themselves with music of their own? And if male rulers and scholar-officials are to civilize the world by ordering the female realm, should they not listen to women's innermost voices before proceeding to teach them morality?

Such contradictions can be resolved, hypothetically, by the argument that females made good as well as bad music and that what should be banished was the latter. Indeed, many fathers and husbands recognized the goodness of music produced by their nurturing mothers, virtuous wives, and filial daughters in the inner quarters. Although evidence from the earlier periods is scarce, in the sixteenth and seventeenth centuries there is some indication that gentry daughters learned to play the *qin*-zither from fathers and teachers as part of cultural literacy.[32] The didactic use of female music was most evident in the case of the Ming emperor Shizong (r. 1522–66) who commanded, in 1530, blind female musicians to the palace to sing exhortations of female virtues to his court ladies.[33] Still, this recognition of the didactic potential of music for women does not detract from the conceptual ambiguity: how to distinguish the undesirable female music and musicians from the good?

The banishment of female musicians and music is an urgent task for the Confucian scholars who authored the musical treatises in spite of, or perhaps because of, these conceptual ambiguities. For, as I contend below, the alluring musical voices of women expose a certain remoteness and limitation of proper music, not to mention its lack of direct sensuous appeal. Proper music is intellectual and distant. As described in the *Analects*, it "begins with playing in unison. When it gets into full swing, it is harmonious, clear and unbroken. In this way, it reaches the conclusions." Confucius was said to have his senses overwhelmed: after hearing "Shao," he did not notice the taste of precious meat for three months. He exclaimed: "I never dreamt that the expressiveness of music could reach such height."[34]

There is no gainsaying, however, that few of his followers could feel what Confucius experienced. Although scholar-officials were supposed to be conversant with the cosmological and musical attributes of proper music and familiar with descriptions of historical examples, their personal exposure to the restrained sounds, performed during state sacrifices and court functions, was in fact rather limited. Proper music was heard only by court musicians who had the license to practice the music and by officials and staff summoned to performances held in such controlled venues as imperial altars and palace halls. Its learned expressions were intelligible only to specialists who were ritual and musical masters.

As practiced, proper music was essentially a male and courtly affair. Only male scholars were recruited to fill the offices of Musicians, Sacrificers, and Erudites in the prestigious Court of Imperial Sacrifices (*taichang si*), the bureau in charge of state sacrifices and music. And since women were barred from bureaucratic appointments, it goes without saying that the ranks of scholar-officials attending such functions were male. Thus official music—proper music—was androcentric in practice.

Besides the social context of gender separation in which it functioned, proper music was also limited by its own aesthetics and requirements. It was effective only when heard in the proper settings as part of a larger ritual, as evinced by its performance in the Han court. No notated sources of Han proper music are extant, but the dynastic histories record one useful example. The ritual and music designed by the scholar Shusun Tong (fl. ca. 206 B.C.E.) projected the dignity of the founding emperor Gaozu; its performance stopped rowdy officials in their tracks during ceremonial functions.[35] First performed in 200 B.C.E. during a ceremony celebrating the completion of a new palace, the ritual and music guided the officials to take their appropriate positions at the eastern and western sides of the palace hall with solemnity and announced the emperor's entry into the space with dignity.

Large-scale participatory performances of such proper music, however, only occurred during special occasions and state sacrifices, many of which were annual events. Infrequent performances made the music unfamiliar to many, a problem aggravated by the distant and abstract subject matter and antiquated styles. For example, the songs that Emperor Gaozu used to accompany offerings during his state sacrifice to imperial ancestors emulated ancient chants and were sung without instrumental accompaniment. Even professionals had difficulty understanding this state music. In the beginning of the Han, hereditary musicians from the former Lu state, the homeland of Confucius, were drafted to compose sacrificial music for the new dynasty. They could remember the resonant sounds of their tradition but not their supposed meanings.[36]

In contrast, vernacular music from the same period appears to have been delightfully appealing and accessible, offering auditory and visual pleasures. It is easy

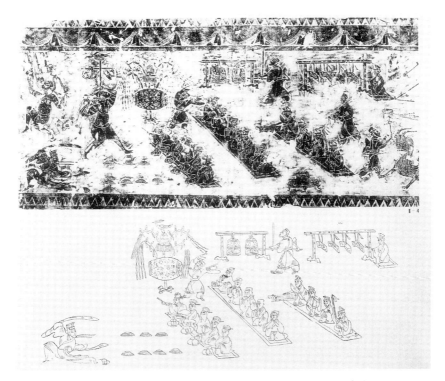

Figure 4.1. Female Drummers. Courtesy of Music Research Institute of Chinese Academy of Arts.

to imagine which kind of music the male audience preferred. Jihuanzi, the Lu statesman whose indulgence in singing girls caused Confucius to retreat from his court, was but one of numerous men who made their choices clear, moral censure notwithstanding. At the most basic level, the Confucian strategy of banishment and retreat is unrealistic because of this contradiction in male desires.

Although no notated sources of Han vernacular music are extant, its appeal is vividly captured by inscribed artifacts. A stone relief from the end of the Eastern Han period (ca. second century C.E.) shows female drummers beating out a rhythm to accompany flowing dance movements (see Figure 4.1). Another relief in a Han brick shows dramatic movements by a pair of female and male performers dancing to panpipe music (see Figure 4.2). The lyrics of Han vernacular music are found in the *Collected Music Bureau Poems* (Yuefu shiji). Although today one can only picture these scenes from afar and without "sound track," it is not hard to imagine the expressiveness of the tunes.

One Han emperor, Ai (r. 7 B.C.E.–1 C.E.), sought to put the Confucian program into practice. In 6 B.C.E. he dismissed 451 out of 824 musicians staffing the Music Bureau (*yuefu*, which supplied musicians for court functions), all of whom were per-

Figure 4.2. Male and Female Dancers and Panpipe Players. Courtesy of Music Research Institute of Chinese Academy of Arts.

formers of vernacular music. When he was a young prince, the emperor was said to dislike the popularity of vernacular music and detested the ways noblemen fought over female musicians.[37] Emperor Ai's banishment of vernacular music from the court, however, is a rarity in history.

Most Confucian scholars had neither the power nor the will to implement such measures. Faced with the ambiguities and conflicts inherent in official Confucian stricture, they adopted a form of *textual* banishment and retreat. Female music was banished from the pages of official treatises—dismissed as not worthy of discussion—but not from social life. The absence of females in the textual and musical traditions that ensued worked as a camouflage for conflicted male desire for and fear of female sensuality. The effective operation of banishment and retreat as rhetorical strategies means that the canonical texts retreated into a space of their own, increasingly detached from social life.

### LOCATING THE MUSICAL FEMALE (*NÜYUE*)

Thus the relationship between Confucian proper music and the sounds and presence of women was extremely ambivalent. For this reason, an exploration of the conceptual and social locations of female music in its own right, with or without references to the discourse of proper music, is needed. First it is crucial to emphasize the performative nature of traditional Chinese music and clarify the meaning of the Chinese term *nüyue*, rendered broadly here as the "musical female." Music operates with ephemeral sounds, and before the invention of phonographs it could only be sonically experienced during an actual performance. This experiential quality is highlighted and celebrated in traditional Chinese music. Musicians and audience alike tended to discuss music in contextual terms—in terms of specific musicians and the performance process—paying secondary attention to such textual elements as composition structure and notation. It is thus difficult to identify a repertory of female music—one supposed to have feminine characteristics—by a set of structural criteria.

Although the boundaries of androcentric proper music are clear, the same is not true for female music. Indeed, the very ontological status of "female music" is unstable. Does it mean music composed by women? Performed by women? In a female voice? By no means can one assume that all music made by women or in a female voice is a direct expression of female experiences and perspectives. The problem of the shifty female musical voice is related to a similar problem, that of the female literary voice.[38] To be sure, there are many pieces in the historical Chinese music repertoire that adopt a first-person female voice, or purport to represent female perspectives. Well-known examples include the *qin*-zither composition "Barbarian Pipe Music" (Hujia shibapai), the folk song "A Widow Mourns Her Husband for Seven Cycles of Seven Days" (Ku qiqi), and the song "The Young Widow at Her Husband's Grave" (Xiao guafu shanfen). Given the popularity of male impersonators in female roles in Chinese operas, however, it is difficult to establish a direct correlation between the narrative voice of a musical composition and the gendered social identity of its performer.

The vexing issue of the female musical voice—its relationship with social gender and its place in the history of music—awaits further research. This task may be aided by clarifications in the terminology of *nüyue* (lit., "female-music"), which is deliberately ambiguous. It can refer to female musicians, or to the music that ensued from the interaction between female musicians and their male audience. It can even refer to social and sexual liaisons between the two. Using such phrases as "female musicians," "musical females," or "female music" does not imply the existence of a shared essential characteristic among these performers and types of music.

Whatever its nature, *nüyue* was often categorically condemned in official discourse. For example, the author of a seminal encyclopedia, *Music Treatise* (Yueshu), Chen Yang (fl. ca. 1094–1104), took *nüyue* to mean female musicians. He equated them with entertainers (*changyou*, lit., "prostitutes and actors") and defined their music as a departure from that of the ancient kings. It is not surprising that Chen adopted the classic Confucian censure that the music should be banished and the entertainers persecuted.[39]

The practice of *nüyue* was more complicated. In their social locations, musical females can be subdivided into two types: "female-exclusive," which produced and consumed music for women only; and "male-female interactive," which entertained both men and women. The former were mostly respectable mothers, wives, and daughters, whereas the latter were women of dubious social standing such as maids, concubines, courtesans, and actresses. The music made by women can also be subdivided into two types according to its channels of circulation: "restricted" and "accessible." The former is represented by wedding and funeral laments that are primarily produced and consumed by females; the latter includes almost all genres of traditional Chinese music played in front of male or mixed audiences.

These matters of terminology underscore the ironic omnipresent yet circumscribed existence of women in Chinese music history and society. Also evident is the slippage between the categories suggested above. The bridal daughter's lament, a popular genre in southern China into the 1980s, was intended for her female relatives and boudoir friends but could of course accidentally fall on male ears. Nonetheless, the categories proposed here help to refine our understanding about the location of the musical female inside and outside of the Confucian discourse. One can also clearly perceive the bias on which the strategy of inclusion and exclusion in the official treatises was based.

Neither "female-exclusive" musicians nor their "restricted" music that circulated in the inner quarters posed a threat to the Confucian order. They were thus tacitly allowed to exist but seldom described, entering into official discourse only when they aroused male sentiments and concerns. For example, Lady Qi of the Han sang to protest her imprisonment by Empress Lü after the death of Emperor Gaozu; Xijun, daughter of a Han nobleman, sang to lament her diplomatic marriage to an old king of Qiuzi. Such laments were documented because these women functioned in a male public domain.[40] Similarly, when moralists raised objections to the frequent practice of keeping blind female singers in upper-class Ming households to entertain wives and concubines, the practice made its entry into public records.[41] Ironically, the most respectable female music was the least visible socially and textually.

The presence of women who entertained at "male-female interactive" functions with "accessible" music is understandably more visible in the archives. Their appearance, however, bespeaks their marginalized status and low social standing. All were maids, courtesans, entertainers, and prostitutes, singing in banquet halls, mansions, entertainment quarters, and private homes. Furthermore, these occasions were, strictly speaking, not considered "musical" events but rather social entertainment. With this compartmentalization, Confucian scholars could participate in them, and occasionally they were moved to describe in writing female musicians of unique artistic achievement and physical charm. Such descriptions were nonetheless often written as short and random comments of passion and nostalgia tinged with social concern, as in the genre of "blue brower" literature. The name of this genre derived from the *Blue Brower Collection*, which consists of the scholar Xia Tingzi's biographical notes of some 117 female musicians and actresses in Yuan dynasty (1260–1368) theater and brothels. They were written as reminiscences of a prosperous age and as warnings of the social turmoil that ensued.[42]

Both the practice and the textual presence of female music changed in the dynasty that followed, the Ming. The flourishing of Ming southern drama (*chuanqi*) as both a literary genre and a performative art drew scholarly attention to *nüyue* and gave female musicians unprecedented textual presence.

## ZHU ZAIYU, A MING PROPONENT OF CONFUCIAN MUSIC

Proper music continued to be transmitted and developed in a ritual and textual space of its own, with scant reference to the theater and vernacular tunes. The extensive music chapters in the official histories, the *History of the Song Dynasty* (Songshi) and the *History of the Ming Dynasty* (Mingshi), offer detailed descriptions of music events at court and preserve complete texts of state sacrificial songs but hardly mention female musicians and music.[43] The strategy of textual banishment and retreat remained the operating principle that skewed the archives.

The crowning achievement of the proper music tradition is Zhu Zaiyu's *Collected Works of Music Theory* (Yuelü quanshu) of 1595, a monumental compendium of late-imperial Chinese knowledge of proper music. This multivolume collection of musical treatises covers all known topics of Confucian music history, theory, and practices. Included are, for example, discussions on the origin of music, comments on various historical theories and experiments of music, an exposition of one of the world's earliest theories on equal temperament, dance pictograms, and detailed music scores that describe performance techniques, rhythm, melodic patterns, and other musical features. Except for a brief reference to the proper music of palace ladies (*fangzhong yue*) in historic courts, Zhu discussed neither female music nor popular songs and operas of his time.[44]

Instead of describing the late Ming music world comprehensively, Zhu wrote his treatises to promote the use of proper music as a means of governance and cultivation of virtues among the populace. His exposition of equal temperament is not only a theoretical and practical exercise to resolve musical problems of tuning; it is also an idealistic pursuit of physically and cosmologically accurate pitches needed to harmonize the world. To activate accurate correspondences among the human and natural entities, proper music must have accurate pitches. By the same token, his detailed scores and dance pictograms not only reflect certain contemporaneous practices of proper music but also demonstrate his understanding of ancient music and dance.

The Confucian reasoning behind Zhu's treatises is succinctly summarized in his *Essentials of Music Theory, the Inner Chapters:*

> In ancient times, the sagely kings instituted ritual and laws, implemented cultivation of virtues, used the three bonds (*sangang*) to rectify the nine practices of governance (*jiuchou*) and to harmonize people and things alike.[45]

The three bonds, a key Confucian tenet, refers to the reciprocal obligations that structure relationships between ruler and subject, father and son, and husband and wife. Its overarching importance in China and Korea is discussed later, in the chapters by Du Fangqin and Susan Mann and Martina Deuchler. Meanwhile, it is important to note how Zhu Zaiyu construed music to have a direct impact on these key social relationships:

Then the sagely kings composed music to air the eight winds (*bafeng zhi qi*) and to pacify emotions of the world. This is why proper music is calm (*dan*) and not sad (*shang*); harmonious and not excessive. When such music enters people's ears and reaches their hearts, they become calm and harmonious. With calmness in their hearts, their desires would be pacified; with harmony in their minds, their worries would be relieved. As people become gentle, relaxed, peaceful and moderate, virtues flourish; as the world becomes cultivated and moderate, governance reaches its peak. This is why people say that the zenith of ancient times occurred when the world matched with the Way.[46]

Sounding a familiar note, Zhu reiterated the political and cosmological significance of proper music:

Music originates from governance. When governance is benevolent and the populace peaceful, the world would be harmonious. Then the sages would make music to air harmonious hearts, and let their emotions reach heaven and earth. As the *qi* between heaven and earth corresponds, the cosmos becomes harmonious. Then all beings would operate smoothly; deities and spirits would come to the human world, and birds and animals would be domesticated. People who are confused would not understand this principle of music, and they would only see music as sequential sounds or remnants from the Tang and Song dynasties. How can these views be worthy of discussion on the way of the great harmony (*dahe zhi dao*)?[47]

Zhu composed many antiquated melodies himself, setting them to lyrics from the *Book of Odes* (see Music Example 4.1). Repetitive and structurally simple, these tunes exemplify the limited appeal of proper music and explain why it was only intelligible to masters of Confucian ritual and music. How could such music compete in popularity with Ming folk songs or dramatic arias? As demonstrated by "How Many Provinces Does the Moon Shine Upon?" (Yuezi wanwan zhao ji zhou), a tune that contrasts the happiness of united families with the sadness of broken ones (see Music Example 4.2), Ming folk songs are replete with sentimentality and smooth melodies. More elegant but no less enticing are Kun arias, the most popular genre in the late Ming theater, which feature long and florid melodies (see Music Example 4.3). Such tunes captured the hearts and minds of late Ming men and women.

### MING THEATER AND FLOURISHING FEMALE MUSIC

Female musicians and their music constituted an undeniable force behind the blossoming of Ming vernacular music. A keen observer of Ming social life, the scholar Shen Defu (1578–1642), wrote that "Tune of the Five Night Watches" (Wugengdiao), "Twisted Silver Threads" (Yinniusi), and other tunes were widely popular because they were sung and listened to by all, be they men or women, old or young, respectable or otherwise. Shen also stated that courtesans in the capital frequently performed the music of "Sheep on the Slope" (Suluo shanboyang), which were

Music Example 4.1. "Yuezi wanwan zhao ji zhou?"

Music Example 4.2. A Kun Aria

Music Example 4.3. Zhu Zaiyu's Setting of a Poem from the *Book of Odes*

arias from the north.[48] Another scholar of the time, He Liangjun (1506–73), es-
teemed songs sung by contemporary female commoners so much that he compared
them to the so-called National Airs (*guofeng*) in the *Book of Odes*, both being natural
expressions of genuine emotions.[49]

Female musicians became so common that they even performed in Emperor
Shizong's sericultural ceremonies between 1530 and 1556. The choice of musicians
was not as unusual as it may seem. Although state sacrificial music was a male mo-
nopoly, sericulture was considered a female occupation and state sacrifices to silk
deities were presided over by the empress. Eventually, the emperor lost interest in
the ceremony and had it canceled.[50]

In the Ming women also became visible as members of the audience. Scholar
and famed dramatist, Xu Wei (1521–93), traced the musical roots of southern operas (*nanxi*), the predecessor of Ming *chuanqi* opera, to tunes freely improvised by
commoners, male and female. Xu also declared that no operatic arias were successful unless children, maids, and women young and old could understand what
was being sung.[51]

This open recognition of women's taste was part and parcel of a changing definition of womanhood and the new texture of domestic life. So popular was the theater that many elite Ming households brought the stage back to their domestic
spaces. When the scholar He Liangjun visited the home of Huangfu Fang
(1503–82), for example, the host entertained him with a domestic performance of
female music and dance.[52] When rich Ming families procured young girls to serve
as concubines and maids, musical skills became a major consideration. In addition to household and sexual services, concubines and maids were expected to perform music to entertain their male owners and female superiors. Even the least
talented girls would learn to play a tune or two on the *qin*-zither and to sing songs
like "Jade Abdomen Wrap" (Yubaodu) and "Gathering of Honored Guests" (Ji-
binxian).[53]

The ubiquity of music in Ming domestic life is most vividly depicted in *The Plum
in the Golden Vase* (Jinpingmei), a novel about the harem of Ximen Qing, a local
merchant of some means. It provides a gold mine of information on domestic and
social lives. When Ximen presented his new concubine Li Ping'er to his friends and
relatives, four professional musicians were hired to sing auspicious marital songs.
Ximen and his male guests enjoyed the show in the front hall, whereas his wife
and concubines sat in the back room of the hall, behind a curtain (Figure 4.3). Afterward, Pan Jinlian, the fourth concubine, complained to the principal wife, Yueniang, that the performance was inappropriate: since Li was only a concubine, the
musicians singing of her as a wife was disrespectful. Implied in Pan's comments was
a cultural understanding that music should befit the social station and occasion.
Yueniang, the wife who happened to be a pious lady, agreed and felt disturbed.[54]

On another occasion, when the family gathered in the garden, Ximen asked
Meng Yulou, the second concubine, and Pan to entertain him with music. Pan refused on the pretense that she was not a hired musician; she would sing only if Li,

Figure 4.3. A Music Party in Ximen Qing's House

the new concubine, joined them. It was not until the patriarch made Li play the clappers to mark rhythm that Pan and Meng began to sing.[55] This negotiation not only underscores music making as a routine activity but also reveals the roles, hierarchy, and interactions of musical females inside Ming homes.[56] It was perhaps understood that wives and concubines, but not a junior concubine, would entertain the husband; only hired musicians entertained their audiences without such concern for hierarchy.

The women in Ximen's house also entertained and amused themselves in female-exclusive spaces. For example, one night when Pan could not have the husband's company, she consoled herself by singing and playing the *pipa*-lute, rehearsing familiar tropes associated with an abandoned woman pining for her lover's

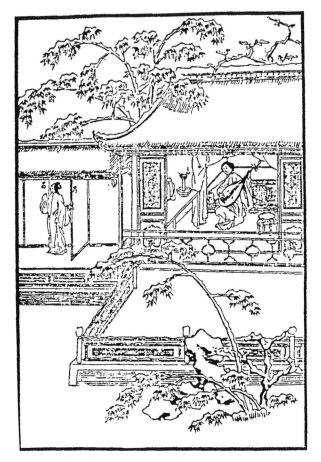

Figure 4.4. Pan Jinlian Singing and Playing the *Pipa*-Lute

return (see Figure 4.4).[57] These tropes recurred in late Ming and Qing popular songs. For example, the song entitled "A *Pipa*-Lute Hanging on the Wall" (Yimian pipa qiangshang gua) was particularly provocative. To console herself, a lovesick woman took down the *pipa* hanging on the wall, fingered the strings, and played a few notes. She then began to cry on realizing that the lute was no substitute for her man.[58] Another song, "No Need for Wooden Clappers" (Buxu tanban), describes a woman urging her lover to join her in drinking and singing.[59]

So popular was the domestic theater that it was not uncommon for elite households in the wealthy Yangzi delta to maintain family troupes as markers of cultural capital (See Figure 4.3).[60] There is some evidence that a handful of these troupes were female. The troupe kept by aficionado Qian Dai, for example, included twelve female performers trained in a wide range of theatrical roles and singing styles. It was guided by two female music teachers. One was Madame Shen, who hailed from the family troupe of Prime Minister Shen Shixing's (1535–1614) household. She was both a master composer and a performer. Even in her sixties, she could sing clearly and rhythmically. With the disguise of costume and makeup, her presence on stage was comparable to that of much younger actors. Madame Xue, the other teacher, was particularly skilled in playing wind and string instruments.[61] It is perhaps no accident that both teachers were natives of Suzhou, a city with thriving theater and literary scenes.

Suzhou also boasted some of the empire's most accomplished courtesans who were musicians, poets, and painters. A handful of the most talented courtesans were eulogized in a respectable anthology, *Collection of Poems from the Dynasties*. In its *Biographical Notes* (Liechao shiji xiaozhuan), its compiler, Qian Qianyi (1582–1664), praised six courtesans noted for their music skills and knowledge: Qi Jingyun, Hu Wenyu, and Ma Wenyu were skilled at playing the *qin*-zither; Yu Sulan knew music theories; Zhu Wuxia learned music and dance when young; and Ma Xianglan taught maids operatic music and dances and hosted banquets that featured singing and playing of *pipa* and drums.[62]

It is obvious that music and poetry were central to the courtesan culture of the late Ming. If there were courtesans who used music to advertise their sensuousness, there were also those who used music, poetry, painting, and calligraphy to engage their male scholar-companions as equals.[63] The respectability and visibility of female musical and poetic voices were a hallmark of the urban culture in the sixteenth and seventeenth centuries.

### CONCLUSION: GENDERING MUSIC IN CHINA

This chapter aims at exposing the Confucian strategy of banishment and retreat, as well as clarifying the nuanced meanings of *nüyue*, female music. It is clear from the preceding discussion that despite such a strategy, female musicians and music from the past are still knowable to some extent. Han E, Madame Wan, Concubine Yu, Lady Tangshan, Empress Zhao, Madame Shen, and Madame Xue are but examples of those whose extraordinary skills earned them a place in the historical records. Some of them were even admired. For example, Cai Yan, a *qin*-zither musician and theorist who inspired composition of the "Barbarian Pipe Music," was widely admired not only as a good mother and filial daughter but also as an excellent musician and theorist.[64]

It is a truism that the extraordinary would not stand out without reference to the ordinary. Therefore, if there was only one Zhang Honghong in Tang China, who could notate complex music after one listening, there were probably many others who had proficient musical memory and skills of music notation.[65] If Li Ye, a Tang courtesan whose poems are analyzed later, in chapter 10 by Suzanne Cahill, could master *qin*-zither music and vividly describe its sounds with literary images of towering cliffs and flowing rivers, there were probably many others who could play the instrument and were conversant with the terms of music appreciation.[66]

Although this chapter focuses on the early and late imperial periods, it proposes a reading strategy that could yield information about female musicians and music in the intervening periods from the third to fifteen centuries. Descriptions are scattered in poems, memoirs, gazettes, miscellaneous notes, and novels, awaiting scrutiny. For example, in his poem "Passing the Drooping-Rainbow Bridge" (Guo chuihong), the famous composer and music theorist Jiang Kui (1155–1221) casually mentioned that his concubine Xiaohong sang to his playing of the flute.[67] Only painstaking research into official and informal sources can balance the biased picture projected by canonical texts. At best, the latter constitute a partial view and half-truth about Chinese music. At worst, they distort historical understanding of it. Music has been not only a means of governance and self-cultivation but also a vehicle of sociabilities and emotional resonance.

Knowledge about female musicians and music would also rewrite narratives of Chinese music history. What roles did female musicians and female audiences play in the development of traditional Chinese music? Did they help to promote practices of improvisation, oral transmission, and subjective interpretations of musical works? Did they shape stylistic changes of various musical genres? Some preliminary answers are already evident, including the caveat that "female music" was not a monolith. The more publicly visible female musicians hailed from the lower classes, and they had neither the resources to produce notated sources nor the need to objectify what they performed. Indeed, it was wise for them to refrain from categorical descriptions of their music so that they could control ownership of it, change it as needed, pleasing their audience in the process of performance.

The theory and practice of music in China were gender- and social status–specific. Above all, gender affected the production of musical treatises and notated sources, which helps to explain the bias of the musical archives extant today. There is a substantive collection of treatises and notated sources for state sacrificial music, *qin*-zither music, Kun operatic music, and other genres that Confucian males publicly practiced.[68] In contrast, to the best of my knowledge, no authentic notated sources of "restricted" female music performed in the inner quarters have been preserved.

Although speculative, it may not be too far-fetched to contend that a distinct female musical voice did exist. The stylistic differences between male and female arias in Chinese operas, such as Peking opera, would be a fruitful point of departure for future investigation.[69] At the least, the gap between the historical presence of female music and its illusory absence in the canon discussed in this chapter is a poignant reminder that there are many realities and voices in historical, gendered, and musical China. Unless those realities are investigated and the multiple female voices heard, our understandings of China will remain androcentric and incomplete.

## NOTES

1. *Confucius: The Analects*, trans. D. C. Lau (London: Penguin, 1979), pp. 133–34, 149.

2. For a discussion of the historiographic issues of Chinese women's history, see Susan Mann, *Precious Records: Women in China's Long Eighteenth Century* (Stanford: Stanford University Press, 1997), pp. 1–18, 201–26; Patricia Buckley Ebrey, *The Inner Quarters: Marriage and the Lives of Chinese Women in the Sung Period* (Berkeley: University of California Press, 1993), pp. 1–20. For samples of musicological discussions, see Carol Robertson, "Power and Gender in the Musical Experiences of Women," in *Musicology and Difference*, ed. Ellen Koskoff (Urbana: University of Illinois Press, 1987); Ruth Solie, *Musicology and Difference: Gender and Sexuality in Music Scholarship* (Berkeley: University of California Press, 1993); Mu Yang, "Music and Sexual Customs in Multi-Ethnic China," *Asian Studies Review* 18, no. 2 (1994): 63–144; Nora Yeh, "Wisdom of Ignorance: Women Performers in the Classical Chinese Music Traditions," in *Women, Gender, and Culture*, ed. Marcia Herndon and Susanne Ziegler (Wilhelmshaven: Florian Noetzel Verlag, 1990); and Su Zheng, "Female Heroes and Moonish Lovers: Women's Paradoxical Identities in Modern Chinese Songs," *Journal of Women's History* 8, no. 4 (1997): 91–125.

3. "Yueji," in *Liji*, in *Baihua shisanjing* (The Thirteen Classics, with vernacular translation) (Beijing: Guoji wenhua chuban gongsi, 1996). "Yueshu," in Sima Qian, *Shiji* (Beijing: Zhonghua shuju, 1962). The modern reprint used by the present author is *Yueji pizhu* (The record of music, annotated edition) (Beijing: Renmin yinyue chubanshe, 1976). A convenient collection of Chinese reference materials is *Yueji lunbian* (The record of music, with critical translations and comments) (Beijing: Renmin chubanshe, 1983). For an introduction in English, see Scott Cook, "Yue Ji—Record of Music: Introduction, Translation, Notes, and Commentary," *Asian Music* 26, no. 2 (1995): 1–96.

4. Ji Liankang, ed., *Qin Han yinyue shiliao* (Music sources of the Qin and Han dynasties) (Shanghai: Shanghai Wenyi chubanshe, 1981), pp. 61–62, 81–82. The *Offices of Zhou*, also known as the *Rites of Zhou*, is a description of the administrative structures of the royal state of Zhou.

5. *Suishu* (Beijing: Zhonghua shuju, 1975), 13.3286.

6. "Yueben bian," in *Yueji pizhu*, p. 7.

7. "Yueli bian," in *Yueji pizhu*, p. 23.

8. "Yueyan bian," in *Yueji pizhu*, p. 39.

9. "Wei Wenhou bian," in *Yueji pizhu*, p. 60.

10. Ibid., p. 63.

11. Cheng Junying, *Shijing yizhu* (Book of odes, with translations and annotations) (Shanghai: Guji chubanshe, 1985), pp. 149, 153. What these images signify is a vexing question. Some Confucian scholars explained the images away as sheer allegories, reading the amorous relationship between man and woman as an allegory for intimacy between ruler and subject. The purpose here, however, is not *Odes* hermeneutics but retrieving hints of female music.

12. Ji Liankang, ed., *Chunqiu zhanguo yinyue shiliao* (Music sources of the Spring and Autumn and Warring States periods) (Shanghai: Wenyi chubanshe, 1980), pp. 2–3, 13–14.

13. Ji Liankang, ed., *Lüshi chunqiu zhong di yinyue shiliao* (Music sources in the Spring and Autumn of Master Lü) (Shanghai: Wenyi chubanshe, 1983), p. 34.

14. Ibid., pp. 50, 57.

15. Ibid., pp. 27–28.

16. "Tang wen," *Liezhi yizhu*, annotated by Yang Beiming and Yang Jie (Shanghai: Guji chubanshe, 1986), pp. 127–28.

17. *Fengsu tongyi jiaozhu*, annotated by Wang Liqi (Beijing: Zhonghua shuju, 1981), pp. 592–93.

18. Ji, *Qin Han yinyue*, p. 2.

19. Ibid., p. 50.

20. Ibid., p. 101.

21. Ibid., p. 176.

22. Ibid., p. 23.

23. Ibid., pp. 104, 109.

24. Ibid., p. 25.

25. *Analects*, pp. 93, 67.

26. *Kongzi jiayu* (The school sayings of Confucius) (Beijing: Yanshan chubanshe, 1995), p. 210.

27. *Analects*, p. 71.

28. Ibid., p. 67.

29. Ibid., p. 146.

30. This interpretation follows the premises stated in the "Yueben pian" and "Yueli pian" of the document (*Yueji pizhu*, pp. 1–12, 20–25). For other interpretations, see Yang Yinliu, *Zhongguo gudai yinyue shigao* (Draft history of ancient Chinese music) (Beijing: Renmin yinyue chubanshe, 1981), pp. 88–92, 133–37; and "Yueji," in *Zhongguo yinyue cidian* (Dictionary of Chinese music) (Beijing: Renmin yinyue chubanshe, 1985), pp. 481–82.

31. *Yueji pizhu*, p. 33.

32. One gentry daughter who learned the *qin*-zither from her father was Chai Jingyi. See Dorothy Ko, *Teachers of the Inner Chambers: Women and Culture in Seventeenth-Century China* (Stanford: Stanford University Press, 1994), p. 244.

33. Shizong shuhuangdi shilu (Veritable records of Emperor Shizong) (Taipei: Academica Sinica, 1962–67), 118.3b.

34. *Analects*, p. 89.

35. *Hanshu* (Beijing: Zhonghua shuju, 1975), 43.565.

36. Ibid., 22.469.

37. Ji, *Qin Han yinyue*, pp. 65–70.

38. There is no theoretical discussion on the musical female voice in China; for discussions of the literary voice, see Maureen Robertson, "Voicing the Feminine: Constructions of the Gendered Subject in Lyric Poetry by Women of Medieval and Late Imperial China," *Late Imperial China* 13, no. 1 (June 1992): 64–110.

39. Chen Yang, *Yueshu, Siku quanshu* edition, 90.4a. See also the entry "*nüyue,*" *Zhongguo yinyue cidian*, p. 288.

40. Ji, *Qin Han yinyue*, pp. 99–100, 103.

41. Wang Liqi, ed., *Yuan Ming Qing sandai jinhui xiaosuo xiqu shiliao* (Forbidden and destroyed sources of fiction and theater of Yuan, Ming, and Qing, expanded ed.) (Shanghai: Guji chubanshe, 1981), p. 256.

42. Xia Tingzi, *Qinglou ji*, in *Zhongguo gudian xiqu lunzhu jicheng* (Collected works on the Chinese classical theater) (Beijing: Zhongguo xiju chubanshe, 1959), p. 3.

43. *Songshi* (Beijing: Zhonghua shuju, 1977), 126–131.2937–3066; *Mingshi* (Beijing: Zhonghua shuju, 1974), 62.1519–57. For a survey of other Ming music treatises crucial to the development of the proper music tradition, see Joseph S. C. Lam, "Creativity within

Bounds: State Sacrificial Songs from the Ming Dynasty," (Ph.D. dissertation, Harvard University, 1988), pp. 662–702.

44. For reference to *fangzhong yue*, see Zhu Zaiyu, *Yuexue xinshuo*, in *Yuelü quanshu* (Collected works of music theory), in *Shangwu guoxue jiben congshu* (The Commercial Press collectanea in Sinology) (Taipei: Shangwu yinshu guan, 1968), p. 62. For Zhu's biography and works, see *Dictionary of Ming Biography*, ed. L. Carrington Goodrich and Chaoying Fang (New York: Columbia University Press, 1976), s.v. "Chu Tsai-yü"; and Fritz A. Kuttner, "Prince Chu Tsai-yu's Life and Work: A Re-evaluation of His Contribution to Equal Temperament Theory," *Journal of Ethnomusicology* 19 (1975): 163–204. For a general survey of Ming music theory, see Joseph Lam, *State Sacrifices and Music in Ming China: Creativity, Orthodoxy, and Expressiveness* (Albany: State University of New York Press, 1998), pp. 75–97.

45. Zhu Zaiyu, *Lülü jingyi neibian*, *Yuelü quanshu*, 6.173.

46. Ibid.

47. Ibid.

48. Shen Defu, *Wanli yehuo bian* (Miscellaneous notes of the Wanli period) (Beijing: Zhonghua shuju, 1959), p. 647.

49. Li Kaixian, *Cixue* (Discourse on song lyrics), in *Zhongguo gudian xiqu lunzhu jicheng* (Beijing: Zhongguo xiju chubanshe, 1959), p. 287.

50. Lam, *State Sacrifices and Music*, p. 72.

51. Xu Wei, *Nanci xulu* (An account of southern dramas), in *Zhongguo gudian xiqu lunzhu jicheng* (Beijing: Zhongguo xiju chubanshe, 1959), pp. 239, 243.

52. Chen Tian, ed., *Mingshi jishi* (Anthology of Ming poetry, with historical notes) (Shanghai: Guji chubanshe, 1993), 8.1526. See also Paul Ropp, "Love, Literacy, and Laments: Themes of Women Writers in Late Imperial China," *Women's History Review* 2, no. 1 (1993): 107–41.

53. Shen, *Wanli yehuo bian*, p. 597.

54. *Jinpingmei cihua*, fasimile of Wanli ed. (Hong Kong: Taiping shuju, 1982), 20.10a–b. For an excellent English translation of the first twenty chapters, see Xiaoxiaosheng, *The Plum in the Golden Vase*, vol. 1, trans. David Tod Roy (Princeton: Princeton University Press, 1993); *The Plum in the Golden Vase*, vol. 2, *The Rivals* (Princeton: Princeton University Press, 2001).

55. *Jinpingmei*, 27.6a–6.

56. For a discussion of female hierarchies, see Francesca Bray, *Technology and Gender: Fabrics of Power in Late Imperial China* (Berkeley: University of California Press, 1997), pp. 351–68. On female jealousy, see Ko, *Teachers*, pp. 103–12.

57. *Jinpingmei*, 38.9a-10a.

58. Wang Tingshao, *Nichang xupu*, in *Ming Qing minge shidiao ji* (Shanghai: Guji chubanshe, 1987), 4.10a.

59. Feng Menglong, *Jiazhutao*, in *Ming Qing minge shidiaoji* (Shanghai: Guji chubanse, 1987), 1.22b–23a.

60. For family troupes, see Hu Ji and Liu Zhizhong, *Kunju fazhanshi* (History of Kun opera) (Beijing: Zhongguo xiju chubanshe, 1989), pp. 188–224; Lu Eting, *Kunju yanchu shigao* (Draft history of Kun opera performances) (Shanghai: Wenyi chubanshe, 1980), pp. 116–32, 155–69.

61. For female troupes, see Hu and Liu, *Kunju*, pp. 195, 200.

62. Qian Qianyi, *Liechao shiji xiaochuan* (Shanghai: Gudian wenxue chubanshem 1957), pp. 745–46, 765–67, 773; Paul Ropp, "Ambiguous Images of Courtesan Culture in Late Imperial China," in *Writing Women in Late Imperial China*, ed. Ellen Widmer and Kang-i Sun

Chang (Stanford: Stanford University Press, 1997). Kang-i Sun Chang has argued persuasively that the chapter on female poetry in this anthology was edited by Qian's concubine, Liu Shi, a former courtesan and famous poet. See her "Ming and Qing Anthologies of Women's Potery and Their Selection Strategies," in Widmer and Chang, eds., *Writing Women*.

63. Yan Ming, *Zhongguo mingji yishushi* (History of the arts of famous courtesans) (Taipei: Wenjin chubanshe, 1992), pp. 108–14, 119–23.

64. Ji, *Qin Han yinyue*, p. 156.

65. Duan Anjie, *Yuefu zalu* (Miscellaneous notes of music and musicians), in *Zhongguo gudian xiqu lunzhu jicheng* (Beijing: Zhongguo xiju chubanshe, 1959), p. 47.

66. Liu Yin, Sun Anbang, and Pan Shen, eds., *Lidai mingji shiciqu sanbaishou* (Three hundred poems by famous courtesans of past dynasties) (Taiyuan: Shanxi renmin chubanshe, 1992), p. 32.

67. This is deduced from a poem entitled "Guo chuihong": "Softly Xiaohong sings as I play the flute" (Xiaohong dichang wo chuixiao). Xia Chengtao, ed., *Baishi shici ji* (Beijing: Renmin wenxue chubanshe, [1959] 1998), p. 46.

68. See *Zhongguo yinyue shupuzhi* (Bibliography of Chinese music books and notated sources) (Beijing: Renmin yinyue chubanshe, 1984), currently the most comprehensive catalog of Chinese musical sources.

69. For a discussion of arias for male and female roles in Peking opera, see Liu Jidian, *Jingju yinyue gailun* (Introduction to the music of Peking opera) (Beijing: Renmin yinyue chubanshe, 1981), pp. 136–40.

# PART TWO

# Propagating Confucian Virtues

# CHAPTER FIVE

# Women and the Transmission of Confucian Culture in Song China

*Jian Zang*

This chapter focuses on the development of Confucian culture during the Northern and Southern Song dynasties (960–1279), taking rural culture as its point of departure. Its purpose is to explore how social attitudes held by people with similar locations in local society—a society formed by the nexus of blood and territorial relations—became crystallized as taken-for-granted habits.[1] These habits, in turn, influenced Confucian ethical thinking on gender relations and women. Furthermore, without positing a dichotomous relationship between "elite culture" and "peasant culture," or between orality and the written canon, this chapter is concerned with the transmission of norms between the various sociocultural spheres in Chinese society, transmissions that had an indelible impact on women's lives. It concludes with preliminary thoughts on the intersection of gender and class illuminated by our focus on lower-class women.

## COMPLICATING "CONFUCIAN CULTURE" AND "WOMEN"

My interest in local society and nonelite women stems from my understanding of two key concepts: "Confucian culture" and "women." Under the rubric "Confucian culture" I include an array of ethical thinking and practices that constituted the orthodoxy in imperial China. The central tenets of classical Confucian learning are embedded in the ethical concepts "Rites-Music-Humanity-Righteousness" and "Three Bonds–Five Relations." They were formulated by Confucius (551–479 B.C.E.) and Mencius (390–305 B.C.E.) and later systematized by the Han philosopher Dong Zhongshu (180–115 B.C.E.) Their purpose was to rationalize and naturalize status hierarchies.

Confucian culture underwent major developments in the Song dynasty. Although Song Confucian learning was built on the foundation of Han learning, it differs from the latter in the depth and scope of its explorations of the origins and principles of nature and human society. Song learning, which encompasses such diverse elements as analytic philosophy and social ethics, constitutes an integral theoretical system.

It is important to note, however, that Confucian ethical thinking is more than the product of intellectual contemplation or upper-class existence. To a great extent, it reflects the social mores held by the masses in an agrarian society. The *Zuo Commentary* (Zuozhuan) identifies filial piety, a natural sentiment, as "the beginning of Rites (*li*)." The *Book of Rites*, in turn, states that the origins of Rites can be sought from "properly behaving husband and wife" and such human impulses as "drinking and eating."[2] We may hypothesize that the early Confucians took values and practices already prevalent at the grass roots, such as a filiality-based ethics, a concept of descent, and the production of sons as the normative expression of wifely filial piety, and transformed them into Confucian ethical culture.[3] Furthermore, this transformation involved processes of systematization and theorization that served the interests of the educated ruling class.

Having been systematized, this ethical culture was practiced in the upper echelons of society and among the ruling class. Then by way of education it was promulgated to the entire society as the means by which social relations could be maintained and regulated. Traditional Chinese culture, especially Confucian culture, put priority on the establishment and improvement of human character, hence its special emphasis on moral education. From Confucius to the Neo-Confucians in the Song and Ming dynasties, philosophers of the Confucian School were predominantly professional educators. Most of them did not serve as officials for long; they either resigned to teach in academies or took up popular education in the countryside. Perhaps it can be said that in China one cannot be a Confucian without being an educator. The deep penetration of Confucian culture into society went hand in hand with the development and popularization of education.

Education is not a top-down process. We should not forget that it was *human* relationships evolving from *blood* and community ties that were at the roots of Confucian ethical ties codified as father-son, elder brother–younger brother, uncle-nephew, maternal nephew–uncle, mother-in-law–daughter-in-law, and neighbor-neighbor. Moreover, the rituals that reproduced these relations were born of profound human emotions: affinities, adoration, sympathy, resonance, respect, and so on. Through the years, these mentalities and mores molded and guided social behavior in a spontaneous and taken-for-granted manner. Popular sentiments and consciousness were thus far-reaching and long-lasting, forming habits day after day, generation after generation.

In focusing on Confucian thinkers, philosophical treatises, and the written canon, scholars have by and large neglected to investigate the contributions of popular culture and consciousness to systems of thought. Nor have they explored the processes and mechanisms through which Confucian culture filtered down and influenced rural societies, bringing about changes in secular values and behavior.

Toward the end of this chapter, I examine the Song civil service examination system as one mechanism that facilitated this process of cultural interpenetration.

The second motivating factor for this chapter is my interest in expanding our understanding of "women." Previous studies in Chinese, limited by the nature of historical sources, tended to focus on empresses and princesses of the ruling class or women in upper-class gentry families.[4] Yet the vast majority of the female population were working women who lived in villages and small towns. Their lives and mentalities were different from those of the ruling class if not entirely at odds with them. Their thoughts belonged more to the realm of popular consciousness—customs born of the local soil, stemming from popular desires, and handed down from generation to generation.

This chapter is my preliminary attempt to make sense of the lives of this invisible majority who left no written records. My premises are two. First, although individual lives may not be knowable in their local specificities, we may gain information about the common denominator shared by Song commoner women: the centrality of the family in structuring their lives. Second, such male-authored didactic texts as family instructions can yield insights, however speculative, on female interests and incentives as women eked out an existence in the family system.

## OF BLOOD AND SENTIMENT: THE SONG FAMILY

Our search for the texture of a Song commoner woman's life has to begin with the family, or lineage-family to be exact. In anthropological parlance, a "lineage-family" ( *jiazu* ) is a grouping made up of family ( *jiating* ) cells; it performs rites to a common male progenitor, and its various branches and generations are knitted together by differentiated blood relations. A lineage-family often resides in the same village or locale. After the collapse of the extended aristocratic families that prevailed before the Tang (618–907), Song lineage-families tended to assume two organizational modes. The first type comprised families who lived together and shared property for several generations; their members numbered from several scores to more than one hundred.

The *History of the Song Dynasty* records fifty such lineages that were recognized by the government. For example, Zheng Yi, a native of Pujiang, Wuzhou, was said to "manage his family with respect and solemnity; they shared the same stove for nine generations." Another patriarch, Yao Zhongming, a native of Yongle, Hezhong, received repeated imperial rewards for keeping several generations under one roof. "His village was renamed 'Filial Piety and Sibling Respect,' his community (*she*) 'Integrity and Righteousness,' and his neighborhood 'Respect and Compassion.' "[5]

The second type is composed of small families created from sons dividing their father's property who then established new residences in the vicinity. These units were loosely organized into a corporate entity by way of shared ancestral halls, genealogies, and charitable fields. This latter form of lineage-family was more common in the Song. Its beginnings can be traced to the reforms enacted by the Qin minister Shang Yang (ca. 390–338 B.C.E.). Shang's reforms stipulated that "Commoners who have more than two sons and do not divide property will have their taxes doubled." Later, it was even more clearly stated that "Father, sons, and male siblings are prohibited from sleeping in the same chamber."[6] That is to say, once the sons married and had children, the family was not to live together. This precedent of sons dividing up father's property signified the collapse of the major-lineage-dominated (*zongfa*) system. Toward the end of the Southern Song, Fang Hui (b. 1227) wrote about Shang's reforms and lamented the demise of filial piety that resulted: "This is the beginning of commoners caring for their wives but not their parents."[7]

Small families were less the products of coercive policies than the natural outgrowth of economic development and population increase in an agrarian society. Small families born of father-son division were common by the fifth century, as evinced by a memorial submitted during the Xiaojian reign (454–56) in the Southern Dynasties: "In seven out of ten official (*shidafu*) families, brothers live apart while their parents are still alive; in five out of ten commoner families, father and son own separate properties."[8] It was also observed that in the seventh century, commoner fathers and sons in the regions of Sichuan, Shaannan, and Jiangnan customarily dwelled in separate residences.[9]

It should be noted briefly that from the Former Han to the mid-Tang, or roughly the first to ninth centuries, peasants in small families remained attached to big landlords. Deprived of an entry in the state household registration, they did not enjoy independent political and legal status. This kind of dependency did not weaken until the period between the mid-Tang and the Song, with the development of a small peasant economy.

By the tenth century, with brothers vying to divide up the stove, the deprivation of aging parents had become a social problem that attracted imperial attention. "In extreme cases, [father and sons] do not know of each other's plights or death; when hungry and cold they do not come to each other's aid."[10] Hence Emperor Taizu of the Northern Song issued a 968 edict: "Before the grandparents' and parents' death, commoner sons and grandsons are not to establish separate domiciles and divide property." In the following year, he specified that "In Sichuan and Shaanxi, the establishment of separate domicile and property division during one's parents' lifetime is punishable by death."[11] Another edict issued by the Emperor Zhenzong in 1009 declared: "Those who entice sons and brothers to divide up property . . . will be pursued by local officials, captured, and exiled."[12]

Although there are no accurate statistics of family size and structure in Song rural society, it was said that an average poor family "consisted of five people";[13] the normal range was probably five to seven members. The husband-wife constituted the main trunk of the household; the husband was usually in charge. Family members included their unmarried sons and daughters and occasionally aging parents or preadult younger siblings. In certain regions it was not uncommon for married brothers to live in separate households before their parents' death, as evinced by Emperor Taizu's prohibition edicts mentioned above.

## FEMALE INTERESTS AND FAMILY DIVISION

The reasons for family division can be sought in a complex of demographic, economic, customary, and emotional factors. The sine qua non of household division is the equal claim of sons to their parents' property. The lack of primogeniture in Chinese customs in effect meant that household divisions were inevitable. Moreover, human relationships in a large family were complicated; conflicts were frequent between mother-in-law and the bride, among sisters-in-law, between stepmother and stepsons, among stepbrothers, and so on. At the death of the household head, fights often broke out between brothers, even resulting in murder. It is clear that despite official prohibitions, family divisions continued to be practiced in private. When sons and grandsons insisted on division, fathers and grandfathers often obliged without notifying the government.

The complexity of motivations was elided in the descriptions of Song writers, who overwhelmingly put the blame on women. According to a common saying, "When family members drift apart, the culprit is always women." Or, "Discord arises in families mostly when women provoke their husbands and peers with words."[14] Liu Kai (945–1000) put it more bluntly: "In any family, the brothers are always righteous. It is only after they bring in brides that people of different surnames have to live together. They start to fight for advantages great and small, quarrels break out, people stow away private endowments, and in the end they break up, dividing doors and windows while treating each other as if they were thieves. This is all caused by women."[15] These harsh words have to be understood as expressions of elite men's support for the big-family ideal, which maximizes patriarchal authority.

At the same time, there were compelling incentives for wives to divide the stove. As the outsider, the bride occupied the lowest position in the family. She had to show filial respect to the in-laws while tending to her husband's younger siblings. If the elder brother and his wife were around, she also had to be careful not to offend them. With the slightest mistake, everyone from above and below would complain or reprimand her. As she was not related by blood to the husband's family, it is only natural that she was less than intimate with its members. "The so-called in-laws, uncles, and sisters-in-law are all fictive relations. Although one addresses them with terms of endearment, these are not natural or inborn relations. It is therefore easy to sever obligations or bear a grudge."[16] Once the slightest conflict of interest arose, the contradictions would reverberate. It is no wonder that the wives of the firstborn or his younger brothers were the main instigators of family division: only thus could they gain more independent power for themselves.

The results of family division were manifold. To begin with, the dispersal of wealth heightened status fluidity and increased the number of small producers in society. Furthermore, human relations became simplified in this kind of small-family-based lineage, as members of one household shared basic interests. Property ownership by the husband and wife team lessened the potential for conflicts with the parents-in-law and sisters-in-law. Hence, ironically, family divisions enhanced peace and harmony within lineages and neighborhoods. An additional advantage is that members of small families, especially women, lived under less restrictive rules.

In general, the women's charge—managing the inner realm (*zhunei*)—referred to demarcations in living space as well as the allotment of domestic power and responsibilities. This could mean that in practice women held considerable economic power in the family. Examples of women's household responsibilities were furnished by Yuan Cai (ca. 1140–95), who acquired an intimate understanding of local disputes and sentiments while serving as county magistrate. According to *Mr. Yuan's Precepts for Social Life:*

> Some women whose husbands are stupid and unworldly can manage the family on their own, keeping account of monies paid in and out, and people cannot take advantage of them. Some whose husbands are inept can share management with their sons and manage to keep both family and property intact. Some whose husbands die when their sons were young can nourish and teach their sons, stay on good terms with inner and outer affinal kin, perform household chores and even bring the family to prosperity.[17]

Still, the inner-outer gender division of labor varied according to family size. In general, the actions of women in large well-to-do families were more restricted, whereas in small conjugal families the mother was de facto manager of domestic affairs. Moreover, in small families the boundary between inner and outer responsibilities was more flexible. At the death of the father, the mother became the household head, hence assuming a superior status position in relation to her sons and grandsons.[18] In according power and authority to the mother over her male descendants, family ethics allowed seniority to supersede gender after the patriarch's demise.

After a woman married, although she became a daughter-in-law in her husband's family, her social relations with her natal family would not end. Often her concern for her paternal family was stronger: "If her natal family is rich and marital family is poor, she would want to take some of the former's wealth to aid the latter; if her marital family is rich and natal family is poor, she would want to take some of the former's wealth to aid the latter."[19] In large families sharing common property, this wish was difficult to realize because of strict regulations. But wives in small families enjoyed more room to maneuver.

### DISCIPLINING SONS AND WIVES: FAMILY INSTRUCTIONS

In a large multigenerational family, the maintenance and unity of the family depended on the economic strength of the whole unit—corporate estates farmed by members collectively—and a set of family instructions enforced by the patriarch. As elite families in the Song became incorporated into lineage organizations, the need for regulations to discipline members grew.

The extent of the discipline needed to engender lineage order is evinced by the scholar Shao Bowen. During the reign of the Song emperor Huizong (1101–25), Shao visited Yongle in Hedong county, Hezhong prefecture, where he observed the enactment of lineage rites in the family of filial son Yao. In the mornings and evenings, as lineage members gathered for meals, "males and females sat in different rows and infants sat on a floor mat; they took their food from a communal wooden trough. As soon as the meals were over, the kitchen door would be locked and no one could eat on his or her own. The males kept their clothes on one rack and the females on another without a sense of individual [ownership]." Of special mention was the extent to which daughters-in-law abided by lineage rules: "A newly married son brought his wife some delicacies from the market. Refusing his favor, she took it to the elders and asked them to give him a flogging."[20] She may or may not have turned him in voluntarily, but one thing is certain—her fear of the regulations.

Scores of family instructions from the Song are extant today. Some were couched in terms of bequeathed words for sons and did not mention female conduct. The genre of family instructions pertinent to females can be divided into two types: *Mr. Yuan's Precepts*, cited above, is an example of precepts written for broad dissemination, often by magistrates; the *Zheng Family Instructions*, discussed below, is an example of regulations issued by and for a particular family. The latter type became popular in the Song and flourished in subsequent centuries, functioning as a channel for disseminating Confucian culture into the female quarters.

Elsewhere I have examined extant Song family instructions and argued that they established the parameters of female behavior in five areas: the priority of filiality, duties involved in managing the inner realm, separation of males and females, rights of property inheritance, and conjugal relations.[21] In their local specificities and possibility of personal supervision, family instructions probably exerted a greater impact on everyday lives than such didactic works as *Precepts for Women* (Nüjie) and *Analects for Women* (Nü lunyu).

A graphic example was the *Zheng Family Instructions* (Zhengshi guifan), compiled in the fourteenth century by the descendants of Zheng Yi (fl. 1127–30) of Pujiang, Wuzhou, in eastern Zhejiang. Family memory honored Zheng Yi as the progenitor of a prosperous lineage who admonished his descendants not to divide the stove at his deathbed. Although we do not know if Zheng Yi left any written instructions, his great-great-grandson Zheng Dezhang (1245–1305) mandated monthly readings of a set of hundred-word regulations. Dezhang's son, in turn, committed a set of fifty-eight regulations to writing, forming the core of the text extant today. In light of this cumulative process, we may take these regulations as indicative of the norms governing the lives of Zheng women from the late Song to the Yuan dynasty.

The *Instructions* consists of 168 stipulations, of which 24 were directed toward "Wives" and another 23 pertained to other aspects of female conduct. Admonitions were supposed to be issued orally every morning to a gathering of males and females. The warnings to women are as follows:

The harmony of the family or the lack thereof depends entirely on the goodness of the women. What is "goodness" (*xian*)? Serving the parents-in-law with filial piety; serving the husband with respect; treating sisters-in-law with gentleness; receiving sons and grandsons with compassion; and so on. What is the opposite of "goodness"? Engaging in licentious or jealous behavior; boosting one's own strength and bullying the weak; stirring up gossip; being reckless and indulging in selfish deeds, and so on. . . . The Heavenly Way is very near; it will bless the charitable and bring calamity upon the licentious. Women should not take this lightly.[22]

In addition to these principles of conduct, the regulations include minute stipulations on the dos and don'ts of everyday life. Females were construed to be selfish and jealous by nature and inclined to side with their natal families:

The mother-in-law has to admonish any who are jealous or gossipy; reprimand them if they carry on; divorce them if they still refuse to stop. If wives chat endlessly about shameless things, or if they muddle in affairs outside the inner quarters, they should be asked to perform punitive bowing to shame them. When women work they should stay in one place together, each taking up spinning or weaving according to her strength. This will not only allow one to discern the lazy from the hard-working, it will also diminish their selfish incentives. Wives have a large number of relatives; they should not be allowed to visit with those other than the closest kin from the same branch. Sons and daughters older than eight (*sui*) are not allowed to accompany their mother during her visits to her natal family. In my case, I would not allow even visits to very intimate families, and the offending mother should be severely punished.[23]

Also important are regulations to enforce gender separation in spatial and functional terms, a key Confucian tenet:

Males and females must not share toilets or baths to forestall any suspicion. Males and females must not take or receive from each other directly—this is the expectation of propriety. The women are not to shave off fine hair from their faces with razor blades [like a man].[24]

In the Song, family instructions served to discipline members of multigenerational families that shared residence, mostly rural elite families. Lineage heads promoted such Confucian virtues as loyalty, filiality, and righteousness, for these values were useful to the fostering of family cohesion. So powerful were these families that they received repeated imperial commendations, as in the example of the Zhengs. As moral exemplars, lineages could exert considerable influence in local society.

### FILIAL AND UNFILIAL WIVES: A MATTER OF FAMILY SURVIVAL

As immutable as family precepts may seem on paper, it is difficult to ascertain their circulation and social impact in the Song outside of elite families. Scattered evidence suggests that in the lower levels of society, pragmatic concerns overrode ideo-logical strictures. Indeed, in the realm of local practice the boundaries between "Confucian" and "un-Confucian" behavior could become so blurred that the la-bels lost their usefulness.

Feelings about family and kinship mores are at the core of the mentalities in the countryside. The former is expressed in three related areas: ancestral rituals and filial piety, conjugal relations, and the passing on of the line. Filiality, the ba-sis of ethics and morality, found its concrete expression in ancestral rituals that signified the continuation of the family. The same is true of conjugal relations and line of descent, as both were concerned with the proliferation of descendants. Arising out of desires for family survival and continuation, the appreciation for filiality, ancestral rites, and lines of descent was unspoken and deeply ingrained in rural society. Its spontaneous and widespread existence provided the psycho-logical foundation for the ethical and ritual systems of Confucian culture. In a sense, the very function of Confucian learning was to transform this awareness into an ideology.

It goes without saying that in a family structured by the father (lineage stem)–son (branch) ties, the ancestors being honored were men. In such patri-archical families governed by agnatic descent, women were dependents of men, serving as instruments for furthering the male line. This was equally true of women in scholar-official and commoner families. Women shouldered the important re-sponsibility of maintaining and proliferating the family. The ultimate goal of filial piety, ancestral rites, and husband-wife ties was none other than the perpetuation of the family line. This is why the belief, "there are three unfilial acts, and the lack of descendants was the most serious," was widely held. The earlier the mar-riage, the earlier the birth; the more births there were, the more productive labor there would be: these were the necessary conditions of the survival and growth of a family. Therefore, it is natural that a woman who gave birth to many sons would be valued by her family. And a barren woman or a woman who bore only daugh-ters was seen as the culprit of family extinction. The characteristics of the family institution itself determined the position of women in each family.

Although Confucian theory stipulated that one of the seven legitimate reasons to divorce a wife was being sonless, this practice was not common in Song society. The Confucian thinker Sima Guang explained: "Some scholar-officials who di-vorced their wives were criticized by society as having done wrong, hence they did not divorce lightly."[25] Although Cheng Yi, another philosopher, held the opinion, "There is no harm in divorcing a wife who lacks goodness," he pointed out that "[p]opular custom deems divorcing a wife as indecent behavior, so one dares not do it."[26] From the words of these Confucian scholar-officials we learn of a gap be-tween what should be and what was. As divorce was generally frowned on by so-ciety, it is not surprising that many barren wives in elite families volunteered to pro-cure concubines for their husbands.

## WOMEN WHO SERVED MORE THAN ONE MAN

Indeed, what people did was often what made sense to them; whether an action was condemned or commended by Confucian thinkers was beside the point. How else would one read an unusual story of a man who lent his serving woman (*pi*) to a friend? According to unofficial history, Chen Shengshu, father of Liaoweng, was close friends with the father of Pan Lianggui. One day, when the senior Pan lamented that he was sonless, Chen Shengshu lent him the birth mother of Liaoweng without hesitation. Not long after, she gave birth to Pan Lianggui. Henceforth, the mother shuttled between the two families.[27] This story extols male friendship and dramatizes the desire for sons in elite families. It also serves as a reminder that for those less privileged families who could hardly afford the expenses of brideprice and wedding, a wife was a precious commodity. They would not send her out lightly even if she could not bear a son.

The value of a wife—literally, in terms of bride-price—was in fact the corollary of a seemingly contradictory practice among poor families, the preference for boys. Both were strategies to maximize the family's chances for continuing its line. The popular sentiment of valuing boys and slighting girls was rooted in the tradition of patrilineal descent and the needs of blood relations. In the Song, infanticide was entrenched in villages in the south, especially female infanticide. The scholar Su Shi (1036–1101) once cited Wang Tianlin, who said that in the regions of Hubei and Hunan "it was a taboo to raise daughters; hence in society women were few but single men were numerous."[28] Another scholar, Fan Zhengda (1126–93), mentioned in a memorial that in Chuzhou "in some villages there are no brides available and villagers have to buy them from other districts."[29]

Infanticide was a result of poverty. Because a girl was deemed a member of someone else's family, naturally parents opted for keeping the boy. In this sense the popular concept of valuing boys and slighting girls may resemble the patriarchal concept held by the elites that the male was superior and the female inferior, but they were different in origin and implications. The former stemmed from a strategy of survival in the face of scarcity; the latter dictated that family property be held in male hands. Neither implied that daughters were not loved by their parents.

It should be mentioned that unmarried daughters in the Song often enjoyed the same privileges in wedding expenses as sons. This practice was clearly influenced by the Song legal codes, which stipulated that unmarried daughters enjoyed inheritance rights. As Zhao Ding (1085–1147) recorded in his *Written Instructions for My Family:* "For weddings, everyone is to receive a full total of 500 *guan;* the same for boys and girls." The Confucian statesman Fan Zhongyan (989–1052) also stipulated in his *Rules for the Fan Family Charitable Estate* that "At a daughter's first marriage, the sum of 30 *guan* 77 *mo* would be paid out; 20 *guan* for remarriage. At a son's first marriage, 20 *guan* would be paid out; no payment made for remarriage."[30] That marrying a daughter cost more than taking in a bride was another reason the Song people were unwilling to raise many daughters. Also, the discrepancy in the subsidy awarded to a widow who remarried and a son who married a second time suggests that Fan intended to support the former.

Popular customs in the Song did not deem a woman's remarriage after divorce or widowhood shameful. Remarriages were in fact very common, even in official families that were supposed to adhere to Confucian norms. For example, the Southern Song poet Lu You (1125–1210) took Tong Wan as wife; although "the couple was intimate," because of conflicts between Tong and her mother-in-law Lu divorced her. Later Tong remarried a Zhao Shicheng, an heir of a local Zhao family.[31] Or, another official Cao Yong had a fierce wife. She "first married a local degree holder also surnamed Cao. The two became estranged, and she married Cao Yong."[32]

The economic motivation for widow remarriage in fact stemmed from the patriarchal nature of the family institution. Because men were the primary economic producers and held the economic fortunes of the household, after they died the widowed wife and children were imperiled. If her parental family was poor she would have no one to turn to. The Northern Song writer Zhang Qixian (943–1014) related: "In the environment of Luoyang a villager by the surname of Liu died suddenly and left behind two daughters and one son, the eldest barely ten years old. His widow was concerned that the tax burden was heavy and she had no one to rely on. The villagers being ignorant of propriety, she wanted to bring in one man as husband. In local parlance he was called 'the continuing husband.'"[33]

When a widow married a man by bringing *him* into *her* household, he was called a "continuing husband" (*jiejiao*, lit., "a relayer"; or *jiejiao fu*, "a relaying husband"). This term recurred in Song documents, and the existence of such a man was recognized by the government. According to the *Administrative Documents of the Song*, on the death of a husband "if his widow is still alive, she can summon a second husband to work on the first husband's manorial land. The wife is appointed the head; no new household name is to be established under the second husband's name."[34] One can deduce that this was not an uncommon practice.

The reasons for the custom of "relaying husband" may be sought from the lopsided sex ratio in the countryside. Men from poor families were said to be mostly "left without a bride" or "aging but without wives." A widow remarrying or bringing in a second husband was considered normal in society. Cheng Yi's famous admonition against widow remarriage, "it is a small matter to starve to death, but it is a grave matter to lose one's integrity," was uttered exactly because the practice was common.[35] In a society where women could only survive as men's dependents, widow remarriage was a necessity. Because a woman's livelihood depended on it, few considered it shameful. This situation, however, was to change drastically in the late imperial times with the rise of the chastity cult, as the chapter by Fangqin Du and Susan Mann demonstrates.

"Thrice Following" thus has multiple, contextual meanings in the Song. On paper, this Confucian dictum mandated that a woman served her husband as his inner helpmate and remained loyal to him unto death. Yet in real life, people's opinion of and expectations from women were tempered by practicality. For example, the scholar Yuan Cai did not think that the requirement that "women should not meddle in outer affairs" was universally applicable. If "her husband and sons are good, then surely there is no need to mind outer matters." But if one's husband and sons were reckless in wandering, gambling, or selling land or even their house, while the woman was still unconcerned, the outcome for her would be unfortunate indeed.[36] This view was representative of the prevalent social opinion at the time.

### URBAN-RURAL DIFFERENCES AND CLASS HIERARCHIES

The gap between theory and practice makes it extremely difficult to generalize about the position of females in and out of the family. Also salient is the distance between the practices of ruling-class and lower-class families. Take, for example, the issue of gender separation. Peasant families did not dwell in mansions with hidden inner chambers and spacious grounds. Their poverty and backward state of productivity mandated that women participate in productive labor with men. They worked in the fields with bare feet or went about selling things; there was nothing shameful about being seen in public. Moreover, the villagers' social circles tended to be narrow, confined to relations and neighbors. This kind of relationship built on kin and territorial networks was more intimate than urban sociabilities. The taboos between the two sexes were not as complicated as those observed by the educated elites. Indeed, the comingling of males and females was the usual mode of social intercourse among rural people.

Nowhere is the public visibility of rural women more evident than the realm of popular religion. One popular Song goddess was Mazu, whose cult was widely practiced on the coast of Fujian in the Song and persisted for generations. Mazu's surname was Lin; she was a rural woman who was born into a fishing village and grew up on the seashore. Being skilled in spiritual healing, she healed many villagers. Moreover, her expertise in astronomy, in reading the signs of the weather and the nature of water, and in the navigation of boats enabled her to save the needy at sea.

The good-hearted deeds of Daughter Lin won her the deep respect of village people. After her death, they built a shrine in her memory on Meizhou Island. Her cult spread from the island to the coast, and she was widely worshiped as "the Protector at Sea." In 1135 Emperor Gaozong canonized her and named her "Bright Efficacy" and "Exerted Fortune," hence lending her official recognition.[37] Daughter Lin was neither an ancient goddess nor a mythical figure; she was a commoner woman in the Song. That a shrine was built for her after her death means that Song rural women could enjoy important positions through their spirituality. In productive activities they were as skilled in water and with boats as men. In Song society it was common for women to participate in productive labor and social activities just like Daughter Lin. But their lives were not being recorded in writing.

Although the above examples pertain primarily to rural women, a few words should be added about the lot of commoner women in the flourishing Song cities. The commercial development in the Song and beyond enabled women to become participants in the urban economy, as owners of restaurants, wine shops, and tea-houses in the Northern Song capital of Bianjing and the Southern Song capital of Lin'an.

Yet it was in the city that the impact of class differentiation was most visible. The lives of urban daughters from poor and lowly families grew increasingly apart from those in the upper classes. Hierarchies developed not only between commoner and elite women but among the former as well. In Lin'an girls from families with deprived or middling means were initiated into the gradation system that was to determine their station in life at a tender age:

> They would be taught a skill and craft according to their endowment, trained to become servers or entertainers for scholar-official families. They go by various names: attendant-by-the-side, attendant-to-be-called, seamstress, attendant-in-the-hall, servants for the troupe, laundry maid, zither-girl, chess-girl, and kitchen maid. They were grouped neatly in a hierarchy.[38]

There was no sharper status gap than that between maids or servants and the women in their masters' families who were admonished not to step outside their middle gate. The former had to perform all kinds of manual labor, not to mention dealing with male masters and male servants.

If we consider the status and power differential between wives and maids, the class hierarchy implied in the dictum "master superior and servant inferior" is more relevant than any sense of shared womanhood implied in the Confucian dictum "male superior and female inferior." In other words, a woman's position was less determined by gender than by class. From the perspective of the maids and servant girls who occupied the "inferior" subject position in both hierarchies, gender distinction was reinforced by class distinction.

## EDUCATION AND THE POPULARIZATION
## OF CONFUCIAN CULTURE

To summarize the discussion thus far, I have examined the idealized norms in the first means of propagating Confucian virtues, family instructions. We have seen that whereas females from elite lineages were exposed to them, the realities of commoner Song families were dictated more by expediency. A second channel of the transmission of Confucian culture was popular education and the related development of the civil service examination system since the Sui and Tang dynasties. The latter, I argue, played an important role in maintaining the vitality of Confucian culture by reproducing male elites. Its impact on women, however, was more tenuous.

From its inception in the Sui-Tang period to its end in modern times, the examination system lasted more than a millennium. As a channel of recruitment for the bureaucratic elite, it was indispensable to the cultural and social lives of traditional China. Through its operation a certain cultural stasis was maintained. Before the Sui and Tang dynasties, a hereditary system served to limit both the recruitment of elites and the transmission of cultural norms to within the aristocratic ranks. The examination system created mobility between the classes: sons from landlord or commoner families could become scholar-gentry (*shishen*), and the latter could ascend to the ranks of the bureaucratic elite if they passed the higher examinations. Such social mobility was crucial to the reproduction and development of cultural norms.

Mainstream scholarship in the People's Republic of China has by and large emphasized the negative effects of the examination system: the closure of the mind and the hegemony of Confucian learning. In a recent study, the historian Xiao Gongqin offered a revisionist view by arguing for the sociocultural mobility thus engendered. First, the examination system ensured an endless supply of fresh talent for the ranks of the bureaucratic elite. Second, it created fluidity within the elite ranks as well as mobility between the upper and lower classes. Third, it created a high degree of homogenization in social values and norms. When students immersed themselves in the Confucian canon in pursuit of degrees and power, they were also socialized into Confucian ethical and behavioral norms. "The high degree of mobility *within* the three elite strata of scholar-gentry (*shishen*), bureaucrat, and landlord facilitated the popularization of Confucian values. As a result, Confucian culture became dominant in society."[39]

The significance of the examination system extended beyond the fluidity of the elites and the creation of a dominant Confucian culture. The permeability of the elite ranks also meant that ideas flowed up from the lower strata of society. To a certain extent, the examination system served as a conduit for the upward transmission of mentalities from the villages. In other words, upward and downward social mobility was coupled with cultural transmission in both directions. This interpenetration continued to inject dynamism into "dominant" Confucian culture, a key factor in its resilience and longevity.

Lower degree holders served as intermediaries in this traffic between the village and the metropolis. In the Song only about one-third of the candidates became advanced degree holders (*jinshi*, or Presented Scholar). Most of the lower degree holders (*gongshi, juren*) who failed to advance returned to the countryside to serve as teachers or to become members of the local gentry. They thus became the bridge between rural culture and metropolitan elite culture. Because the examination curriculum consisted mostly of Confucian texts, as candidates advanced through prefectural and departmental examinations they became immersed in the culture of the educated class. On returning to their native villages, they promoted these concepts through various means. Popular consciousness in the countryside was thus continuously influenced by elite systems of thought brought back by examination candidates.

This interpenetration was facilitated by institutional developments in education. During the Song, the development of the examination system went hand in hand with a marked growth in the number of schools at all levels throughout the country. Since the reign of Emperor Renzong (r. 1023–63), the Northern Song government continued to build schools in counties, districts, and prefectures. One observer remarked that in the Qingli era (1041–48), "it was rare to find a district without a school."[40] By the Southern Song, in and out of metropolitan centers not only were there government schools, "there were also village schools, family schools, study centers, and reading groups." "In every lane and alley one could find at least one or two of these. The crisp sounds of recitation could be heard everywhere."[41] Even in the countryside, "winter schools" emerged to educate farm boys after harvest. The poet Lu You described one such school in the rural areas of Shaoxing prefecture: "In the Tenth Month farming families would send their sons to the so-called winter school. [They studied such primers as] 'Miscellaneous Words' and 'Hundred Family Names' and called them 'village books.' "[42] This steady development of education opened up new channels for the penetration of the ideas of the ruling class into society.

### EPILOGUE: DEVELOPMENTS FROM SONG TO MING

Although few commoner girls enrolled in schools during the Song, the major Confucian philosophers paid attention to the problem of female education in their discourse on Confucian ethics.[43] For example, Sima Guang's *Family Instructions* and Zhang Zai's *Hengqu's Admonitions for Women* abound with teachings for women. It is difficult to ascertain the extent to which these precepts circulated in female quarters during the Song. We do know, however, that instruction books for women proliferated in the Ming (1368–1644) and Qing (1644–1911) dynasties. Nearly fifty kinds of female didactic texts circulated in the Ming. Illustrated and easy to read, many were accessible to the less educated classes.

Besides formal and informal schooling, the other channel for the propagation of Confucian culture, family instructions, also began to take shape in the Song and blossomed in the Ming and Qing. The developments of these two channels were in fact causally linked. The fluidity introduced by the examination system coupled with the lack of primogeniture created extreme fluctuations in the fortunes of elite families. A family could not count on its ability to perpetuate its elite status through several generations. Lineage regulations became a means of instilling a modicum of stability in the face of insecurities.

As I have argued, family instructions—when effectively enforced by the patriarch—served as a conduit for the transmission of Confucian ethics to the female quarters. It is important to note here that the content of Confucian norms promulgated on the pages of these instructions changed from the Song to the Ming. In the earlier period, restrictions on women were more relaxed: "Give filiality and friendly respect priority in the female quarters"; "Sons and wives, do not keep private property"; "In serving in-laws, rise at the crack of dawn"; and so on.[44]

As time went on, the strictures became much more tedious and severe. For example: "Male-female distinctions depend on separation between inner and outer. Hence obviously it is improper for a woman to venture outside"; "Within three months of a bride's arrival, and when a daughter reaches eight *sui*, she should be taught *Lessons for Women* (Nü jiao) and *Biographies of Women* (Lienü zhuan) by rote so that she will know the woman's way. But she should not be allowed to be skilled in the writing brush or to learn poetry and prose"; "A housewife's job is to prepare food and wine. She should be skilled in cooking and knowledgeable in matters of rice and salt. Do not step away from the stove." The consequences for noncompliance were grave: "If a female has erred and committed adultery, give her a knife and a rope and lock her up in the cowshed; let her kill herself. If her mother interferes, divorce her. If her father interferes, take him to the officials and have him exiled. Erase his name from the genealogy and cast him off from the ancestral shrine in life and death." And so on.[45]

From the pages of family regulations that proliferated in the Ming and Qing dynasties, one gets the clear impression that late imperial women were more burdened by Confucian strictures than were Song women. The Yuan as a crucial transitional period and the subsequent rise of wifely fidelity as a paramount female virtue are central themes in the chapter by Du and Mann later in this volume. Meanwhile, a clear topography of the variety of emphases in family instructions from different periods and locales awaits future research. Also illuminating would be case studies of the connections among the content of instructions, domestic spatial arrangements in that particular family, and the texture of local cultures that made the small world meaningful to its male and female inhabitants.

*Translated by Dorothy Ko*

## NOTES

*Editors' Note:* Zang Jian is a pioneer woman historian in the PRC. She belongs to a generation of younger scholars who have sought to develop a gendered analysis in their respective disciples in the second half of the 1980s. This chapter outlines her vision and method for integrating women and gender into medieval Chinese history.

Within PRC historical scholarship, Zang's vision represents several breakthroughs: a more positive assessment of the civilizing potential of Confucian culture, a nuanced conception of "gender," and a concern with processes of cultural transmission instead of economic relations.

Some of Zang's terminology, such as "ruling class," "masses," and "tradition," are conventional in the PRC. We retain them in translation to preserve the integrity of her arguments.

1. The nature of "rural" or "local" society in the Song is a matter of ongoing debate among historians in the PRC. Previous consensus was that a full-blown rural gentry society did not emerge until the Ming and Qing periods. Recently, a younger generation of schol-

ars has argued that the development of lineage organizations, ancestral halls, local gentry, and village convenents in the Song signaled the beginnings of a rural gentry society. This chapter is more concerned with the issue of cultural transmission than with the nature of local society itself.

2. *Zuozhuan* (The Zuo commentary) (Beijing: Zhonghua shuju, 1980), vol. xia [2]: 1839. "Properly behaving husband and wife" is from the "Neize" chapter, *Liji Liji* (The book of rites) (Beijing: Zhonghua shuju, 1980), vol. *xia* [2]: 1468; "drinking and eating" is from the "Liyun" chapter, *Liji*, vol. *xia* [2]: 1415.

3. On the development of early Confucian thought, I have been inspired by the recent work of Yan Buke, who argues that the origins of rites (*li*) were customs (*su*). See Yan, " 'Lizhi' zhixu yu shidafu zhengzhi de yuanyuan" (The relationship between ordering by rites and scholar-official politics), *Guoxue yanjiu* 1 (1993): 293–331.

4. Recently, Chinese, Japanese, and U.S. scholars have begun to make important contributions. They include, among others, Patricia Ebrey, Yanagida Setsuko, Zhu Ruisi, Yuan Li, and Deng Xiaonan (see citations in notes below).

5. *Songshi* (History of the Song dynasty) (Beijing: Zhonghua shuju, 1977), 456:13415, 13402–3.

6. Sima Qian, *Shiji* (Records of the Grand Historian) (Beijing: Zhonghua shuju, 1959), 68:2230.

7. Fang Hui, *Xu gujin kao* (Matters old and new, a sequel), in *Siqu quanshu*, vol. 853, 6: 201. For a discussion in English of Song ideas and debates about the lineage system, see Patricia Ebrey, "Conceptions of the Family in the Sung Dynasty," *Journal of Asian Studies* 43, no. 2 (May 1984): 219–45. The development of new kinship institutions in the Song is discussed by Ebrey in "The Early Stage in the Development of Descent Group Organization," in *Kinship Organization in Late Imperial China*, ed. Patricia Ebrey and James L. Watson (Berkeley: University of California Press, 1986), pp. 16–61. Robert Hymes's article, "Marriage, Descent Groups, and the Localist Strategy," in the same volume (pp. 95–136), discusses how kinship institutions and marriage strategies were used in tandem to enhance the local social position of elite families. Both articles suggest that what Hymes calls a "lineage orientation" developed gradually over the course of the Song, with kinship institutions such as ancestral halls, genealogies, and charitable estates becoming increasingly widespread by the late Yuan period. For Song uses of charitable estates, see Linda Walton, "Charitable Estates as an Aspect of Statecraft in Southern Sung China," in Robert P. Hymes and Conrad Schirokauer, eds., *Ordering the World: Approaches to State and Society in Sung Dynasty China* (Berkeley: University of California Press, 1993).

8. Gu Yanwu, *Rizhi lu*, in *Siqu quanshu*, vol. 858, 13:704. In this, the Song government followed the Tang Code, which stipulated that sons must not set up separate households before their parents' deaths. See Wallace Johnson, trans., *The T'ang Code* (Princeton: Princeton University Press, 1979), p. 75.

9. *Suishu* (History of the Sui dynasty) (Beijing: Zhonghua shuju, 1973), 29:830.

10. Gu Yanwu, *Rizhi lu*, 13:704.

11. *Songshi*, 2:27, 30.

12. Ibid., 7:140.

13. *Song huiyao: Shihuo* (Administrative documents of the Song: Economics section) (Taipei: Xinwenfang chuban gongsi, 1976), p. 5185.

14. Zhou Dunyi, *Zhouzi tongshu* (The comprehensive book of Master Zhou), in *Gujin tushu jicheng: Minglun huibian; jiafan dian*, vol. 321 (Beijing: Zhonghua shuju, 1934), 2:7a; Yuan Cai, *Yuanshi shifan* (Mr. Yuan's precepts for social life), Zhibuzu chai congshu edition, 1:16b.

15. Liu Kai, *Hedong ji* (Collected works of Liu Kai), Sibu congkan chubian edition, 14: 6a–7b. The work of anthropologists of Chinese society has suggested that it was indeed to a woman's advantage to get her husband to "divide the stove" with his siblings and set up their own conjugal unit. See Margery Wolf, *Women and Family in Rural Taiwan* (Stanford: Stanford University Press, 1972).

16. Yuan Cai, *Yuanshi shifan*, 1:16b. For an English translation of the text cited here, see Patricia Ebrey, *Family and Property in Sung China: Yüan Ts'ai's Precepts for Social Life* (Princeton: Princeton University Press, 1984), p. 206.

17. Yuan Cai, *Yuanshi shifan*, 1:24b–25a. For women's property rights, see Yanagida Setsuko, "Nanshōki kasan bunkatsu ni okeru joshōbun ni tsuite" (The female allotment in family property division in the Southern Song period), in *Ryū Shiken hakushi shōju kinen Sōshi kenkyū ronshū* (Research on Song history to commemorate the birthday of Dr. James Liu), ed. Kinugawa Tsuyoshi (Tokyo: Dōhōsha, 1989). See also Yuan Li, "Songdai nüxing caizhanquan shulun" (An analysis of female property rights in the Song dynasty), *Songshi yanjiu jikan* 2 (1988): 271–308. Women in elite families of Suzhou were known to have managed enterprises or aided needy relatives as husbands' deputies or independently. See Deng Xiaonan, "Songdai Suzhou shiren jiazu zhong de funü" (Women in the gentry families of Song Suzhou), paper delivered at the Third International Workshop on Women, Beijing University, 1994. For discussions of the economic roles of Song elite women in English, see Ebrey, *Family and Property*, p. 221; Patricia Ebrey, *The Inner Quarters: Marriage and Lives of Chinese Women in the Song Period* (Berkeley: University of California Press, 1993), pp. 117–19; Joseph P. McDermott, "Family Financial Plans of the Southern Sung," *Asia Major*, 3d ser., vol. 4, pt. 2 (1991): 15–52. McDermott has also written more extensively on women's roles in family management in later imperial China: see his "The Chinese Domestic Bursar," *Ajia bunka kenkyū* (November 1990): 15–52.

18. Gao Shiyu, "Zhongguo gudai funü jiating diwei zhouyi" (The position of women in traditional Chinese families), *Funü yanjiu congkan* 3 (1996): 33–37. See also Zhu Ruisi, "Songdai funü de shehui diwei" (Social positions of Song women), in *Songdai shehui yanjiu* (Studies of Song society) (Zhengzhou, Henan: Zhongzhou shuhuashe, 1983).

19. Yuan, *Yuanshi shifan*, 1:27a. See also Ebrey, *Family and Property*, p. 225.

20. Shao Bowen, *Henan Shaoshi wenjian qianlu* (Things heard and seen by Mr. Shao of Henan) (Beijing: Zhonghua shuju, 1983), 17:187.

21. Zang Jian, "Songdai jiafa yu nüxing" (Song family regulations and women), in *Qingzhu Deng Guangming jiaoshou jiushi huadan lunwenji* (Essays commemorating the nintieth birthday of Professor Deng Guangming), ed. Tian Qingyu (Shijiazhuang: Hebei jiaoyu chubanshe, 1997).

22. Zheng Taihe, *Zhengshi guifan* (Regulations of the Zheng family), in *Congshu jicheng chubian*, vol. 975, p. 2. For English-language scholarship on the Zheng family, see John W. Dardess, "The Cheng Communal Family: Social Organization and Neo-Confucianism in Yuan and Early Ming China," *Harvard Journal of Asiatic Studies* 34, no. 1 (1974): 7–52. See also John D. Langlois Jr., "Authority in Family Legislation: The Cheng Family Rules," in *State and Law in East Asia: Festschrift Karl Bunger* (Weisbaden: Otto Harrassowitz, 1981).

23. Zheng, *Zhengshi guifan*, pp. 16–17.

24. Ibid.

25. Sima Guang, *Jiafan* (Family instructions), 1626 edition, 7:22a.

26. Cheng Hao and Cheng Yi, *Er-Cheng ji* (Collected works of the Cheng brothers), vol. 1 of *Henan Chengshi yishu* (Bequeathed books of the Chengs from Henan) (Beijing: Zhonghua shuju, 1981), p. 243.

27. Zhou Mi, *Qidong yeyu* (Unofficial words from Qidong) (Beijing: Zhonghua shuju, 1983), pp. 294–95.

28. Su Shi, *Dongpo wenji* (Collected writings of Su Dongpo), Sibu congkan chubian edition, 46:5b–7b.

29. *Lidai mingchen zouyi* (Memorials by famous statesmen through the dynasties) (Shanghai: Shanghai guji chubanshe, 1989), 108:1447.

30. Zhao Ding, *Jiaxun bilu* (Written family instructions), hand-copied manuscript in the Lishi collection, Beijing University Library, entry 21, no page [4a]; Fan Zhongyan, "Fanshi yizhuang guiju" (Regulations of the Fan family charitable estate), in *Shuofu*, ed. Tao Zhongyi (Shanghai: Shanghai guji chubanshe, 1988), vol. 6, p. 3336.

31. Zhou Mi, *Qidong yeyu*, pp. 294–95.

32. Cao Yong, *Xianxiu tang manlu*, cited in Wang Chutong, comp., *Lianshi xuanzhu* (Selections from a history of the toilette), ed. Li Yonghu (Beijing: Renmin daxue chubanshe, 1994), pp. 22–23. On the topic of widow remarriage in the Song, see Ebrey, *Inner Quarters*, pp. 204–12.

33. Zhang Qixian, *Luoyang jinshen jiuwen ji* (Old hearsays by a gentleman from Luoyang), in *Siqu quanshu*, vol. 1036, 5:9a.

34. *Song huiyao*, p. 5888.

35. Cheng, *Er-Cheng ji*, p. 243.

36. Yuan, *Yuanshi shifan*, 1:24a–b.

37. On recent research in Chinese on Mazu, see special issue, *Shehui kexue zhanxian* 4, 1990. The essays were first presented at the First International Conference on Mazu Studies, Putian, Fujian, April 21–25, 1990.

38. Liu Yingzhong, *Jiangxing zalu* (Miscellany from Jiangxing), in Congshu jicheng chubian, vol. 2882, p. 5.

39. Xiao Gongqin, "Cong keju zhidu di feichu kan jindai yilai di wenhua duanlie" (On cultural rupture in modern China after the abolishment of the civil service examination), *Zhanlüe yu guanli*, no. 17 (1996): 11–17.

40. Peng Dayi, *Shantang sikao*, in *Siqu quanshu*, vol. 975, 78:471.

41. Nai Deweng, *Ducheng jisheng* (Famous sites of the capital), in *Siqu quanshu*, vol. 590, 12.

42. Lu You, *Lu You ji*, in *Lu You ji; Jiannan shigao* (Collected writings of Lu You), Sibu bieyao edition, 25:280.

43. For women's education in the Song, see Bettine Birge, "Chu Hsi and Women's Education," in *Neo-Confucian Education*, ed. Wm. Theodore de Bary and John W. Chafee (Berkeley: University of California Press, 1989).

44. Zhao Ding, *Jiaxun bilu*, entry 1, no page [1a]; Sima Guang, *Susui jiayi*, in *Gujin tushu jicheng: minglun huibian; jiafan dian*, vol. 325 (Beijing: Zhonghua shuju, 1934), 57:41a.

45. Xu Xiangqing, *Xu Yuncun yimou*, in Congshu jicheng chubian, vol. 975, p. 6; Cao Duan, *Jiagui jilüe* (Family instructions), in *Cao Yuechuan xiansheng yishu* (Posthumous works of Mr. Cao) (n.p., 1832), 13b–14a.

# CHAPTER SIX

# Propagating Female Virtues in Chosŏn Korea

*Martina Deuchler*

Women do not figure prominently in Korean historiography past or present. To be sure, biographies of "virtuous women" (*yŏllyŏ*) constituted a separate historiographical category since Chinese-style writing of history was adopted in Korea. The earliest extant examples are contained in Kim Pusik's (1075–1151) *History of the Three Kingdoms* (Samguk sagi), discussed in this volume by Lee Hai-soon. The short preface that introduced the biographies of virtuous women (*yŏllyŏjŏn*) in the mid-fifteenth-century *History of Koryŏ* (Koryŏsa) states:

> In olden times, when a girl was born, she received education from a nurse; when she grew up, she received instruction from a [female] teacher. Thus, she became a wise daughter in her natal home, and when she got married, she became a wise daughter-in-law, and when she met adversities, she became a virtuous woman. In later times, instruction for women did not reach the inner chambers, and thus [for women] to establish themselves firmly and, when confronted with disaster or in the face of blank weapons, not to change their resolve, whether they were to live or to die, can be said to be difficult indeed. [For this reason] we have compiled biographies of virtuous women.[1]

In the absence of proper instruction, these early stories about women who selflessly risked their lives for their husbands were to convey an educative message. The spotlight of the historian was on the heroic deed illustrating Confucian notions of womanly behavior rather than on women as agents of their own will.

This chapter deals with elite women of the Chosŏn dynasty (1392–1910) and in particular explores the extent to which they absorbed and embodied the new social values and norms imposed on them by the Neo-Confucian legislators at the beginning of the dynasty. In Chosŏn Korea, elite women rarely participated in nondomestic activities, and their lives, therefore, were confined to the domestic realm. Although it is clear that many women were literate and thus, at least indirectly, communicated with the outside world through books and letters, it was not thought proper for a woman to make her concerns, let alone her feelings, known to outsiders. This chapter, then, is principally based on official government sources as well as on tomb inscriptions, biographies, and exhortatory literature compiled or written by high officials for their kinswomen between the sixteenth and eighteenth centuries. This type of literature has largely determined the subjects discussed—subjects that, in the men's view, were crucial for highlighting a woman's "virtue" as manifested in her handling of human relationships and in the performance of her daily duties.

### THE IMPACT OF DYNASTIC CHANGE ON WOMEN

Unlike in China where dynastic transitions seldom changed the rules that affected women's lives, the establishment of the Chosŏn dynasty in 1392 had a profound impact on elite women. The introduction of Neo-Confucianism as the new state ideology altered their social standing, their place within family and kin group, and their relations to the nondomestic outside world.

Under the Koryŏ dynasty (918–1392), women enjoyed a great deal of social and economic freedom. Sharing the ancestral patrimony equally with her brothers, a woman possessed a high degree of liberty in decision making and action. Her economic power rendered uxorilocal residence for her husband attractive. Her bond with her brothers thus often lasted for a lifetime, while an incompatible husband could be easily deserted, making divorce an easy affair without negative social or economic consequences. As a result of such close intrafamilial economic interdependence, marriage within the group, for example, with a cousin, was common. Widowhood did not lower a woman's attractiveness as a marriage partner, and no social stigma was consequently attached to remarriage. The uncomplicated gender relations found ready expression in the Koryŏ love songs, which unabashedly celebrated courtship and sensuality.[2]

The Confucian transformation initiated at the beginning of the Chosŏn dynasty changed all this. The implantation of a highly structured patrilineal social paradigm demanded that women be firmly incorporated into their husbands' descent groups. As a consequence, women eventually lost their inheritance rights and became entirely dependent on affinal wealth. Moreover, the new system introduced a ranking order for women. While in Koryŏ a man's wives (plural marriage was common) had not been ranked because they originated from similar social backgrounds, in a Chosŏn patriline only one wife, the primary wife, could become the mother of the lineal heir(s). A law enacted in 1413 legalized the strict distinction between primary and secondary wives. This was perhaps the most consequential piece of legislation for women: by throwing into bold relief a primary wife's elevated position within her husband's descent group, it automatically degraded to secondary status the other wives her husband may have had. It thus institutionalized a special kind of female inequality that laid the domestic realm open to potential rivalry and conflict.

The strict distinction between primary and secondary wives did not result solely from a close interpretation of patrilinearity, however. Korean society was an aristocratic society that attached highest esteem to social status based on descent and heredity. Typical for Koryŏ, elite social status derived from both the father's and the mother's side—a bilateral calculation that still remained valid in Chosŏn. Although in the new Confucian scheme descent was fixed patrilineally, status ascription remained bilateral. In other words, the juxtaposition of patrilinearity and bilaterality created a unique social system in which descent was traced through the male line while status was determined bilaterally. Clearly, only women from certified elite families could satisfy the vital social demands put on primary wives. By linking two elite patrilines, such wives alone could guarantee full legitimacy to their offspring. To demonstrate a bride's proper background, an elite wedding took place, in contradiction to Confucian etiquette, in her natal home, and she retained her father's surname throughout her life. Her sons, their father's legitimate heirs, would secure lineal succession, take charge of ancestral worship, and inherit the major parts of the patrimony. Primary sons alone were admitted to the civil service examinations and thus were given access to political participation and economic advancement.

In contrast, secondary wives, usually originating from commoner or slave backgrounds, lacked social prestige and thus had little or no significance for their husbands' patrilines. Secondary wives could challenge primary wives as sexual partners of their husbands but not as mothers of male offspring. Secondary sons were restricted, often completely excluded, from domestic rituals and (until the latter part of the dynasty) from public life and thus could not rival primary sons.

The inequalities imposed on women and their offspring by Confucian ideology, thus, were much more pronounced than in China. The Confucian social system as it emerged in Korea tightened the native criteria of aristocratic status and reached its fullest elaboration in the second half of the dynasty. Despite important economic developments in late Chosŏn that gave rise to a degree of social diversification, Korean society remained highly stratified and never had the fluidity and mobility of late imperial China. Moreover, Confucianism in Korea was tied more closely than in China to the definition of upper-class status—a fact that left its deep imprint on the lives and thought of elite women. To fit women into the dominant discourse, indoctrination was of strategic importance, and the early legislators did not hesitate to set in motion a major propaganda campaign.

## LITERATURE FOR INDOCTRINATION

In Confucian thought, the propagation of virtues was a process of transformation (*hwa*). Deviant customs had to be reformed or replaced by new values and norms. In short, the transformation aimed to create a new social consciousness that eventually would express itself in behavior that conformed to Confucian values. In early Chosŏn, the Confucian scholar-officials looked on the Koryŏ past with scorn and praised the Confucian precepts for their reformative power. They propagated the kind of literature they thought would best describe Confucian morality and give practical advice about how to emulate it. Confucian didactic literature such as the *Classic of Filial Piety* (C: Xiaojing; K: Hyogyŏng) had been known and read in Korea long before the Chosŏn dynasty, but it gained its full significance as an illustration of a normative system only in conjunction with Confucian legislation. The book, then, no longer contained mere tales of morality. Its message took on a sharper prescriptive tone demanding that each individual reader find his or her proper place in family and society.

Throughout the Chosŏn period the most influential textbook of moral education was the *Elementary Learning* (C: Xiaoxue; K: Sohak)—a slim work that the Chinese Neo-Confucian philosopher Zhu Xi himself had compiled in 1189. Brought to Korea presumably in the early fourteenth century, it was adopted as compulsory reading for beginners in 1407. This primer, containing elementary rules of personal conduct and interpersonal relationships, was thought to introduce the reader to the more advanced Confucian literature, in particular the Four Books. The work was considered so fundamental for the transformation of the country's mores that its instruction was made a legal requirement for lower officialdom. For this reason, the book was reprinted several times during the reign of education-minded King Sejong (r. 1418–50).

The propagation of the *Elementary Learning* was intensified at the beginning of the fifteenth century when, in 1518, thirteen hundred copies were printed and distributed as gifts to court officials and some select members of the royal house.[3] As long as the text was available only in classical Chinese, however, it could not be as widely circulated and absorbed as the "deteriorating customs" of the time would have demanded. The Office of the Special Counselors (*hongmungwan*) therefore memorialized in summer 1517 as follows:

> The *Elementary Learning* is of critical importance in everyday use. Yet, the simple people in the alleys and the women who are unfamiliar with writing find it difficult to read and practice it. We beg that those books most instrumental for everyday use like the *Elementary Learning* be translated into the vernacular, printed, and distributed inside and outside the capital so that no one from the palace and the capital officialdom down to the little people in the alleys is ignorant of it and does not read it. If all the families in the land are corrected, the evil atmosphere will cease and heavenly harmony will prevail.[4]

A translation appeared the following year. The *Elementary Learning* thus remained a much praised classic of moral education until the end of the dynasty.[5]

Whereas the *Elementary Learning*, despite its simplicity, demanded full literacy, another morality book, the *Illustrated Guide to the Three Bonds* (Samgang haengsilto) included full-page illustrations that provided the reader with a visual aid to comprehend the three cardinal human relationships (between ruler and subject, father and son, and husband and wife). When it was first compiled in 1432, its didactic message seems to have been directed primarily to the elite. It was again King Sejong who took a special interest in the distribution of this work. In an edict of 1434, he ordered the capital and provincial officials to search for learned individuals who would be able to teach the book's basic message to all members of society regardless of social status. Women would have to be instructed by their kinsmen. With everyone developing his or her basic human nature, sons would be preoccupied with fulfilling filiality, subjects loyalty, and spouses their special relationship. The book's impact, however, apparently remained slight, because some fifty years later, in 1481, King Sŏngjong (r. 1469–94) expressed his deep concern about the "unreformed" state of elite women. He ordered a vernacular version of the "chaste women" (*yŏl-lyŏ*) section to be distributed for the education of women within and outside the capital.[6]

The *Illustrated Guide* became one of the dynasty's most celebrated moral guidebooks and was variously supplemented and augmented. In 1514, during the Chungjong period when pessimistic views about society's moral bankruptcy prevailed, a supplement (*Sok samgang haengsilto*) was completed. This work incorporated a greater number of exemplary cases from the Chinese Ming and Chosŏn periods than its predecessor and thus stressed the indigenous potential for moral transformation. A few years later, in 1517, however, some high officials felt that the *Illustrated Guide* related only extraordinary deeds by individuals in response to crisis situations and therefore was not useful as a guide for everyday behavior. For this reason, they suggested to the king that "practical books" such as the *Elementary Learning*, the *Biographies of Women* (Lienü zhuan), the *Precepts for Women* (Nüjie), and the *Rules for Women* (Nüze) be translated into Korean so that "there will be no one in the palaces and aristocratic houses as well as among the common people in the alleys who does not know and recite them." This request was granted, and the translations were distributed throughout the country.[7]

Although the inculcation of Confucian norms and values was a task to be directed at the entire society, from the above choice of literature recommended for translation it is clear that the officials regarded the instruction of women as fundamental "for setting the domestic realm in order." It also posed specific problems as access to elite women was permitted only to their closest kinsmen or affines. Through the strict separation of domestic and public spheres, accentuated by the spatial arrangement of domestic architecture, women were confined to the inner quarters and at least ideally had little contact with the outside world. If women were to be reached by beneficial influences from the outside, these had to be packaged appropriately. Teaching materials specifically aimed at women, therefore, developed into a separate genre of morality literature.

One of the earliest Korean works exclusively directed at women was the *Instructions for Women* (Naehun) compiled by the mother of King Sŏngjong, Queen Consort Sohye, Lady Han (1437–1504), in 1475 (see Figure 6.1). Worried about female ignorance and the lack of appropriate instructional materials, Sohye excerpted "important passages" from such Chinese works as the *Elementary Learning*, the *No-*

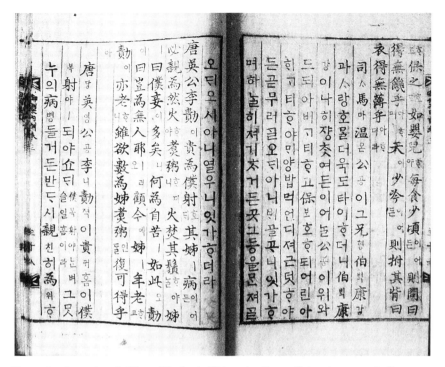

Figure 6.1. *Instructions for Women* (Naehun), Written by Queen Sohye (1437–1504). Courtesy of the Academy of Korean Studies.

*table Women* (Lienü), the *Lessons for Women* (Nüjiao), and the *Mirror of Sagacity* (Mingjian) and called her work *Naehun*. She then added to the Chinese text a Korean translation "in order to facilitate comprehension." Famed for her own exemplary lifestyle, the author stated in the preface:

> All human beings are born with the spirit of Heaven and Earth, and all are endowed with the virtues of the Five Relationships. As to principle, there is no difference between jade and stone, yet whether [a human being resembles] an orchid or a bitter smelling shrub depends entirely on the method of self-cultivation. . . . The rise or fall of the political order, although connected with the husband's character, also depends on the wife's goodness. She therefore must be educated. . . . Generally, men let their hearts wander in passions and amuse themselves with all kinds of subtleties, [yet] because they naturally distinguish between right and wrong, they are able to keep themselves [on the right track]. Do they need to await our instruction to behave [properly]? This is not so with women. Women only concern themselves with the quality of their embroidering skills and are ignorant of the urgency of virtuous conduct. This is what worries me daily![8]

Because she deplored the inferior natural qualities of women, Sohye was convinced that female education was not a luxury but a necessity; it was imperative for rectifying the womanly nature and bringing it in line with the moral exigencies of a Confucian society. Education was empowerment. Only educated women were prepared for their exacting roles as daughters-in-law, wives, and mothers. Education, Sohye believed, was all the more urgent because a woman's "goodness" influenced, beyond the domestic realm, the moral condition of public life.

*Naehun* was divided into seven chapters, covering what Sohye considered the essentials of womanly conduct: proper speech and behavior, filial devotion to parents and parents-in-law, the wedding rite, the husband-wife bond, motherly duties, intrafamilial relationships, and frugal living. It is a collection of stories that depict the dutiful life of the young girl growing up in her natal home and the supportive and devoted role of the married woman in her husband's family. Quoting celebrated precedents from history, the book highlighted how human impulses and emotions could be transformed into disciplined disposition of character sustaining behavior appropriate to Confucian social values.[9] *Naehun* was popular reading throughout the Chosŏn dynasty and underwent several printings.

In the second half of the dynasty, the perceived deficiency of female nature was analyzed in Neo-Confucian terms: fettered by turbid mind-matter (*ki*) and consequently controlled by material desires, women easily strayed into evil. For this reason, they needed special education to recover their fundamentally good nature (*ponsŏng*) and become "wise" (*hyŏn*) and "virtuous" (*suk*) members of society.[10] The Neo-Confucian scholar Yi Sangjŏng (1710–81), on the other hand, thought that women's lack of development was caused by their limited opportunities. He wrote in a postface to *Biographies of Chaste Daughters-in-Law* (Yŏlbujŏn):

> Moral principles are rooted in a person's heart; whether they are fully or poorly developed does not depend on being high or low in status, or male or female. Thus, without instruction of books and practice, or without the guidance of teachers and friends, it is not possible to develop innate nature. Loyalty, filiality, righteousness, and chastity can therefore be found in abundance in men, but are rarely heard [to be] in women; they are abundant in the elite, but rarely found in the lower classes. It is not that the heaven-bestowed talents are different. It is alone the circumstances that make them so.[11]

Whatever the reasons thought to account for female inferiority, moral pressure on elite women increased. In 1736, for example, a high official, Yi Tŏksu (1673–1744), was ordered by King Yŏngjo (r. 1724–76) to translate the so-called *Four Books for Women* (Nü sishu)[12] into Korean. The translation was published under the title *Yŏsasŏ ŏnhae* (Vernacular version of the Four Books for Women). In a brief preface the king stated that having come across a Chinese version of this compilation by chance, he thought it would be of particular educative value for women, if read in conjunction with Sohye's *Naehun*. Except for changing the sequence of the four works, the translation faithfully followed the Chinese originals.[13]

In sum, the instructional texts designed exclusively for women formed an important part of the Chosŏn dynasty's morality literature. Based on the conviction that even women could be transformed into moral beings, this state-sponsored literature significantly provided women with a choice: they could either follow its precepts and become virtuous or risk the censure of society if they remained impervious to moral instruction. For women who were unable to read the Chinese originals, the perusal of these manuals was facilitated by vernacular versions. Illiterate women could easily absorb their essence by recitation (*kusong*), a favored method for memorizing exhortatory materials. Whatever the method, training in virtue had to start from an early age in the natal home and continue later in the husband's family.

### INDOCTRINATION AND LEARNING IN THE INNER CHAMBERS

Enlightened parents taught both their sons and their daughters the Confucian ways. A conscientious father instructed his sons and daughters in ritual matters,[14] or, loving his daughter's obedient nature, he hand-copied for her *Basic Regulations for Women* (Yŏbŏm).[15] It was never too late to begin or to reinforce education. On the day when a bride was presented to her parents-in-law, she might be given a copy of *Naehun*.[16] As an eighteenth-century writer put it, "Not to teach one's sons leads to the ruin of one's own house. Not to teach daughters leads to the ruin of someone else's house. Not to be prepared for education, therefore, is the parents' fault."[17]

A number of biographies, thus, begin, "At a young age, she read the *Illustrated Guide to the Three Bonds* and was able to understand its general meaning."[18] Or, "When she was ten, her father bought her a *Biographies of Women*."[19] Frequently mentioned was the *Elementary Learning*. As a woman in the late seventeenth century described her own experience:

> When I was young, I received the *Elementary Learning* from my father. Loyal ministers, filial sons, brotherly brothers, chaste women—their good words and admirable deeds I always recited and pondered in my mind. These are all matters pertaining to one's duties. If we can act accordingly, we do not need to do anything extraordinary and still can reach [the accomplishments of] the people of old.[20]

Song Siyŏl (1607–89) wrote admiringly of his paternal aunt, Madame Song (b. 1571):

> The Songs have for generations instructed sons and daughters in rites and laws. . . . The domestic rules (*kabŏp*) are very strict and severe as is fit for an elite house. Since Madame Song received instruction from wise (*hyŏn*) parents, her natural alertness and smartness were heightened. When her brothers received instruction, she listened from the side, remembered everything, and understood the meaning in her heart even better [than her brothers].

When, at the age of seven, Madame Song wanted to witness some festivities, her father made his permission dependent on the condition that she be able to recite a book of two thousand characters the next morning.

> She read through it under a lamp several times, and the next morning her recitation was perfect. Her father exclaimed in amazement: "I am unhappy that you are not a

boy!" From then on, her learning progressed even faster, and she came to have an extensive understanding of the classics and history. With her brothers she also progressed in the law of writing.

Even in old age Madame Song read such books as the *Illustrated Guide to the Three Bonds.*[21]

Learning was a lifelong pursuit for some women. Of the elder sister of the famous poet Chŏng Ch'ŏl (1536–93), for example, it is said that she read the *Elementary Learning*, the *Great Learning* (C: Daxue; K: Taehak), and other books and "acquired some general understanding of their greater meaning. In later years she devoted herself even more earnestly to scholarship and wished to understand the *Doctrine of the Mean* (C: Zhongyong; K: Chungyong), but she was unable to finish her studies."[22] Other women were encouraged to read, in addition to the *Elementary Learning* and the *Four Books for Women*, the *Book of History*, the *Analects*, and the *Book of Odes* and to memorize the names of sages and worthies.[23] Of a seventeenth-century descendant of the famous Neo-Confucian pioneer scholar Yi Saek (1328–96), it was said:

> She was clever and remembered the theories of the classics and history. What she heard once, she never forgot again. As to the *Odes* and the *Mencius*, she could recite them completely and also understood their meaning in broad terms. She was equally familiar with all great families and descent groups of Korea. At times she discussed past and present in terms of success and failure, of wisdom and unwisdom, and her arguments rarely ever missed the point.[24]

Despite such praise of female erudition, it was not thought appropriate for a woman to show her learning openly beyond the walls of the inner quarters. Therefore, a woman's intellectual capacity was often greatly understated, as in the following example:

> She learned to write and had some understanding [of written texts]. Yet, this remained inside [the house] and did not get known outside. Her sons went to a teacher, and one [of the sons] talked about his mother, and only then, for the first time, did outsiders learn that she was literate. Such was her virtue.[25]

Although her nature was thought to prevent a woman from grasping the deeper meaning (*taeŭi*) of classical texts as fully as a man could, excessive learning was regarded as a cause of misfortune. The eminent scholar-official Yun Chŭng (1629–1714) wrote of his aunt that when she was young she was praised as a "female scholar" (*yŏsa*). Later, however, she was pitied because she lost her husband early and was childless. The verdict of her generation: "A wise daughter-in-law (*hyŏnbu*) has virtue, yet is bereft of good fortune."[26] Yun Chŭng's contemporary, Yi Ik (1681–1763), well known for his Practical Learning (*sirhak*), equally warned that "teaching women scholarship (*hangmun*) will lead to disaster."[27]

While excessive learning was deemed dangerous, a carefully supervised classical education prepared elite women for their essential role as educators of their offspring. A great number of biographies testify to the fact that mothers imparted elementary knowledge to their young sons and daughters. Even an old grandmother could instruct her grandchildren.[28] If the sons' advanced education became the responsibility of their mother alone, however, the outcome was considered doubtful. The example of Yi T'oegye's (1501–70) mother's fortitude was often cited. Widowed at an early age, she constantly reminded her two sons that they would have to make an effort a hundredfold greater than that of the other children to avoid the popular slander that "a widow's offspring are uneducated." Both her sons vindicated their mother's efforts by successfully passing the civil service examinations and entering the bureaucracy.[29]

"The True Story of Madame Chang of Andong" (Andong Chang-ssi silgi),[30] provides further evidence that scholarly talent was considered a natural gift that could be enhanced by education and training but did not, for women, constitute a value in its own right. Madame Chang (1598–1680), an only daughter, was instructed by her father, Chang Hŭnghyo (1564–1633), himself educated by one of Yi T'oegye's most prominent disciples. In this scholarly and sober milieu she is said to have delighted in the "maxims of the sages and the worthies" and tried to live accordingly. This spirit of devotion is evident in the nine short poems she wrote before marriage. One is entitled "The Sage":

> If not born at the time of a sage,
> I cannot see a sage's face;
> [Yet,] a sage's words can be heard,
> and [thus] a sage's heart becomes visible.

Madame Chang not only wrote poetry but also developed such a forceful brush stroke that her calligraphy was taken for Chinese! However, as soon as her hair was pinned up and she got married, she reportedly stopped writing poems and practicing calligraphy because such activities were not thought befitting a married woman.

At the age of nineteen Madame Chang became the second wife of Yi Simyŏng (1590–1674) and settled in a remote village to the east of Andong. Simyŏng also adhered to T'oegye's school. Thus Madame Chang entered a house whose intellectual orientation was similar to her own. Her husband, disgusted with factional politics in the capital, retired to the countryside and lived the rest of his life in obscurity, devoting himself to self-cultivation, scholarship, and the instruction of his sons.[31]

Not surprisingly, Madame Chang is depicted as an exemplary wife, daughter-in-law, and mother. Her virtue and wisdom were likened to that of the mother of the famous Cheng brothers of the Song period: two of her six sons passed the civil service examinations and entered officialdom. True to her upbringing, she was a strict disciplinarian and taught her sons to take the words and deeds of the sages and worthies as their models. She instilled in her offspring the meaning of the classics and guided them with the basic values of interpersonal relationships. Her favorite term was *sŏn*, "to be good"—a concept that encapsulated for her correct moral conduct within the human bonds (*illyun*), behavior that, if pursued with perseverance, would eventually lead to sagehood. To Madame Chang, sagehood was the outcome of constant moral practice (*sŏnhaeng*). She once told her sons that she did not care about their literary fame but that she would rejoice if they were to become known for their righteousness and moral acts.

Madame Chang died in 1680 at the age of eighty-three and was, because of a son's official position, given the posthumous title "virtuous wife" (*chŏng puin*). The most befitting epitaph was written by one of her many descendants: "Through the support she gave by disciplining herself and regulating the inner quarters, her contribution to an ordered world was indeed not small!"

A woman's literacy and classical learning thus often evoked ambivalent feelings among her kinsmen and affines. Although not supposed to become common knowledge during her lifetime, a mother's, a sister's, or a wife's mastery of classical texts was proudly mentioned in her obituary. Surely, filial devotion and affection may have compelled many compilers and writers to allude to the high standards of education reached by their kinswomen. This cannot be the full explanation for such posthumous praise, however. Rather, by referring to their educational accomplishments, men acknowledged the women's crucial role in transmitting elite standards and norms from one generation to the next. Primary wives not only were brokers of elite status and as such conferred full legitimacy on their sons, they also were the guardians of Confucian norms in the inner realm. Women were not admitted to the civil service examinations, but, as the first teachers of their sons, they laid the emotional and intellectual foundation for their offspring's long road to success. Equally, from behind the scenes (*naejo*), a woman could advance her husband's career as an official or a scholar. Her reward was a posthumously granted honorific title commensurate to her husband's achievements in the outside world. Literacy was not, of course, necessarily and always correlated with virtue, but the combination of the two gave an elite woman unusual empowerment even within the narrow confines of the inner chambers.

The number of highly educated women in Chosŏn Korea cannot be estimated, but we may assume that the degree of their educational refinement largely depended on the scholarly milieu of their natal homes. Even if classical scholarship may not have been a widespread phenomenon, a large number of elite women could at least read and write the native alphabet, *han'gŭl*. It was for them that the vernacular versions of the classics and morality books were prepared.

That women were prolific letter writers, using the vernacular, provides clear evidence of female literacy.[32] Indeed, a woman's correspondence was often her most important link to the outside world. For this reason, women were encouraged to acquaint themselves with the primer *Proper Sounds for the Instruction of the People* (Hunmin chŏngŭm)[33] in order to improve their writing skills.[34] Letters were frequently exchanged with distant parents and husbands (when they were on duty away from home). They were usually brief inquiries into the recipient's well-being (*munan*). Lady Hyegyŏng's *Memoir of 1795*, for example, starts out by stating: "From the time

I came to the palace as a child, each morning and evening I exchanged letters of greetings with my parents."[35] At times letters were treated like "unauthorized" visitors. Because a woman was not supposed to receive visitors in her husband's absence, she would await his return before opening a letter from an old acquaintance.[36]

## MORALITY IN INTERPERSONAL RELATIONSHIPS

Although as far as the outside world was concerned the male household head was responsible for controlling and mediating peace and harmony in the domestic domain, it was the primary wife (*ch'ŏ*) who in fact was the steward of family affairs. Selected by a prestige marriage as the (potential) future mother of the lineal heir, she held a unique position of honor within her husband's descent group. Her rank was unassailable because she was inducted into her new home with public acclaim of her natal group's high social status.[37] Her prestige became even greater if she was married to a first son.

Nevertheless, a bride entered her husband's house as a complete stranger and started her marital life against a backdrop of potential misgivings and even hostility, especially from the other women in the household. By affirming the moral values of her education, the newcomer began to define her place in the intricate web of human relationships that characterized the inner domain. Biographies and obituaries tell the tale of how elite women established themselves in their new surroundings as wives and mothers.[38]

Foremost among the many obligations a primary wife was expected to fulfill was her devotion to her parents-in-law. Confucian morality demanded that she transfer filiality (*ihyo*) from her own parents to her husband's parents—a transaction that more than anything else tested her emotional stability. This transfer usually is fictionalized as the most dramatic action dictated by an oppressive Confucian system that severed a woman from her natal bonds and forced her to give priority to an untested human relationship. Although this depiction indeed highlights the severity of this experience, the evidence suggests that women maintained contact with their own parents and were even praised for doing so. It is said, for example, that "she married early, yet her filiality toward her own parents did not diminish at all."[39] At times, although quite rarely, divided loyalties posed a threat to the marital bond, as in the following biography of Madame Yi:

At that time [when she lived with her husband in Seoul], Madame Yi's mother, Madame Ch'oe, was ailing. Consequently, she took leave from her mother-in-law, Madame Hong, and returned east to take care of her sick mother. She personally nursed her fever spells, administered medicine to her, and did not sleep at night. She devoted all her energy to filial piety. . . .

Her husband came and wanted her to return with him to Seoul. Madame Yi, in tears, said: "Because a woman has the three obediences [C: *sancong;* K: *samjong*], I cannot disobey you. However, my parents are old, and I am their only daughter. If one

morning I am gone, on whom will they be able to rely? Moreover, my mother has
been sick for a long time and is still on medication. How would I bear to leave her?"

Despite the fact that Madame Yi invoked the "three obediences" according to
which she would have had to bow to her husband's demands, the dilemma was
solved when the husband agreed to return to the capital to care for his own parents while Madame Yi stayed on with her mother until the latter died. This arrangement resulted in a sixteen-year separation for the couple.[40]

Whereas the above case may indeed present an unusual occurrence, the tradition of the husband's uxorilocal residence, still strong throughout the first half of
the Chosŏn dynasty, may have at first tolerated such compromises. Women then
entered their affinal homes at a mature age with children of their own, presumably
at a time when their parents-in-law were about to hand over their responsibilities
to the next generation. Nevertheless, when in later times the uxorilocal living
arrangements disappeared and the bride entered her new home at an early age,
she was advised to "overcome her emotions" and to be all the more obedient and
submissive under the more oppressive conditions of her new surroundings.[41]

The inner quarters of elite households were complex female communities within
which diverse human relationships and interests had to be reconciled and harmo-
nized in conformity with the moral dictates of Confucianism. As the wife of a first
son, a woman may have had to deal with the wives of her husband's younger brothers living in the same household or in close proximity. Although status differences
as well as the birth sequence of their husbands may initially have ranked these
wives, ritual primogeniture, gaining prominence in the seventeenth century, most
probably also affected their economic standing. Second sons (i.e., the first son's
younger brothers) rarely lost their right to inherit parts of the patrimony, yet with
the passage of time, their shares tended to shrink. This development—accelerated
by the growing shortage of cultivable land—introduced economic inequality
among brothers and opened the door to potential jealousy and misgivings among
their wives. Even though Confucian morality addressed the problem by emphasizing brotherly hierarchy, that is, the subordination of younger brothers to their
older sibling, in the late Chosŏn brotherly love (*che*) was propagated as one of the
five human imperatives (*oryun*) with ever greater urgency.[42]

Economic inequality among brothers was often at the root of intrafamilial discord, and sisters-in-law were admonished to make common cause rather than fight
over the distribution of resources. Equally, sisters-in-law were not to be treated according to the economic standing of their natal families, namely, generously when
rich but shabbily when poor. "If there is a rift between them, the poor will be resentful, the rich haughty. The decline of the domestic way will certainly originate
from here."[43]

Whereas potential conflict among primary wives in the same household arose
from economics, the cause of inequality among the primary wife and the secondary wives the husband might have taken into his household was primarily social

and cultural. In Chosŏn Korea, an unbridgeable status gulf separated these women. Primary wives invariably came from elite families and often had enjoyed extensive education, whereas secondary wives were of commoner or slave origin. Such social and cultural differentiation was accentuated by marked ritual incongruity. Moreover, while in the early period of Chosŏn sons of commoner concubines might have been called on, in the absence of a primary son, to assume the ancestral responsibilities of the ritual heir, this substitution was no longer tolerated in later times. Sonlessness of the primary wife was then remedied by adoption. Even though many secondary sons may have enjoyed an education similar to that of primary sons, their scholarly achievements did not lead to prestigious careers in the bureaucracy because they were barred by law from taking the civil service examinations.[44] In short, the discrimination against secondary sons created a high degree of frustration and unhappiness that manifested itself poignantly in tension and conflict in the inner chambers.

It was therefore the task of the primary wife to accommodate and harmonize the diverse interests and expectations and, above all, to curb her own sympathies or aversions. As an eighteenth-century observer put it from the perspective of the main wife:

> A concubine is inferior to the primary wife, yet she is liked by my husband and thus should not be despised and maltreated. Her sons are my sons' brothers and brought forth by my husband. Thus, they have the same blood as the parents-in-law. Would it be proper not to love them like my own?[45]

Undue jealousy climaxing in "beating a concubine like an ox or horse, or despising her like an enemy," was since olden times one of the "seven instances of extreme disobedience" (*ch'ilch'ul*) for which a wife could be expelled from her husband's household.[46]

In contrast, in case of sickness or barrenness a "wise wife" was advised, even against her husband's protestations, to encourage him to take a secondary wife and to herself search "for a good and virtuous woman, teach her some manners, and make her take her place." If the relationship between the two women was guided by both kindness and authority, the domestic way was secure. "If, however, there is only kindness, the concubine turns haughty and oversteps her status; if there is only authority, the concubine hates it and plots harm. A wise concubine (*hyŏnch'ŏp*) surely is not like this."[47]

At the very bottom of the domestic scale were the slave women (*pi*), who were assigned to the heaviest manual duties. Rarely affected by the dictates of morality, they are pictured as having been the greatest challenge to a primary wife's human skills and patience. It was therefore often remarked as a distinct sign of her virtue if a primary wife "did not beat a female slave when the latter did wrong, but reprimanded her."[48] Or, "In front of Madame Hong [her mother-in-law] she never scolded the female slaves. Her words were invariably warm, and her expression calm. . . . The slaves all respected her."[49] If the noise of scolding or beating was heard outside the female quarters, this was taken as a sure sign of domestic decline. If, on the contrary, "upon entering a house, there is the sound of spinning and weaving in the inner quarters, and the sound of reciting the *Odes* and reading the *Book of History* in the men's quarters, one knows that the house is in order."[50]

Poverty, even among the elite, became a problem in later Chosŏn, and well-to-do households had to provide shelter for various destitute relatives, in particular orphaned children. To act generously toward poor kin and impoverished neighbors was noted as a distinct mark of wifely benevolence and by extension as a manifestation of the kin group's public standing. Nevertheless, "a wife who enjoys giving to others is not good news. . . . Although giving to others earns a good reputation, the property of the master of the house should not be wastefully spent. Poor and destitute relatives and neighbors should appeal to the master of the house, and it is proper for him to assist."[51] In sum, the managerial circumspection and the leadership qualities—both hedged in by the strictures of Confucian morality—demanded of a primary wife a natural disposition as well as a proper education that would make her fit for her multifarious tasks. A felicitous combination of the two could earn a woman high praise and even an occasional gift of an extra slave.[52]

### MORALITY AND ECONOMIC MANAGEMENT

The primary wife, once installed in her function as administrator of her husband's household, was expected to lead a disciplined and just regime (*ch'i'ga*). In her endeavors she was often guided by "domestic laws" (*kabŏp*) that detailed her various responsibilities and the house's particular customs. To everyone she was expected to be a living example of virtue, and it was in terms of "virtuous behavior" and her domestic management skills (*kyubŏm*) that she was judged by her affines and the outside world. In the words of an eighteenth-century observer:

> The daughter-in-law is the one upon whom the prosperity or doom of the house depends. Her responsibility is indeed great. If she is wise and makes the "domestic way" (*kado*) prosper, her affines will respect her, and later generations will take her as a model. If she is not wise and causes the domestic way to deteriorate, her affines will hate her, and later generations will be ashamed of her. Indeed, the way of a daughter-in-law is to be feared![53]

In practical terms, a primary wife controlled the domestic purse strings, thus enabling her husband "who did not pay attention to domestic affairs"[54] to devote himself entirely to his official career or scholarly pursuits. In this domain, "virtue" was directly correlated to frugality. A wise wife economized expenditure (*chŏl chaeyong*) and kept an eye on the inventory, avoided debts, and above all took care of the ancestral property (*po chongmul*). By preserving (*su*) the family's patrimony, she greatly contributed to the economic maintenance of her children's social status—an issue that became especially pressing in the second half of the dynasty.

The praise that was lavished on "wise" and "virtuous" women who prudently managed their husbands' financial resources stands in stark contrast to the frequent references to the darker side of a woman's inclination to covet riches and profit. Many fathers and husbands warned their daughters and wives to beware of turning into "extravagant women" (*nangbu*) who would gamble away domestic assets by lending them for profit or borrowing beyond their means. Such misconduct naturally played on Confucian sensibilities against profit seeking. Financial speculation, especially involving close kin, was apt to lead to acrimonious exchanges with tardy or defaulting debtors and in the worst cases gave rise to litigations that dragged the conflicts into the public sphere. This was the way to ruin family fortunes and, worst of all, family reputations.[55] Moreover, standing between two family groups, a daughter-in-law could find herself tempted into dangerous financial transactions:

> If she is after the wealth of her natal family in order to enrich her husband's family, she might ruin her own family, or if she freezes her affines in order to maintain her brothers, she might bankrupt her husband's family. This is not the womanly way. In case one family is rich, and the other poor, there must be a balance.[56]

Split loyalties as much as the inability to "know how to measure money, grain, and cloth" could bring about a family's doom.

Whereas wealth had to be managed with wisdom, poverty was expected to be endured with stoicism. Indeed, remaining unaffected by economic adversities was noted with praise, as in the following example:

> Being the wife of a poor scholar (*hansa*), she insisted on eating coarse food and dressing plainly. Would others be able to bear this? . . . She was resolute and persevering; she suppressed her feelings and disciplined herself. By nature she was frugal and did not enjoy fancy and elegant things."[57]

Undoubtedly, often a painful adjustment to new economic circumstances tested a woman's steadfastness of character: "She grew up in a rich house and was used to beautiful ornaments. After marriage, she adjusted herself to the modest means of her husband's house and never had a different countenance than before."[58]

To alleviate hardship, it was not dishonorable for the wife of a poor scholar to engage in such "basic" pursuits as weaving or raising silkworms. Even keeping a few chickens and ducks and collecting various nuts for oil that could be sold was considered within the bounds of honesty but with this express caveat: "If women get carried away with seeking profit, engage in superficial activities, and distance themselves from matters of human feelings, would this be the behavior of a wise and virtuous woman?"[59] The economic well-being of a household, thus, depended on a wife's human and managerial skills that she had to exercise within the constraints of Confucian morality. Given the woman's alleged natural predilection for riches and extravagance, it was easy for her to violate these boundaries. It was therefore a special kind of praise when her affines noted on her tombstone that "all her life long, she did not covet riches," or "when someone mentioned wealth, she politely turned away as if she did not want to listen."[60]

The counterpart of the wise householder was the lazy woman who got up late and, by spending her time on reading novels and "queer stories," neglected her duties. Even more damaging was her habit of wasting money on borrowing such despicable literature, thus ruining her household.[61]

### WOMEN'S RELIGIOUS CHARGE

Although the Confucian patriline did not involve women in its ancestral cult, women were nevertheless instrumental in assisting their husbands and sons behind the scenes, and "serving the ancestors" (*pong chesa*) was routinely mentioned as a major responsibility of the primary wife. Her attitude toward the ancestors was thought to influence the earnestness and devotion with which her household served them. Noteworthy is a mother's admonition to her sons that they should conduct the ancestral rites with undivided reverence lest Heaven become resentful.[62] A resolute only daughter even built an ancestral shrine (*sadang*) to gather her kinsmen and reactivate a "cold genealogy" (*naengbo*).[63]

Primary wives had to oversee all practical preparations for the offerings. Ritual handbooks as well as instruction by parents and parents-in-law familiarized a woman with the intricacies of preparing and presenting the sacrificial food. Strict rules demanded absolute cleanliness of body and spirit during the process. No talk or laughter was to be heard, and the slave servants, if they were to assist at all, were not to be scolded. Indeed, at times ambitious women seem to have used the solemn ancestral rites as opportunities to flaunt wealth and prestige. If they deemed their economic resources insufficient, they borrowed in order to lavish gifts of propitious ancestral food on kinsmen and neighbors. Would the ruin of the house, a critic of such devious practices asked, be the will of the ancestors?[64]

While male-oriented ancestor worship did not satisfy women emotionally, the many references to "superstitious practices" (*ŭmsa*) make clear that women tended to seek, against the dictates of Confucian morality, yet apparently often with their husbands' tacit blessing, religious gratification for themselves and their families in shamanic ceremonies or visits to Buddhist temples.[65] To resist such diversions gave proof of Confucian education and mental fortitude, often admiringly noted by biographers: "She hated superstitious practices, and shamans did not enter her house."[66] Or, "During her whole life, she did not go near shamans and did not believe in spirits." Or, "When her mother died, her family wanted to have a shaman ceremony to amuse the soul of the dead. She declined, saying that her mother had never held such a ceremony."[67]

Instead of believing in spirits, some elite women seem to have resigned themselves to "fate" (*myŏng*) or put their trust in the mercy of Heaven. Often a certain kind of fatalism, not at all alien to Confucian thought, permeates their life stories.

When an eldest son died, for example, his mother attributed his demise to "fate."[68] Praying to Heaven for assistance and good fortune, on the other hand, was a more positive act that could result in relief of mental anguish and fulfillment of a sincere supplication. The "Record about How Madame Yi Moved Heaven" (Yi-ssi kam-ch'ŏn-gi) gives a splendid illustration. Madame Yi, who lived apart from her husband for many years to serve her own parents, soon was confronted with the serious illness of her husband. The story goes:

> [Grieving about her bad fate,] she burnt incense and prayed to all spirits above and below continuously for seven days and nights. She did not close an eye. Then she took a bath and cut her nails. Secretly taking a little knife with her, she climbed the mountain behind her maternal great-grandfather's grave and put up a little table and burned some incense. Bowing to Heaven, she said in tears, "Heaven, Heaven, luck is good, and misfortune is bad: this is Heaven's principle. To collect good deeds and to pile up bad deeds: this is man's affair."

After enumerating the virtuous acts of her husband as a filial son, she continued her lamentation:

> I am meeting disaster. My mother has already died, and my husband is gravely ill. If his illness cannot be cured, I shall be alone with no one as support. Heaven and man belong to the same Principle—there is not the slightest difference between them. August Heaven, august Heaven, show pity!

Thereupon she took out her little knife and cut two joints of her middle finger of her left hand. Looking up to Heaven and beating her breast, she exclaimed:

> My sincerity and reverence go to such an extreme. I received my body from my parents; I do not dare destroy it. However, what I consider my heaven is my husband. If this heaven goes to ruin, how can I live all by myself? I wish to take upon myself my husband's fate. August Heaven, august Heaven, look down upon this small sincerity.

When she had finished her prayer, she descended to her ancestor's grave, bowed, and said:

> While you were alive, you were a wise minister; dead, you are certainly a good spirit. Help to carry my supplication to Heaven.

> Afterwards she returned home and did not show a changed expression [on her face] for fear that her husband might find out.

Although at the time there was a severe drought, black clouds suddenly appeared, and it began to thunder and rain. In a dream, a female spirit told the husband that medicine would come forth from Heaven. When this prediction became true, all the villagers were surprised and ascribed it to the wife's sincerity. When the matter was reported to the throne, the wife was rewarded with a commemorative arch.[69]

By recording this story of his maternal grandmother, Yi Yulgok (1536–84) intended to provide later generations with models for "wise husband" (*hyŏnin*) and "sagacious wife" (*ch'ŏlbu*). In Yi's judgment, Madame Yi acted according to humaneness (*in*) and etiquette (*ye*) and by exemplifying the "wifely way" (*pudo*), set virtuous standards for the inner chambers, with her sincerity even moving Heaven.

### THE CHASTE WOMAN AS A CONFUCIAN IDEAL

An essential part of the "wifely way" was to observe the rules of "chastity" (*chŏngnyŏl*) extolled in the Confucian literature. It was a specific challenge to womanly steadfastness of character and morality that, when successfully met, conferred honor. "Chastity" took many forms—from venturing outside the house only in the dark with the face hidden behind a cloak to self-mutilation and even suicide. The ideological basis of this dictate was not the protection of female vulnerability. On the contrary, the female body was liable to mutilation for manifesting a wife's allegiance to only one husband: as a loyal minister could not serve two rulers, so could a loyal wife not serve two husbands. Chastity, thus, was a special form of loyalty the pursuit of which was regarded as an indispensable constituent element of female virtue. Indeed, chastity was propagated in all morality books for women—in the *Four Books for Women*[70] as well as in the *Illustrated Guide to the Three Bonds*.

In Chosŏn Korea, "chastity" was enshrined in the legal stipulation that the sons of twice married women were not admitted to the civil service examinations. This law in effect prohibited the remarriage of widowed elite women, and when a remarriage occurred for economic reasons, it was usually a secondary marriage.[71] Celebrated, in contrast, were the cases of young widows who resisted the calls of their families for remarriage, instead kept vigil at their husbands' graves, and after the completion of the mourning period dedicated their lives to the service of their parents-in-law. Even more dramatic were the examples of women who when faced with assailants took their own lives rather than lose their honor.

Preservation of female honor by committing suicide after the husband's death—the counterpart to a loyal minister's sacrificial death for his ruler—was praised as a "beautiful custom" (*misok*),[72] and throughout the dynasty the government allowed the kinsmen of such honorable women to erect commemorative arches (*chŏngp'yo* or *chŏngmun*) to celebrate and display the examples of extraordinary morality in their midst. Because the rewards reaped by the dead woman's affines were, besides a reputation for high moral standards, exemption from taxes and corvée labor, it is not unlikely that young childless widows were at times put under pressure to do away with themselves. Whereas in the two first centuries of Chosŏn the majority of women who killed themselves after their husbands' death belonged to the upper class, in later times occasional cases of commoner and even slave women became known—a sure sign that Confucian behavioral norms had begun to be emulated by the lower classes, or, conversely, that government propaganda had become more extensive.[73] A similar process was at work in China (see chapter 9).

Criticism of female suicide as a questionable expression of virtue[74] was rare, and the eminent scholar Chŏng Yagyong (1762–1836) seems to have been rather isolated in his attack on the system:

> If, upon the husband's death, the wife also dies, this is called "faithful wife." Then the sideposts of the entrance gate [of their house] are brightened, a red certificate is issued, the household exempted from tax, and her descendants relieved from forced labor. What is this? This has nothing to do with a "faithful wife." This is nothing but a tragedy. This is a contraction of feeling, and the authorities have not thoroughly investigated the case. Did she intend to seek fame? No, there was no such intention.

Chŏng went on to find fault with the mental disposition that made such a gruesome act possible. In his view, it had nothing at all to do with "chastity" because "among the worst things in the world was killing oneself." Suicide, Chŏng maintained, could be justified only in some specific cases (see Figure 6.2):

> When the husband is pursued by a tiger or robber, and the wife follows and dies while protecting her husband: this is a chaste woman. Or, if she herself is pursued by robbers or bad men and, under the threat of being abused, dies by defending herself: this is a chaste woman. Or, if she is widowed early and her parents and brothers try to force her into remarriage, yet she refuses and, unable to resist them, dies: this is a chaste woman. Or, if, after the husband had died with a grudge, the wife discloses the facts and is therefore punished and dies: this is a chaste woman. However, nowadays it is not like this. The husband dies quietly in the bedroom according to the years allotted to him by Heaven, and the wife follows him and dies: this is killing oneself and nothing else. It does not conform to reason.

Rather than commit suicide, Chŏng continued, it was the duty of a widow to look after the parents-in-law and after their death conduct the ancestral rites and raise the children to maturity. Would it not be an utter failure in filiality and motherly love if a woman neglected her duties by hanging herself?[75]

Even Chŏng Yagyong, thus, did not condemn the practice of wifely suicide as long as it conformed to "reason," that is, was committed in response to extraordinary circumstances. By the end of the Chosŏn period, the ideal of the "chaste woman" had undoubtedly become the most powerful manifestation of a woman's subordination to men as demanded by Confucian social doctrine.[76]

There is no clear evidence that the normative expectations of womanly behavior held by the government or by individuals changed significantly over time. The dictates of Confucian morality dominated the official discourse on society and regulated all aspects of everyday conduct, eventually even affecting the nonelite. Indeed, if anything, the normative pressure on women of all classes increased in late Chosŏn. Yet this picture of a solidly Confucianized society had a reverse side. The popular novel, emerging in the eighteenth century, questioned, criticized, and even ridiculed Confucian norms.[77] "Queer stories," reportedly so

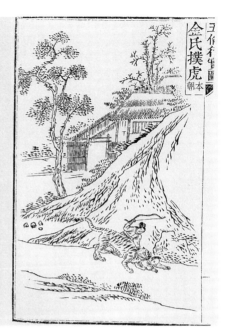

Figure 6.2. A Faithful Wife Saves Her Husband from a Tiger, from *Illustrated Guide to the Five Relations* (Oryun haengsilto). Courtesy of Kyujanggak Archives, Seoul National University.

popular with some upper-class women, depicted an alternative and unconventional world: lovers braving adverse conditions, the domestic realm rent by intrigue, heroic deeds requited with unexpected rewards, and fantastic resolutions of hopeless adventures with the help of Daoist or Buddhist magic. However antihegemonic, these marvelous tales, usually centering on one or two protagonists, did not build up "moral worlds" of their own. The delight they evoked in their readers stemmed from their making light of the existing order—at times subverting it, at times transcending it, and often, in the end, restoring it.[78]

Although popular novels may have given voice to deep-seated feelings repressed by Confucian principles and thus revealed ambivalent attitudes toward the dominant discourse, it was nevertheless the hegemonic standards to which everyone— including women of all social classes—seems to have aspired, regardless of the cost. In particular, the image of the "chaste woman" was an enduring one, perhaps exactly because of the spectacular hardship and sacrifice required for attaining it.

## EXCEPTIONAL BIOGRAPHIES

Elite women were educated so that they had a good grasp of the values and norms embodied in the classical literature and could transmit them to their offspring. Their primary role being that of educators, women were rarely encouraged to be creative. Nevertheless, despite consistent disavowal of female creativity, a small number of women whose works have survived prove that Chosŏn dynasty women, even under severe social and moral restrictions, did create unique and original works. Surely, their works are of exceptional quality, but what makes them even more exceptional are the circumstances under which they survived: their transmission to posterity depended entirely on the care and interest of male kinsmen. Only a few named works of art, literature, and philosophy have thus been preserved as extraordinary exhibits of female artistry and scholarship anonymously pursued in the inner quarters.

Foremost among these exceptional women is Sin Saimdang (1504–51),[79] the most famous female painter of the Chosŏn period.[80] Saimdang was born into an elite family, and her early education was guided principally by her maternal grandfather. Her biography, written by her son, Yi Yulgok, briefly mentions her precocious grasp of classical literature, her calligraphic and painting skills, and her unusual dexterity with the needle, but its largest part describes her outstanding filiality, her devotion to her mother-in-law, and her dedicated management of the household. Her artistic work is recalled only in the last few sentences.[81] In her usually small-scale paintings Saimdang depicted "female" topics such as flowers, plants, fruits, vegetables, birds, and insects.[82] Her painting tradition was continued by her eldest daughter, Maech'ang (1529–92), and one of her granddaughters. Sin Saimdang's fame as a painter was established, perhaps exclusively, because she happened to be the mother of Yulgok and because her memory was later maintained and even propagated by the adherents of Yulgok's school of thought. In contrast, Maech'ang was remembered on her husband's epitaph only for her knowledge of the classics and history. No written record exists for the granddaughter.[83] Yulgok's slightly older contemporary, Ŏ Sukkwŏn (n.d.), summarized the generally ambiguous attitude toward female painters:

> Now there is Madame Sin of Tongyang [P'yŏngsan]. Since her youth she has been painting well. Her grapes and landscapes are outstanding, and people who evaluate her work say that she ranks second [only] to An Kyŏn.[84] How is it possible that [some] slight [her work] as "a woman's paintings," and how come others even reproach her, saying that [painting] is not something a woman should properly do?[85]

A younger contemporary of Sin Saimdang was the poetess Hŏ Nansŏrhŏn (1563–89), the elder sister of the famous writer and statesman Hŏ Kyun (1569–1618). Finding no happiness in marriage, she expressed her sorrow and frustration in what is now regarded as a specifically female genre of melancholic poetry. Shortly before her death she destroyed most of her work, and the remaining poems were collected by her brother and given to a Chinese envoy to have them printed in China (a printing in Korea obviously would have been unthinkable).[86]

While contemporary opinion disparaged artistic and poetic skills of elite women, the pursuit of Neo-Confucian philosophy must have been thought completely beyond female capability. In fact, to date only one female scholar, Im Yunjidang (1721–93), is known to have left collected works, *Bequeathed Works of Yunjidang* (Yunjidang yu'go). Containing some forty items, the collection comprises tracts on Neo-Confucian questions, interpretations of classical works, and historical discourses.[87] Yunjidang was born into a family with a long history of scholarship and office holding. Her early training was deeply influenced by her brothers, Im Sŏngju (1711–88) and Im Chŏngju (1727–96), both of whom were outstanding exponents of eighteenth-century Neo-Confucian thought in the Yulgok tradition. Sŏngju, in particular, became known as an articulate advocate of Yulgok's emphasis on the primacy of material force (*ki*). Because Yunjidang lost her parents at an early age, her elder brother saw to her education. Together with her brothers, she studied the classics and the histories and reportedly developed into a skilled debater. She is said to have regretted that she had not been born a man. At the age of nineteen she was married to Sin Kwangyu (n.d.) of the powerful P'yŏngsan Sin but was widowed after eight years. Without children of her own, she continued to live in the family of her younger brother-in-law, Sin Kwangu (n.d.), who had passed the civil service examinations and served as a high official. After devoting herself to filial and ritual duties, she reportedly resumed her studies—which she had abandoned after marriage—in old age. She remained close to her brothers, with whom she exchanged frequent letters.

Greatly molded by the men around her, Yunjidang does not seem to have developed a specifically female attitude toward what she studied. On the contrary, she reminisced: "[A]lthough what men and women do, differ, the human properties bestowed by Heaven are at first not different at all. Thus, when I studied the classics and had questions about their meaning, my elder brother instructed me in a caring manner until I came to a complete understanding." Consequently, in Yunjidang's view, all human beings possess the potential to become sages (*sŏngin*), if they are able to recover their innate nature. To assist this process education was of primary importance, but for women, Yunjidang seems to have upheld the conventional emphasis on the primacy of wifely tasks. She said: "For women, to immerse themselves in books or to make efforts at various writing styles goes against their essential roles. However, it is beneficial for them to read the *Elementary Learning* and the *Four Books* and to use these materials for training themselves." During her active life, this is the course Yunjidang herself reportedly followed. Her brother-in-law recalled: "After coming to our house as a bride, she was never seen with books, she devoted herself entirely to wifely duties. Only after she had become old and had some time off from her daily routines did she open the classics she had bought and read them stealthily in a low voice."[88] It is not clear whether Yunjidang thought that just as scholarship and self-cultivation were means to attain sagehood for men, the faithful performance of wifely tasks would lead women to sagehood. She did not see her own scholarship as a unique achievement and pursued it within the boundaries set by Confucian norms for women of her age. She herself may rather have wished to be remembered for the "wifely virtue" (*pudŏk*) she so highly valued.

## CONFUCIAN WOMEN

Education for women constituted an integral part of the sociopolitical program of the Chosŏn state. Indeed, the adoption of a Neo-Confucian patrilineal ideology necessitated the construction of a new gender model for women. The weight of this transformational process was particularly heavy on elite women, who had to be fitted into a novel social scheme that in so many ways ran counter to earlier indigenous traditions. Women were taught to assume pivotal roles as guardians and transmitters of Confucian norms and values and to embody the ideal of female virtue as one of the axial elements of the Confucian hegemonic system. Taking up these charges, elite women found their own agency. The enactment of "virtue" provided space to express individual interpretations and solutions. However hegemonic the discourse, circumspect women always found ways to balance the conflicting demands put on them. Ultimately, a woman's worth was judged according to her ability to avoid friction and conflict within the family, to create harmony in the larger domestic realm, and thus to contribute to "an ordered world."

Nevertheless, the sphere of activities available to Korean elite women was more restricted than that of their Chinese contemporaries. Not only were the boundaries of the inner quarters more strictly observed, but most elite women lived in isolated villages remote from towns and marketplaces. Ideological and geographic distance, thus, prevented women from building up the kind of female networks so celebrated for the urbanized and commercialized Lower Yangzi, or Jiangnan, region in China. Women did communicate with the outside world by letter. *Han'gŭl* was an easy medium of writing, but one that also separated most women from the dominant Chinese-bound male culture.

The documents consulted for this chapter, written by men, naturally picture elite women as compliant students and executors of Confucian ideals. Nevertheless, for most women it cannot have been a question of merely surviving in a patriarchal society. Although rarely known or recorded, elite women were apt to develop an inner disposition that allowed them not only to find a meaningful place in this order but also to retain a sense of their own identity. Self-confident in their ability to fulfill successfully the charges of daughter, wife, and mother, they, no less than men, contributed to the perpetuation of the Confucian system well into the twentieth century.

## NOTES

I would like to thank Dorothy Ko and JaHyun Haboush for their critical reading of an earlier version of this essay.

1. The *Koryŏsa* was compiled on royal orders by Confucian scholar-officials and completed in 1451. It contains twelve biographies of virtuous women.

2. For the details, see Martina Deuchler, *The Confucian Transformation of Korea*, Harvard-Yenching Monograph No. 36 (Cambridge, Mass: Council on East Asian Studies, Harvard University, 1992), pp. 51–73.

3. *Chungjong sillok*, 34:3a.

4. *Chungjong sillok*, 28:21b–22a.

5. For a brief overview of the publication history of *Sohak* in early Chosŏn, see Yun Pyŏnghŭi, "Chosŏn Chungjongjo sap'ung kwa *Sohak*," pp. 41–78. In 1797, King Chŏngjo (r. 1776–1800) still praised the educational value of the *Sohak*. See his *Yunŭm* (Royal Pronouncement).

6. *Sejong sillok*, 64:19a–b; *Sŏngjong sillok*, 127:7a.

7. *Chungjong sillok*, 28:21b–22a. The classic biographical collection *Lienü zhuan* was compiled by Liu Xiang (77–6 B.C.E.). Liu divided his biographies into seven sections: correct deportment of mothers, virtue and wisdom, the benign and wise, the chaste and obedient, the chaste and righteous, those able in reasoning and understanding, and the pernicious and depraved (see Susan Mann, *Precious Records: Women in China's Long Eighteenth Century* [Stanford: Stanford University Press, 1997], pp. 205, 211; also see Katherine Carlitz, "The Social Uses of Female Virtue in Late Ming Editions of *Lienü zhuan*," *Late Imperial China* 12.2 [December 1991]: 117–48). The *Nüjie* is the work of the famous Ban Zhao (died 116 C.E.) of the Later Han, a book of long-lasting influence throughout East Asia. The author of *Nüze* was Tang Taizong's empress.

8. Preface, *Naehun* in *Naehun-Yŏsasŏ* (rpt. Seoul: Asea munhwasa, 1974). The earliest extant edition of *Naehun*, preserved in a Japanese library, was reprinted by Kim Chiyong, ed., *Naehun* (Seoul: Yŏnse taehakkyo, Inmun kwahak yŏn'guso, 1969).

9. Kim Chiyong has pointed out that Sohye made no reference to and thus may not have known the Chinese work with the same title compiled by the consort of the second Ming emperor in 1405 and printed two years later. For a discussion of the publication history of the Korean *Naehun* and a brief comparison with the Chinese work, see Kim Chiyong, ed., *Naehun*, pp. 5–9.

10. Yi Tŏngmu, *Sasojŏl*, trans. Kim Chonggwŏn (Seoul: Myŏngmundang, 1985), pp. 199–200. This work dates from the late eighteenth century.

11. Yi Sangjŏng, "Sŏ Im Yŏlbujŏn hu," *Taesan sŏnsaeng munjip*, 45:19a–b. I was unable to identify the book to which Yi refers.

12. Written by women for women, the *Nüjie* (Precepts for women) by Ban Zhao, *Neixun* (Instructions for the inner quarters) by the consort of the Yungle emperor (r. 1403–24), the *Nü lunyu* (Analects for women) by Song Ruozhao (Tang dynasty), and the *Nüfan jielu* (Concise account of basic regulations for women) by Wang Xiang's mother were combined into the *Nü sishu* by Wang Xiang (Qing dynasty). For some notes on these works, see Sharon Shih-jiuan Hou, "Women's Literature," in *The Indiana Companion to Traditional Chinese Literature*, ed. and comp. William H. Nienhauser Jr. (Bloomington: Indiana University Press, 1986).

13. Yi Tŏksu put these books in chronological order: *Yŏgye*, *Yŏnonŏ*, *Naehun*, and *Yŏbŏm ch'ŏmnok*. He also added brief biographical notes on the authors at the beginning of each work. A reprint was published by Asea munhwasa in 1974.

14. Yu Hŭich'un, *Miam sŏnsaeng-jip*, 4 (no pagination).

15. Song Siyŏl, *Songja taejŏn*, 211:21a.

16. Yun Chŭng, *Myŏngjae sŏnsaeng yu'go*, 32:23a.

17. Yi Tŏngmu, *Sasojŏl*, p. 238.

18. Yi I, *Yulgok chŏnsŏ*, 18: 31a.

19. Song Siyŏl, *Songja taejŏn*, 187: 43b-35a.

20. Ibid., 211:28a–b.

21. Ibid., 215:26b–27a.

22. Yi I, *Yulgok chŏnsŏ*, 18:62a.

23. Yi Tŏngmu, *Sasojŏl*, p. 271.

24. Song Siyŏl, *Songja taejŏn*, 211:24a–b.

25. Ibid., 187:11b–12a.

26. Yun Chŭng, *Myŏngjae sŏnsaeng yu'go*, 32:29a–30b.

27. Yi Ik, *Sŏngho saesŏl*, as quoted by Kim Yongsuk, "Yijo yŏinsang yŏn'gu," *Asea yŏsŏng yŏn'gu* 10 (1971): 124.

28. For an example, see Yi I, *Yulgok chŏnsŏ*, 17:20a.

29. Yi Hwang, *T'oegye chŏnsŏ*, 46:4b–5a (Yi's tomb inscription of his mother); Yi Tŏngmu, *Sasojŏl*, p. 237. A similar example is in Song Siyŏl, *Songja taejŏn*, 200:7b.

30. The *Andong Chang-ssi silgi* is preserved as a woodblock print, dating from the mid-nineteenth century. One of the main compilers was Madame Chang's nonagnatic great-great-grandson, Yi Sangjŏng, who was famous as a scholar and an official.

31. For Yi Simyŏng's biography, see *Andong punmyo* (Andong: Andong munhwawŏn, 1994), pp. 611–22.

32. In recent years a growing number of women's letters have come to light. It is clear that from the time of its invention *han'gŭl* was widely used for official and unofficial purposes despite the scholar-officials' preference of classical Chinese as the "language of culture." From the late seventeenth century, the native script was widely used especially by women. The oldest extant *han'gŭl* letter written by a woman dates from 1571. This material has not yet been fully analyzed by historians. For details, see Kim Ilgŭn, *On'gan ŭi yŏn'gu* (Seoul: Kŏnguk taehakkyo ch'ulp'anbu, [1989] 1991).

33. The *Hunmin chŏngŭm*, Korea's indigenous alphabet, was created under the guidance of King Sejong (r. 1418–50) and promulgated in 1446. It later came to be known as *han'gŭl*.

34. Yi Tŏngmu, *Sasojŏl*, p. 272.

35. *Hanjungnok* (Records written in silence), available in an English edition as *The Memoirs of Lady Hyegyŏng: The Autobiographical Writings of a Crown Princess of Eighteenth-Century Korea*, translated with an introduction and annotations by JaHyun Kim Haboush (Berkeley: University of California Press, 1996), p. 49.

36. Song Siyŏl, *Songja taejŏn*, 187:12a.

37. For a description of the Korean wedding ceremony, see Deuchler, *Confucian Transformation of Korea*, pp. 251–57.

38. For a description of life in the husband's household at the beginning of the Chosŏn, see Deuchler, *Confucian Transformation of Korea*, pp. 258–64.

39. Song Siyŏl, *Songja taejŏn*, 187:32b.

40. Yi I, *Yulgok chŏnsŏ*, 14:28a–b.

41. Yi Tŏngmu, *Sasojŏl*, pp. 246–47.

42. According to the Janellis, the relationship between Korean brothers is generally characterized by mutual help and cooperation, not by hostility, despite unequal inheritance. See Roger L. Janelli and Dawnhee Yim Janelli, *Ancestor Worship and Korean Society* (Stanford: Stanford University Press, 1982), pp. 104–6. This interpretation differs to some extent from my historical data that document fraternal conflict over land and eventual separation. For this reason, moral pressure on brothers to cooperate and work together is very strong in Korea.

43. Yi Tŏngmu, *Sasojŏl*, pp. 251–52.

44. The law was relaxed in the second half of the eighteenth century, and a number of secondary sons did take the examinations. For details, see Martina Deuchler, " 'Heaven Does Not Discriminate': A Study of Secondary Sons in Chosŏn Korea," *Journal of Korean Studies* 6 (1988–89): 121–63.

45. Yi Tŏngmu, *Sasojŏl*, p. 254.
46. See Deuchler, *Confucian Transformation of Korea*, pp. 273–76.
47. Yi Tŏngmu, *Sasojŏl*, pp. 200–201, 255.
48. Song Siyŏl, *Songja taejŏn*, 211:20a.
49. Yi I, *Yulgok chŏnsŏ*, 18:35a–b.
50. Yi Tŏngmu, *Sasojŏl*, pp. 211, 226.
51. Ibid., p. 261.
52. Yun Chŭng, *Myŏngjae sŏnsaeng yu'go*, 37:34b.
53. Ch'oe Hŭngwŏn (1705–86), *Paekpuram sŏnsaeng-jip*, 7:2a.
54. Yun Chŭng, *Myŏngjae sŏnsaeng yu'go*, 38:27a; Yi I, *Yulgok chŏnsŏ*, 18:35b.
55. Yi Tŏngmu, *Sasojŏl*, pp. 260–61.
56. Ibid., pp. 255–56.
57. Chŏng Ku, *Han'gang-jip*, 10:12b.
58. Song Siyŏl, *Songja taejŏn*, 211:19a.
59. Yi Tŏngmu, *Sasojŏl*, p. 259.
60. Song Siyŏl, *Songja taejŏn*, 200:12a–b; 211:28b.
61. Yi Tŏngmu, *Sasojŏl*, pp. 228, 272.
62. Yun Chŭng, *Myŏngjae sŏnsaeng yu'go*, 37:34b.
63. Song Siyŏl, *Songja taejŏn*, 187:22b–23a. This was the daughter of Hong Ikhan (1586–1637), a Namyang Hong. Hong-ssi also collected her father's papers.
64. Yun Chŭng, *Myŏngjae sŏnsaeng yu'go*, 35: 1a; Yi Tŏngmu, *Sasojŏl*, pp. 256–58.
65. Yi Tŏngmu, *Sasojŏl*, pp. 258–59. For a discussion of women's response to Confucianism and shamanism, see Boudewijn Walraven, "Popular Religion in a Confucianized Society," in *Culture and the State in Late Chosŏn Korea*, ed. JaHyun Kim Haboush and Martina Deuchler, Harvard East Asian Monographs No. 182 (Cambridge, Mass.: Asia Center, Harvard University, 1999), pp. 160–98.
66. Yi I, *Yulgok chŏnsŏ*, 17:20a.
67. Song Siyŏl, *Songja taejŏn*, 187:28b; 215:29b.
68. Ibid., 215:28a.
69. Yi I, *Yulgok chŏnsŏ*, 14:27b–30b. This piece is dated 1553.
70. For an example, see *Yŏsasŏ*, 4:20a–b.
71. *Kyŏngguk taejŏn*, pp. 34, 208; Deuchler, *The Confucian Transformation of Korea*, pp. 276–80. This law was not applicable to secondary wives.
72. For an example, see Yi Ik, *Sŏngho saesŏl* (rpt. Seoul: Kyŏngin munhwasa, 1970), vol. 1, p. 249.
73. For a discussion of governmental policy concerning commemorative arches, see Pak Chu, *Chosŏn sidae ŭi chŏngp'yo chŏngch'aek*. Pak gives statistical evidence for the fifteenth through seventeenth centuries based on the *Chosŏn wangjo sillok*.
74. The physical aspects of virtue are a subject that deserves further study. In the literature examined for this chapter, references to physical violence inflicted by women on their own bodies are rare indeed.
75. Chŏng Yagyong, *Tasan nonch'ong*, trans. Yi Iksŏng (Seoul: ŭryu mun'go 91, 1972), pp. 119–24.
76. A study of female suicides during the colonial period (1910–45) suggests as further motives difficulties with mothers-in-law, jealousy of concubines, and childlessness after five years of marriage. See Homer Williams and Laurel Kendall, "Women and Suicide in Colonial Korea: A Comparative Perspective," unpublished paper, 1982.

77. For a discussion of vernacular literature, see JaHyun Kim Haboush, "Filial Emotions and Filial Values: Changing Patterns in the Discourse of Filiality in Late Chosŏn Korea," *Harvard Journal of Asiatic Studies* 55.1 (June 1995): 129–77.

78. For the authorship, dating, and brief content summaries, see W. E. Skillend, *Kodae Sosŏl: A Survey of Korean Traditional Style Popular Novels* (London: School of Oriental and African Studies, 1968).

79. Saimdang is Madame Sin's pen name. Her personal name is unknown, as a woman was recorded in her family's genealogy only under her husband's name. For a detailed account of her life and work, see Yi Sŏngmi, "Chosŏn sidae yŏryu hwaga yŏn'gu," *Misul charyo* 51 (June 1993): 98–149.

80. Some seventeen female painters are known to have been active from the late Koryŏ to the end of the Chosŏn. But the works of only five have survived. Yi Sŏngmi, "Chosŏn sidae yŏryu hwaga yŏn'gu," p. 98.

81. Yi I, *Yulgok chŏnsŏ*, 18:35a–36b.

82. Landscapes were rarely topics treated by women, animals and people never. Yi Sŏngmi, "Chosŏn sidae yŏryu hwaga yŏn'gu," pp. 102–5.

83. Yi Sŏngmi, "Chosŏn sidae yŏryu hwaga yŏn'gu," pp. 138–46.

84. An Kyŏn (n.d.) was a famous painter at the beginning of the Chosŏn dynasty.

85. Ŏ Sukkwŏn, *P'aegwan chapki* as quoted in O Sech'ang, *Kŭnyŏk sŏhwajing* (rpt. Seoul: Sinhan sŏrim, 1970), p. 84. Yi Sŏngmi's article drew my attention to this quote.

86. *Han'guk inmyŏng taesajŏn*, p. 1009. Translations of her "A Woman's Sorrow" (Kyuwŏn ka) and "Poor Woman" (Pinnyŏ ŭm) are in *Anthology of Korean Literature from Early Times to the Nineteenth Century*, comp. and ed. Peter H. Lee (Honolulu: University of Hawaii Press, 1981), pp. 116–18, 158; Yi Yongsuk,"Yijo yŏinsang yŏn'gu," p. 125. Some 140 poems are extant. There is also a Japanese edition.

87. These summary remarks on Im Yunjidang are based on Yi Yŏngch'un, "Im Yunjidang ŭi sŏngnihak," *Ch'ŏnggye sahak* 12 (April 1996): 125–75. Her correspondence in *han'gŭl* and her poetry were apparently left out by the compilers of her work.

88. Cited in Yi Yŏngch'un, "Im Yunjidang," pp. 129, 135.

# CHAPTER SEVEN

# State Indoctrination of Filial Piety in Tokugawa Japan

*Sons and Daughters in the* Official Records of Filial Piety

*Noriko Sugano*

The household (*ie*), a corporate unit comprising ancestors, family members, and descendants, constituted the basic socioeconomic unit in early modern Japan, also called the Tokugawa period (1600–1868). This principle held true for the shogun at the apex of government (who distinguished himself from his kin by using Tokugawa as his surname), the daimyo who ruled their domains at the shogun's behest but without his interference, and the warriors (samurai) who served them and ran their administrations from the cities and castle towns, as well as the commoners—peasants, merchants, and artisans. In practice, the organization of the household varied from class to class; for example, concubinage was common among the rulers but rare among commoners. But this does not detract from the importance of the household for all.

The household constrained the choices open to both men and women, because this was a society in which status and residence were fixed from one generation to the next. No movement from peasant to samurai or from rural areas to urban was permitted, at least in theory. Marriage in the case of rulers and ruled was supposed to be for the sake of the household, with scant regard for individual inclinations. Women, and men too, spent their lives under the supervision and control of the patriarchal system, symbolized in ceremonies performed for the ancestral spirits by the male head of household (although he might well have been adopted if no direct descendants were available) and in the virtue of filial piety, the obedience and respect owed to parents.

Given the importance of the *ie*, it is not surprising that the ruling authorities considered its maintenance over time crucial to governance and the stability of the realm. In their vision of the ideal world, all the families in existence in 1600 would continue to perpetuate themselves at the same political, social, and economic level indefinitely. In reality, however, during the course of the commercial developments of the seventeenth and eighteenth centuries, some houses, especially among the commoner classes, became increasingly wealthy, and others declined or disappeared. Meanwhile, many members of the ruling class found themselves sinking into genteel poverty. Unable to control the effects of economic growth, the shogun and daimyo resorted to didactic measures intended to shore up the individual's sense of responsibility and commitment to his parents, his ancestors, and his descendants. Among the most popular were a system of rewards for exemplars of moral virtues and the use of education to spread the knowledge of these rewards throughout the country.

To examine the strategies that the Tokugawa shogun and daimyo used to indoctrinate the commoner classes, we need to pay special attention to filial piety, one of the five virtues that established in Confucian thought the proper order of the five basic human relationships, or the "five relations": lord-retainer (loyalty), parent-child (filial piety), husband-wife (chastity), elder brother–younger brother (harmony), and friend-friend (affection).[1] In the case of women, both parents and parents-in-law were considered appropriate objects of filial piety. The problem of women's divided loyalty that vexed the Chinese imperial officials, analyzed in chapter 9 in this volume, did not seem to be of concern to the Tokugawa authorities.

This chapter discusses the ways in which the shogun's government, the *bakufu*, tried to propagate the virtue of filial piety and its specific meanings. I have used for my source materials the *Official Records of Filial Piety* (Kankoku kōgiroku). This collection documents the awards given by the Tokugawa *bakufu* and the daimyo, usually rice or money, or on rare occasions a tax reduction or a grant of land, to people who had performed virtuous deeds. In that it was widely disseminated as a text for commoners to study and learn, it can be said to reflect the educational policy of the state. Although the recipients listed in this record were commended for various types of virtuous deeds, the reason most frequently cited was that they were people who performed filial acts (*kōkōmono*).

I am particularly interested in the ideological goals of the *bakufu* in giving awards to filial people and publicizing their virtues through the *Official Records*. Whereas the vast majority of cases in this voluminous text pertained to men, I focus on some of the cases involving women, especially insofar as they suggest changes in women's marriage options from the seventeenth through the eighteenth century. My conclusion is that both the awards for filiality and the publicity concerning them served the primary purpose of shoring up the *ie* as a key social institution. Furthermore, this accent on filiality suggests a class variation in the moral landscape. The ethos of the samurai ranks was dominated by loyalty, which came to mean a commitment to maintaining the lord's house. It becomes clear from reading the didactic texts aimed at commoners, however, that the defining value for them was not loyalty but filial piety.

## THE TEXT OF THE *OFFICIAL RECORDS OF FILIAL PIETY*

The *Official Records* was a product of the so-called Kansei reform decade of the 1790s. Whereas "Biographies of Filial Subjects," which record the many people who were rewarded for good deeds, can be found all over Japan and from many different periods, the *Official Records* was the first text compiled and published by the *bakufu* as part of an educational policy directed at commoners. The Kansei reforms represent the *bakufu*'s second attempt to rejuvenate itself by returning to its founding principles, with emphases on reviving the economy, restoring the morale of the samurai administrators, and promoting the practical application of Confucian ethics. On the advice of the Confucian scholar Shibano Ritsuzan (1736–1807), Matsudaira Sadanobu (1758–1829), the chief senior councillor whose mandate was to restore the *bakufu* to its days of greatest glory, ordered scholars at the *bakufu* academy headed by the Hayashi family to work on this project.

In 1789 the *bakufu* issued a directive throughout Japan requesting names from existing records of exemplars who had performed good deeds. The request was couched in all-inclusive terms:

> Regardless of whether people reside on *bakufu* or private land, or dwell in cities or villages, if there be people who have been rewarded for filial acts or extraordinary good deeds, the officials should copy and turn over their names, their geographical location, and their words and deeds found in any record from the past.[2]

In the decade that followed, local officials submitted troves of names and deeds. The *bakufu* organized this information and issued it in 1801 under the title *Official Records*. The text consists of fifty chapters organized by domain and covers all of Japan, except, for unknown reasons, the Hida domain.

The *bakufu* intended to make the *Official Records* widely available for sale in local bookshops. Anecdotal evidence suggests that a variety of people ended up acquiring it, including women. Precise information about the dissemination of the text, however, is scarce. Thus far I have not located any indication of the total number of copies produced. We know, however, that a complete string-bound edition from 1801 is housed in the National Diet Library in Tokyo today and that every prefectural and local library possesses at least the chapter pertaining to its region. This suggests that instead of the entire text the *bakufu* sold or sent only the relevant chapters to each domain.

The total number of virtuous individuals listed in the *Official Records* is well over 8,600.[3] About 900 of them, involved in 787 cases, were presented with short biographies detailing their commended deeds. Whereas the oldest award is dated 1602, very few cases were entered into the official record for the next eighty years. In the early 1680s, however, the *bakufu* evidently stepped up the strategy of indoctrinating the populace by means of awards for exemplary behavior. Thereafter commendations were made every year, and the number of awards increased as time progressed.

In the *Official Record*, each commended individual is listed under the domain that gave the award, as well as by county, village, and the period in which the individual lived. Also recorded is the recipient's name, occupation, social status, and age and the reason for the award. In a few cases, some of these categories are left blank, as are some of the biographical entries. As stated in Item 11 of the "Rules of Compilation," this is because officials were sometimes unable to find accurate data. They left spaces in the hope of filling in the relevant information later, suggesting that the authorities considered this an open-ended text, with sequels to follow.[4]

The uniform format of the *Official Records* creates an impression of a unified political and moral realm. At the beginning of each chapter devoted to a domain appears a list of all commended individuals residing there. A circle next to a certain name indicates that a biographical commentary for that individual can be found in the pages that follow. These narratives contain descriptions of virtuous acts as well as information on the awarding authority, date of conferral, and words of praise. This uniform format belies the fact that the process of recording the stories and the system of rewards varied from domain to domain.

To illustrate the general trajectories of the geographic distribution of commended behavior and change through time, I have compiled the aggregate data from the *Official Records* in two tables. Table 7.1 presents the total number of cases in the text organized according to time periods and categories of virtue; Table 7.2 presents the same information for selected cases about which biographical information is known.[5] The overarching and growing importance of filial piety is evident from both.

## INDOCTRINATION OF COMMONERS

Despite its name, the *Official Records* is not devoted exclusively to filial piety. In fact, eleven categories of virtuous deeds were deemed noteworthy: filial piety, loyalty, loyal filiality, chastity, harmony between siblings, harmony in household, harmony in lineage, compliance with prevailing customs, purity, extraordinary acts, and diligence in agriculture. Notably, expressions such as "filial piety," "loyalty," and "chastity" refer to Confucian virtues found also in didactic texts in Korea and China, but such categories as "extraordinary acts" or "diligence in agriculture" were used only in Japan (see Table 7.1 and the Glossary).

The first category, "filial piety," comprised the majority, or more than 60 percent, of the cases. Moreover, it was often considered an overarching virtue under which other virtues can be subsumed. In the case of "loyal filiality," a composite virtue referring to sincerity in serving one's lord and parents, filial piety was construed as coextensive with loyalty. The centrality of filiality for males and females is explicitly stated in Item 2 of the "Rules of Compilation" of the *Official Records*, albeit females were admonished to be both filial and chaste:

> Since filial piety is very important to the norms of human conduct, even if a filial individual performed many other virtuous acts, his case would be listed under the category of filial piety. For women, however, filial piety and chastity are of equal weight. Thus their virtuous acts will be listed under whichever category was considered to be more prominent in their deeds.[6]

TABLE 7.1 Total Number of Cases in the *Official Records of Filial Piety*, by Reign Eras and Categories of Virtue

| Reign Era | Filial Piety (kōkō) | Extraordinary Acts (kitoku) | Loyalty (chūgi) | Loyal Filiality (chūkō) | Diligence in Agriculture (nōgyo shiussei) | Chastity (teisetsu) |
|---|---|---|---|---|---|---|
| 1602 | 1 | | | | | |
| 1615–23 | | | | | | |
| 1624–43 | | 1 | | | | |
| 1644–47 | 1 | | | | | |
| 1648–51 | | | | | | |
| 1652–54 | 27 (11) | 7 (1) [1] | | | | |
| 1655–57 | 6 (1) | 3 (1) | 5 | 1 | | |
| 1658–60 | 1 | | 1 | | | |
| 1661–72 | 10 (1) | 20 (1) | | | 1 | 4 (4) |
| 1673–80 | 4 (1) | 2 | | | 3 | |
| 1681–83 | 7 | 1 | | | | 1 (1) |
| 1684–87 | 23 (7) | 7 | 1 | | 3 (1) | 1 (1) |
| 1688–1703 | 75 (12) | 24 (1) | 9 (2) | 6 | 14 (1) | 3 (3) |
| 1704–10 | 32 (10) | 14 | 2 | 1 | 2 (1) | 1 (1) |
| 1711–15 | 16 (5) | 3 | 1 | | | |
| 1716–35 | 329 (87) | 78 (6) | 39 (6) | 10 | 10 | 11 (11) |
| 1736–40 | 108 (37) | 33 (2) | 11 (1) | 2 (1) | 2 | 6 (6) |
| 1741–43 | 82 (23) | 12 (3) | 17 (4) | 1 | 6 (1) | 3 (3) |
| 1744–47 | 182 (47) | 37 | 29 (4) | 5 | 2 (1) | 6 (6) |
| 1748–50 | 99 (19) | 22 (1) | 14 (4) | 2 (2) | 6 | 5 (5) |
| 1751–63 | 627 (178) | 128 (4) [1] | 64 (11) | 5 | 18 (1) | 10 (10) |
| 1764–71 | 534 (145) | 113 (1) [2] | 41 (8) | 9 (1) | 26 (3) | 23 (23) |
| 1772–80 | 815 (246) [1] | 183 (3) [7] | 69 (13) | 6 | 55 (12) | 60 (60) |
| 1781–88 | 1352 (384) | 400 (21) | 188 (32) | 16 (3) | 188 (19) [1] | 42 (42) |
| 1789–97 | 1149 (288) | 322 (9) [3] | 73 (9) | 8 (1) | 64 (3) [2] | 33 (33) |
| Era not known | 10 (1) | 10 (1) | | | 7 | 1 (1) |
| TOTAL | 5490 (1503) [1] | 1420 (55) [14] | 564 (94) | 72 (8) | 407 (42) [4] | 210 (210) |

( ) Number of female awardees included.
[ ] Number of cases in which multiple individuals were commended.

| Harmony between Sibs (kyōdai mutsumaji) | Harmony in Household (kanai mutsumaji) | Harmony in Lineage (ichizoku mutsumaji) | Compliance with Prevailing Customs (fūzoku yoroshi) | Purity (keppaku) | Subtotal |
|---|---|---|---|---|---|
|  |  |  |  |  | 1 |
|  |  |  |  |  | 1 |
|  |  |  |  |  | 1 |
|  |  |  |  |  | 34 (12) [1] |
|  |  |  |  |  | 15 (2) |
|  |  |  |  |  | 2 |
| 7 |  |  | 3 [3] |  | 45 (6) [3] |
|  |  |  |  | 1 | 10 (1) |
|  |  |  |  |  | 9 (1) |
| 1 (1) | 2 |  |  |  | 38 (10) |
| 9 | 7 |  |  | 1 | 148 (19) |
| 2 |  |  | 1 [1] |  | 55 (12) [1] |
|  |  | 2 |  |  | 22 (5) |
| 18 | 3 |  | 1 [1] |  | 499 (110) [1] |
|  | 4 [1] |  |  | 1 | 167 (47) [1] |
| 1 |  | 1 |  | 1 | 124 (34) |
| 2 | 5 |  | 1 [1] | 1 (1) | 270 (58) [2] |
| 3 |  |  | 3 [3] |  | 154 (31) [3] |
| 13 | 6 [1] |  | 17 [8] |  | 888 (204) [10] |
| 7 | 10 [2] |  | 9 [2] | 2 | 774 (181) [6] |
| 10 (2) | 13 (4) [1] | 11 | 73 [6] | 3 (1) | 1298 (341) [15] |
| 35 (2) | 16 |  | 21 (1) [4] | 10 (2) | 2268 (506) [5] |
| 12 (1) | 14 [5] |  | 22 [10] | 6 (1) | 1703 (345) [20] |
| 2 |  |  |  |  | 30 (3) |
| 122 (6) | 82 (4) [10] | 12 | 151 (1) [39] | 26 (5) | 8556 (1928) |

TABLE 7.2 Selected Cases in the *Official Records of Filial Piety*,
Showing Gender Division and Cases with Multiple Awardees

| Period | Filial Piety | Extra-ordinary Acts | Loyalty | Loyal Filiality | Diligence in Agriculture | Chastity |
|---|---|---|---|---|---|---|
| 1644–47 | 1 | | | | | |
| 1648–51 | | | | | | |
| 1652–54 | 3 (1) | | | | | |
| 1655–57 | 5 (1) | | | | | |
| 1658–60 | | | | | | |
| 1661–72 | 3 | | | | | 2 (2) |
| 1673–80 | 1 | | | | | |
| 1681–83 | 5 | 1 | | | | |
| 1684–87 | 8 (3) | 3 | 1 | | | |
| 1688–1703 | 15 (1) | 3 (1) | 4 (1) | 4 | | 2 (2) |
| 1704–10 | 9 | 2 | 2 | | | 1 (1) |
| 1711–15 | 1 (1) | | 1 | | | |
| 1716–35 | 43 (6) | 5 | 13 | 1 | 1 | 5 (5) |
| 1736–40 | 23 (7) | 3 | 4 (1) | 1 (1) | | 3 (3) |
| 1741–43 | 7 (4) | 1 | 4 (1) | 1 | 1 | 1 (1) |
| 1744–47 | 25 (7) | 7 | 3 (1) | 2 | | 4 (4) |
| 1748–50 | 11 (4) | 4 | 2 (1) | 1 (1) | | 1 (1) |
| 1751–63 | 72 (20) | 9 | 9 | 1 | 2 | 1 (1) |
| 1764–71 | 51 (20) | 10 | 8 (1) | 2 (1) | 1 | 6 (6) |
| 1772–80 | 61 (20) | 9 | 6 (3) | | | 9 (9) |
| 1781–88 | 94 (22) | 21 (5) | 10 (4) | 3 | 5 (2) | 9 (9) |
| 1789–97 | 134 (39) | 11 (1) | 10 (1) | 6 (1) | | 5 (5) |
| Era not known | 7 (2) | 1 | | | | 2 (2) |
| TOTAL | 579 (158) | 90 (7) | 77 (14) | 18 (4) | 14 (2) | 51 (51) |

( ) Number of female awardees included.
[ ] Number of cases that involve multiple individuals.

| Harmony between Sibs | Harmony in Household | Harmony in Lineage | Compliance with Prevailing Customs | Purity | Subtotal |
|---|---|---|---|---|---|
| | | | | | 1 |
| | | | | | 3 (1) |
| | | | | | 5 (1) |
| 1 | | | | | 6 (2) |
| | | | | | 1 |
| | | | | | 6 |
| | | | | | 12 (3) |
| 2 | | | | | 31 (5) |
| 2 | | | | | 16 (1) |
| | 2 | | | | 4 (1) |
| 5 | 3 | | | | 76 (11) |
| | | | | | 34 (12) |
| | | 1 | | | 16 (6) |
| 1 | | | | | 42 (12) |
| | | | | | 19 (7) |
| 1 | 2 | | | | 97 (21) |
| 3 | 1 | | 7 | 1 | 90 (28) |
| 1 | 2 (1) | 11 | | | 99 (33) |
| 8 (1) | 1 | | | 7 (1) | 158 (44) |
| 1 | | | 6 [2] | 3 | 176 (47) [2] |
| 2 | | | | | 12 (4) |
| 27 (1) | 11 (1) | 12 | 13 [2] | 12 (1) | 904 (239) [2] |

The second largest category after filial piety is the rather amorphous category of extraordinary acts. Then follow the categories of loyalty, diligence in agriculture, and chastity. Because of the proximity between filial piety and loyal filiality for both sexes and the relevance of chastity for females, I take all three categories into account whenever possible in the case studies below.

The paramount importance of filiality in the *Official Records* is not an accident. The *bakufu* exercised editorial control over the content, relegating some recipients of domainal awards to the Appendix or excluding them from the text altogether.[7] In Item 7 of the "Rules of Compilation," for example, the *bakufu* compilers cautioned that vendettas avenging wrongs against one's parents were not to be encouraged as "filial" acts; at best they would appear in the Appendix as "extraordinary deeds." An even more extreme case was described in Item 8: "In the streets of Edo, a man severed the fingers of his hands and the toes of his feet in order to convey his desperation over his father's dire circumstances. Although he received a local award, his case was excluded here because it cannot serve as a model for others to follow."[8] In the process of collecting and compiling records of virtuous deeds, the *bakufu* was establishing a set of normative criteria for commoners to emulate. The *Official Records* is not a random collection of virtuous words and deeds. It is a deliberate instrument of indoctrination used by and for the *bakufu*.

To facilitate the reception of the *Official Records, bakufu* compilers used colloquial and dialectal expressions in the biographical commentaries. This rhetorical style suggests that the *bakufu* intended to make the *Official Records* accessible to commoners. That ordinary people constituted the *bakufu*'s target audience is also indicated by the choice of awardees. Item 6 of the "Rules" states:

> Although there have been many wealthy peasants, townspeople, and monks who saved those who suffered from poor harvests, they are not included in *Official Records.* The cases in which Shinto priests and physicians were rewarded for their service, or because of their seniority, are also excluded. In short people of higher social ranks and those who come to the aid of others out of professional duty are excluded. Among retainers, only those of the *wakatō* rank and below are included. In turn, junior warriors of the *kachi* rank—that is, those not allowed to ride on horseback—and above are excluded.

The *wakatō* rank is that of the most lowly retainer status, only slightly above foot soldiers. This exclusion of most of the warrior ranks, professionals, and members of the merchant class bespeaks the expansive didactic purpose of the *Official Records:* if commoners would but make the effort to be virtuous, even they could be honored. As part of a general educational drive, the *Official Records* encouraged commoners to follow examples presented on a nationwide scale and to make these cases the norm for their everyday lives. After 1843 in particular the *bakufu* urged teachers to extend instruction to noble and base, to men and women alike. The aim was not only to impart the basic skills in reading, writing, and math needed to advance in life but also to promote the lofty Confucian goals of reforming local customs and moral fiber.[9] The *Official Records* was to serve as an instrument of indoctrination under the rubric of popular enlightenment and renewal.

## *KŌKŌMONO* IN THE *OFFICIAL RECORDS*

In the Tokugawa period, *bakufu* and domainal directives repeatedly admonished people to study the *Classic of Filial Piety*. Therein filial piety—serving one's parents well—is presented as a principle permeating the realms of Heaven, earth, and humans. The constituent of an unchanging order, filiality is said to govern the rightful conduct of people everywhere.[10] Such tenets served the purposes of political manipulation across time and geography in East Asia.

In compiling its *Official Records*, the *bakufu* highlighted the political and moral primacy of filial piety. But what kinds of behavior did the Tokugawa *bakufu* consider filial? A close examination of the stories of filial children in the *Official Records* reveals that the exact meaning of this virtue is not as immutable as the classics imply. We should note at the outset that the designation *kōkōmono* refers to sons and daughters who performed filial acts; "child" defines a person's social station in relation to his or her parents irrespective of sex or age.

I limit my preliminary case study here to *kōkōmono* from the following regions: (1) Yonezawa domain, Dewa Province; (2) the *bakufu*'s domain in Musashi Province (Edo); (3) Hiroshima domain, Aki Province; and (4) Kumamoto domain, Higo Province.[11] The aggregate data of these four regions is presented in Tables 7.3 through 7.6. In each table the data from each domain are shown in two charts, one by categories of virtue (A) and the other by reign period (B). A cursory reading of the tables reveals that the temporal patterns of commendation varied greatly from domain to domain. In Higo, awards were given evenly throughout the seventeenth and eighteenth centuries. In Dewa and Aki, awards were made only during the eighteenth century. In Edo, they cluster in the Kansei period (1789–1800), that is, the decade during which the *Official Records* was produced.

Below my analysis focuses on those *kōkōmono* in the four domains whose deeds were described in some detail in biographical commentaries. This sample is even more skewed than that of the general list. Personal biographies appeared only after the Meiwa era (1760s) in Dewa and during the Kansei era in Edo, with one exception. In contrast, all the biographies for Higo referred to awards made before the 1780s. I do not analyze these temporal variations here because a lengthy discussion of changes in domainal politics would be required.

In compiling the tables from the narrative biographies, I discovered that many filial children were rewarded for more than one virtuous deed. It is often difficult to determine which deed was considered primary. It might also be the case that while a singular deed might not have garnered a reward, an accumulation of deeds tipped the scales. In spite of such ambiguity, I have concluded that in practice the virtue of filial piety can be boiled down to seven acts that recur frequently:

TABLE 7.3 *Kōkōmono* in Yonezawa Domain, Dewa Province

*(A) By Category of Virtue*

| Category of Virtue | Kōkōmono | Male | Female | Cases with Biography | Cases with Multiple Awardees |
|---|---|---|---|---|---|
| Filial piety | 57 | 39 | 18 | {11} | 14 |
| Extraordinary acts | 10 | 10 | 0 | 0 | 4 |
| Harmony in household | 6 | 5 | 1 | 0 | 3 |
| Chastity | 1 | 0 | 1 | 0 | 0 |
| TOTAL | 74 | 54 | 20 | 11 | 21 |

*(B) By Period of Commendation*

| Period of Commendation | Kōkōmono | Cases with Biography (Male and Female) | Cases with Biography (Female Only) |
|---|---|---|---|
| Kyōhō period (1716–35) | 1 | 0 | 0 |
| Kampō period (1741–43) | 2 | 0 | 0 |
| Enkyō period (1744–47) | 1 | 0 | 0 |
| Kan-en period (1748–50) | 1 | 0 | 0 |
| Hōreki period (1751–63) | 4 | 0 | 0 |
| Meiwa period (1764–71) | 20 | 2 | 1 (wife) |
| An-ei period (1772–80) | 25 | 5 | 3 (mother and daughters) |
| Temmei period (1781–88) | 17 | 3 | 0 |
| Kansei period (1789–1800) | 3* | 1 | 0 |
| TOTAL | 74 | {11} | {4} |

{ } Cases analyzed in this chapter.
*All three people commended in 1789.

(i) Performing memorial services for ancestors; tending the graves of parents; showing respect to mementos (*katami*) of deceased parents
(ii) Preservation of the *ie* household; the establishment or revival of a household (including one's employer's household, *shuka*)
(iii) Sustenance and care of parents, parents-in-law, or younger siblings
(iv) Dedication to family occupation or business, by working hard or learning a new skill
(v) Practicing familial morality, including performance of father-son rites, showing gratitude to parents, fostering harmony in the household, and abiding by parent's words

TABLE 7.4 *Kōkōmono* in Edo (Bakufu Domain, Musashi Province)
*(A) By Category of Virtue*

| Category of Virtue | Kōkōmono | Male | Female | Cases with Biography | Cases with Multiple Awardees |
|---|---|---|---|---|---|
| Filial piety | 77 | 68 | 9 | {17} | 7 |
| Extraordinary acts | 33 | 32 | 1 | 2 | 1 |
| Loyalty | 19 | 18 | 1 | 5 | 1 |
| Chastity | 6 | 0 | 6 | {1} | 0 |
| Loyal filiality | 3 | 3 | 0 | {3} | 0 |
| Harmony between sibs | 1 | 1 | 0 | 0 | 0 |
| Purity | 1 | 1 | 0 | 1 | 0 |
| TOTAL | 140 | 123 | 17 | 29 | 9 |

*(B) By Period of Commendation*

| Period of Commendation | Kōkōmono | Cases with Biography (Male and Female) | Cases with Biography (Female Only) |
|---|---|---|---|
| Kyōhō period (1716–35) | 3 | 0 | 0 |
| Gembun period (1736–40) | 3 | 0 | 0 |
| An-ei period (1772–80) | 1 | 0 | 0 |
| Temmei period (1781–88) | 1 | 1 | 0 |
| Kansei period (1789–1800) | 132* | 20 | 3 |
| TOTAL | 140 | {21} | {3} |

{ } Cases analyzed in this chapter.
*All commended between 1789 and 1797.

(vi) Compliance with the strictures of public morality, including showing respect for one's lord, abiding by laws and compacts, frugality, paying the annual rice tax, and performing corvée labor
(vii) Miscellaneous deeds such as saving a life or preserving strong family bonds

A closer examination of concrete examplars of *kōkōmono* is now in order. As stated above, the first subcategory involves dutiful performance of memorial services for ancestors, whereas the second involves assiduous work in maintaining or reviving the household. A case that combines the two involves Jintarō, an Edo townsman who, at the age of fifty, received an award for loyalty and filial piety in 1796. For fifteen years, since the age of eleven, Jintarō had been apprenticed to a blacksmith named Jūbei. After completing his apprenticeship, he remained as

TABLE 7.5 *Kōkōmono* in Hiroshima Domain, Aki Province

*(A) By Category of Virtue*

| Category of Virtue | Kōkōmono | Male | Female | Cases with Biography | Cases with Multiple Awardees |
|---|---|---|---|---|---|
| Filial piety | 77 | 56 | 21 | {19}* | 10 |
| Extraordinary acts | 5 | 5 | 0 | 2 | 1 |
| Loyalty | 8 | 8 | 0 | 0 | 1 |
| Chastity | 1 | 0 | 1 | 0 | 0 |
| Loyal filiality | 1 | 1 | 0 | 1* | 0 |
| Harmony in household | 3 | 2 | 1 | 0 | 2 |
| Compliance with prevailing customs | Multiple | Unclear | Unclear | 1 | 2 |
| TOTAL | 95+ | 72+ | 23+ | 23 | 16 |

*(B) By Period of Commendation*

| Period of Commendation | Kōkōmono | Cases with Biography (Male and Female) | Cases with Biography (Female Only) |
|---|---|---|---|
| Kyōhō period (1716–35) | 29 | 4 | 0 |
| Gembun period (1736–40) | 2 | 1 | 0 |
| Kampō period (1741–43) | 1 | 0 | 0 |
| Enkyō period (1744–47) | 5 | 0 | 0 |
| Kan-en period (1748–50) | 1 | 1 | 0 |
| Hōreki period (1751–63) | 3 | 1 | 0 |
| An-ei period (1772–80) | 3 | 1 | 1 |
| Temmei period (1781–88) | 13 | 3 | 1 (sister) |
| Kansei period (1789–1800) | 40 | 8 | 3 |
| TOTAL | 97 | {19} | {5} |

{ } Cases analyzed in this chapter.
*One man was commended for both "filial piety" and "loyal filiality."

Jūbei's day laborer and was so hardworking that he revived his master's declining business. This was commended as an act of loyalty. In addition, for decades Jintarō routinely kept up memorial services for his parents by honoring their tablets, keeping fresh flowers on the altar, and making monthly offerings. These simple observances were commended as expressions of filiality.[12]

*Kōkōmono* who served their parents when the parents were alive constitute the third subcategory of filiality. One exemplar was Ichitarō, an Edo man who was eighteen years old when he was commended in 1795. His biography conveys the extent of his devotion: "Rokubei [Ichitarō's father] grew senile and often wet or

TABLE 7.6 *Kōkōmono* in Kumamoto Domain, Higo Province

*(A) By Category of Virtue*

| Category of Virtue | Kōkōmono | Male | Female | Cases with Biography | Cases with Multiple Awardees |
|---|---|---|---|---|---|
| Filial piety | 79 | 56 | 23 | {29} | 1 |
| Extraordinary acts | 12 | 12 | 0 | 3 | 1 |
| Loyalty | 9 | 7 | 2 | 4 | 0 |
| Chastity | 2 | 0 | 2 | 0 | 0 |
| Harmony between sibs | 3 | 3 | 0 | 0 | 1 |
| Diligence in agriculture | 2 | 1 | 1 | 1 | 0 |
| TOTAL | 107 | 78 | 28 | 37 | 3 |

*(B) By Period of Commendation*

| Period of Commendation | Kōkōmono | Cases with Biography (Male and Female) | Cases with Biography (Female Only) |
|---|---|---|---|
| Kan-ei period (1624–43) | 1 | 0 | 0 |
| Kambun period (1661–72) | 2 | 1 | 0 |
| Jōkyō period (1684–87) | 13 | 5 | 3 |
| Genroku period (1688–1703) | 1 | 0 | 0 |
| Shōtoku period (1711–15) | 1 | 1 | 1 |
| Kyōhō period (1716–35) | 11 | 5 | 1 |
| Gembun period (1736–40) | 4 | 2 | 0 |
| Kampō period (1741–43) | 1 | 0 | 0 |
| Enkyō period (1744–47) | 4 | 2 | 0 |
| Kan-en period (1748–50) | 3 | 0 | 0 |
| Hōreki period (1751–63) | 40 | 8 | 1 |
| Meiwa period (1764–71) | 3 | 1 | 0 |
| An-ei period (1772–80) | 21 | 3 | 2 |
| Temmei period (1781–88) | 3 | 1 | 1 |
| TOTAL | 107 | {29} | {9} |

{ } Cases analyzed in this chapter.

soiled his bed. Ichitarō cleaned it during the night without telling anyone else. And he never contradicted his father. This conduct is indeed rare among people of the lower classes."[13]

Then there is the case of the twenty-eight-year-old Mitsu, a townsman's wife from Aki. Mitsu lived with her husband's eighty-seven-year-old adopted mother, who had become almost blind and had difficulty walking. In her better days she was a fast spinner, but in old age her abilities had diminished, and she was greatly troubled. To cheer up the old woman, Mitsu quietly stuffed the thread spun by her eight-year-old daughter into her mother-in-law's thread box. Mitsu was rewarded not for her material or bodily care of the parent but for her thoughtfulness. It is also interesting to note that both grandmother and granddaughter were portrayed as diligent spinners, an important attribute of Confucian womanhood in Chinese didactic texts.

The idealized depiction of women as textile workers is also evident in the story of the filial son Chūhachi, a sixty-year-old hunter from Aki commended in 1760. The commentary reads: "Chūhachi's mother became one hundred years old this year. She is still healthy and weaves hemp cloth to keep herself busy. It is to the credit of Chūhachi's filial care that his mother has lived to be a centenarian."[14] The same kind of care extended to young siblings in lieu of parents was included in this category of filial act. Nurturing young siblings was recognized as equally relevant to the continuation of the household.

The importance of gainful employment for all was underscored in the fourth subcategory, which includes children who took over the family occupation from their fathers, people who strived to live on their own despite a handicap, or those who helped disabled family members learn practical skills. In this category we also find unemployed people scrambling to support themselves. A case in point is the thirty-eight-year-old Edo woman Sayo, who suffered multiple tragedies: her mother-in-law had been blind for twenty years, her fifteen-year-old daughter also lost her eyesight, her son had died three years before her commendation, and then she was widowed. Sayo supported her mother-in-law and daughter by selling branches from the shikimi tree and incense sticks, both popular offerings at Buddhist graves, in the daytime and by taking in sewing jobs at night. In addition, "Sayo had her blind daughter learn acupuncture and massage because she was worried about the daughter's future and thought that learning a skill would help."[15] Sayo's industry and concern for her daughter's livelihood won her a commendation in 1793.

Hana, a forty-four-year-old commoner from Aki, commended in 1780, was another hardworking filial woman. After the death of her husband, she labored in the paddy fields to provide for her grandmother-in-law, parents-in-law, and five daughters, who were either too infirm or too young to help. Single-handedly Hana worked a rice field the size of four *tan* and three *se* (approximately one acre) from morning until night. Unable to afford hired hands, she did everything from plowing to carrying night soil.[16] Like Sayo, Hana was filial in eking out a living for herself and her family.

In addition to providing for the ritual and material needs of one's family, filial piety entails the maintenance of familial and public morality, as evinced in cases grouped under the fifth and sixth subcategories. It is not surprising that the *bakufu* was particularly inclined to promote these kinds of moral deeds, emphasizing as they do the connection between the cultivation of minds and social order. This connection is encapsulated in such phrases as "the rites of father and child" and "the way of father and child," which recurred in the commentaries in the *Official Records*. Implied in the concept of rites or way is the normative expectation that a child must obey the parent even when the latter imposes unreasonable demands. In this insistence on obedience we glimpse the Confucian tenet that familial filiality and public loyalty are intimately linked, a theme that also recurs in this book.

The filial son Daikichi, a thirty-nine-year-old commoner from Dewa, illustrates what compliance to the way of father and child may entail. All the members of his family obeyed Daikichi's father as the household head, but Daikichi walked the extra mile. Whenever the father stepped out or returned home, Daikichi dropped whatever work he was doing to offer proper greetings. When father and son went out together, Daikichi never stepped on his father's shadow, nor did he walk in front of his father. Daikichi received an award in 1769.[17]

It is important to note that on a certain level the filial bond was construed as gender-neutral. Not only were daughters expected to be as filial as sons, but also, as we have seen, mothers received equal attention as the object of filial devotion. The story of Tōichi, a forty-two-year-old hunter from Higo, demonstrates that mother and father shared parental authority: "One day when Tōichi wanted to go out, it was at times sunny and at times cloudy. His father told him to wear high wooden sandals; his mother told him to wear flat straw sandals. So he slipped one kind of sandal on each foot before stepping out the door." This filial son was commended in 1718.[18]

The ideological centrality of the *ie* household emerges from these examples. Filial acts categorized as (i), memorial services for deceased family members, are indispensable for continuing the family line. Cases grouped in (iii) and (iv), caring for parents and siblings or dedication to the family enterprise, exalt efforts on behalf of the family. These deeds often produced the same auspicious results as (ii), the maintenance or reinstatement of the house. At first glance, the behavior that the *bakufu* deemed noteworthy appears diverse, but the underlying rationale for the awards can be reduced to (i), (iii), and (iv). Maintenance and continuation of the household were construed as the highest good for the commoner.

## FILIAL WOMEN

Having argued for the gender neutrality of some categories and their commendees, I focus here on the role of women in maintaining and perpetuating the household. Female recipients of awards in the four regions were by no means as numerous as male recipients. When they did appear, they were concentrated in categories (iii) and (iv). That is, women were commended most often for caring for family members, serving as breadwinners, or eking out a living in the face of adversity. Whereas sheer industry often sufficed, a handful of women displayed impressive income-generating skills to support their families.

One skill demonstrated by female commendees is teaching, as in the story of Sayo, the twenty-eight-year-old adopted daughter of an Edo townsman (no relation to the widow Sayo above). Sayo learned how to read and write and to play the stringed zither while she was in service to a warrior family. After leaving her post, she returned to her neighborhood to educate girls in basic literacy and "the way of the female." Her income allowed her to provide for her ailing parents, for which she was commended in 1791. Yayo, another teacher of women, was a forty-six-year-old from Aki commended in 1790. From her childhood Yayo exerted herself in learning to read and write. She became a teacher at the age of thirteen and managed to support her parents and younger brother for decades. Even while tending her parents she never took leave from her work.[19]

Sayo and Yayo were but two of the many women who served as professional teachers of girls in the late eighteenth century. Chapter 8 in this volume, by Martha C. Tocco, describes the flourishing state of women's education in the Tokugawa period. As far as female filiality is concerned, however, we should note that Sayo and Yayo received recognition not because they were educators per se but because they provided care and sustenance to their parents. We should also note that Sayo and Yayo seem exceptional in their learning: few of the other filial women exhibit such erudition. Most were rewarded for their steadfast devotion to the well-being of others.

Indeed, women were by and large absent from subcategory (ii), preservation of the household by developing a thriving business or bringing in an adopted son. The only case featuring the substantial involvement of a woman is that of Myōki, a fifty-eight-year-old spinster from Higo commended in 1685. Myōki's father, a village official, took the tonsure after a battle with illness and renounced the world. Having "lost" their father, Myōki's family suffered economic hardship. Myōki, who was lauded for her intelligence, reared her younger brother, restored the solvency of the house, and reinstated her brother as village headman. The family grew so prosperous that it could afford male and female servants. Her relatives and neighbors urged her to marry, but she refused and devoted herself to her natal family. When Myōki was fifty-three, her eighty-year-old father finally died, whereupon she immediately took Buddhist vows and became a nun.[20] The narrative dwells on Myōki's dedication to family interest above her own and her efforts to revive the family fortune, not the considerable power she wielded as de facto head of household.

The story of Myōki reinforces the contention that the perpetuation of the house was the paramount concern of the Tokugawa *bakufu* in compiling the *Official Records*. For it was through the *ie* household that the *bakufu* exercised its control over the populace. Insofar as women's filial devotion served to support the household, it was recognized as both a private and a public good, on a par with male filiality. Yet Myōki was more an exception than the rule in the voluminous records. Women's virtual absence from business ventures and decisions affecting the patriline serves as a faint reminder that gender mattered in the social world that produced the filial exemplars.

## MARRIAGE AND FILIAL PIETY

The able manager Myōki resisted social pressure to marry by citing her devotion to the household. This implicit conflict is pervasive in the stories of *kōkomono* in the *Official Records*. In refusing a marriage proposal or pursuing a divorce, many sons and daughters gave the standard justification that they would rather devote themselves to their parents or parents-in-law. This statement, in turn, was often cited as the rationale for the award. Of the eighty or so cases examined from the four regions, I have found eighteen in which men and women made decisions about their marital status. The nature of their decisions can be divided into four categories:

(i) Refusal to marry because of parents
(ii) Refusal to divorce because of parents or parents-in-law
(iii) Refusal to remarry because of parents or parents-in-law
(iv) Compliance with a strong parental wish for marriage

My analysis here focuses on the marital decisions of women only. I propose below that a filial woman may have regarded marriage as interfering with her life choices. Granted, all that we can ascertain from the *Official Records* are the ostensible reasons people gave for their choices, not the complicated negotiations they made with themselves and others. But even on the rhetorical level, we must recognize the apparent tension in justifying such anti-house actions as divorce or rejection of marriage by the ultimately pro-house rationale of filiality.

Of the eighteen decisions regarding marital status in my sample, eight were made by women: of those, six refused to marry and two refused to *re*marry. Among those who refused marriage, three were daughters from Higo who took Buddhist vows in order to remain single for the sake of their parents. We have encountered one of them, the able manager Myōki; the second is Man, the twenty-nine-year-old daughter of a watchman who was commended in 1685, the same year as Myōki; the third is Tatsu, a seventeen-year-old commoner daughter commended in 1713. Although it is not clear why all three came from Higo, it is perhaps not a coincidence that all received awards around the turn of the eighteenth century.

We may also ponder the timing of two other cases of daughters rejecting marriage, Sayo of Edo and Yayo of Aki, commended almost a century later, around 1790. They are rare examples of female teachers who made enough money to support their natal families. Although Sayo and Yayo did not pursue the extreme measure of taking Buddhist vows, their filial devotion was exceptional.

It is admittedly risky to make arguments on the basis of a handful of scattered cases, so I would only offer tentative hypotheses here to encourage further research. Perhaps these daughters signal a shift in the definitions of filiality and female roles from the seventeenth to the late eighteenth century. By the late eighteenth century women like Sayo and Yayo did not have to choose to become Buddhist nuns in order to avoid marriage because the development of a commercial economy meant that they could find other ways to support themselves. To reiterate, in the seventeenth century women took Buddhist vows in order to refuse marriage, which was a refusal to maintain the household. By the late eighteenth century, however, women did not have to choose the life of a nun in order to remain single and filial. They could support their parents and maintain the household at the same time.

The official *bakufu* attitude toward this phenomenon is worth analyzing. A rejection of marriage is in principle a rejection of the perpetuation of the household, because, obviously, not to marry and not to have children means no heirs for the household institution. Thus to praise women who chose to do so seems inconsistent with the traditional policy of the *bakufu* that had made keeping and perpetuating a household a crucial factor in filial acts. However, some women could take care of their parents and help their natal families to survive by deciding not to marry. Therefore, when the *bakufu* praised these examples of filial women, it had to praise the deeds of unmarried daughters at the expense of wives and mothers. The *bakufu* had taken this seemingly contradictory attitude because by the end of the eighteenth century in Japanese society the pattern of the household itself was changing, and the *bakufu* needed to find a way to adapt.

## CONCLUSION

My brief analysis of the *Official Records* provides diverse examples of filial conduct, idealization of which was meant to maintain the household among the commoner classes. There is more that can be said, however. Significant shifts took place from the seventeenth to the eighteenth century regarding the notion of filial piety for women, for the family, and for the household. Women's roles in the family and people's notions regarding these roles also appear to have changed during this period. I consider these changes to have been brought about by the social and economic developments that accelerated in the mid-eighteenth century. These must have had an effect on commoners' concepts of filial piety, family, and household, although the specific dynamics of change await further research.

In the case of daughters in particular, it is striking that what was once undesirable behavior came to be considered filial by the late eighteenth century. This indicates that the social norms governing what ordinary people thought and practiced underwent significant changes. Insofar as the state took its examples of virtuous deeds from the biographies of actual people rather than from canonical texts, this acceptance of new types of filial behavior broadened the range of models of filial piety. In other words, changes in what constituted filial piety stemmed not from the *bakufu*'s efforts to illustrate model filial behavior in the *Official Records* but from the lives of common people, which constituted the basis for the text.

*Translated by Sherri Bayouth*
*Edited by Anne Walthall*

## NOTES

An earlier version of this essay, "17–18 seiki no 'kō' ni tsuite," appeared in *Teikyō shigaku* 12 (1997): 77–96.

1.  As the chapter by Sekiguchi earlier in this volume has described, the ethical system associated with the five relations was introduced into early Japan by way of the Penal and Administrative Codes.

2.  *Zoku Tokugawa jikki* (Tokyo: Yoshikawa kōbunkan, 1966), vol. 1, pp. 48, 9–92. Only handwritten copies circulated; the Tokugawa authorities never issued the *Kankoku kōgiroku* in a printed edition. For a modern typeset edition of the entire text collated by the author, see *Kankoku kōgiroku*, 3 vols. (Tokyo: Tōkyōdō, 1999). All references in this chapter are to this edition. For background information on this compilation, see Sugano Noriko, "Bakufuhan kenryoku to josei," in Sugano Noriko, *Mura to kaikaku* (Tokyo: Sanseido, 1992), p. 223; Sugano Noriko, "17–18 seiki no 'kō' ni tsuite," *Teikyō shigaku* 12 (1997): 77.

3.  The total number of cases is 8,563, some involving multiple participants.

4.  "Rules of Compilation," *Kankoku kōgiroku*, p. 3. In 1807 and again in 1810 and 1811 the *bakufu* issued additional calls for names of people who had received recent commendations or who had been neglected in the previous submission. In 1848 the official Hayashi Akira compiled them into a documentary collection, but the sequel to the *Official Records* was never published. See my *Edo jidai no kōkōmono* (Tokyo: Yoshikawa kōbunkan, 1999), pp. 213–14.

5.  For a table with categories of virtues commended in each of the domains, see *Edo jidai no kōkōmono*, pp. 218–21.

6.  "Rules of Compilation," *Kankoku kōgiroku*, p. 3.

7.  Hayashi Hidekazu, ed., *Kōkyō* (Tokyo: Meitoku shuppansha, 1979).

8.  "Rules of Compilation," *Kankoku kōgiroku*, p. 4.

9.  For opportunities in women's education thus opened up, see chapter 8 in this volume, as well as Sōgō joseishi kenkyūkai, ed., *Nihon josei no rekishi: Bunka to shisō* (Tokyo: Kadokawa shoten, 1993), p. 126. For the transmission of Confucian teachings in Tokugawa Japan, see Sugano Noriko, "Edo jidai ni okeru 'Jukyo' no Nihonteki tenkai," in *Ajia joseishi*, ed. Ajia joseishi kokusai shinpojium jikkō-inkai (Tokyo: Akashi shoten, 1997), p. 228.

10.  For an English translation of the *Classic of Filial Piety* and the *Classic of Filial Piety for Women*, see Susan Mann and Yu-Yin Cheng, eds., *Under Confucian Eyes: Writings on Gender in Chinese History* (Berkeley: University of California Press, 2001).

11.  I selected regions 1, 3, and 4 because they represent diverse areas of Japan governed under different types of domainal controls. Region 2 provides a contrast in being under direct *bakufu* jurisdiction. Furthermore, all four regions supplied a repertoire of cases.

12.  *Kankoku kōgiroku*, p. 150.

13.  Ibid., p. 147.

14.  Ibid., p. 154.

15.  Ibid., p. 143.

16.  For additional information, see Sugano Noriko, "Yōjō to kaigo," in *Nihon no kinsei*, vol. 15, ed. Hayashi Reiko (Tokyo: Chūō kōronsha, 1993), 396.

17.  *Kankoku kōgiroku*, p. 702.

18.  Ibid., p. 1294.

19.  The case of Sayo is in *Kankoku kōgiroku*, p. 132; see p. 1016 for Yayo. For additional information, see Sugano Noriko, "Bakufuhan kenryoku to josei," pp. 237, 252.

20.  *Kankoku kōgiroku*, p. 1291.

# PART THREE

# Female Education in Practice

# CHAPTER EIGHT

# Norms and Texts for Women's Education in Tokugawa Japan

*Martha C. Tocco*

The educational reformer Tsuda Ume (1864–1929) is one of Japan's best known "great women" of the modern period. As the endearing youngest member of the first female delegation sent by the Meiji government to study abroad, six-year-old Ume claimed a permanent place in the affections of subsequent generations of Japanese. She arrived at her destination, Washington, D.C., in February 1872, "in a blinding snowstorm, in ill-fitting, ready-made American garments, and wrapped in [a] big red shawl."[1] Later that spring she sent her mother what appears to have been her first and last letter home that was written in Japanese.[2] The content was fairly ordinary for a little girl writing to her mother: she wrote of her studies, her teachers, and her friends. But Ume's use of characters, grammar, and honorific language was not rudimentary. Her letter provides evidence of the level Ume's education had reached *before* she left Japan, and that level was impressive. What remains puzzling is how Ume, born in the late Tokugawa period (1600–1868) before Japan had a modern school system, came by her education.

The education of Tsuda Ume, daughter of a Tokugawa samurai family, began at her mother's side while she was still a toddler. Ume's mother, Tsuda Hatsu (1843–1909), the youngest daughter of a shogunal vassal family and a product of elite Tokugawa female educational traditions, began teaching Ume her "letters" when she was only three. As a result, Ume could read and write Japanese syllabary and Chinese characters by the time she was six. Although Ume was exceptional in a variety of ways, she was only one of many Tokugawa daughters who began their schooling in reading, writing, and calligraphy at an early age. A government nationwide survey of educational conditions begun in 1883 reported that several local schools (*terakoya*) established before 1868 were managed by women, employed women as teachers, and included girls as students.[3] Tanahashi Aya (1839–1939), one of the original members of the faculty at the government's teacher training school for women, established in 1875, first became a teacher-administrator when she opened her own local school in 1862.[4] Tanahashi, Ume, and other mid-nineteenth-century girls and women were able to study and teach because traditions of female education were firmly established by that time.

Although it is now passé to argue that Tokugawa Japan was stagnant, the period is still widely understood to represent the nadir in the status of Japanese women. Yet there is much evidence to refute this understanding, and the history of women's education is one example. There is substantial evidence of women's education found in a diverse body of Tokugawa materials: the proliferation of moral guides for girls (*jokun*) from the mid-eighteenth century, the inclusion of sections for women's books in publishers' lists of offerings, the increase in the number of educational texts (*ōraimono*) written for women, and women's autobiographies that testify to the level of their education.[5]

Throughout the period education expanded, institutional development increased, and education levels rose. More and more parents sought greater education for daughters as well as sons, increasing enrollments in local schools and private academies (*shijuku*).[6] Traditionally, women instructed young children, other women, and servants in their households; and by the nineteenth century many women taught neighborhood children, boys as well as girls, in these local and private schools. Tokugawa women from the samurai and commoner classes founded and managed local schools and private academies and employed other women there as teachers. These women educators were able to find students whether they taught in castle towns or nearby cities. The increasing visibility of women from both the samurai and the commoner class in the public role of teacher and school administrator shows that teaching had become a suitable occupation for women as a gender group and not just for women of a certain social stratum.[7]

### The Tokugawa Philosophical Canon and Women's Education

Clearly, aspects of Tokugawa philosophy fostered the expansion of education in general and of women's education in particular. Scholars have produced many studies of Tokugawa thought, but ideology about women or women's education has not been included in these. Nevertheless, the historian Herman Ooms's analysis of the earliest stages of Tokugawa ideology has important implications for the history of gender in the period.[8] His reperiodization of the rise in dominance of Tokugawa-era Neo-Confucian thought challenges the plausibility of continuing to assert that women's lives were shaped by one hegemonic discourse throughout the more than two hundred fifty years of Tokugawa governance. It is also clear from his study that female archetypes wielded important symbolic and cultural power in the early ideologies employed to legitimize shogunal rule: they occupied central symbolic positions in early Tokugawa Shinto philosophies; and they retained at least symbolic importance within the imperial family.

In the absence of systematic study, many scholars of Japanese women's history continue to view Japan's versions of Neo-Confucianism in totalizing ways. It is still widely believed that the impact of Neo-Confucian thought on the status of Tokugawa women was devastating, as Confucian tenets confined women within the family, subordinated their interests there, and proscribed their public participation in the political realm. In fact, Neo-Confucian thought on women's education varied greatly, ranging from admonitions that highly educated women posed a danger to the state to warnings that, given their role as mothers, *uneducated* women undermined the stability of the family and by extension the stability of the state. Over the course of the period, many Neo-Confucian philosophers wrote essays on the importance of women's education and commanded parents not to neglect the education of daughters. Among them, Kaibara Ekiken (1630–1714) and Matsudaira Sadanobu (1758–1829) are often quoted to provide evidence of the oppressive influence of Japan's version of Neo-Confucian thought on Tokugawa women's education. Yet in their writings Kaibara and Matsudaira actually recommended that women be well educated.

It is one of the small injustices of history that the remarkable Confucian philosopher and humanist Kaibara Ekiken has for so long been associated with circumscribing women's education in the Tokugawa period. The cause for this misunderstanding rests with a morals text for women (*jokun*) mistakenly attributed to him but actually of unknown authorship.[9] The *Great Learning for Women* (Onna daigaku), with Kaibara listed as author, is still regularly cited as evidence of the inadequacies of women's education in the Tokugawa period. Unfortunately, Kaibara's pedagogical essay, *Methods of Teaching Women* (Nyoshi o oshiyuru hō), written in 1710 as part of his larger work, *Precepts on Japanese Customs for Children* (Wazoku dōji kun), has received little attention. In *Methods of Teaching Women*, Kaibara instructed parents in the proper upbringing and education of girls:

> Boys go outside. They follow the guidance of their teachers, they learn from physical objects, they mix with their friends, and they learn the etiquette of the world with their eyes and ears. They do not learn only from their parents' instruction. The bulk of their education they gain through their eyes and ears. Usually, girls remain inside. They do not go out. In order to learn the etiquette of the world they must rely entirely on the instruction of their father and mother. Fathers and mothers who do not [teach] their daughters properly do not know [how] to love their children. To begin with, the education of girls should not differ from the education of boys.[10]

Boys have the opportunity to learn from the outside world, from teachers and from friends, and can offset unsuitable parental training; but, Kaibara cautions, because after the age of ten girls are not allowed these freedoms, they have no opportunity to correct a faulty education. Therefore, he urged parents to be especially conscientious in the education of their daughters. Kaibara condemned the early-eighteenth-century vogue among men to marry women solely on the basis of physical beauty and implored men to select brides on the basis of intellect and education.

In his introduction to *Precepts for Daily Life in Japan* (Yamato zokkun), Kaibara briefly summarized part of his educational philosophy:

> Thus for the sake of people who are so unfortunate as not to know Chinese characters, I have written in contemporary language about the principles that have been received from ages past. I would only ask that this book be made available for the instruction of husbands and wives who know nothing of worldly matters, and even that it be taught to small children who cannot distinguish beans from barley. I suppose that by trying to teach trivial things and making much use of the abbreviated script of the rustic Japanese of old I will become the laughingstock of scholars who have established a reputation in Confucian studies. But since I have committed myself to this task, I am not fearful of the criticism of others.[11]

Like many Confucian scholars, Kaibara was a committed pedagogue. It is clear from his preface to *Precepts for Daily Life* that he wanted to educate men, women, and children and that he knew that men as well as women often had no education in Chinese characters. Therefore, he made a point of writing in the vernacular in order to teach as large an audience as possible. Women's education benefited from texts like Kaibara's and from the value Tokugawa-era Neo-Confucianisms placed on education as a means to self-cultivation and the means by which to acquire virtue.

As Kaibara did, the Confucian scholar Matsudaira Sadanobu has taken a lashing for writings on women's roles and education that espouse the subordination of women. In Matsudaira's case, the criticism is more appropriate because he is indeed the author of what is attributed to him. He is frequently quoted for having written, "A woman does not need to bother with learning; she has nothing to do but to be obedient."[12] Matsudaira, however, wrote down these thoughts about women's education while still a very young man. At the age of twenty, he wrote *Naniwa'e* (The Bay of Naniwa) as a gift for his new bride, and it is this work that is often quoted as the epitome of Tokugawa thought on women.[13] Although several passages in *Naniwa'e* advocate women's education, this element in his thought has been neglected. For example, Matsudaira urged that women should be educated in the Confucian classics known as the "Four Books"—the *Analects, Mencius,* the *Great Learning,* and the *Doctrine of the Mean*—because these works were preferable to classical Japanese literature as models for moral behavior. He also recommended that women read the *Tale of Genji,* though he eschewed it as a model for conduct.

By the early eighteenth century writings on pedagogy such as Kaibara's *Methods of Teaching Women* reveal that their authors assumed the early education of girls and boys should be similar and should begin at the hands of both parents. None of these texts argued for a link between women's physiological ability to bear children and the ability to teach them. Rather, they assumed that women were appropriate as children's teachers because women were in charge of young children. In other words, women were understood to teach children as an extension of their social role rather than as a consequence of biology.

In Tokugawa Japan concubines often gave birth to the children of elite men. Such a child was incorporated into the father's main household and presented as the child of his official wife. In many cases the children of affluent households were first nourished and nurtured by wet nurses. In such circumstances a child's first teacher might be neither the child's biological mother nor the child's official mother. Long-standing traditions in elite households of concubinage and wet-nursing gave rise to a family culture that included nonconsanguineous members as children's teachers and nurturers. Neither Tokugawa family customs nor advice literature assumed that the physiology of childbearing was the origin of the qualities of nurturance required by child rearing. Rather, parenting in Tokugawa Japan was seen as a skill to be taught. Kaibara Ekiken was only one of several philosophers who attempted to teach parents these skills.

### *Written for Women: The Importance of Readers and Moral Guides*

More than anything else, education in Tokugawa Japan focused on reading and writing, mastering the complicated language that even today requires the lion's share of the time spent in public school. By the late Tokugawa era, images of women reading and writing were everywhere—in the wood-block prints of famous artists, in the illustrations of popular novels, and in the pictures accompanying the basic texts written for women. Noblewomen read and wrote, warrior women read and wrote, commoner women read and wrote, and courtesans (a special class of women in the Tokugawa era) read and wrote as well.

Throughout the Tokugawa period, widely distributed texts provided an element of commonality to women's education at a time when education was not standardized. During the course of their education and throughout their lives, educated Tokugawa women from both the samurai and the commoner class often read the same moral guides and textbooks. The tenets outlined in eighteenth- and nineteenth-century moral guides for girls and women drew heavily on Japan's adaptations of Neo-Confucian ethical principles for their instruction.[14] Although many historians of Japanese women criticize these moral guides because they disagree with what was taught in them, the very existence of these texts, together with publication and republication records, substantiates the breadth and depth of Tokugawa educational traditions for women. The content of women's moral guides has contributed to the negative image of the status of Tokugawa women and of their education, but these guides were only one of several categories of books published for a female audience. Educational texts written specifically for women (*joshi yō ōraimono*) was another category.

According to the historian Ishikawa Ken, the word *ōraimono* was first used to refer to educational texts in the latter half of the eleventh century. Best translated as "basic texts" or "introductory texts," the earliest *ōraimono* provided instruction in basic writing and conveyed general knowledge useful in the daily life of ordinary people.[15] The number, variety, and scope of these texts increased throughout the Tokugawa period, indicating an ongoing expansion of education beyond the narrow circle of nobility and warrior elites to commoner classes. As a distinct category, *joshi yō ōraimono* had existed for noblewomen since the late Nara period (710–84).[16] Before the twelfth century women's education was largely restricted to the noble class and initially consisted of instruction in music, poetry, and calligraphy—the three R's of elite women's education.[17] With the rise of the warrior (*bushi*) class in the twelfth century, women's education expanded to include the women of Japan's new elite.

The historians Ishikawa Ken and Ishikawa Matsutarō have surveyed women's educational materials from the eighth through fifteenth centuries. According to their summaries, over this time women were schooled in the three R's as well as in the graces and civilities that noble and later *bushi* women were expected to acquire before marriage—the rules of etiquette, the maintenance of beauty, and the management of countenance. In addition, young elite women studied practical arts, such as weaving, textile dyeing, and embroidery. The primary goal of this education was to prepare older girls and teenagers for marriage.[18]

From the fourteenth century on, Buddhist and Confucian thought began to influence women's education, and by the end of the seventeenth century, there was additional diversity in women's textbooks. In the early Tokugawa period, Japan's moral texts for women owed a large debt to Chinese Confucian didactic classics. In both China and Japan, such texts included moralistic biographies and novels. Japanese authors adapted popular Chinese-language Confucian texts used to teach morals and ethics to Japanese boys into vernacular editions directed at a female audience. The *Four Books for Women* (Onna shisho), for example, was adapted from the standard Chinese-language work. To facilitate comprehension, this and many other Chinese-language moral texts were presented in *kambun*, Sino-Japanese, or Chinese written by or glossed for reading by Japanese. Japanese philosophers, biographers, and novelists also produced new texts that relied heavily on the Chinese Confucian tradition.[19]

Ishikawa Ken cataloged 1,109 volumes of Tokugawa-period basic texts written for women and divided these into four categories based on content: moral guides, letter-writing manuals, almanacs, and basic academic primers on a single subject such as arithmetic.[20] Ishikawa Matsutarō suggests a different typology. He separates Tokugawa-period women's texts into three categories: one that centered on inculcating social graces and two that centered on inculcating moral principles. Tracts designed to inculcate elite social graces have the longest history of all women's texts, and these often included excerpts from the *Tale of Genji* and poetry from such collections as the *Anthology of [Poems] Old and New* (Kokinshū). Of the texts directed at women's moral and ethical training, one genre presented a straightforward adaptation of Chinese Confucian philosophy. The other emphasized the importance of ethical and moral teachings for women as domestic managers after marriage, a role that Ishikawa Matsutarō suggests gained new importance in the

Tokugawa era. For much of the period, moral guides, particularly this new type, dominated textbook publishing aimed at women.[21]

From the mid-seventeenth century until 1868, when the Tokugawa period ended, the subjects of texts written for women expanded and appealed to a wider female audience. This is especially true from the beginning of the nineteenth century. While the earliest guides to letter writing were limited to examples of formal correspondence, later guides contained information on daily note writing and more popular epistolary forms, indicating an expansion of literacy into daily life. For the whole of the period, Ishikawa Ken cataloged 377 texts that he classified as moral guides. Toward the end of the eighteenth century, however, the number of academic texts for women on subjects such as geography was twice that of moral texts; and in terms of the number published, academic texts for women more than held their own against moral texts during the remainder of the Tokugawa period.[22]

### *The* Great Learning for Women: *One Example of a Tokugawa Moral Guide*

The *Great Learning for Women* was among the most widely published of Tokugawa texts for women and was one of the first of these books to be translated into English in the late nineteenth century.[23] Editions of the *Great Learning for Women* have been in print continuously since the early eighteenth century, but the exact date of its initial publication and its authorship remain unclear. Ishikawa Matsutarō has argued convincingly that Kaibara Ekiken could not have been its author. He also underscored the importance of women's education in the Tokugawa period. According to Ishikawa, the earliest known reference to the *Great Learning for Women* appears in a 1729 catalog of recently published books. The catalog, published in Kyoto, ran to four volumes and included some 3,300 titles; the fourth volume included a section entitled "Reading Material for Women" (Onna shorui) that was devoted exclusively to books for women. One entry in this section cited the *Great Learning for Women Treasure Chest* (Onna daigaku takarabako).[24] The oldest extant copy of the work itself dates from 1733, and it too is entitled the *Great Learning for Women Treasure Chest.* As evidence that Kaibara was not the author of the *Great Learning for Women,* Ishikawa points out that this oldest extant version ends with the phrase "as related by our teacher Ekiken Kaibara" and that the publisher's colophon states that "the *Great Learning for Women* [was] written from the lectures of our teacher Kaibara."[25] This suggests that Kaibara considered women's education important enough to include in his lectures to disciples. Ishikawa examined Kaibara's earlier work, *Methods of Teaching Women,* to see if it mentioned the *Great Learning for Women.* As it did not, Ishikawa concluded that it was improbable that the *Great Learning for Women* was written before 1710. Kaibara died in 1714, and from 1710 until his death, it is well known that he was devoted to other writing projects. Based on this evidence, Ishikawa concludes that the *Great Learning for Women* first appeared after Kaibara's death but before 1729.[26]

Ishikawa argues further that the vocabulary, prose style, and complexity of the *Great Learning for Women* bear little resemblance to Kaibara's other work, but more important, he maintains that the philosophy of women's education espoused in the *Great Learning for Women* differs from that espoused by Kaibara in *Methods of Teaching Women*. According to Ishikawa, the latter work reveals that Kaibara ignored gender differences, asserted the dignity of human nature, and insisted that men and women, without exception, had both a right and a duty to be educated.[27] It seems likely that the *Great Learning for Women* was ascribed to Kaibara to associate his reputation as a Neo-Confucian scholar and pedagogue who advocated women's education with this new moral text. The strategy of the unknown author(s) was successful: the *Great Learning for Women* has been in print for more than two hundred sixty years.

Most examinations of the *Great Learning for Women* and other moral guides have focused on their content and overlooked other aspects. In the Tokugawa period, these guides were used not simply as moral tracts but as textbooks in basic literacy. The moral guides were designed to be used as copybooks to teach vernacular Japanese, and their primary value was educational rather than philosophical. The *Great Learning for Women*, for example, was a primer for women in the reading and writing of Chinese characters.[28] Customarily, women's texts from earlier eras had been written in cursive syllabary. Because the *Great Learning* was written in both the phonetic *kana* syllabary, the simplest form of the Japanese alphabet, and Chinese characters and because almost all of those Chinese characters were glossed with additional phonetic *kana* spellings (*furigana*), instructing the student in the proper Japanese reading for each Chinese character, it and texts like it represented an innovation in women's educational literature. By attaching Kaibara's name to this text, Tokugawa booksellers were able to launch a primer in Chinese characters designed to expand the reading and writing skills of young Japanese girls from both samurai and commoner classes.[29]

Because Tokugawa-era moral texts prescribed a subordinate position to women in the family and in politics, many historians have used them to argue that women's position in society was lower than in any other period of Japanese history.[30] These tracts certainly contain admonitions on proper female conduct. They caution women against extravagance and admonish parents against overindulging their daughters. The *Great Learning for Women* exhorts parents to raise daughters appropriately so that when they marry and enter their in-laws' household the rigid customs that prevail in their new household will not be unbearable.[31] *Women's Imagawa* (Onna Imagawa), a didactic text that dates from the late seventeenth century, cautions women against gossip, envy, extravagantly expensive clothes, arrogance, and a variety of other character flaws many parents still caution their children about today.[32] Both texts encourage women to treat their parents, in-laws, and husbands with respect and to be fair in their treatment of servants.

### Reception of Moral Texts and Gender Difference

Tokugawa women were not the only members of society urged to practice morally correct behavior in a context of hierarchical roles. In many aspects exhortational tomes written for men were similar to those written for women. Tokugawa moral guides for men and boys exhorted them to treat their superiors with proper respect and encouraged them to avoid boldness, loquaciousness, gossip, loose talk, idleness, evil companions, and a variety of other defects. Men and boys were admonished to treat their parents and their teachers with utmost respect.[33] Moral literature directed exclusively at male members of the samurai class exhorted them to devote themselves to duty—to honor their obligations to their lord, friends, parents, siblings, and wives.[34]

Whether they were written for women or for men, subordination was clearly one element in Tokugawa moral guides, and the proliferation of moral texts for women suggests that women were expected to inhabit the same moral world as men.[35] To some degree, the various Neo-Confucian approaches to education in Tokugawa Japan had the same moral goals for both sexes. Not through prayer, or meditation, or good works but only through study could one acquire virtue. Learning, for men and women, was the way to virtue and by extension the way to stability of family and of the country as a whole.

Popular Tokugawa moral guides for women were often published as "miscellanies," or anthologies of women's literature and sold in multivolume editions with one illustrated text printed at the top of the page and another at the bottom.[36] Many editions of the *Great Learning for Women Treasure Chest*, for example, included excerpts from the *Tale of Genji* and a selection of poems from the medieval poetic miscellany *One Hundred Poems by One Hundred Poets* (Hyakunin isshū), as well as advice on beauty, etiquette, and proper letter writing; all of these added to the moral guidance suggested by the title. This format, which mixed educational traditions from previous centuries with Tokugawa moral tracts, diffused the impact of Neo-Confucian moralizing. Repeated exposure diluted it further.

Other aspects of the publishing history of women's moral guides also affected their impact. The historian Joseph Levenson once argued that ideas that do not seem to change over time in fact do so because the context surrounding them changes.[37] Needless to say, the context of women's education changed considerably during the Tokugawa period. The *Great Learning for Women* could not have had the same meaning when read by a young girl in 1865 as it had in 1730. For one thing, the presentation of the text itself was different, and the illustrations that accompanied the text changed with contemporary fashions in illustration to appeal to new generations of readers.[38]

Presenting the Tokugawa moral guides as one part of illustrated, highly glossed anthologies contributed substantially to the popularity they enjoyed. Women's moral guides and other books were published on thick Japanese paper so as to withstand the wear of repeated use. Filled with luscious illustrations, basic primers like the *Great Learning for Women Treasure Chest* were lovely to behold. By the nineteenth century various textbooks designed to be attractive to children were widely available for use in girls' earliest education. Texts such as Matsudaira's *Naniwa'e* and Kaibara's *Methods of Teaching Women* did not enjoy the wide circulation of women's texts and moral guides. Sturdy, brightly colored editions that juxtaposed moral essays with beauty hints and classical romantic poetry held the young reader's attention in ways that sober essays on morality or pedagogy alone would not have done. By the end of the Tokugawa period, more and more women were reading a variety of popularly published materials. Textbooks for the education of girls and women were ubiquitous, and women's moral texts had become part of popular culture. While the essays of Kaibara and Matsudaira moldered in scholarly collections, colorful anthologies of moral guides and textbooks for women were so popular that tiny models of them appeared among the appurtenances in annual doll festival displays.

By the late Tokugawa period, most educated women had studied the *Great Learning for Women* and other popular moral guides under similar teaching methods, and as a result, these women shared significant common ground. Although Tokugawa women's education followed no single pattern, it shared certain features. Daughters from wealthier families, whether they were from the samurai or the commoner class, had richer educational opportunities. Daughters of the imperial family and daughters of domain lord families had some educational traditions all their own, but there was still a good deal of overlap between traditions. Elite marriage customs, which promoted blurring at the edges of class lines, dispersed educational traditions across class boundaries. Imperial princesses married shoguns; women from the shogunal Tokugawa family married emperors; daughters from merchant and well-to-do farm families married samurai. When affluent Tokugawa women married, they carried a multitude of possessions with them to their new households. One of these was their education. At the same time, other factors influenced women's access to education, and not all Tokugawa women (or men) were educated.

### VARIETIES OF LATE-TOKUGAWA WOMEN'S EDUCATION

Although popular texts such as the *Great Learning for Women* circulated widely, geography, region, and locale still presented severe barriers to women's education.[39] These barriers often proved more of an impediment to women's education than did social class. The urban centers of Tokyo, Osaka, and Kyoto, for example, had a larger number of local schools administered by women, higher ratios of girls' attendance at school, and higher numbers of women teachers.[40] Evidence suggests that in central urban areas almost all samurai women were literate and moderately to highly educated. Some cities and towns could boast large numbers of educated women from a variety of classes; but at the same time there were villages and hamlets where seemingly no women and few men were educated.[41] In general, education was more widely available to women who lived in and around major cities and in the castle towns of the Tokugawa domains.

### *The Education of Samurai Women*

Samurai women of the highest rank almost always lived in a castle town. Their education began at home when they were quite young. Houses of upper-class samurai were rambling and spacious, and families were large. Everyone in the household participated in the earliest education of an upper-class samurai daughter. Before she was old enough to hold a writing brush, grandmother or grandfather might tell her valorous tales of the family's warrior past. Mother would read to her heroic stories that exemplified the bravery and discipline required of samurai women. Servants would lull her to sleep with fantastic fables drawn from Shinto traditions. Samurai fathers, often away on official business, would write letters home encouraging the education of their daughters.[42] By the time her lessons in the written syllabary began, the stories she copied would already be familiar to her; by the time she began to write passages from the *Tale of Genji*, she would know them by heart; and by the time she began reading the Four Books with a learned tutor, their ethical precepts would already be part of her moral fabric.

Sugimoto Etsu describes her education in her autobiography, *A Daughter of the Samurai*. Although born after the Meiji Restoration, her experience was typical of nineteenth-century samurai women, and her education began at home.

> We did not have kindergartens when I was a child, but long before the time when I could have been admitted to the new "after-the-sixth-birthday" school, I had acquired a goodly foundation for later study of history and literature. My grandmother was a great reader, and during the shut-in evenings of the long, snowy winters we children spent much time around her fire-box, listening to stories. In this way I became familiar, when very young, with our mythology, with the lives of Japan's greatest historical personages and with the outline stories of many of our best novels.[43]

While initially a samurai daughter's education took place under the tutelage of her mother or grandmother, her academic education might also be supervised by a Buddhist priest or nun, or by a local scholar. The educational history of Aoyama Chise (1857–1947) follows this pattern. Aoyama was the daughter of a middle-ranking retainer of Mito domain, Aoyama Nobu(hisa),[44] and the granddaughter of the Neo-Confucian scholar Aoyama Nobuyuki (1776–1843), one of the Mito scholars who worked on the *History of Great Japan* (Dainihonshi).[45] Chise's father, like his brothers, followed in her grandfather's scholarly footsteps and assisted with the compilation of this history. Chise's formal education with a local scholar began, as her mother's had, at the age of six, apparently the standard age at which Mito samurai daughters' educations shifted from the home to private academies outside.

In 1864 Chise went to study in the private academy run by a neighbor woman named Kozawa, whose eldest son, the same age as Chise, was a student in Chise's father's private academy. There were ten students in Chise's all-girl class, and just as in private academies for boys, such as the one Chise's father ran, Kozawa's students did little from early morning until afternoon but copy handwriting models over and over again. In addition to managing her academy, Kozawa managed her household and children. She did not stay in the classroom, as Chise's father did. Rather, Kozawa would write the day's calligraphy model, read it aloud, and then set the girls to practicing their writing. This accomplished, she would leave to take care of other responsibilities, checking on her students' progress intermittently. When a student became bored, she was at liberty to rest or play for a while and then resume her work. At first the students practiced their writing on pieces of paper already completely blackened with ink. At irregular intervals, Kozawa would give the girls white pieces of paper so that she could check their skill in writing. Once everyone's execution of the model was acceptable, Kozawa would draw the next model and set them to practicing again on black paper.[46]

The students began by learning to recite and write the *i-ro-ha*: the ABC's of the phonetic, forty-seven-character Japanese syllabary. Once the syllabary was mastered, the students would then study the poems of the *One Hundred Poems by One Hundred Poets*. After finishing these basic introductory exercises, students would begin to copy lengthier documents from among the anthologies of basic texts and moral guides that constituted the schoolbooks of girls' elementary education. Almost all of the girls who learned to read and write in this period used the same basic readers: *Women's Imagawa*, the *Great Learning for Women*, *Household Precept Letter Writer for Women* (Onna teikin), and the *Classic of Filial Piety for Women* (Onna kōkyō).[47] Beginning with the first syllable of the first word of the first line, Kozawa would prepare the daily calligraphy model from these texts. First, the students would listen to the teacher read the text out loud, and then they would begin copying it over, syllable by syllable, line by line, repeating the words to themselves silently. In addition to copying textbooks, students' elementary lessons included memorization through recitation, and they learned to recite the names of the Tokugawa domain lords and the names of the fifty-three stations on the Eastern Sea Road circuit (Tōkaidō) by heart, chanting them over and over again as if they were singing a song.

In the 1860s, when political strife plunged Mito domain into chaos, Chise left Kozawa's academy to become the student of a woman by the name of Matsunobe, the highly educated daughter of a Kumamoto domain Confucian scholar. She had been trained in Chinese language, the Chinese classics, sword wielding, and horsemanship; and her husband was the skilled calligrapher Matsunobe Michimaru (Den), who served as Mito domain lord Tokugawa Nariaki's (1800–1860) official physician and confidant. Chise studied with Matsunobe for two years. Under her tutelage, she began reading the Chinese classics—the *Classic of Filial Piety*, the *Great Learning*, and the *Analects*—in Chinese. To read these texts, Matsunobe taught Chise *kambun*, and every evening Chise and her elder brother (who was also learning *kambun*) would study side by side at their father's desk. Matsunobe also introduced Chise to classical Japanese and the serious study of Japanese poetics, using the Kamakura-period *New Anthology of [Poems] Old and New* (Shin Kokinshū) as their text. Chise's course of study—learning Chinese and reading the Chinese classics—was similar to that of the typical samurai boy in a domain academy.[48] The curriculum Chise studied with Matsunobe grounded her in the basics of Tokugawa higher education.[49]

"Granny Matsunobe" was exceptionally well trained, but she was not the only well-educated woman in Mito. Other Mito women living near the Aoyama family enjoyed reputations for scholarship and were models of the benefits of women's higher education. Even the most curmudgeonly Mito samurai father expected his daughter to be literate. At the very least, samurai daughters in Mito learned to read and write, and in the course of such learning, they were exposed to poetry and Confucian moral philosophy. Beyond this, when parental attitude permitted, there were opportunities to pursue higher education. Well-educated women expected to marry, and education seems to have presented no bar to eligibility as a marriage partner. On the contrary, as local academicians, private tutors, and school administrators, it seems that well-educated married women added to their domestic duties professional responsibility for educating daughters of the community.

Natural talent—or parental recognition of natural talent—also influenced the extent of a young samurai girl's education. For example, Hatoyama Haruko's (1863–1938) parents recognized her academic talent and encouraged her rigorous training. Hatoyama (née Watanabe), the youngest child of a large, high-ranking samurai family in Matsumoto domain (now Nagano prefecture), recalled her childhood education in the late Tokugawa era in her autobiography. As with other samurai daughters, Haruko's mother was her first teacher. Haruko's education began with the *i-ro-ha* and proceeded to the poems of the *One Hundred Poems by One Hundred Poets*, which she memorized by playing a card game over and over with her mother and by herself and by copying the poems repeatedly.[50] When Haruko was about ten, she told her mother that she wanted to learn to read the Chinese classics, and with her permission Haruko went to study with a neighborhood scholar of Chinese learning.[51] There Haruko began studying calligraphy and *kambun* and reading the *Analects* and *Mencius*. Hatoyama's parents, who valued education, believed that educational opportunities in rural Matsumoto were limited. Earlier they had sent their only son to Tokyo to study at the famous educator Fukuzawa Yukichi's private academy, Keiō Gijuku; and when Haruko had exhausted neighborhood educational opportunities, she too went to Tokyo to continue her studies.

In addition to parental recognition of natural talent, even religious custom could extend women's education in the Tokugawa period. Sugimoto Etsu remembered the role religious custom played in setting the course of her education:

> My sister received the usual education for girls, but mine was planned along different lines [because] I was supposed to be[come] a nun. I had been born with the navel cord looped around the neck like a priest's rosary, and it was a common superstition . . . that this was a direct command from Buddha. Both my grandmother and my mother sincerely believed this, and since in a Japanese home the ruling of the house and children is left to the women, my father silently bowed to [this] earnest wish. . . . He, however, selected for my teacher a priest[,] . . . [a] scholarly man, who spent little time in teaching me . . . temple worship, but instructed me most conscientiously in the doctrine of Confucius.[52]

Although Etsu did not become a nun, her preparation included training in the classics, "from books intended only for boys," and gave her access to her father's extensive library.

Tokugawa-period evidence suggests that almost all samurai women were literate, but when family encouragement or religious customs did not support additional education, a samurai daughter's basic literacy made it possible for her to continue to study and even to learn the Chinese classics on her own. The classical canon of Japanese education, written in Chinese, was glossed in vernacular Japanese for young Japanese readers, and most of the popular Confucian moral texts were available at bookstores and lending libraries in the Tokugawa period. In many samurai families, the household library was open to all children, but even if it was not, the ready availability of glossed textbooks in urban centers, coupled with the basic literacy provided by samurai women's childhood education, gave these women the tools to continue their own educations.[53]

Samurai women's education took place at home and in neighborhood academies. This education began with basic literacy and often continued to include mastery of *kambun* and Confucian classics, exposing them to an educational canon that paralleled their brothers'. The education of samurai daughters instilled in them the same notions of loyalty and duty characteristic of the men of their class and prepared them for management and service in their marital households. Although samurai women in the Tokugawa period were restricted from the exercise of direct political authority, through similar educations women and men of the samurai class came to inhabit the same moral and ethical world.

### The Education of Commoner Women

Many of the traditions that operated to promote samurai women's education also promoted the education of elite and middle-class urban commoner women. Even in agricultural families, if there was enough discretionary income, money would be diverted to daughters' educations.[54] Two late-eighteenth-century diaries kept by Numano Kokkan and his daughter, Mine, who lived in Kishū, the castle town of Wakayama, suggest one educational course for commoner women in urban settings.[55] The Numano family was extremely wealthy. They owned a local pawnshop and probably functioned as the castle town's local bankers, as wealthy pawnbrokers often did. The head of the Numano house held the hereditary position of village elder, which carried with it the right to an annual audience with the Kishū domain lord. Audience with the lord was a right granted to very few commoners, even wealthy ones. In 1770 Numano Taka, heiress to the main branch of the Numano family, married Rokubei Kokkan, who was adopted into her family to be her husband. Their only daughter, Mine, was born the following year. Taka died when Mine was four, and her father continued to raise her alone.

In his diary Kokkan revealed his affection for his daughter and his sorrow at the loss of his wife. Interwoven with his personal revelations, he recorded information on Mine's early childhood education. After her fifth birthday, Kokkan described Mine's aptitude for learning: "These days Mine has become really good at remembering [everything]. She expresses herself clearly and is very clever. It is a blessing beyond anything. She has been learning the [*One Hundred Poems by One Hundred Poets*] and she already knows twenty poems by heart." When she was eight, Mine began to study reading and writing with a local teacher named Maeno Tame. That same year her father died, and his record of Mine ended. Unfortunately, we have no further direct record of her early education.

At fifteen Mine married the son of a local rice merchant family, the Yukawa family, and the son was adopted into her family as her husband. Her diary from 1791 recounts the daily life of a young, wealthy, merchant wife of twenty-one. That Mine kept a diary, together with the diary's contents, indirectly indicates the level of her education and the role that education played in her adult life. In her summary of Mine's 1791 diary, Hayashi Reiko highlights Mine's educational attainments revealed therein. Mine was sufficiently literate to read Takizawa Bakin's rendition of the Chinese novel *The Water Margin* (Suikoden) for pleasure before retiring for the night.[56] Although most of the responsibilities for the family business were discharged by her husband and employees or servants, Mine was responsible for much of the family correspondence and helped with the bookkeeping when business was unusually hectic. Mine and her husband entertained themselves by reading poetry (*waka*) to each other. As mistress of the household, Mine supervised the servants in the preparation of food used as ceremonial gifts, and she kept the records of gifts given and received, an important family social function. She often referred to the state of the family business and her husband's and son's activities for the day, providing a picture of close-knit family involvements that integrated personal, economic, and urban social life.[57]

The long and well-documented relationship between the national learning scholar Tachibana Moribe (1781–1849) and the provincial artisan family of Yoshida Seisuke (b. 1794) and Yoshida (Kamiyama) Sato (b. 1804), who were his students, provides a wealth of information about commoner education in the early nineteenth century.[58] Tachibana, born in an Ise village and the son of the village headman, worked for a time for an Osaka merchant before establishing himself as a teacher. He spent several years teaching in the village of Kiryū in the Jōshō district (now Gumma prefecture) before moving to Edo in 1829 to establish his own national learning (*kokugaku*) academy. In Edo he became a well-known academician, and his students were primarily wealthy farmers, merchants, and artisans. Yoshida Seisuke and Kamiyama Sato, residents of Kiryū, married in 1823 and worked together in Seisuke's silk-weaving business: Seisuke wove, and Sato did the bookkeeping. In 1824 their daughter, Ito, was born.[59] Moribe's educational philosophy influenced the Yoshidas' child-rearing practices, and eventually they sent Ito to Edo to complete her education under Moribe's tutelage as a member of his household.

Tachibana Moribe was an eclectic, humanistic scholar with a perceptive philosophy of the education of children—both girls and boys. About the time Ito was six years old, Moribe sent to Kiryū a treatise outlining his precepts for early childhood education. In this treatise, entitled *Jimon zatsuki*, Moribe distilled his philosophy on child rearing and childhood education. He wrote this text for students he knew well and whose households he understood, and he filled it with parenting advice:

> [You] should always appear to be interested in your children's conversations even when their conversation does not particularly interest [you].... It is the parent's responsibility to create a close, intimate relationship. Then, should you need to reprimand a child who has done something wrong, the child will comply [with your admonition] if you have established a relationship based on intimacy.

He also suggested ways to establish a foundation for children's future education:

> If you are thinking about making your children study, [begin by] telling them tales, like Momotarō, or by giving them picture books or pictures to copy (*utsushi e*) while they are still little, so that a fondness for books becomes a habit. If, after they grow older, you abruptly start insisting "Study! Study!" children will utterly loathe books.[60]

When Ito was eight years old, she was sent to study at Shōseidō, a private academy in Kiryū. Tamura Kajiko, reputed to have been Moribe's best student, founded and managed Shōseidō, a local coeducational school. Ito, together with other Kiryū girls and boys, spent six years in Tamura's academy studying reading and writing, poetry, Japanese grammar, and the principles of protocol or formal manners (*reigi sahō*). When Ito was fifteen, her parents sent her to Edo to live with the Tachibana family and to continue her education under the direction of Moribe himself.[61]

In Edo Ito studied calligraphy directly with Moribe. Moribe was an advocate of moral self-cultivation, and to this end he had Ito keep a journal in which she recorded her daily struggles with self-improvement. Moribe regularly reviewed her efforts at strengthening her own character. Tachibana Futeru, one of Moribe's children, lectured Ito on the eighth-century poetry anthology, the *Ten Thousand Leaves* (Man'yōshū), as well as on the *Tale of Genji*, and taught her complex forms of Japanese poetry. Ito's studies also included training in the polite arts. She learned to play the *koto*-zither and the string instrument *shamisen*. Moribe believed that musical accomplishments and proficiency on a musical instrument had important educational value, especially in terms of music's contribution to spiritual enrichment, and Ito spent a good deal of her time practicing *koto*. She also studied tea ceremony and flower arranging and learned sewing and housekeeping. Ito spent two and a half years studying with the Moribe family. She returned to Kiryū in 1840 and married in 1843 at the age of twenty. Throughout her marriage, Ito maintained close ties with her teacher and his family. Ultimately, the two families' ties grew closer when Ito's former teacher, Tachibana Futeru, adopted one of her children.[62]

Yoshida Ito was the daughter of a Kiryū weaving family. Ito's first teacher outside her family, Tamura Kajiko, was the daughter of a merchant family from the same area. Both of these early-nineteenth-century commoner women left their families and went to Edo to study—one in the household of an academician of the school of national learning, the other in the women's quarters of the Tokugawa shogunal palace. When they returned, both were absorbed back into the activities of village life, both married, and both kept up their ties to their teacher, Tachibana Moribe. Education acquired in the distant reaches of Edo did not prevent these two women from being reintegrated into village economic and social life.

Both urban and rural middle-class women acquired educations that went beyond basic literacy, and suburban commoner women did as well.[63] Not every middle-class commoner daughter was sent to the shogunal capital to study. Basic and advanced levels of education were available in a variety of urban and suburban centers built around Tokugawa castle towns. The diaries of Ōba Misa (1833–1905) suggest the educational level attained by one early-nineteenth-century commoner raised in an agricultural setting on the edge of Edo. Misa, the daughter of a wealthy farm family named Kaburagi, was born in 1833 in what is now the Shinagawa area of Tokyo.[64] In 1857, when Misa was twenty-five, she married thirty-one-year-old Ōba Yoichi (1827–65), intendant (*daikan*) of the Setagaya District in Hikone domain (Setagaya ward of modern-day Tokyo). Yoichi was a samurai retainer of the domain lord Ii Naosuke (1815–60). Because the Ōba family had long held the position of intendant, their family records have been collected and preserved.

In addition to the official records of the Intendant office and genealogies of the Ōba family, the Setagaya ward archives contain the thirty-two volumes that remain from Ōba Misa's forty-five-volume diary, which she kept from 1860 through 1904. Of the remaining volumes, nine covering the period from 1860 through 1871 were published in 1988 as the first volume of *Ōba Misa no nikki*. Unfortunately, very little information remains about Misa herself, only the sketchy information recorded in birth, marriage, and death records. But from her diaries we know that she bound each journal by hand and almost never used new paper. Instead, with a frugality that seems to have been characteristic, she used the blank sides of discarded letters and documents for diary pages, which she bound together with handmade paper twine. And perhaps to conserve space further, she wrote in dense strings of Chinese characters, using little of the phonetic *kana* script alphabet assumed standard in Tokugawa women's writing. Because our record of Misa's diary keeping begins after she married, her diaries provide no direct information about her early education. The form, content, style, and syntax of her diary entries, including her extensive knowledge of Chinese characters, are all that are left to attest to the superior level of this wealthy farm daughter's education.

In her diaries Misa preserved for modern readers many of the social and political aspects of the life of district officials in Setagaya. Through them she reveals a precise awareness of geography and national and local politics. Located very near Edo, Setagaya was integrated into the political and economic activities of the shogunal capital and took on added importance whenever the Hikone domain lord Ii Naosuke resided in Edo. Misa moved to Setagaya in 1857 and began her diary in 1860, the year that Ii Naosuke was assassinated. Her first volume records the frightening events that were reshaping the nation, including the assassination of Ii. As part of her daily routine she also noted her husband's interactions with the various headmen of the villages in Setagaya, and from Misa's first diary, we learn of the spread of the news of Ii's assassination to Setagaya and of the local response to his death. Later, in 1861, Misa records the pageantry of the procession of Kazunomiya, imperial princess and sister of the emperor, as it passed through Setagaya on its way to Edo in preparation for the marriage arranged between Kazunomiya and the shogun, Tokugawa Iemochi.[65] Because she was able to record her observations (and because this record has been preserved), Misa's diaries remind us that some Tokugawa women were conscious of and concerned about the political events engulfing the nation at the end of the period.

Misa's journals also chronicle, interspersed among political observations, both family and official life. The comings and goings of many of the members of the extended Ōba and Kaburagi families weave in and out of Misa's catalog of daily events. Although they were not of samurai status, several of Misa's Kaburagi relatives held official posts in the local administration, and Misa's diary provides a glimpse into the activities of this stratum of Tokugawa-era gentry. Misa's family were wealthy farmers, while the Ōba family had samurai status; yet the connection between the two families was of long standing. The Ōba and Kaburagi family trees crossed before the marriage between Misa and Yoichi. Both Misa's paternal grandmother and great-grandmother were descended from the Ōba family. The close connection between these two families indicates that the barrier between commoner and samurai was a permeable one—and had been, perhaps, throughout the Tokugawa period.

In her diaries Misa kept records that assisted her—as Mine's diaries did—with the many duties of a district intendant's wife. It is clear from the diaries that Misa herself was an important functionary in and acute observer of the machinery of district administration.[66] In addition to her duties in support of administration, Misa acted as one of her husband's advisers; and it was Misa who solved the problem of succession occasioned by her husband's untimely death at the age of thirty-eight. In order for her brother to succeed to her husband's official position, Misa first arranged for her brother's adoption into another family of samurai rank. Then, from that status, he could be adopted into the Ōba family to inherit the position of intendant from his former brother-in-law.[67] Misa understood and personally manipulated the conventions that surrounded samurai status. She orchestrated family decisions (which were sometimes political decisions) in her husband's absence and during his final illness.

The centrality of education to Ōba Misa's life is revealed through her diaries: education made it possible for her to keep them, education determined their epistolary style, and education contributed to the scope of their contents. Nothing suggests, given her family and class, that Misa's education was exceptional. On the contrary, her diaries, together with other records, suggest that in the late Tokugawa period prosperous commoner women were often highly educated.

## CONCLUSION: THE GOALS OF
## TOKUGAWA WOMEN'S EDUCATION

Several rationales existed in the Tokugawa period to support women's education, but the most common one was the importance of preparing a woman for the domestic responsibilities she would assume after marriage. Tokugawa educational philosophies reflected demographic realities in assuming that women would marry. As a result, a large part of women's education prepared women for the complex duties that followed marriage; and these included a managerial and an ethical component and sometimes, as in the case of Misa, a political one. Japanese women's educations were similar in many respects; and regardless of class, all women received a foundation in Neo-Confucian ethical precepts. There seem to have been differences, however, in the emphasis placed on ethical training in the higher educations samurai and elite commoner women received.

One important component of all samurai education in the late Tokugawa period was instruction in Japan's version of the Neo-Confucian principles of duty, service, and loyalty. In the code of behavior idealized for members of the samurai class, there was no distinction between private and personal conduct. In several ways, this offset distinctions made on the basis of gender. It could be said that the major purpose of *all* samurai education—whether for women or for men—was a vocational one. Samurai education was role based. It was designed to train members of this class for careers that were inherited, not chosen. It is important to remember that in Tokugawa Japan there was similarity as well as divergence between the roles of women and men of all classes: merchant women and men together managed enterprises; agricultural women and men cooperated in agriculture; and both the women and the men of the samurai class were restricted from merchant and farming activities. Samurai men managed political affairs, samurai women managed domestic affairs, but always domestic affairs had significant political import and represented the interior circle of the nested concentric circles of public affairs.

A samurai woman's education presumed that she would marry into a samurai household and after marriage, that she would serve her husband's family and their interests in the same way that her husband served the domain lord who paid the family's salary. A samurai woman's training in duty and service often began, as a samurai man's did, with the discipline of early education. Samurai women were educated to fill domestic managerial roles that often involved complicated household arrangements and large numbers of servants. These managerial roles had a practical, aesthetic, and ethical component, and samurai women were expected to function as the custodians of moral training for members of the household compound, including their husbands. And in special circumstances, such as when the castle compound was under attack or when a spouse met with an untimely death, traditional male samurai responsibilities could devolve to females of the samurai class, whose educations had prepared them for such responsibilities. Samurai women's personal accounts indicate that they took pride in the discipline and moral training their education entailed, and many took greatest pride in mastering the difficult *kambun* texts of Confucian morality that formed the canon of men's higher education in early modern Japan.

Commoner women also were educated in Japan's tradition of Neo-Confucian ethics, but their education appears to have focused on popular moral tracts for women. Instead of mastering the difficulties of Chinese and such classics as the Four Books, the records of Ito's and Mine's education suggest that elite commoner women's education had a slightly different focus. Of course, their education increased their competence to assume the social and economic responsibilities of the domestic household, including financial management, record keeping, and gift giving. Elements of their education assisted them in the performance of responsibilities that were at once a concomitant of marriage and of their social status as middle- and upper-class urban, suburban, or village elites. Mine's diaries reveal a close network of personal and economic ties connecting residents in the urban setting of a Tokugawa castle town. Misa's diaries reveal her involvement in district administration and her understanding of the searing political events of her day. But elite commoner women's education did not stop with preparation for official duties; their education was useful, ethically, professionally, and personally. Ito and Mine were educated in the enjoyable pastimes of music and poetry. In Ito's case, it is clear that this part of her education was intended to enrich the quality of her personal life. In Mine's case, training in traditional poetry enriched her life in the same way, whether it was intended to or not. Evidence drawn from the records of Mine's and Ito's educations suggests that personal satisfaction was perhaps a more explicit element in the education of elite commoner women.

Over the course of the Tokugawa period, basic educational opportunities became available to a growing number of women, and education became an important and increasingly common aspect of their lives. Whether education took place informally at home or in a nearby local school or private academy, women's education shared a common canon and a common discipline required by mastery of the complexities of written Japanese. Beyond this, family traditions and individual inclination determined Tokugawa women's higher education. When both converged, women received educations comparable to men of their class.

The availability of education for women varied, however, according to class and geographic area, and wealthy, urban women had greater educational opportunities. Female members of the nobility and of the domain-lord class lived in their own sections of their respective estates and were educated at home by their parents or by tutors. Ladies-in-waiting to both types of households were often selected on the basis of education, while at the same time serving as a lady-in-waiting was one means of acquiring still higher education. Wealthy daughters from the commoner class were taught by parents or by notable scholars from the community, or they might be sent to board in the household of a scholar in a distant city if a desirable scholar was not available nearby. Village daughters from middle-class families were educated in local schools or private academies, and some were also tutored privately. In the Tokugawa period, private academies developed around different philosophical schools of thought, and academies of the "heart learning" (*shingaku*) and national learning schools educated women as well as men. From the early 1800s, Japanese women increasingly received some kind of education, be it at home, in a village school, or in a private academy.

By the end of the Tokugawa period, few if any educators or philosophers argued that women should be ignorant and illiterate. In many cases, where education was valued, it was valued for men and women from the same class, even though that did not mean education was identical for men and women. Despite the conservative tone of moral texts, such as the *Great Learning for Women*, their use as primers for teaching reading and writing promoted women's education. By the end of the period, elite women's education often extended to higher levels, and some women had the advantage of a "man's education." Although women trained in *kambun*-Chinese and in the classics of Chinese literature might describe this aspect of their education as drawn from male traditions (as Hatoyama and Sugimoto did), facility with "men's learning" did not contravene gender boundaries to such a degree that women so educated were rendered social or educational pariahs.

Because education did not transgress established gender boundaries, most girls and women educated in the Tokugawa period did not have to study in secret. The content of their education was publicly acknowledged, and women with higher levels of education taught others without stigma. As a result, educated girls and women shared more than the content of their education; they shared a common process. Although some students studied individually with tutors, many did not. Instead, they came together in schoolrooms or at their tutors' houses. There they joined their voices in recitation, endured the tedium of repetitious copying, and shared the difficulties of acquiring literacy. The educational process itself, the routines of women's education, was in many ways more important than its content. Education publicly acknowledged women's educability to themselves and to society at large.

NOTES

1. *Tsuda Umeko monjo*, rev. ed., ed. Yoshiko Furuki, Akiko Ueda, and Mary E. Althus (Tokyo: Tsuda juku daigaku, 1984), pp. 18, 83, 556, 581; Yamazaki Takako, *Tsuda Umeko* (Tokyo: Yoshikawa kōbunkan, 1962), pp. 16, 20, 67–68. Tsuda's birthdate is given as the twelfth month, third day, 1864, by the lunar calendar; and as December 31, 1864, by the solar calendar (*shinreki*). Tsuda's age is usually given as seven when she was a member of the Iwakura Mission. She was six when the mission sailed from Yokohama in late December 1871. When she arrived in Washington, D.C., in February 1872, she had turned seven. See also Yoshikawa Riichi, *Tsuda Umeko den*, rev. ed. (Tokyo: Tsuda juku dōsōkai, 1956). The details of Tsuda's life can be found in the above-cited biographies.

2. *Monjo*, pp. 581–82. Later letters that remain are in English.

3. Sugano Noriko, "Shomin josei no kyōiku," in *Nihon joseishi*, ed. Wakita Haruko, Hayashi Reiko, and Nagahara Kazuko (Tokyo: Yoshikawa kōbunkan, 1987), pp. 150–51; and

R. P. Dore, *Education in Tokugawa Japan* (Berkeley: University of California Press, 1965), pp. 256–70.

4. "Ochanomizu joshi daigaku hyakunenshi," in *Ochanomizu joshi daigaku hyakunenshi*, ed. Ochanomizu joshi daigaku hyakunenshi kankō iinkai (Tokyo: Ochanomizu joshi daigaku, 1984), p. 14.

5. Ishikawa Ken, *Joshi yō ōraimono bunken mokuroku* (Tokyo: Dainihon yū benkai kōdansha, 1946), pp. 1–13. See also Ishikawa Matsutarō, "*Onna daigaku* ni tsuite," in *Kaibara Ekiken, Muro Kyūsō*, vol. 34 of *Nihon shisō taikei*, ed. Araki Kengo and Inoue Tadashi (Tokyo: Iwanami shoten, 1970–85), p. 531.

6. Sugano, "Shomin josei," pp. 150–55; Ishikawa Ken, *Terakoya* (Tokyo: Shibundō, 1960); Dore, *Education*, pp. 252–70; Richard Rubinger, *Private Academies of Tokugawa Japan* (Princeton: Princeton University Press, 1982). By midcentury educational advisers in a few Tokugawa domains recommended establishing domain academies for girls (*han jogakkō*) to parallel those for boys, and a few domains began to establish such academies. See Naka Arata, Uchida Tadashi, and Mori Takeo, eds., "Kōtō jogakkō," in *Gakkō no rekishi*, vol. 3, *Chū gakkō, kōtō gakkō no rekishi* (Tokyo: Daiichi hōki shuppan, 1979), pp. 79–85.

7. Hayashi Reiko, "Edoki no josei gunzō," in *Edoki josei no ikikata*, vol. 10 of *Jimbutsu Nihon no joseishi*, ed. Enchi Fumiko (Tokyo: Shūeisha, 1977).

8. Herman Ooms, *Tokugawa Ideology: Early Constructs, 1570–1680* (Princeton: Princeton University Press, 1985).

9. Ishikawa Matsutarō, "*Onna daigaku* ni tsuite," pp. 531–45.

10. Kaibara Ekiken, *Nyoshi o oshiyuru hō*, in *Yōjō kun, Wazoku dōjikun*, ed. and rev. Ishikawa Ken (Tokyo: Iwanami shoten, 1962), pp. 264–80.

11. Kaibara Ekiken, *Yamato zokkun*, trans. Mary Evelyn Tucker, in Mary Evelyn Tucker, *Moral and Spiritual Cultivation in Japanese Neo-Confucianism: The Life and Thought of Kaibara Ekiken (1630–1714)* (Albany: State University of New York Press, 1989), p. 134.

12. Quoted in Joyce Ackroyd, "Women in Feudal Japan," *Transactions of the Asiatic Society of Japan*, 3d ser., 7 (November 1959): 56.

13. Dore, *Education*, p. 333, gives the date of *Naniwa'e* as 1779. Herman Ooms, *Charismatic Bureaucrat* (Chicago: University of Chicago Press, 1975), pp. 22–24, gives a date nearer to 1775, when Matsudaira was sixteen.

14. For an introduction to Japanese adaptations of Neo-Confucian thought in the Tokugawa period, see Masao Maruyama, *Studies in the Intellectual History of Tokugawa Japan*, trans. Mikiso Hane (Tokyo: Tokyo University Press, 1974); and Ooms, *Tokugawa Ideology*.

15. Ishikawa Ken, "Hakko no kotoba," in *Ko ōrai*, vol. 1, pt. 1, of *Nihon kyōkasho taikei ōraihen*, ed. Ishikawa Ken and Ishikawa Matsutarō, pp. 1–2. In the Meiji period, such texts were renamed *kyōkasho* (textbooks) by the Ministry of Education.

16. Ishikawa Ken, *Joshi yō ōraimono*, pp. 1–10. Basic instructional writings often had no gender designation and were meant to be read by everyone. Some were directed specifically at girls and women, others specifically at boys and men. According to Ishikawa Ken, neither women nor men exclusively read only gender-appropriate texts. Both read texts for women, texts for men, and general texts.

17. Ishikawa Matsutarō, ed., *Nihon kyōkasho taikei ōraihen*, vol. 15, *Joshi yō*, p. 12. Ishikawa Ken, *Joshi yō ōraimono*, pp. 1–2.

18. Ishikawa Ken, *Joshi yō ōraimono*, pp. 1–2. Ishikawa Matsutarō, *Joshi yō*, p. 12. The assessments of pre-Tokugawa women's texts by Ishikawa Ken and Ishikawa Matsutarō are sketchy and do not link women's educational practices to the history of women in earlier

times. Other studies document aspects of Heian or Kamakura life in which elite women's education played an important role. Heian-period histories note the pervasive influence elite women authors exerted on the production of classical literary forms. Kamakura-period historians document the importance of elite women's participation in almost every aspect of Kamakura institutional life through their extensive involvement in land transactions, their voluminous wills, and the numerous lawsuits they brought. Although they do not discuss elite women's education directly, Jeffrey Mass, Hitomi Tonumura, and Haruko Wakita suggest either that elite medieval women's educational practices went beyond beauty, arts, and social graces or that education in those things, which were intended to "prepare older girls and teenagers for marriage," had importance for elite women as fiscal and legal actors. See Mass, *Lordship and Inheritance in Early Medieval Japan: A Study of the Kamakura Sōryō System* (Stanford: Stanford University Press, 1989); Tonomura, "Women and Inheritance in Japan's Early Warrior Society," *Comparative Studies in Society and History* 32 (July 1990): 592–623; and Wakita, "Marriage and Property in Premodern Japan from the Perspective of Women's History," *Journal of Japanese Studies* 10, no. 1 (Winter 1984): 77–99.

19. Ishikawa Matsutarō, *Joshi yō*, pp. 13–14. He cites as examples *Joshi kun* by Kumazawa Banzan (1619–91), *Hiragana retsujo den* by Kitamura Kigin (1624–1705), and *Honchō retsujo den* by Takizawa Bakin (1767 1848).

20. Ishikawa Ken, *Joshi yō ōraimono*, pp. 6–13. The 1,109 editions of women's texts from the Tokugawa period that were cataloged by Ishikawa Ken in 1946 were found to be distributed across the four categories: 377 morals texts, 207 letter-writing texts, 136 almanacs, and 389 academic texts. See Ishikawa Matsutarō, *Joshi yō*, pp. 18–36.

21. Ishikawa Matsutarō, *Joshi yō*, pp. 11–18, 46. Ishikawa Matsutarō connects the appearance of these new morality handbooks for women to the Tokugawa-era consolidation of the family system. He argues that this consolidation was essential to the centralization of the Tokugawa state and that a specific type of married woman was essential for the consolidation of the family. He also maintains that in this period the goal of women's education became training as household managers (*shufu*) rather than as elegant, beautifully groomed, dilettante brides.

22. Ishikawa Matsutarō, *Joshi yō*, p. 46. For the Tokugawa period as a whole, however, handbooks on female morality outnumbered any other single type of women's textbook.

23. For a late-nineteenth-century English translation of *Women's High Education*, see Basil Hall Chamberlain, "Educational Literature for Japanese Women," *Journal of the Royal Asiatic Society of Great Britain and Ireland*, n.s., 10, no. 3 (1878): 325–43. Chamberlain criticizes the work ascribed to Kaibara in his article.

24. Ishikawa Matsutarō, "*Onna daigaku* ni tsuite," pp. 531–45. The full citation read, *Onna daigaku takarabako—Kaibara Atsunobu*, literally, "the *Onna daigaku* treasure chest—Kaibara Atsunobu" (punctuation added).

25. *Ekiken Kaibara sensei nobe; Kaibara sensei no jussaku Onna daigaku*. See Ishikawa Matsutarō, "*Onna daigaku* ni tsuite," pp. 532–34.

26. Ishikawa Matsutarō, "*Onna daigaku* ni tsuite," p. 532. For an English analysis of Kaibara Ekiken's philosophy, see Tucker, *Moral and Spiritual Cultivation*. A discussion of *Wazoku dōji kun* appears on pp. 114–21 and includes a brief description of Kaibara's thought about teaching women. This description conflated *Onna daigaku* and *Nyoshi o oshiyuru hō* and mistakenly suggests that Kaibara was the author of *Onna daigaku*.

27. Ishikawa Matsutarō, "*Onna daigaku* ni tsuite," pp. 544–45. It is now generally accepted by the Japanese academic community that Kaibara Ekiken did not write *Onna daigaku*. Here

and elsewhere, Ishikawa argues that the ideals of women's education and the domestic role presented in *Onna daigaku* represent a shift in Tokugawa thought from Kaibara's humanistic approach to one that emphasized women's duties as household managers, occasioned by new political pressures on women's roles in the family.

28. *Onna daigaku*, an example of a *jokun* used as a copybook, is reprinted in *Kaibara Ekiken, Muro Kyūsō*, pp. 202–27.

29. Ishikawa Matsutarō, "*Onna daigaku ni tsuite*," p. 532.

30. Global terms of comparison such as "lower" and "higher" refer to the status of women in history as if it were a unitary construct. They therefore artificially consolidate different women's experiences into one totalizing generalization. All women's lives do not change at the same time, in the same way, or to the same degree. While some women's "positions" might have been "lower" in the Tokugawa period, others' lives remained unchanged and still others' lives improved.

31. *Onna daigaku takarabako*, reprinted in *Kyōiku*, vol. 4 of *Nihon fujin mondai shiryō shūsei*, ed. Mitsui Tametomo (Tokyo: Domesu shuppan, 1976), pp. 99–102.

32. Chamberlain, "Educational Advice Literature for Women." The women's handbook *Onna imagawa* takes its name from the advice literature written by the fourteenth-century warrior and poet Imagawa Ryōshun.

33. Basil Hall Chamberlain, "A Translation of the *Dou-zhi keu:* Teachings for the Young," *Transactions of the Asiatic Society of Japan* 9 (1881): 223–48. An alternative romanization for *dou-zhi keu* is *dōjikyō*.

34. For an example of exhortations directed at samurai males, see Yamaga Sokō, *The Way of the Samurai*, in *Sources of Japanese Tradition*, vol. 1, ed. and trans. Ryusaku Tsunoda et al. (New York: Columbia University Press, 1958).

35. Although they occupied the same moral world, they did not occupy the same position in that world.

36. This term is taken from Chamberlain, "Educational Literature for Japanese Women."

37. Joseph Levenson, *Modern China and Its Confucian Past* (New York: Doubleday, 1964).

38. For a discussion of the varied styles of presentation in editions of *Onna daigaku*, see Ishikawa Matsutarō, "*Onna daigaku ni tsuite*," pp. 533–41.

39. Regional editions of *Onna daigaku* appeared in Sendai in 1807, according to Ishikawa. See his "*Onna daigaku ni tsuite*," pp. 534–35.

40. Sugano, "Shomin josei," pp. 150–55; Dore, *Education*, pp. 229, 257, 264.

41. Dore, *Education*, p. 205 passim.

42. See, for example, Yamazaki, *Tsuda Umeko*, pp. 23–25.

43. Etsu Inagaki Sugimoto, *A Daughter of the Samurai* (New York: Doubleday, Page, 1926; rpt. 1990), p. 17.

44. Yamakawa Kikue, *Buke no josei*, reprinted in *Yamakawa Kikue shū*, vol. 10 (Tokyo: Iwanami shoten, 1946–81). The pre- and postwar socialist Yamakawa Kikue (1890–1980) drew on family reminiscences and the diaries and records left by her grandfather to record the daily life of Tokugawa samurai women. For an English translation of this work, see Yamakawa Kikue, *Women of the Mito Domain: Recollections of Samurai Family Life*, trans. Kate Wildman Nakai (Tokyo: University of Tokyo Press, 1992).

45. Compilation of the multivolume historical record *Dai Nihon shi* was begun in 1657 by the Mito daimyo, Tokugawa Mitsukuni (1628–1700), and it was finally completed in 1906.

46. Yamakawa, *Buke no josei*, p. 25. The details of Chise's life are drawn from *Buke no josei*.

47. According to Ishikawa Ken's classification system, these four texts can be classified as follows: *Onna Imagawa*, moral guide, first published circa 1692; *Onna daigaku*, moral guide, first published circa 1716 [*sic*]; *Onna teikin*, calligraphy, composition, and manners, first published circa 1661; *Onna kōkyō*, moral guide, first published circa 1656, as an abridged version of *Kōkyō*, the *Classic of Filial Piety*.

48. For a review of domain academy education, see Dore, *Education*, pp. 124–52.

49. Chise's studies of the *Shin Kokinshū*—one of the main texts of the national learning school, which emphasized original Japanese classics over texts based on imported Chinese philosophy—augmented the standard educational program. For texts used in *kokugaku* academies, see Rubinger, *Private Academies*, pp. 158–73.

50. Hatoyama Haruko, *Jijoden*, reissued as vol. 7 of *Nihonjin no jiden* (Tokyo: Heibonsha, 1981), pp. 327–29. The details of Hatoyama's life were taken from this autobiography.

51. Hatoyama, *Jijoden*, p. 330.

52. Sugimoto, *Daughter*, pp. 17, 19. Sugimoto recalled that her training in Confucian classics included the Four Books of Confucius.

53. For a discussion of glossing of Tokugawa-era Chinese texts, see Dore, *Education*, pp. 127–38; for glossing Chinese characters in girls' texts, see Ishikawa Matsutarō, "*Onna daigaku* ni tsuite," pp. 531–45. A reproduction of a 1733 edition of *Onna daigaku* with glossing appears in this same volume, pp. 206–27.

54. Walthall, Anne, "The Life Cycle of Farm Women," in *Re-creating Japanese Women*, ed. Gail Bernstein (Berkeley: University of California Press, 1991), pp. 46–50.

55. This discussion is based on the excerpts and analysis of the two diaries presented in Hayashi, "Edoki no josei gunzō" pp. 219–26. Hayashi cites volume 5 of the multivolume history of Wakayama City, *Wakayama-shi shi*, as her source for the texts of the two diaries.

56. It was imported into Japan in the early to mid-seventeenth century. Takizawa Bakin (1767–1848), perhaps the greatest novelist of the Edo period, wrote the version of *Suikoden* that Numano Mine read. The Bakin version was written in both *hiragana* and Chinese characters, which were further glossed with correct readings. For an introduction to this novel and the myriad versions of it that have appeared in Japanese since the mid-seventeenth century, see Takashima Toshio, *Suikoden to Nihonjin: Edo kara Shōwa made* (Tokyo: Taishūkan, 1991).

57. Mine's diary also suggests the close relationship between biological mother and wet nurse. When Mine's six-year-old son fell against the *kotatsu* and injured his hand, Mine went to notify her former wet nurse of his injuries before she went to the local pharmacist for medicine. Hayashi, "Edoki no josei gunzō," p. 223.

58. Takai Hiroshi, "Tempōki no aru shōnen to shōjo no kyōyō keisei katei no kenkyū," pt. 1, *Gumma daigaku kyōiku gakubu kiyō: Jimbun kagaku hen* 13 (1964): 139–56. This series of articles continues through nine parts (vol. 23, 1973), entitled in English by the author, "A Study of the Process of the Acquirement of Culture by Motojiro Yoshida (boy) and Ito Yoshida (girl) in the Tempo-era (1830–1844)." See also Hayashi Reiko, "Edoki no josei gunzō," pp. 209–46. See also Sugano, "Shomin josei," pp. 150–54.

59. Takai's work is summarized in Hayashi, "Edoki no josei gunzō," pp. 209–46. The following discussion in text and notes was taken from Takai's work and from the summary by Hayashi.

Yoshida Seisuke was the second son of a prosperous merchant family that had become bankrupt. Takai, "Tempki no aru," p. 139, lists the causes of the bankruptcy as (1) the Temmei-era eruption of Mount Asama; (2) the subsequent widespread famine; and (3) *bakufu* economic retrenchment policies. In addition, Seisuke's father seems not to have had a head for business. To support himself, Seisuke studied silk weaving as an apprentice in Kyoto. He returned to the Jōshū village of Kiryū in 1820 at the age of twenty-seven to start his own weaving business. Three years later he married Kamiyama Sato, then nineteen. Seisuke, who had studied with various poets and scholars in Kiryū, became Tachibana Moribe's student in 1827. Although Moribe moved to Edo two years later, he maintained frequent contact with his Kiryū students and corresponded regularly with the Yoshidas. The Yoshidas' long relationship with Tachibana provides evidence of one approach to commoner female education and documents the influence of Tokugawa education on child-rearing practices. It also indicates one route for transmitting educational philosophy from urban center to provincial town.

60. Both excerpts are quoted in Hayashi, "Edoki no josei gunzō," pp. 213–14.

61. Hayashi, "Edoki no josei gunzō," pp. 214–16. Tamura Kajiko, the eldest daughter of a Kiryū merchant family that dealt in woven goods, left Kiryū at seventeen to serve as a private secretary ( *yūhitsu*) in the back palace ( *ō'oku*) of the Tokugawa shogunal compound in Edo. When she returned to Kiryū at thirty-one, she married a man adopted into her family for her and opened her own private school. Yoshida Ito was hard of hearing, probably from birth or an early childhood illness. Moribe adjusted Ito's education to accommodate this physical limitation. He kept detailed notes of Ito's lessons because he did not want to risk that she would not hear and therefore not understand what he was trying to teach her.

62. Hayashi, "Edoki no josei gunzō," p. 218. Ito and Yasubee's son took the name Tachibana Michiyasu; he became a middle-Meiji-era *kokugakusha*.

63. Rural women's access to education depended on family economics and the location of their home village. Female literacy was lowest in the remotest villages and hamlets of Tokugawa Japan and highest in urban and suburban areas.

64. Tokyo-to Setagaya-ku kyōiku iinkai, *Ōba Misa no nikki* (Tokyo: Tokyo-to Setagaya-ku kyōiku iinkai, 1988), vol. 1, pp. 285–86. Although Misa's family was a very old one, with records dating back to the mid-sixteenth century, it was a commoner family of farmers, albeit farmers of the highest class. See also Tokyo-to Setagaya-ku kyōiku iinkai, *Setagaya joseishi* (Tokyo: Tokyo-to Setagaya-ku kyōiku iinkai, 1980), vol. 1, pp. 151–59 ff. The following discussion of Ōba Misa's life is taken mainly from *Ōba Misa no nikki*, vol. 1.

65. *Ōba Misa no nikki*, vol. 1, pp. 67–68. The marriage took place in 1862.

66. In her diary Misa recorded special assistance, social calls, and gifts received. She noted gifts prepared for exchange and recorded reciprocating calls and gifts.

67. *Setagaya joseishi*, vol. 1, pp. 157–60. Misa's husband, Yoichi, died before they had a male child to assume the hereditary post of *daikan*. Misa recorded in her diary her efforts to ensure the continuation of an heir in this position. After Yoichi's death, Misa's brother became the last *daikan* of Setagaya *ryō*.

# CHAPTER NINE

# Competing Claims on Womanly Virtue in Late Imperial China

*Fangqin Du and Susan Mann*

Virtue, in China's Confucian culture, was displayed in action. Rarely were the Confucian virtues filial piety (*xiao*), righteousness (*yi*), loyalty (*zhong*), or fidelity (*jie*) defined in the abstract. Accordingly, biographies in China's official dynastic histories were arranged by category, to illustrate specific Confucian virtues.[1] As the virtuous conduct expected of men differed from that expected of women, official biographies provide the historian with a map charting shifts in gender and virtue through time. Male virtues remain relatively constant throughout the historical record, featuring three paradigmatic forms of exemplary conduct. Sons are honored for filiality; officials are honored for loyalty; and male community members are singled out for "righteousness," usually conceived as generosity or leadership that contributes to the common good. By contrast, womanly virtues in early historical records are both varied and contradictory, revealing competing claims on the emotional commitments and the moral will of individual women.[2] Moreover, the record of womanly virtue changes significantly over time, particularly after the Tang-Song period.

The analysis that follows traces these changes and analyzes competing claims on Confucian womanly virtue, focusing on the late imperial period, when concepts of female virtue were dominated by the so-called chastity cult. The late imperial chastity cult defined a woman's ultimate moral obligation as her obligation to the patriline into which she married. This commitment was embraced by women themselves, even by young girls who, confronting the death of a fiancé, proclaimed their determination to serve his parents unto death, in defiance of their own parents' wishes. By resolving a woman's conflicting filial obligations to her parents and to those of her spouse, the late imperial chastity cult effectively reduced an abiding tension in the Chinese family system—the tension embodied in brides who moved from one patriline into another.[3] To what extent these changes in the conceptualization and representation of virtue are attributable to Confucianism remains a subject of discussion and debate, as scholars trace the complex processes that produced competing claims on women's virtue in Chinese history.

The chastity cult that flourished in China during the Ming-Qing period honored two female virtues: purity and martyrdom. The first virtue, termed *jie*, referred not simply to sexual purity but to absolute fidelity to one husband, expressed in a refusal to remarry and lifelong devotion to the parents and heirs of the deceased spouse. The second, *lie*, meant that a woman's absolute commitment to fidelity and sexual purity might require self-sacrifice ending in death or suicide. These womanly virtues were often likened to the male virtue of loyalty (*zhong*). Even though females and males shared the same obligation to be "filial" (*xiao*) toward parents[4] and even though biographies of exemplary women in earlier dynasties honor filial daughters as well as faithful wives and chaste martyrs, by the Ming-Qing period the twin themes of *jie* and *lie* (fidelity and martyrdom) far overshadowed any celebrations of daughters' filiality in biographies of exemplary women. *Xiao* as a womanly virtue, which was important and arguably central to the Confucian didactic texts of the Song period, was subsumed in mid-Qing times into a discourse that focused on marital fidelity and sexual purity.

These shifts in celebrations of womanly virtue accompany shifts in the organization of the family, changes in the laws and decrees of the imperial state, and a growing self-consciousness about female virtue—shared by men and women—during the centuries after the Song period (approximately 1300–1900). The Song discourse emphasizing filiality for both sons and daughters was compatible with the family system of that era, which Patricia Ebrey once dubbed "slightly cognatic."[5] By Ming and Qing times, by contrast, discourses on virtue change along with what Ebrey describes as the patrilineal tilt of the post-Song family system. In the Ming-Qing period, when a daughter "married out" to reside permanently with her husband's parents, she was understood to have transferred her filial duties from her own parents to her husband's. Once married, a woman's childbearing obligations, her mourning duties,[6] her role in ancestor worship (as worshiper and worshiped), and her participation in such filial acts as *gegu* (cutting her own flesh to prepare healing medicines for a parent) and *gong ganzhi* (offering special delicacies for aging palates) were understood to focus not on her parents but on her parents-in-law.

As a wife, every woman became the necessary partner to her husband's filiality: she was the mother of all his sons. Every male was expected to father sons in order to fulfill his filial obligations to his own father. The first step toward this end was the elaborate marriage ceremony presenting the future mother of his sons to his parents and his ancestors. This binding ritual incorporated every wife into the ancestral line of her spouse and removed her from the descent line of her natal family. Other women might later serve to reproduce heirs for her husband, but they could do so only as concubines; all the sons they bore would call *her* mother. The wife and her spouse, moreover, became potential progenitors of their own branch

descent line, itself ranked in relationship to the descent lines of her spouse's brothers, both older and younger. Generational lines marked patrilineal cousins—the
sons of brothers—as a cohort while setting off each sibset as a distinctive line within
the cohort. These sibling hierarchies and generational lines made it unthinkable
for a woman to remarry within her husband's lineage in the event of his death.
For this reason, unlike many other patrilineal descent systems, China's has never
espoused a levirate. On the other hand, if a widow remarried outside her late husband's lineage, she literally split her ancestral body in two, the nightmare prospect
of which became a powerful theme in one of Lu Xun's finest short stories criticizing the oppressive customs of the past.[7]

Beliefs about marital fidelity sustained by family practice were also supported
by the status hierarchies and the state power structure of the late imperial period.
Because skewed sex ratios favored bride-givers in China's marriage market, a
woman marrying for the first time could count on marrying "up," or at least
"matching doors." A widow could expect the opposite. In addition, beginning in
the Yuan dynasty, the imperial state—and the emperors themselves—became
deeply involved in campaigns to celebrate and reward faithful wives. The Ming and
Qing emperors presented certificates of merit, sums of silver, and personal commendations written in the emperor's own hand to families who could document
the fidelity of a chaste widow.

With these powerful incentives in place,[8] the Ming-Qing period also saw distinctive historical changes in the meaning and practice of womanly virtue. Whereas
under Ming rule a woman who committed suicide to defend her chastity (*lie*) was
singled out for special praise, the Qing government promoted chastity (*jie*)—especially faithful service to a deceased husband's patriline—but condemned suicide
as self-indulgent or misguided. Most striking among the historical changes of this
period is the appearance, for the first time, of young women engaged to be married who, confronting the death of a fiancé, defy their parents' wishes and vow
fidelity to his patriline for the rest of their lives. These "faithful fiancées" sparked
heated debate among scholars. Should a young woman once betrothed refuse a
second betrothal if her fiancé was declared unfit or if he died before the wedding?
And should she do so in blatant disregard for her parents' own authority?[9] Writings left by women hint at their own agonized response to the competing claims
on virtue during this period, showing us that the debates about these issues were
hardly academic. Contradictory moral values forced women—and sometimes very
young girls—into moral decisions, often a choice between two kinds of misery: pain
in death or suffering in life.[10] In the narratives and poems describing these decisions, we find hints of women as historical agents who embraced and celebrated
the values of the age.

What motivated men and women in rural and urban China to identify themselves with this chastity cult? And why, when the virtues of fidelity and martyrdom
were celebrated during both the Ming and Qing periods, did distinctive patterns

of change persist? These changes, which appear to mark shifts in the cultural meaning and the social practice of women's virtue, are the subject of the discussion that follows. We base our analysis on historical evidence of the female chastity cult from the Ming-Qing period (roughly 1500–1800). In our conclusion, we return to broader questions about historical change.

## WOMANLY VIRTUE BEFORE THE MING-QING PERIOD

The Chinese family system based on ancestral rites traces its roots to the Western Zhou period (ca. 1000 B.C.E.). The earliest classical records, however, do not emphasize a woman's commitment to her husband and his descent line. To be sure, early texts condemn women for licentious behavior or promiscuity. But the focus on female chastity and the ideal of widow suicide, both of which dominate late imperial tales of womanly virtue, are absent from the most important early writings on the subject of women.[11] Liu Xiang's (ca. 16 B.C.E.) Han dynasty *Biographies of Women* presents both positive and negative examples of womanly behavior, without holding up chastity as an exclusive goal.[12] Fan Ye (398–445), the historian who was the first to enter "Biographies of Women" into an official dynastic history, stressed that he was selecting women of high talent and outstanding virtue, without any particular reference to chastity or martyrdom.[13] Lisa Raphals's study of representations of women in Han and pre-Han texts stresses that the earliest construction of female roles is relatively evenhanded, portraying women in a correlative, complementary, or balanced position vis-à-vis men. At the same time, Raphals notes that as early as the first century B.C.E., with the rise of correlative cosmologies, dichotomies like *yin* and *yang*, or "inner" and "outer," began to be understood hierarchically, with "male" becoming associated with *yang* and "outer" above "female," which was conflated in some texts with *yin* and "inner."[14]

This tendency to portray women as subordinates of men, or even as tragic martyrs or victims, can be found throughout the historical record. From the Six Dynasties era to the Tang and Song periods, official dynastic histories include stories of women enduring hardship or adversity who committed suicide for a righteous cause, or who sacrificed their lives to uphold an ideal of Confucian honor represented by purity, fidelity, and chastity. But none of these compare with the tales of chastity and suicide that dominate the official histories of the Ming and Qing periods. Statistical data illustrate these patterns persuasively. Table 9.1 shows the contrast between the indifferent attitude toward female chastity before the Song and the obsession with female chastity and suicide during the Yuan, Ming, and Qing dynasties.

Previous studies addressing the problem of historical change in female biography have focused mainly on cultural and economic factors. T'ien Ju-k'ang, for example, has argued that fierce competition for success in the civil service examinations led men from certain highly competitive areas to displace their anxieties by celebrating the martyrdom and self-sacrifice of women.[15] Patricia Ebrey has

TABLE 9.1 Incidence of Female Chastity and Suicide in
Historical Records from the Zhou through the Qing

| Dynasty | Jie *(chastity)* | Lie *(martyrdom)* | Total |
|---|---|---|---|
| Zhou | 6 | 7 | 13 |
| Qin | 1 | | 1 |
| Han | 22 | 19 | 41 |
| Six Dynasties | 29 | 35 | 64 |
| Sui Tang | 32 | 29 | 61 |
| Five Dynasties | 2 | | 2 |
| Liao | | 5 | 5 |
| Song | 152 | 122 | 274 |
| Jin | | 28 | 28 |
| Yuan | 359 | 383 | 742 |
| Ming | 27,141 | 8,688 | 35,829 |
| Qing | 9,482 | 2,841 | 12,323 |

SOURCE: Dong Jiabin, "Lidai jiefu lienü de tongji" (Statistics on chaste widows and female martyrs through history) (1937), reprinted in *Zhongguo funüshi lun ji* (Collected essays on the history of Chinese women), ed. Bao Jialin (Taipei: Daoxiang chubanshe, 1979), vol. 1, p. 112.

stressed the importance of Neo-Confucian thought and its influence among the scholar-gentry families of the Song period, especially with respect to the increasing value attached to chaste widowhood (observed, as she notes, more in the breach than in the observance).[16] Neo-Confucian instructions for organizing lineages and supporting ancestor worship, which proliferated in the Song, strengthened the patrilineal family system and by late imperial times sometimes provided an economic basis for female chastity through support for chaste widows.[17]

But attributing the spread of the chaste widow ideal to Neo-Confucian thought raises further questions. How did Neo-Confucianism become the dominant school in the official ideology during this period? And how did Neo-Confucianism affect women's own beliefs about chastity and their propensity to commit suicide?

All evidence suggests that critical changes during the Song period combined to provide the larger context for the spread of these new beliefs.[18] These changes, which increased the importance of the male descent line and the patrilineal family system, were associated with the growing free market in land, the development of the commercial economy, the intensification of urbanization, and the expansion of a gentry class whose power was enhanced by civil service degrees. The new lineage organizations sponsored by this gentry class, with their substantial corporate estates and their multiple interlocking marriage networks, had profound implications for class and gender relations and for interpersonal relationships as well. The "family instruction books" setting out proper norms of conduct for members of these lineages supply intimate glimpses of these relationships, as Zang Jian has discussed earlier in this volume.[19]

The Chinese family system described in these texts displays the tilt toward patrilocality and patrilineality that Ebrey identified in Song times and that continued through the Ming-Qing period. Evidence from Song legal codes suggests that a woman's ties to her natal family were more important under the law in dynasties that preceded the Song. The Tang code stipulated that even a daughter who had married out could inherit property if all other heirs had died, and an unmarried daughter, according to the code, could also inherit the family wealth if her parents and brothers had died. In the Song, daughters in elite families still commonly claimed inheritance rights, especially in the form of dowry, whereas by Ming and Qing times property inheritance was almost exclusively patrilineal.[20] In Song times, similarly, an unmarried daughter could inherit the property of her natal family provided all other heirs were dead. Though technically speaking the same was true in later dynasties, after the Song it was more acceptable to adopt a male heir than to pass property to females.[21]

Other important changes in the law occurred in the transition from Tang to Song. Laws through the tenth century, for instance, tolerated cross-cousin marriage; by contrast, in later periods cross-cousin marriage was legally banned.[22] Bans on cross-cousin marriage—even though they were often overridden by local custom—underscored the ritual significance of the male descent line, because they applied only to patrilateral cross-cousin marriage; marriage between a son and his mother's sibling's daughter was still tolerated. Still another example of the patrilateral tilt in the Chinese family system during the Tang-Song transition comes from legal definitions of collective family responsibility for crimes. Pre-Tang conventions of collective family responsibility held a woman responsible for crimes committed by kin in either her natal or her marital family. After the Tang, however, women were legally responsible only for infractions by relatives through marriage.[23]

Finally, mourning rituals in Song times show signs of a shift favoring patrilineal bonds. Although the ritual guides of the period stipulate that a woman's mourning obligations to her husband's kin should be one degree lower than his own, in practice wives often performed the same mourning as their husbands.[24]

Ebrey has pointed to a rising intolerance for widow remarriage in the documents of the Song period.[25] Song officials and historians, she notes, likened a widow's fidelity to a son's filiality: "Determined widows were . . . treated like the heroes of filial piety who endured unusual austerity in mourning, sliced off a piece of their thigh to prepare medicine for an ailing parent, or maintained an undivided household for five more generations."[26] Ebrey's observation invites us to view the tilt toward patrilineality in Song times as a shift in focus, from daughters to wives and widows, in the hagiographic literature on female virtue.

The Neo-Confucian values invoked by families of the Song called for revitalizing the three bonds and five constant virtues, promoting the regulation of the family as a prerequisite for governing a well-ordered country, and emphasizing introspective self-cultivation in order to uphold and sustain Heavenly principle (*tianli*) while suppressing human desires (*renyu*). In the context of the joint family system, such ideas enhanced the power of husbands, fathers, and the ruler and provided a basis for ensuring social order at a time when economic and social change was rapid. By the same token, women became subject to new interventions and constraints.

From the perspective of women, in fact, the changes of the time were especially dramatic. The traditional relationship between a married daughter and her natal family was transformed, as married women came increasingly to be regarded as members of the family of the husband. This transformation intensified a woman's dependence on her husband's family and increased the latter's dominance over her. At the same time, a husband-centered marriage gave wives more duties and more responsibilities. Accompanying these new duties and responsibilities was a growing recognition that a wife was due special protection from her husband's family and that her sons owed her special reverence as their mother. These changes in the family system of the governing class reached upward into the imperial court, with the result that Song emperors would eventually order every princess to pay ritual homage to her parents-in-law and to follow her husband's family regulations, regardless of her royal status. And whereas the dowager empresses of the Song dynasty took on themselves the responsibility of maintaining the power of the royal house, never under the Song did female rulers dominate court affairs, nor did the relatives of imperial consorts control court politics.[27]

Signs that these values were being embraced in practice among the Song elite appear in anecdotes such as the story of the newly widowed young daughter-in-law of Bao Zheng who, when she was encouraged by Bao Zheng and his wife to remarry, wept and declared, "[H]aving lived as the wife in the Bao family, I shall die as a Bao ghost!"[28]—testifying to her conviction that her permanent place was in the family of her late husband. At the same time, the valorization of wives and mothers remains an important theme in the story of many upper-class Song women. For example, the meritorious careers and literary works of the Su family (Su Xun and his two sons, Su Shi and Su Che) are often associated with the success of Su Xun's wife, Lady Cheng, in managing family affairs, assisting her husband, and teaching her sons.[29]

These Neo-Confucian family values emerged in the context of Song family life absent any attempt by the government to promote them. By contrast, during the Yuan dynasty, when Neo-Confucianism was adopted as government ideology, the state became involved for the first time in explicit campaigns to promote and reward particular models of female virtue. Yuan rulers adopted a self-conscious strategy to follow the injunctions of the early classical text the *Great Learning*, which held that regulating the family was the first step in administering the state. Under this political strategy, the Yuan government began to promote female chastity and wifely sacrifice. Yuan rulers drew an explicit parallel between a wife who dedicated herself to her husband and a subject who was absolutely loyal to his ruler: "a man

TABLE 9.2 Biographies of Women
from the *History of the Song Dynasty*

| | |
|---|---|
| Suicide in war or violence | 34 |
| Suicide following husband | 2 |
| Suicide resisting rape | 3 |
| Filial service to in-laws | 3 |
| Resist/escape violence or danger | 5 |
| Other* | 3 |
| TOTAL | 50 |

SOURCE: See *Songshi* (History of the Song dynasty; annotated edition)
(Beijing: Zhonghua shuju, 1977), *juan* 46, pp. 13477–93.

*For example, resisting forced prostitution.

dies for his country and a woman dies for her husband; this is *yi* [righteousness]."[30]
Under these policies, records of widows who refused to remarry in order to fulfill
their filial obligations to their parents-in-law greatly increased over those of the
Song dynasty.

An equally striking shift in the Yuan period is the emphasis on the female body,
which should not serve two husbands. In the strictest interpretation of the Yuan injunctions on chastity, a woman who was touched anywhere by a man other than
her husband was so disgraced—and the humiliation suffered by her husband's family was judged so dire—that she ought to die. This compulsion to commit suicide
was heightened in the violence and warfare of the Yuan period, when countless
women threatened with rape or violation made martyrs of themselves.

An analysis of the examples in the "Biographies of Women" in the official histories for the Song and Yuan provides dramatic evidence that it was the Yuan dynasty that supplied the precedents for state policies promoting female chastity and
suicide under the subsequent Ming and Qing regimes. Note in the Yuan records
the prominence of women who commit suicide following a husband in death, the
large proportion of cases involving suicide to resist rape, and the new attention paid
to widows who refuse remarriage (see Tables 9.2 and 9.3).

Jennifer Holmgren's research on the Yuan dynasty proscriptions on widow remarriage shows that they were part of a strategy to reconcile Mongol marriage
practices, which promoted the levirate in order to concentrate wealth in the hands
of the ruling tribal elite, with Chinese values. Holmgren shows that by promoting
widow celibacy and insisting that a widow's dowry be retained by the family of
her late husband—instead of being returned to her natal family as was customary
in the Song—the Mongols sought to "protect fragile Mongol institutions" threatened by Chinese custom. Holmgren's argument dramatizes the ironic success of
astute government policies that gained legitimacy by canonizing Confucian values.
As she puts it, "[W]idow-celibacy where the woman lived with the husband's par-

TABLE 9.3 Biographies of Women
from the *History of the Yuan Dynasty*

| | |
|---|---|
| *Chaste* | |
| Refuse remarriage | 25 |
| Chaste and filial | 18 |
| *Suicide* | |
| Follow husband | 48 |
| Resist rape or violence | 85 |
| *Other* | |
| Filial daughters | 13 |
| Heroic deeds | 4 |
| TOTAL | 193 |

SOURCE: See *Yuanshi* (History of the Yuan dynasty; annotated edition)
(Beijing: Zhonghua shuju, 1976), *juan* 200–201, pp. 4483–516.

ents to care for them in their old age gradually became an all-embracing philosophy in China, usurping the place of piety to the natural parents as the chief virtue
for women."[31]

## THE CHASTITY CULT IN MING-QING TIMES

The celebration of female chastity and of suicide in the name of chastity grew to
unprecedented levels in the Ming-Qing era. Not only do Ming and Qing histories
report unprecedented numbers and varieties of cases in the lists of women's biographies. In addition, Ming and Qing records of female virtue marginalize tales of
filial daughters who serve their own parents while foregrounding stories of filial
daughters-in-law. Unprecedented in women's biographical records are the suffering and horror described in Ming and Qing biographical narratives and the strange
or bizarre situations the narrators recount. Finally, women in Ming and Qing biographies appear more willing than ever before to accept and to identify themselves
with Confucian virtues. Biographies in the Ming-Qing period are unique in providing explicit, sometimes graphic accounts of women's will and agency, testimony
to their own moral commitments.

To begin with the sheer numbers, the data in Table 9.1—which are incomplete
since they tabulate only cases recorded in official dynastic histories—indicate the
sharp increase in reported cases of female martyrs and paragons of chastity in the
Ming-Qing era. Proliferating categories of virtue are displayed and recorded. Under the category "chaste," for example, appear not only women who remained
faithful widows in order to serve their parents-in-law, or to raise an heir who would
succeed the deceased, but also women who purposely mutilated themselves, de-
stroying their physical appearance, in order to reduce pressures to remarry. Under

the category "martyr," similarly, are listed widows who commit suicide as a demonstration of loyalty to a deceased husband, or to avoid "humiliation" during periods of war and banditry, alongside new sorts of martyrs, including women in towns as well as rural areas who committed suicide because a vicious husband or parent-in-law tried to seek profit by selling a wife's or daughter-in-law's body. In still other cases, women die to dramatize their purity when they were being sexually harassed by powerful members of the local gentry or by bullies or vagrants. Finally, in addition to widows who died for a deceased husband, Ming and Qing biographies supply the first records of betrothed girls who committed suicide as "virgin martyrs" on the death of a fiancé.

During the Ming and the Qing dynasties, dramatic displays of female virtue occur in tales of *lie*, or martyrdom. Women determined to preserve their purity find extraordinary or unusual ways to commit suicide: no longer simply death by hanging (which remained common), but also drowning by jumping into wells, rivers, ponds, or even large water jars. To keep the body inviolate even in death, before committing suicide many women first sewed their garments tightly about them so their clothing could not be loosened. Group suicides are reported, among women facing threats from marauding soldiers or bandits. Loving mothers kill their daughters before committing suicide themselves. Meanwhile, as if to compound the hardships of chaste widowhood, young widows slash their faces with knives or cut off their fingertips to show their determination to resist remarriage. Then they serve a deceased husband's parents and raise the heir, toiling year after year at spindle and loom until the parents-in-law are properly buried and the family line secured. Sonless widows adopt an heir to continue the family line, raise the boy to adulthood, see to his marriage, and celebrate the birth of a grandson before judging their duty fulfilled.

In virtually all of these stories, women martyrs take the initiative themselves and reveal no misgivings or regrets. This marks a contrast that sets the biographies from Ming and Qing times apart from their counterparts in the Yuan period, which generally reveal some coercion by male or even female relatives or superiors. For example, in the story of Bo Tie'mu'er's wife, recorded in the biographies of the "Loyal and Righteous" in the *History of the Yuan Dynasty* (Yuan shi), we learn that when Ming armies besieged their city in 1367, Bo led his wife and concubines to the balcony of their home and declared that he would die for the realm, and they should die for him:

> "Now the city has fallen and I will surely die here; can you follow me?" They all answered: "We have no will but to die." So saying, all six hung themselves.[32]

By contrast, in the Ming and Qing periods the record shows a sharp rise in women's self-awareness and volition in decisions about following a husband in death. Here, as an example, is the story of one such person:

> The woman martyr Zhang was the wife of the scholar———. She married him when she was eighteen. Four years later, he grew ill. With her welfare in mind, he urged

her to release herself from her obligations to him. But she objected, weeping: "Do you think I have two hearts? If we had a son, I would preserve my chastity and rear him as your heir, which is the duty of any wife. Having no son, a wife's purity may only be preserved by following her husband in death." So saying, she removed the sash from her garments, wrapped it about her neck, and hung herself. Within a few days, her husband was dead too.[33]

Other stories from the Ming show women committing suicide in front of ailing husbands who are about to die, including the story of Lady Zheng, wife of Zhao Ren, whom we are about to meet.[34] Such women of the Ming and Qing periods appear to have embraced directly the Song Neo-Confucian tenet that "a widow who remarries loses her moral integrity." This is evident in the tale of Lady Sun, the wife of Huang Yizhao, who—after the death of her husband and their son—remained a faithful widow devoted to the guidance of her daughter-in-law and grandsons, insistent that they work hard and pay their taxes. When an official asked her why she would rather face a difficult life than remarry, she quoted the Song philosopher Zhu Xi: "Starving to death is a minor matter; whereas losing one's chastity is an extremely important matter."[35]

Social pressure clearly played a role in this growing self-consciousness about widow morality. The disdain for remarried women among the Ming and Qing upper classes left women who moved in those circles no alternative but to remain faithful to a deceased husband or commit suicide. These pressures are illustrated in another story about Lady Zheng, who once received the present of a teacake from a remarried widow. Outraged, Lady Zheng not only had her family members throw away the cake, but she also personally berated the sender, scolding her severely for the affront. When her husband joked that this was a stand she could afford to take only because he was still alive and gently suggested that she should not reprimand a remarried woman, Lady Zheng vowed that he need never worry that she would do the same thing. The tale comes full circle when Zhao Ren himself later becomes seriously ill and from his deathbed stares fixedly at his wife until she takes the hint and kills herself, upon which Zhao closes his eyes and dies.[36]

With this anecdotal and empirical evidence in mind, let us now turn to a more detailed investigation of historical change in the ideals of chaste martyrdom and widow fidelity during the Ming-Qing period itself.

### FEMALE SUICIDE IN THE MING DYNASTY

The four hundred women whose lives are recorded in the "Biographies of Women" in the official *History of the Ming Dynasty* (Mingshi) were selected from among more than thirty thousand "model women" mentioned in the *Ming Veritable Records* (Ming shilu) as well as in local gazetteers of the period (see Table 9.4). But even this small sample suggests that suicide was singled out more for praise than other kinds of virtuous behavior.

Table 9.4 arrays the four hundred cases from the *History of the Ming Dynasty* under different categories. It dramatizes the overwhelming importance attached to suicide during the Ming period. Some of these data suggest that what appear to be high suicide rates are a direct function of the disorder of the period: 67.2 percent of women who committed suicide died during a sudden and unexpected threat of violence, by contrast to the 32.8 percent who killed themselves under apparently "normal" circumstances. On one level female suicide in the face of a violent invasion is a continuation of Yuan dynasty beliefs that a woman must display her integrity and moral conviction (*zhi*) by dying for her husband, just as her husband died for his country; or, put another way, that "loyal ministers do not serve two sovereigns, and faithful wives do not serve two husbands." The difference in the Ming records is the prominence of mass suicide, with groups of women killing themselves together with members of their own families, lineages, or communities.

Another striking feature of the Ming records is the testimonial of women themselves, often recorded as a direct quotation:

> Chastity is the most important part of being a good wife. Faced with calamity, a good wife has two choices: water or metal. Remember this! (Wife of You Quan, addressing her daughter)[37]

> If bandits come and I do not die, I am not faithful; if I do not die at the appropriate time, I lack righteousness. (Lady Zhao, wife of Tang Zuqi)[38]

This kind of moral conviction was an implicit reminder that in such situations death was preferable to survival, and we find many women refusing to seek protection when they might have done so. Thus, when the city of Taikang was sacked, Tang Zuqi's wife told her husband to bear his mother on his back and flee; she remained behind and tried to hang herself over the protest of her remaining relatives, until eventually she was killed by the invading bandits. Mothers generally did not teach their daughters ways to survive under duress; instead they gave the sort of advice we hear from Lady Zhang, above. As Lady Ye, wife of Jiang Hua, put it to her sister-in-law: "Even if I were to survive, the judgements that would be made about me make death better."[39] From such fragments we may begin to understand that many women chose to die not in the name of fidelity but out of dread at the humiliation that might accompany survival. A "good wife" understood that she bore the weight of her husband's family's reputation.

But what of women who were not threatened with violence? What was the motivation for widow suicide under ordinary conditions? Here we can only speculate that some women were led to perceive the act of suicide as more noble and glorious than simply living on in chastity. Dramatic suicide drew attention and caused excitement; the more harrowing the death, the more celebrated the act, as we see from the attention lavished on female suicide by men who were keepers of the historical record. In some cases, we find women making explicit statements about a hierarchy of alternatives open to widows. When Gao Wenxue of Tongcheng, An-

TABLE 9.4 Types of Virtuous Behavior in Biographies
of Women from the *History of the Ming Dynasty*

| | |
|---|---|
| *Suicide* | |
| Ordinary | 103 |
| Wartime | 211 |
| Total | 314 |
| Percent | 78.5 |
| *Chastity* | |
| Wife | 47 |
| Daughter | 7 |
| Total | 54 |
| Percent | 13.5 |
| *Filiality* | |
| Total | 17 |
| Percent | 4.25 |
| *Virgin* | |
| Total | 2 |
| Percent | 0.5 |
| Righteous wife | 8 |
| Righteous maid | 5 |
| Total | 13 |
| Percent | 3.25 |
| TOTAL | 400 |

SOURCE: *Mingshi* (History of the Ming dynasty; annotated edition)
(Beijing: Zhonghua shuju, 1974), *juan* 301–3, pp. 7689–763.

hui Province, died, his wife's mother, Wang Daomei, gave her widowed daughter the following advice: "Do not mourn excessively. There are three courses open to you. The first is martyrdom: to follow your husband in death. The second is fidelity: to keep yourself pure as ice and frost, in order to serve your parents-in-law. The third is to do what ordinary people do [i.e., remarry]."[40] The mother here echoes clearly the sentiments of Zhu Xi, who granted that "ordinary women" might have to seek remarriage but that women who truly understood their wifely obligations would judge death a "small matter" when purity was at stake.

Ming records of exemplary women, with their obsessive attention to suicide, reveal that a wife's fidelity to her husband often took precedence over all other obligations. Thus we find young widows professing their determination and killing themselves within three to seven days after the death of a spouse so that, as one said, "I may meet my husband in the underworld." This happens regardless of whether she is pregnant or has children, even sons. Consider the case of Lady Gong. Her husband and her mother-in-law both died, and the family was too poor to bury them. A person who offered to donate coffins to assist the young widow aroused her suspicions about his intentions, upon which she entrusted her six-year-old son and three-year-old daughter to her own mother's care and burned herself to death together with her husband's corpse.[41] Lady Tan, whose husband died three months after her son was born, was admonished by her mother-in-law and her mother not to commit suicide. She waited a few more years until he was seven and old enough to attend school. Lady Tan then entrusted the son to her mother-in-law and, telling herself with satisfaction, "I can now fulfill my wishes," she hanged herself.[42]

In some cases of widow suicide, it appears that the widow was motivated by her deep love of her husband (*qing xun*). Stories of such cases describe talented women who enjoyed not only a deep emotional tie but also a spiritual bond with a husband. For example, Lady Jiang, wife of Jiang Shijin from Danyang, Jiangsu Province, took poison several times after her husband died; every time she was saved by others in the family. Later she accepted the responsibility given to her by the brother of her grandfather-in-law, Jiang Bao, a minister in the Board of Rites, to write a sequel to Liu Xiang's *Biographies of Women*. After the book was completed, she drowned herself in a large water jar. Lady Jiang was also the author of "Weeping for [My] Husband" (Ku fu wen) and of a prose poem entitled "Dreaming of My Husband." Learned women like Lady Jiang were deeply influenced not only by their emotions but also by the social circles in which they moved, as members of distinguished families, and by their study of the classics and the moral ideals they internalized when studying. While she was young, Lady Jiang was greatly annoyed when people compared her with the female Song poets Li Qingzhao and Zhu Shuzhen. As she put it, "Li Qingzhao remarried and Zhu Shuzhen was dissatisfied with her husband. Although they were good at writing poetry, they lacked any firm commitment to fidelity."[43] Obviously, in the case of Lady Jiang, the decision to commit suicide for her deceased husband was informed by her learning, her class consciousness, and her emotions.

By contrast, of course, we find cases in which a widow committed suicide for a husband who mistreated her. Lady Xuan, wife of Zhang Shutian from Jiading, Jiangsu, was always treated rudely and violently by her husband. After Zhang died she expressed her determination to kill herself, and others tried to dissuade her by pointing out that she had an unworthy husband. Her response was to sigh and say "I know how to be a good wife; what does that have to do with the kind of person my husband was?" before she hanged herself.[44]

Among the many cases of female suicide recorded in the *History of the Ming Dynasty* are those in which a betrothed girl chooses to commit suicide when her fiancé dies.[45] One such case described in detail is the story of the daughter of the Liu family of Yingzhou who, on hearing that her fiancé had died, wept blood and refused to eat, declaring to her father that she intended to observe three years of mourning for him and then follow him in death as soon as her younger brother had grown to adulthood. When she learned one year later that her father was making plans to betroth her to someone else, she opened up the chest containing the clothing sent to her as betrothal gifts by her deceased fiancé's family, selected a sash, and hanged herself.[46] A still more extreme case is that of Weng Yingzhao's fiancée, Lady

Li. Following Weng's sudden death, she tried to burn herself to death several times but was rescued by her parents. At length she moved in with the Weng family to serve her late fiancé's parents and asked them to arrange an adopted son for her. She then set up her intended husband's wooden tablet and kept it near her at all times, sleeping and waking. She even sat face-to-face with the tablet while eating her meals. One day, after her late fiancé's parents had died, a fire broke out in the neighborhood. She embraced the wooden tablet and waited for the fire to spread to her house, allowing the flames to engulf her.[47]

Whereas such cases appear to result from the voluntary or affirmative agency of women acting out of moral conviction, countless others suggest that women committed suicide to escape unbearable misery at the hands of violent or abusive husbands, parents-in-law, or lineage members. Drunkenness, gambling, and other forms of addiction, not to mention greed, figure in stories in which young women are pressed to remarry or even to enter a brothel. One of the most famous of these cases was that of Tang Guimei of Guichi, whose story was immortalized by the scholar Li Zhi in a biography that provoked heated debate among literati at the time about pressures on women. Tang Guimei was married into the Zhu family. Her mother-in-law was involved in an adulterous relationship with a rich merchant who took a fancy to Guimei and bribed Guimei's mother-in-law to persuade Guimei to receive his advances. When Guimei resisted, the angry mother-in-law beat her brutally in an attempt to force her to surrender; meanwhile, the merchant bribed officials at the local yamen to throw her into prison, where she was nearly tortured to death before she was released. Guimei remained resolute, and she never disclosed her mother-in-law's adultery. In the end she chose to hang herself.[48]

Sexual abuse of this sort, either at the hands of a mother-in-law or at the hands of a ne'er-do-well husband who prostitutes his wife, appears in many tales of wifely suicide.[49] Outside the family, delinquent local youths and idlers were a constant threat, harassing women sexually and even forcing women into compromising relationships by blackmail. Women caught in these situations used suicide as the only way to protest their integrity. In turn, their short lives provided the narratives with which critics of late Ming commercialism attacked declining morals and abusive human relationships.

## THE SHIFT FROM MARTYRDOM TO FIDELITY: EXEMPLARY WOMEN IN QING BIOGRAPHIES

Although the early Qing government continued to promote both martyrdom and fidelity as the wifely values most crucial for women, the claims on womanly virtue shifted. The shift foregrounded filiality—service to parents-in-law—as the core wifely virtue, the logical consequence and overriding rationale for absolute fidelity. In the process of celebrating the filial duties of faithful daughters-in-law, the Qing government praised "correct" (*zheng*) and "constant" (*yong*) virtues, which were contrasted unfavorably with those newly labeled "bizarre" (*qi*) or "extreme" (*ji*). The

TABLE 9.5 Exemplary Women in the Biographies
of the *Draft History of the Qing Dynasty*

| | |
|---|---:|
| *Suicide / Martyrs* | |
| Married | 70 |
| Unmarried | 23 |
| Unrest | 275 |
| Sexual harassment | 41 |
| Abuse | 39 |
| Starvation | 4 |
| Total | 452 |
| Percent | 60 |
| *Chaste / Faithful* | |
| Married | 128 |
| Unmarried | 26 |
| Total | 154 |
| Percent | 20 |
| *Filial* | |
| Total | 66 |
| Percent | 9 |
| *Talented* | |
| Total | 21 |
| Percent | 2 |
| *Other* | |
| Coll | 61 |
| Percent | 8 |
| TOTAL | 754* |

SOURCE: See *Qingshi gao* (Draft history of the Qing dynasty; annotated edition) (Taipei: Guoshiguan, 1986), *juan* 515–18, pp. 11639–760.

*Percentages may not total 100 due to rounding.

ideal, a combination of filiality and fidelity (*xiao jie*), was touted as the norm most
exemplifying the "middle path" toward harmonious human relationships advocated by Confucian teachings. By contrast, martyrdom and suicide were criticized
as cowardly acts by which individuals sought to escape their most important human responsibilities.[50] These shifts are reflected clearly in the biographies of women
who were singled out for praise during the Qing period, as summarized in Tables
9.5 and 9.6.

The turning point in Qing policies appears to be the much-cited edict issued in
1728 by the Yongzheng emperor, calling a halt to what was termed the "use of death
to avoid all responsibilities" and stressing that a widow had two grave responsibilities: caring for her husband's parents and rearing her own son or adopted heir.[51]
The edict's effect on record keeping was immediate: cases of widow suicide in

TABLE 9.6 Female Suicide during Peacetime:
Ming-Qing Comparisons

|  | Ming Dynasty | Qing Dynasty | Total |
|---|---|---|---|
| *Suicide / Martyr* | | | |
| Married | 75 | 70 | |
| Unmarried | 14 | 23 | |
| Coerced | 14 | 80 | |
| Other | 0 | 4 | |
| Total | 103 | 177 | 280 |
| Percent | 65.6 | 53.5 | 57.4 |
| *Chaste / Faithful* | | | |
| Married | 47 | 128 | |
| Unmarried | 7 | 26 | |
| Total | 54 | 154 | 208 |
| Percent | 34.4 | 46.5 | 42.6 |
| TOTAL *(Percent)* | 157 (100) | 331 (100) | 488 (100) |

peacetime reported in the *Draft History of the Qing Dynasty* (Qingshi gao) come mainly from the period before the Yongzheng reign or after the Jiaqing and Daoguang reigns. Even so, the Qing government continued to confer insignia of imperial recognition, including memorial arches, on women who died during periods of violence, as Table 9.5 shows. Throughout the Qing period, women who committed suicide continued to win posthumous honors, sometimes on an exceptional basis, as in the 1740 case of Lady Zhang, who committed suicide after accompanying her criminal husband to exile in Guangxi.[52] Stories of female suicide in the Qing continue to describe women overwhelmed by the demands of ritual propriety, women ruined by men who squander family resources, women coerced into becoming prostitutes, widows forced to remarry so in-laws can claim their property, and sexual harassment. Perpetrators range from spouse or parent-in-law to local bullies, yamen personnel, and Buddhist monks and Daoist priests. In this manner a story of a woman's suicide becomes a critique of the persons or the social conditions that drove her to it.

A particularly ironic example is the story of the "five *lienü* of the Song family." The five Song women (four daughters and one granddaughter) belonged to the family of a tenant farmer. Because the women were attractive, the owner of the land the father tilled tried to coerce them to become his concubines. One night in 1695, the five young women committed suicide together. When the case was brought to the county magistrate, who feared the power of the landowner and dared not report it to his superiors, the girls were buried instead in a tomb provided by the government, over which was a stone tablet with the inscription "Tomb of the Five Song

*Lienü.*[53] In a similar case in 1716, the widow Zhang, wife of Fan Tingzhu in Xiangcheng, Hubei Province, was raped and killed by two bullies who were registered military men from the same county. Her neighbors brought the case to court, but the county magistrate was afraid of the power of the two bullies and their families, so he blamed the widow's death on alleged advances by a younger brother-in-law. So many people protested this obvious fabrication that the magistrate was forced to alter his final report on the case, changing the verdict to "insoluble."[54]

Despite the continued practice of suicide even after it was publicly condemned by the Qing court, clear differences between patterns of female suicide in Ming and Qing biographies can be identified. First, reported cases of female suicide dropped dramatically in Qing times, especially after the bans on widow suicide published by the Yongzheng (r. 1723–35) and Qianlong (r. 1736–95) emperors. Second, Qing records of widow suicide tend to stress that the woman honored for fidelity had fulfilled all of her duties to her late husband's family—in particular, seeing to the establishment of an heir—before she killed herself. An elaborate example is the story of Lady Li, betrothed to a man named Wu Du and reared in the Wu family from the age of eleven. Six years later, Wu Du drowned in a well. Although the marriage ceremony had not yet taken place, Li pinned up her hair in the manner of a married woman and began to serve Wu Du's mother as her mother-in-law. She also asked the family to adopt a son for her to rear. When at last she had sent her younger brother-in-law through school and arranged a marriage for her younger sister-in-law and her own adopted son, she announced to her late husband's older brother: "Now my late husband's parents have died, and our family has enough people to carry on the rites for them in our ancestral hall. The person in the well [Wu Du] has waited for me for a long time. I should follow him." Twenty-one years after her fiancé's death, on his birthday, she jumped into the same well and drowned herself. Lady Li's biographers make it clear that her suicide, following this extraordinary record of faithful service, was an especially virtuous deed.[55]

Other examples show how the Qing preoccupation with filial duty rather than suicide was embraced by women of all ranks within elite families. When Lady Zhang, wife of Liu Kun, became aware that the city where she lived had been sacked and her husband had died, she killed her two daughters and told her late husband's concubine, named Wu, to hide the three-year-old heir so that he could carry on the Liu family line. The concubine first arranged for her son's nanny to carry the boy away to safety, then she committed suicide together with her late husband's wife.[56] After the death of Ma Xiongzhen, his wife, Lady Li, presided while her late husband's concubine, her daughters-in-law, and her daughters all killed themselves. She then arranged for their bodies to be placed in a proper sequence, proclaiming, "These women would not allow their bodies to be humiliated. Like them, I go to my death without regret!"—whereupon she too committed suicide.[57]

During the post-Yongzheng era, as the ideal of the faithful widow replaced the glorification of the suicidal martyr, rhetoric of family and state focused increasingly on the stability of the family as the foundation of the polity. As the preface to the

"Biographies of Exemplary Women" (Lienü zhuan) in the *Draft History of the Qing Dynasty* points out:

> A state is formed by the accretion of families, composed equally of males and females. The daughter obeys her parents; the daughter-in-law reverently serves her parents-in-law; the wife assists her husband; the mother guides her sons and daughters; sisters and sisters-in-law fulfill their appropriate [duties.] When every member behaves this way, a family achieves harmony; when every family is harmonious, the state is well governed.[58]

In this context, a widow moved to the center of the family left bereft by her husband's death. Not only was her role as wife and mother foregrounded by Neo-Confucian ideology. In addition, her own beliefs in fate figured in her sense of obligation. She had to assume all of the filial responsibilities for her husband's parents. She had to rear an heir who would ensure the perpetuation of his descent line. And, if possible, she had to educate the heir and see him on his way to scholarly success and an official career through the civil service examination system.

Stories of widows who reared famous scholar-officials fill the records of the Qing dynasty. These stories emphasize the devotion of the learned mother, the high moral standards of the illiterate mother, and the sense of moral worth and pride that steeled widows to endure the loneliness and labor of widowhood in the interests of the family.[59] Lady Dong, who married Hu Yuanqin of Linqing, Shandong Province, was widowed at the age of fifteen and lived on alone for the next eighty years. When a neighbor asked how she managed, she replied:

> When I'm hungry, I eat; when I'm tired, I sleep, and when I'm not tired or hungry, I have to keep working. I never sit and enjoy myself. Before when I was employed as a maid, I always tried to make my work as good as it could be. When I tried to make my work good, I concentrated my mind. When I concentrated my mind, I used all of my energy. When I used all of my energy, I easily got tired. When I was tired, I went to sleep, and after I slept, I got up. I never gave myself even a minute to rest. I have done that for so long now that it's become a habit.[60]

## THE CHANGING MEANING OF FILIALITY
## FOR VIRTUOUS WOMEN IN QING TIMES

Echoing the shift from *lie* to *jie*—from martyrdom to fidelity—in Qing stories of virtuous women is the declining salience of daughterly virtue. Qing temples honoring paragons of virtue (*jiexiao ci*) identify *xiao* (filiality) with men, reserving the complementary term *jie* (fidelity, purity) for women. It appears that the virtue known as filiality was losing its importance for daughters in the Ming-Qing period, to be replaced by *jie*. Often understood as "filiality" and described as such, *jie*, or fidelity, focused on a woman's filial conduct not toward her own parents but toward her husband's.

Some evidence for this change is found in the declining prominence of a book entitled the *Classic of Filial Piety for Women* (Nü xiaojing), written in the Tang period and reprinted with elaborate illustrations during the Song.[61] In marked contrast to the attention the text received in the Song period, and to the explosion of stories about filial boys and girls in Yuan times, during the Qing the so-called *Four Books for Women* (Nü sishu) conspicuously dropped the filiality classic and replaced it with other texts considered more fundamental to women's moral development. In Qing times, young women anxious to cultivate their virtue were expected to study Ban Zhao's *Precepts for Women* (Nüjie) and another early work, the *Analects for Women* (Nü lunyu), along with two didactic Ming texts, *Instructions for the Inner Quarters* (Neixun) and *Female Exemplars* (Nüfan jielu)—but not the filiality classic. Even the official advocate of mid-Qing education for women, Chen Hongmou, did not see fit to include *Filial Piety for Women* in his "bequeathed guidelines" for women's education (*Jiaonü yigui*), compiled in 1742, nor did subsequent editors include it on the list of texts that made their way into expanded later versions of Chen's original work.[62]

Local gazetteers in Qing times provide additional evidence that filiality as a female virtue had been displaced by the virtue *jie* or its equivalents. During this period, stories of exemplary women in local gazetteers often divide their subjects into categories, according to the nature of their virtuous deeds. These categories can be read as glosses on how contemporaries understood the womanly virtues honored by the official discourse and the imperial court. In chapters on virtuous women, where *xiao* appears at all, it is usually paired with *jie* (fidelity or sexual purity).

An excellent example is the "Monograph on Exemplary Women" in the gazetteer *Hanzhou zhi* (Chengdu *fu*, Sichuan Province) of 1812, which was divided into four sections: *jiexiao* (faithful and filial wives), *jielie* (faithful martyred widows), and *zhennü* (pure women) and *lienü* (martyred women). These categories focus exclusively on married, about-to-be-married, or marriageable women. *Xiao* is the term reserved for widows who remain alive after a husband's death to serve their parents-in-law, as distinguished from those who "follow a husband in death." The term *zhennü*, which might appear to mean "pure daughter," refers *not* to *xiaonü* (filial girls) but to "pure girls"—daughters who lose a fiancé before marriage and remain faithful to the betrothal, often transferring residence and service to the home of the deceased, sometimes against the expressed wish of parents. The preface explains:

> A righteous wife who follows one husband all her life, a pure daughter who does not marry for ten years [after her fiancé dies]—how virtuous they are! To prepare tempting foods and offer up the washbasin, to wait upon a father-in-law and mother-in-law, to grasp the broom and hold the towel, to respectfully support a husband and sons: each of these homely tasks has its place; all are prescribed in ritual texts.
>
> And so it is that when a young girl loses her mate and with him her pledge to follow him to the grave through three lifetimes, or when a child's soul is frightened and she suddenly dies resisting assault by a person bent on doing her harm, or when a husband meets a violent end and his wife takes her own life, or when upon hearing some vile and lewd language a woman rises up and sacrifices her life—such women have only these aims: that they not be found wanting in fidelity and righteousness, and that they live up to the weighty responsibilities of family relationships. The white

essence of virtue rises to fill the heavens, as well as appearing in inscriptions on bronze and stone. The vermillion annals record her name, ensuring her perpetual glory. Herewith our monograph on exemplary women.[63]

The editors of the Tai'an county gazetteer in Shandong, following a slightly different model, divided exemplary women's biographies into three categories: the pure and wise (*xianshu*), the faithful and filial (*jiexiao*), and the martyred true ones (*zhenlie*). Once again, the editors reserved honors for filial conduct for widows who served their husbands' parents.[64] A roughly contemporary gazetteer from Boshan county in the same province opens its chapter on exemplary women with the following statement:

> Filial wives have long won fame for their virtue. Living, they bear responsibility for the family's guidance; after death, they join the ancestral spirits. Throughout the thousands of years of unbroken ancestral rites, there has never been a time when they flourish as they do today.[65]

In Guangdong Province, the Longshan district gazetteer (*Longshan xiang zhi*) of 1805 includes both suicidal and faithful widows under the category *jiefu*, contrasting them with *lienü* and *zhennü*. Stories of *jiefu* are the only stories celebrating filiality in this chapter. The others (i.e., *lienü* and *zhennü*) prove once again to be young betrothed women who die resisting rape or who follow their fiancés in death. Filiality does not figure in their stories.

Filial conduct for women certainly remained important in Qing times. Chapters in the *Four Books for Women* discuss filial deeds (*xiao xing*) and describe in detail various ways to both "serve parents" and "serve in-laws." Similarly, a text compiled in 1831 surveying biographies of exemplary women through history—Wanyan Yun Zhu's *Precious Records of the Maidens' Chambers* (Langui baolu)—gives pride of place to the virtue *xiao* in a sixfold classification scheme for women's biographies.[66] As the editor's preface to Chapter 1 explains:

> Filial piety is the impulse behind all action:
> Rising early, stepping quickly,
> Caring well for her father and mother,
> Keenly obeying her father-in-law and mother-in-law,
> With patience and meticulous care,
> Without insolence or excess.
> Nurturing this pure beginning,
> Her performance is always exemplary.[67]

Yet Yun Zhu's own historical analysis of women's virtues through the ages, displayed in the table on the following page, shows that in Qing times filiality for daughters was likely to receive short shrift when compared to fidelity or chastity.

With respect to temporal shifts, Yun Zhu's records dramatize the focus on chastity that emerges in records of women's virtue in the Ming-Qing period. Whereas in Han and Song times, filiality and chastity are relatively evenly balanced in records of women's virtue and whereas filiality is manifestly more important than chastity in Tang and Yuan records, by Ming and Qing times chastity is the virtue distinguishing more than half of all biographies of exemplary women, with filiality reduced to less than one-fifth of all cases (see Table 9.7). Yun Zhu's nine stories of filial girls for the Qing period, moreover, include five that stress a woman's filiality toward her in-laws rather than her parents.

Turning to the individual tales of womanly filial piety selected for inclusion in Yun Zhu's anthology, we find a broad definition of filial virtue for girls. In one story a Manchu woman named Baishun, her parents' only surviving child, vows never to marry so that she can serve and care for her parents.[68] The tale of Wang Wenlan's wife, née Yun, describes how she continued to care for her aging mother even after her marriage.[69] A prepubescent girl dies trying to rescue a father, while another courageous daughter leads troops to avenge her father's death and ultimately wins him justice in the courts.[70]

But Yun Zhu's tales of filial girls seem to be less about filiality itself and more about other, larger lessons. Her stories tell of treacherous servants, of tribal minorities, of Manchu women, of lowly folk. In that way, they dramatize the fact that virtue may cross as well as stop at gender, ethnic, and class lines. Perhaps more important, they show that the imperial grace recognizes virtue wherever it appears. In other words, the virtue of filial piety itself may be less salient than the universalizing message it is intended to convey.

The most telling example of this appears in the story of Ou, wife of Cui Huan, daughter of a tribal chieftain in Guangxi. In the custom of Ou's tribe, all children who reached the age of one year were given a silver necklace to wear for life. This "fate necklace" (*ming juan*) protected the life of the wearer until it broke. In Yun Zhu's story, Ou takes a vow before the gods when her mother-in-law becomes ill, then breaks her necklace and sells it for medicine to heal her mother. Her mother-in-law then recovers, and Ou suffers no ill effect. The story of Ou shows the reader how the civilizing force of Confucian virtue and the healing powers of Confucian medicine override tribal custom and superstition. And a filial girl becomes an emblem of the Confucian civilizing project.[71]

How did "filiality" (*xiao*) differ from "fidelity" (*jie*) as a womanly virtue? If the filial married woman was someone who dutifully served her in-laws, was the faithful widow a filial girl in special circumstances? That is, a daughter-in-law who remained filial after her husband's death? Yun Zhu's biographies of "chaste" (*jielie*) women are helpful here. The thirty stories in the Qing section of Yun Zhu's chapter on "faithful wives" seem on first glance to describe moral exemplars just like the women chronicled in the section on filiality. Included among the tales of women who "follow a husband in death"[72] or die resisting rape,[73] we find a woman saving her mother-in-law from bandits and dying in the attempt,[74] a woman who kills herself after retrieving the bodies of her murdered husband, son, and parents-in-law,[75] and other more or less bizarre tales of death in the name of fidelity and chastity.

TABLE 9.7 Yun Zhu's Exemplary Women in the *Precious Record*,
Showing Total Cases by Dynasty and by Category

| Dynasty | Filial | Wise | Nurturing | Chaste | Strategy | Talented | Totals |
|---|---|---|---|---|---|---|---|
| Qin | 0 | 0 | 0 | 0 | 1 | 0 | 1 |
| Han | 7 | 7 | 6 | 7 | 2 | 6 | 35 |
| Six Dynasties | 10 | 15 | 7 | 11 | 30 | 13 | 86 |
| Sui | 3 | 1 | 3 | 1 | 1 | 2 | 11 |
| Tang | 15 | 13 | 10 | 10 | 8 | 11 | 67 |
| Five Dynasties | 1 | 4 | 0 | 3 | 1 | 1 | 10 |
| Song | 11 | 12 | 19 | 13 | 2 | 4 | 61 |
| Liao-Jin | 4 | 5 | 2 | 4 | 5 | 2 | 22 |
| Yuan | 11 | 8 | 3 | 6 | 1 | 1 | 30 |
| Ming | 15 | 27 | 4 | 53 | 10 | 3 | 112 |
| Qing | 9 | 7 | 6 | 30 | 4 | 5 | 61 |
| TOTAL | 86 | 99 | 60 | 138 | 65 | 48 | |

These tales of virtue show how shifting the focus from the natal to the marital family resolved competing claims on womanly virtue in Qing times, creating a seamless continuity between the state's prescriptions, the family's imperatives, and the behavior of women, whose conflicted loyalties mirror the political conflicts of the age.

## CONCLUSION

The homely virtues of endurance and service honored in the Qing dynasty cult of the faithful widow constitute a denatured, or "civilized," form of the more flamboyant, even sensational virtues celebrated in earlier heroic tales of martyrdom, whether by filial daughters or faithful wives. The power of the imperial state, reaching down to recognize loyal officials and virtuous women, is omnipresent in Yun Zhu's tales of exemplary women, as in the other narratives of Ming and Qing female biography. Especially in Qing times, womanly virtue becomes a mirror on society, a sign of the vigorous moral standards upheld by the Manchus and realized in the lives of even their lowliest, most marginal subjects.

If political messages are as important as moral messages in Yun Zhu's stories of womanly virtue, they explain why wifely fidelity became more important than daughterly filiality during the Qing period. A filial daughter actually does, or may, serve two masters—her parents and her parents-in-law. A faithful widow owes service only to one. If the Manchus were troubled by the ambivalent allegiance of the filial daughter, they could only have been comforted by the unambiguous loyalty of the chaste widow. Filial daughters may have been symbols of the ambivalent subjects of the former Ming who turned to support the Manchus after the conquest. Faithful widows, in contrast, could be carefully chosen to illustrate the absolute fidelity displayed by Ma Xiongzhen's women—celebrated by Yun Zhu as well as by official chroniclers—who scorned the rebel factions in the south to support the new Manchu regime.[76]

*Xiao* as a womanly virtue was important in early periods of Chinese history, when the elite kinship system was still—in Ebrey's words—"slightly cognatic." By late imperial times, though, daughterly filiality was far less important than wifely fidelity, and widows as martyrs (through death or suffering) had become near-cult figures in Confucian didactic texts. How and why did this happen? Confucianism alone clearly cannot answer these questions. Changes in the law that favored patrilineal bonds played a role. Important too were changes in ritual practice (marriage and mourning) and in the philosophical canon. These changes strengthened and also expressed other shifts in economic power and in the symbolic world of emotional and creative expression in Chinese culture. We still know very little about these shifts, but we are beginning to appreciate their complexity. Kathryn Bernhardt's survey of law and women's property rights, for instance, shows how rules of succession, inheritance, and ritual obligation constrained women's claims on property after the Song dynasty. At the same time, she stresses that widows enjoyed particular advantages with respect to property rights until "modern" legal systems that overrode widows' Confucian privileges were introduced after the Revolution of 1911.[77] Francesca Bray has posited a long-term secular decline in the cultural and material value of women's textile production resulting from changes in tax policies and other factors.[78] On the other hand, promoting "women's work" (defined as household spinning and weaving) was a hallmark of Qing dynasty statecraft policy.[79] Other scholars have documented the expansion of commercial entertainment employing female labor, especially courtesans, prostitutes, and performing artists, after the Song period. All were venues where women's talent was necessarily devalued while the prestige of classical scholarly learning remained the measure of cultural success, and where women's sexual behavior became the subject of growing state regulation.[80] Yet female writers and intellectuals of the Ming and Qing periods, who represented the barest fraction of a percentage of the population as a whole, used classical writing and publishing to assert their cultural power and to celebrate their own talent and virtue.[81]

In sum, the complex relationship between Confucianism—the ideology of cultural expression and the bedrock of the family system in imperial China—and the late imperial chastity cult is only part of a larger historical story. That story must also encompass the impact of broad economic transformation, along with the late imperial government's relentless drive to regulate the intimate relations of men and women living in China's diverse local cultures and ethnic groups.

## NOTES

The authors wish to thank Yu-Yin Cheng for her invaluable help in translating the initial draft of Du Fangqin's portion of this chapter. This final jointly written version relied heavily on Cheng's rendering of the original Chinese essay.

1. See the discussion of the didactic purpose of official biographies in D. C. Twitchett, "Chinese Biographical Writing," in *Historians of China and Japan*, ed. W. G. Beasley and E. G. Pulleyblank (London: Oxford University Press, 1961), pp. 95–114.

2. Mark Elvin was the first to call attention to the contradictions, or what he called "ambiguities," inherent in Confucian womanly virtues. See Mark Elvin, "Female Virtue and the State in China," *Past and Present* 104 (1984): 111–52, esp. pp. 138–48. For a discussion of the contradictions between norms and real behavior, see Susan Mann, "Widows in the Kinship, Class, and Community Structures of Qing Dynasty China," *Journal of Asian Studies* 46, no. 1 (1987): 37–56.

3. For discussions of tensions between a woman's obligations to her own parents and the parents of her husband, see Margery Wolf, *Women and the Family in Rural Taiwan* (Stanford: Stanford University Press, 1972), pp. 35, 136, 140, 217; Maurice Freedman, "Ritual Aspects of Chinese Kinship and Marriage," in *Family and Kinship in Chinese Society*, ed. Maurice Freedman (Stanford: Stanford University Press, 1970), pp. 45, 101, 177; Hugh D. R. Baker, *Chinese Family and Kinship* (New York: Columbia University Press, 1979), pp. 127–28. Marriage laments sung by women express the emotional cost of these tensions. See Elizabeth L. Johnson, "Grieving for the Dead, Grieving for the Living: Funeral Laments of Hakka Women," in *Death Ritual in Late Imperial and Modern China*, ed. James L. Watson and Evelyn S. Rawski (Berkeley: University of California Press, 1988), pp. 138–39.

4. *Xiao* referred to every child's obligation to revere and serve parents in life and to continue that reverence and service after death through mourning and ritual offerings (ancestor worship). For males, filial duty was unambiguous and lifelong. It encompassed the full range of obligation from unconditional obedience (in childhood) to fathering sons who would continue the patriline (after marriage) to mourning and ritual offerings (after parents died). Even though hagiographic descriptions of filial piety show daughters as well as sons performing filial deeds, such as cutting flesh from their bodies to make a medicinal broth to heal an ailing parent, the most dramatic public expression of filial obligation was reserved for boys. This public display came during mourning rituals; even the highest official in the imperial bureaucracy retired from office for the full twenty-seven months' mourning period at the death of a parent. Officials who neglected their filial duty were ready targets of impeachment campaigns.

5. Patricia Ebrey, "Women in the Kinship System of the Southern Song Upper Class," in *Women in China: Current Directions in Historical Scholarship*, ed. Richard W. Guisso and Stanley Johannesen (Youngstown, N.Y.: Philo Press, 1981), p. 125.

6. During the Ming and Qing periods, sons and unmarried daughters mourned for a full three years following the death of either parent, but once married, a woman's obligation to mourn her own mother and father decreased to only one year. See Ch'ü T'ung-tsu, *Law and Society in Traditional China* (Paris: Mouton, 1961), p. 31; also Maurice Freedman, *Lineage Organization in Southeastern China* (London: Athlone Press, 1958), pp. 45, 101. Arthur Wolf, however, studying mourning obligations in Taiwan, found considerable disagreement among his informants with respect to a married woman's mourning obligations, despite ritual prescriptions. See Arthur P. Wolf, "Chinese Kinship and Mourning Dress," in *Family and Kinship in Chinese Society*, ed. Maurice Freedman (Stanford: Stanford University Press, 1970), pp. 201–3. Wolf's findings underscore the enduring tension in the relationship between a married women and her natal kin. See also note 3, above.

7. See William A. Lyell Jr., *Lu Hsün's Vision of Reality* (Berkeley: University of California Press, 1976), pp. 141–44.

8. See, for example, Angela Ki Che Leung, "To Chasten Society: The Development of Widow Homes in the Qing," *Late Imperial China* 14, no. 2 (1993): 1–32.

9. One of the most impassioned of these critics was Wang Zhong, whose essay condemning the folly of young girls who insisted on a ghost marriage after the death of a fiancé pointed out that theirs was the most unfilial act of all, because it was usually undertaken in defiance of the heartfelt pleas of their own parents. See Wang Zhong, "Nüzi xu jia er xu si you si ji shou zhi yi," *Shu xue, nei bian* 1 (Taipei: Guangwen shuju, 1970), n.p. Yuasa Yukihiko's review of these critiques stresses that such young women were criticized for their lack of filiality toward their parents, in particular by Wang Zhong, who quoted from the *Classic of Filial Piety* (Xiao jing) in his essay. See Yuasa Yukihiko, "Shindai ni okeru fujin kaihōron: Reikyō to ningenteki shizen" (The discourse on women's emancipation in the Qing dynasty: The teachings of the rites and human nature), *Nihon Chūgoku gakkaihō* 4 (1953): 115.

10. See Susan Mann, *Precious Records: Women in China's Long Eighteenth Century* (Stanford: Stanford University Press, 1997), pp.115–16.

11. See Du Fangqin, "Zhouli zhi xing: Fuquanzhi chujianshi de xingbie guanxi" (The rise of the rituals of Zhou: Gender relations in the early stages of patriarchy), in *Faxian funü de lishi—Zhongguo funüshi lunji* (Discovering women's history: Collected essays on the history of Chinese women) (Tianjin: Tianjin shehui kexueyuan chubanshe, 1996).

12. See Liu Xiang, *Lienü zhuan* (Biographies of women) (rpt. Taipei: Sibu beiyao edition, 1966).

13. See *Hou Han shu jijie* (History of the Later Han dynasty, with complete annotations) (Beijing: Zhonghua shuju, 1984).

14. Lisa Raphals, *Sharing the Light: Representations of Women and Virtue in Early China* (Albany: State University of New York Press, 1998), summary on p. 142.

15. T'ien Ju-k'ang, *Male Anxiety and Female Chastity: A Comparative Study of Chinese Ethical Values in Ming-Ch'ing Times* (Leiden: E. J. Brill, 1988).

16. See Patricia Buckley Ebrey, *The Inner Quarters: Marriage and the Lives of Chinese Women in the Sung Period* (Berkeley: University of California Press, 1993), pp. 194–212, esp. 204–12; and Patricia Buckley Ebrey, trans. and annot., *Family and Property in Sung China: Yüan Ts'ai's "Precepts for Social Life"* (Princeton: Princeton University Press, 1984), p. 99.

17. Jerry Dennerline, "Marriage, Adoption, and Charity in the Development of Lineages in Wu-hsi from Sung to Ch'ing," in *Kinship Organization in Late Imperial China, 1000–1940*, ed. Patricia Buckley Ebrey and James L. Watson (Berkeley: University of California Press, 1986), esp. pp. 188, 204.

18. Over the past decade, Patricia Ebrey has been documenting those changes, which are analyzed and richly documented in Ebrey, *Inner Quarters*.

19. Ebrey, *Family and Property*.

20. Ebrey, "Women in the Kinship System of the Southern Song Upper Class," pp. 118–19; Ebrey, *Inner Quarters*, pp. 103–9; Ch'ü, *Law and Society*, p. 37.

21. Zhao Fengjie, *Zhongguo funü zai falüshang de diwei* (The position of women in Chinese law) (Shanghai: Commercial Press, 1928), p. 13. The problem of female inheritance in the Song is critically examined in Kathryn Bernhardt, *Women and Property in China, 960–1949* (Stanford: Stanford University Press, 1999).

22. Ch'ü, *Law and Society*, p. 95.

23. Ibid., pp. 110–11.

24. Ebrey, *Inner Quarters*, p. 52. As in later times, in the Song period a married woman's mourning obligations to her natal home were reduced one degree, as were her natal kin's mourning obligations to her.

25. Ebrey, *Inner Quarters*, summary on p. 265.

26. Ibid., p. 196.

27. See the discussion in Du Fangqin, "Shengyu wenhua de lishi kaocha" (An historical inquiry into the culture of childbirth), in *Xingbie yu Zhongguo* (Gender and China), ed. Li Xiaojiang et al. (Beijing: Sanlian shudian, 1994), pp. 317–18; also Du Fangqin, "Lixue chujian dui Yuandai funü de yingxiang" (The influence of Song Neo-Confucianism on women in the Yuan dynasty), in *Faxian funü de lishi*, pp. 167–68.

28. See *Songshi* 460, p. 13479, cited in Du, "Lixue chujian," pp. 167–68.

29. Su Shi's biography in the *Song shi* alludes briefly to Lady Cheng's role as a tutor. See *Songshi* 338, p. 10801. Epitaphs supply more detail. See Su Xun, *Jiayou ji* (Collected works of Su Xun) (Taipei: Taiwan Shangwu yinshuguan, 1983–86), vol. 1104, pp. 977–78; and Su Che, *Luancheng ji* (The complete works of Su Che) (Shanghai: Guji chubanshe, 1987), *juan* 22, p. 1410. The former is an epitaph for Lady Cheng herself, written by Sima Guang and inserted in an appendix to Su Xun's collection; the latter is an epitaph for Su Shi in which Su Che mentions their mother's role in their education.

30. *Yuanshi* 196, p. 4433.

31. She dates the formal introduction of these policies to an imperial edict of 1303. See Jennifer Holmgren, "Observations on Marriage and Inheritance Practices in Early Mongol and Yuan Society, with Particular Reference to the Levirate," *Journal of Asian History* 20, no. 2 (1986): 127–92, quotations on p. 183.

32. *Yuanshi* 196, pp. 4433–34.

33. *Mingshi* 302, p. 7716.

34. For all these stories, see *Mingshi* 302, p. 7716.

35. *Mingshi* 301, p. 7697.

36. *Mingshi* 302, p. 7716.

37. Ibid., p. 7718.

38. *Mingshi* 303, p. 7752.

39. *Mingshi* 302, p. 7718.

40. Ibid., p. 7733.

41. *Mingshi* 301, p. 7705.

42. *Mingshi* 302, p. 7731.

43. Ibid., p. 7723.

44. *Mingshi* 301, p. 7704.

45. Examples include the chaste lady (*zhennü*) Lin of Houguan, Fujian (*Mingshi* 303, p. 7739); Lin Duanniang of Ouning, Fujian (*Mingshi* 301, p. 7709); Hu Guizhen of Leping, Jiangxi (*Mingshi* 301, p. 7712; Lady Xiang and Lady Zhang of Xiushui, Zhejiang (*Mingshi* 302, p. 7729; 301, p. 7701); Ouyang Quanzhen of Jiangxia, Hubei (*Mingshi* 301, p. 7701); Lady Chen of Xiangfu, Henan (*Mingshi* 301, p. 7701); Lady Shi of Qi county, Henan (*Mingshi* 301, p. 7708); Lady Peng of Anqiu, Shandong (*Mingshi* 302, p. 7724). All either refused food and starved to death or hanged themselves following the death of a fiancé.

46. *Mingshi* 302, p. 7725.

47. Ibid., p. 7729.

48. *Mingshi* 301, p. 7700.

49. Similar cases include those of Wang Miaofeng of Wu county, Jiangsu (*Mingshi* 301, p. 7700), and Lady Zhang of Jiading, Jiangsu (*Mingshi* 301, p. 7700), both of whom committed suicide because of sexual abuse by a promiscuous mother-in-law; also Lady Wang of Shangyuan and Lady Xu of Songjiang, Jiangsu, whose husbands were drunkards and gamblers who invited predatory male friends into their homes, where they sexually harassed their wives (*Mingshi* 302, pp. 7716–17).

50. *Qingshi gao*, "Lienü xu," *juan* 55, p. 11640.

51. *Qingshi gao*, "Xiao yi," "Li Shengshan zhuan," *juan* 504, p. 11441. The biography of Li Shengshan in the *Qingshi gao* consists entirely of this reprinted (and slightly edited) edict, the original version of which may be found in *Da Qing Shizong xianhuangdi shi lu* (Veritable records of the Yongzheng reign) (Taipei: Taiwan huawen shuju, 1964), *juan* 67, pp. 1043–44.

52. *Qingshi gao* 518, p. 11731.

53. Ibid., p. 11746.

54. Ibid., p. 11745.

55. *Qingshi gao* 516, p. 11693.

56. *Qingshi gao* 517, p. 11707.

57. Ibid., p. 11706.

58. *Qingshi gao* 515, p. 11640.

59. After her husband died, Hong Liangji's mother, Lady Jiang, taught her son to study the *Book of Rites*, drilling him in the proper pronunciation of every character: "[M]other's teaching and son's reciting usually lasted till midnight," according to his biographers. Zhang Huiyan's mother, Lady Jiang, whose husband died young, guided her two sons to well-established scholarly careers. The female scholar and painter Yun Zhu, who married the Manchu Wanyan Tinglu, likewise reared her sons after the death of her husband and was praised for her strictness. Even illiterate widows proved capable of strictly supervising a son's studies. For example, Lady Pan, the widow of Hu Michan of Tongcheng, personally conducted her eldest son to the village school. Because the family was too poor to permit him to complete his schooling, Pan would ask her son to recite texts and she would then explain the texts to him based on her own rudimentary grasp of classical teachings. Thus, the story goes, when she heard her son reading from Cheng Yi's or Zhu Xi's words, she was unceasingly approving, but on hearing him recite Sima Xiangru's prose poem "Praising Beauty," she grew angry and ordered him to stop at once. Lady Tian, wife of Chen Shixia, states in her "Preface to the Instructions from the Jinghe Hall" (*Jinghe tang bixun zixu*) that she remained a faithful widow in order to educate her three sons and one daughter. She said, "[I hope only that] while I am alive I will do nothing that is unworthy of my children and when I am dead I will have done nothing unworthy of my husband." See *Qingshi gao* 515, pp. 11643–44.

60. *Qingshi gao* 516, p. 11672.

61. See Julia K. Murray, "Didactic Art for Women: The Ladies' Classic of Filial Piety," in *Flowering in the Shadows: Women in the History of Chinese and Japanese Painting*, ed. Marsha Weidner (Honolulu: University of Hawaii Press, 1990).

62. It does not appear in the published edition of 1868, nor was it added to the considerably expanded version reissued in 1895. Various editions of the *Nü xiaojing* printed in the Ming-Qing period, in China and in Japan, are described in Yamazaki Jun'ichi, *Kyōiku kara mita Chūgoku joseishi shiryō no kenkyū* (A documentary study of Chinese women's history as seen from education) (Tokyo: Meiji shoin, 1986), p. 341.

63. *Hanzhou zhi* (1812), 32:1a.

64. For the Ming-Qing listings, see *Tai'an xian zhi* (1782), 10 *xia*:6a–25b. The next edition of the gazetteer, dated 1828, follows almost exactly the same pattern.

65. *Boshan [Shandong] xian zhi* (1753) 8:1a.

66. Wanyan Yun Zhu, ed., *Langui baolu* (Precious record from the maidens' chambers), Hongxiang guan edition, printed 1831–32, preface dated the first ten days of the second month of summer, 1831 (approximately mid-June).

67. *Langui baolu,* 1: "Mu lu," 1.

68. Ibid., 1:29a–b.

69. Ibid., 1:30a.

70. Ibid., 1:27b–28a.

71. On civilizing projects, see Stevan Harrell, "Introduction: Civilizing Projects and the Reaction to Them," in *Cultural Encounters on China's Ethnic Frontiers,* ed. Stevan Harrell (Seattle: University of Washington Press, 1995); on the Manchus' own universalizing project, see Pamela Kyle Crossley, "*Manzhou yuanliu kao* and the Formalization of the Manchu Heritage," *Journal of Asian Studies* 46, no. 4 (1987): 761–90.

72. *Langui baolu,* 4:43b–44a, 44a–b.

73. Ibid., 4:44b–45a.

74. Ibid., 4:44a.

75. Ibid., 4:45a–b.

76. Yun Zhu herself, a Han Chinese woman married into a Manchu family and the mother of a prominent Manchu official, would have had strong views on such subjects. See Mann, *Precious Records,* pp. 94–108. For the biography of Ma Xiongzhen's wife, see *Langui baolu,* 4:47a–b.

77. Bernhardt, *Women and Property.*

78. Francesca Bray, *Technology and Gender: Fabrics of Power in Late Imperial China* (Berkeley: University of California Press, 1997).

79. Mann, *Precious Records,* pp. 143–77.

80. Though many studies of opera and of prostitution can be used to document this process, the single work devoted exclusively to the subject of women as entertainers is Wang Shunu's study, *Zhongguo changji shi* (The history of prostitution in China) (Shanghai: Sanlian shudian, [1933] 1988). Also important here is Matthew Sommer's analysis of the criminalization of prostitution and its effects on women's status in the courts of the Qing period. See Matthew Sommer, *Sex, Law, and Society in Late Imperial China* (Stanford: Stanford University Press, 2000).

81. See Dorothy Ko, *Teachers of the Inner Chambers: Women and Culture in Seventeenth-Century China* (Stanford: Stanford University Press, 1994); and Mann, *Precious Records.*

# PART FOUR

# Corporeal and Textual Expressions of Female Subjectivity

# CHAPTER TEN

# Discipline and Transformation

## Body and Practice in the Lives of Daoist Holy Women of Tang China

*Suzanne E. Cahill*

This study investigates an extraordinary group of women who lived in the context of Confucian society: Daoist holy women of the Tang dynasty (618–907). It examines issues of female body and text and highlights the centrality of the body as the location of practice and change. Here I link body, gender, discipline, and liberation in the lives of these women. All the chapters in this volume fracture and complicate our definitions of "Confucianism." This chapter promotes inclusive understandings of Confucianism and discourages superficial contrasts between Daoist and Confucian values.

We begin by admitting the relativity of our terms. Such apparently simple terms as "body," "gender," "discipline," and "liberation" have been regarded in different ways at different times and places. We know that the body has not always been perceived as the same whole we understand now. Nor has it always been dismembered and divided from an internal self. Notions of gender are culturally constructed: some go so far as to claim gender is not a state but a performance. Even sex, which we place in the realm of science and assume we can distinguish clearly, does not escape cultural construction. Discipline, viewed by many today as limiting individual freedom, is regarded by others as a path to individual liberation. When the medieval Chinese holy women considered here disciplined their bodies to achieve liberation, they did so in the context of the Daoist religion.[1]

The terms "Confucianism" and "Daoism" also need definition for the purposes of this discussion. Confucians and Daoists have often been construed as opposites and rivals, with Confucianism representing the hierarchical standards and structures of the Chinese patriarchy and imperium and Daoism embodying more egalitarian, individual, and even eccentric values. The medieval reality is more complex. Tang Confucianism included commitment to the ethical priorities expressed in the ancient Confucian canonical texts and their later commentaries, together with dedication to the ideals of official service in the imperial bureaucracy under the reigning dynasty. Major contributions of Tang Confucianism included expanding scholarship on the canon, linking it to official training and ideology, while at the same time adapting it to harmonize with the institutions of the most sophisticated dynasty yet to rule China. Tang Confucianism attained its maturity as a political and ethical system of thought at the same time Daoism reached a high point in its development as a religion. Tang Confucianism taught people how to be ethical human beings and good leaders of government. Tang Daoism taught them how to become immortal.

Daoism, the native higher religion of China, grew up in China alongside its real rival, Buddhism, during the first five centuries of the Common Era. There were two great Daoist schools by the fifth century. The Shangqing, or Supreme Clear Realm, tradition, named after one of the highest heavens of Daoism from which its sacred scriptures were believed to be revealed, emphasized individual self-cultivation. In contrast, the Lingbao, or Numinous Treasure, school, named for its scriptures, emphasized public ritual. Both schools pursued individual immortality through realizing humans' highest potential. By the Tang dynasty, Shangqing Daoism had grown into an institutionalized religion patronized by the state and favored by the educated official classes, while Lingbao Daoism had provided many of the great state, community, and family rites.

Emerging from and reflecting the medieval Chinese social context, Tang Daoism is distinctly ambivalent about gender. On the one hand, Daoist scriptures begin with the creation of the world by the equal and opposite forces known as *yin* (the dark, female force) and *yang* (the bright, male force). This seems to suggest equity between men and women. The scriptures also teach that all humans are capable of perfection. And modern Daoists have often asserted that men and women are equal in their tradition. On the other hand, the social and institutional reality of medieval Daoism was that men held power, prestige, and material wealth within church hierarchies. On earth, men held important religious offices, performed rituals, and wrote texts. In the heavens, male deities possessed more honored ranks than did female deities. In the textual record, women are few.

The notion that Daoists opposed a "Confucian" social order does not help us to understand Tang historical reality. We often identify lineage and bureaucracy, two ancient values that give order to Chinese society, with "Confucianism." But concern with family and state is older than either Confucianism or Daoism, and central to both. Conflict with values of clan and imperium were not conflicts with "Confucianism" but with broadly held cultural traditions. When Daoist practices seemed to run contrary to these traditions, the Daoists had some explaining to do.

Medieval Daoists, like medieval Chinese Buddhists, had to answer criticism that their faith threatened the Chinese family and the state. Critics claimed that Daoist practices, such as the celibacy and asceticism of monks and nuns, opposed traditional values of filial piety and loyalty. Daoists, like their Buddhist rivals, answered that their religious practices constituted a higher filial piety and loyalty than the ordinary, since their deeds could save multitudes rather than a single family or ruler.

Daoists further argued that the mere presence of a saint was an auspicious omen signifying the legitimacy of the reigning dynasty. The Daoist women studied here would never have considered themselves opposed to what we today call "Confucian" values.

Not only did Daoists claim to support the social order, but Daoist institutions also imitated structures found in the larger "Confucian" society. The convent, for example, resembled a family, with the abbess as mother and the nuns as her daughters. Daoist sects are organized as teaching lineages, substituting the master-disciple relationship for that of blood kin. Where clan relationships are disrupted, fictive kinship is adopted. The process of legitimizing Daoist saints provides another case of institutional borrowing. In verifying saints, Daoists relied on two prestigious and ancient obsessions of Chinese culture: lineage and bureaucracy. To be accepted as a saint, a man or woman had to be placed in a divine lineage and assigned an office in the heavenly bureaucracy after life on earth.[2]

In the end, differences in goal and focus distinguish Confucians and Daoists most clearly. The Confucian aims to be an ethical person and a good subject of the emperor. The ultimate goal of the Daoist religious practitioner or adept was individual immortality; religious acts were believed to nurture an immortal embryo so that the adept became a perfected or realized person (*zhenren*) who ascended to the Daoist heavens to live there forever as a celestial bureaucrat after "death." It was assumed that the Daoist adept was in full compliance with the ethical norms of his or her social context before beginning the religious practices directed toward attaining immortality. The physical practices in question—fasting, ingesting elixirs, sexual or reproductive abstinence, and meditation—involved and transformed the adept's body.

The physical body, identified with the self in medieval Chinese thinking (whether Daoist or Confucian), was viewed as a location, the center of human thought and action.[3] As the source of needs we can interpret and control, and as the site of religious acts, the body provided the adept with opportunities for transcendence. With its desires, impermanence, and social constraints, the body also put obstacles in the path to immortality. The female body, as a location of cultural norms of beauty, health, and duty, presented special choices, special opportunities, and special obstacles. This chapter examines how one group of women faced these choices, opportunities, and obstacles.

Daoist holy women of the Tang removed themselves from the body of society, usually leaving or refusing to enter the household life. They chanted, spoke, and wrote. They availed themselves of Daoist religious practice. They proceeded along an ordered path of religious discipline leading to transcendence, committing acts that went against "common sense" in medieval China but that they and their biographers believed led to transformation and immortality. Their practice required physical discipline. Discipline was viewed by Daoists as necessary for liberation from mortality rather than as a hindrance to individual freedom. The specific disciplines they followed involved controlling or altering the universal human needs of family, nutrition, and sexuality. Practices were enacted through the body; results could be seen on the body. The adept's activities were believed to transform her body into something fragrant and radiant, perfect and permanent, "like metal or stone," that would never decay and would in the end ascend to heaven.[4]

In developing these themes, I discuss our sources and the stories they tell, what difference gender may have made for these sources, Daoist notions of the body, and finally practices of Daoist holy women during the Tang dynasty. I examine the women's acts, assumptions, and goals, in relation to the medieval Chinese social and historical context. The women believed that their religious practice would lead to corporeal transformation and physical liberation. I argue that their practice inverted the usual physical practices of women within the family and society in medieval China, with the clear goal of inverting the usual physical consequence of mortality. I hope this work will illuminate cultural constructions of the female and religious body in medieval China as well as other times and places and stimulate conversation on theoretical approaches to female subjectivities and expression.[5]

## SOURCES

Here I am looking at discipline and transformation in the lives of twelve medieval Daoist holy women who lived from the late sixth to the tenth century. Through the biographies and writings of these women, we can gain a sense of the constraints placed on women in Confucian society. I focus on these women's bodies, noting physical practices and their physical consequences. I consider female bodies in male-authored texts, female bodies as texts with physical practices as forms of writing, and female authors writing with body and brush. My sources, questioned about information they were never intended to provide, include biographies, poetry, and Daoist canonical texts.

Ten of the subjects are linked by inclusion in the "Records of the Assembled Transcendents of the Fortified Walled City " (Yongcheng jixian lu), a collection of biographical records of holy women completed around 910 by the Daoist Master Du Guangting (850–933). I also investigate two Tang dynasty Daoist nuns who wrote poetry: Li Ye (disappeared 756) and Yu Xuanji (844–68). Their poems survive today in a Qing dynasty collection called the *Complete Tang Poetry [Anthology]* (Quan Tang shi). To study what these women were doing, we can also interrogate texts on religious practice contained in the *Daozang*, or Daoist Canon.[6]

Each text has its own take on gender, bodies, discipline, liberation, and holy women. After discussing our sources and the type of information to be found in each, I consider how they treat gender. Let us turn first to Daoist Master Du.

### BODY AND PRACTICE IN DU GUANGTING'S
### DAOIST HAGIOGRAPHY

The most imporant single source for studying Daoist women saints of the Tang is the collection of twenty-seven biographies of Daoist holy women compiled by the

Shangqing Daoist Master and court official Du Guangting, "Records of the Assembled Transcendents of the Fortified Walled City," that appears in the Daoist Canon. The "Fortified Walled City" of the title is located in the Daoist heavens, a residence of the deity known as Queen Mother of the West; the assembled transcendents are female immortals to whom that goddess transmitted her Daoist arts. I have selected the nine women among Du's subjects born during his own era, the Tang dynasty, along with one who began her career during the preceding Sui period (589–618) and lived on into the following dynasty. These are his most detailed and coherent accounts, perhaps because his own primary sources were relatively abundant.

Du uses a form of biography that ultimately derives from biographies of officials in the dynastic histories, with some debt to accounts of exemplary women, biographies of Buddhist monks and nuns, and tales of Daoist transcendents.[7] A typical biography in Du's collection includes the following elements, when available, in order of appearance: name, lineage, offices of male ancestors, social class, places of origin and activity, historical period, childhood practice along with indications of vocation and divine selection, parental reaction to the child's devotion, solution to the dilemma posed by marriage, adult practices and signs of grace, encounters, disciples, transmissions of texts or rituals, circumstances of transformation ("death"), and posthumous position in the celestial bureaucracy.

Du Guangting defines the path to transcendence for his subjects in terms of religious practice. Their path follows an orderly progression from one stage to the next. All practice is preceded and accompanied by attitudes of faith and reverence. These internal states are assumed but not described in detail; practice as Du treats it in this text means external, observable religious activity. This activity may be divided into two main categories: good works and Daoist religious observances. Du's subjects perform several types of good works, often specified as hidden (*yin*): that is, deeds done with no expectation of recognition or reward. These include charity, restoration of holy sites, and defense of the faith. Charity can involve feeding animals or people in need, caring for the sick, or burying abandoned bones. Good works precede and lead to Daoist religious practices, which represent a more advanced state of religious development as well as a more effective means to transcendence. Religious practices include fasting and sexual abstinence, preliminaries for study and meditation. Study and meditation in turn lead to desired fruits of the faith: magical travel, special powers, teaching and textual transmission, and the ultimate reward of ascent to heaven where the Daoist perfected enjoy eternal life and divine office.

Du Guangting's collection of biographies was composed at the imperial court during the tumultuous last decades of the Tang dynasty. His didactic accounts tell stories of exemplary women in order to provide models of the faith, compete with Buddhist saints, present the Daoist church as worthy of imperial patronage, glorify his own Shangqing school, and supply evidence of the efficacy of Daoism in hard times. He aims for universality of class, region, school, and practice. His records supply us with the most reliable data we are likely to find on a variety of women's physical practices. While Du's subjects are extraordinary rather than typical women, their cases tell us about how contemporary people understood women's bodies, their religious activities, and the consequences of such behavior.

## TEN LIVES BY DU GUANGTING

Ten of Du Guangting's entries narrate stories of discipline and transformation in the lives of medieval Daoist holy women. The tales, enchanting in themselves, emphasize physical details. Every detail—a scar, a fragrance, a seed—has meaning. Each story adds to our picture of the body and practice during the Tang dynasty.

Certain elements associated with the body appear repeatedly. These include fasting while feeding others, eating special foods, having an unusual appearance or wearing uncommon clothing, refusing to marry or bear children, regaining health, looking youthful in old age, writing, predicting the time and place of one's own "death," and departing in an extraordinary fashion, accompanied by strange and wonderful fragrances. Each of these elements renounces or inverts the normal life cycle of a medieval Chinese woman. I consider the meanings of these inversions in the concluding section on Daoist women's physical practices. Below I discuss the individual women's lives in the order in which they appear in Du's work. I summarize each biography, translating literally the sections that pertain to body, practice, and physical results.

### Wang Fajin: An Ascetic Who Transmitted Rites and Ascended to Heaven

Wang Fajin (d. 752) revered Daoist images as a child and entered religious life at the age of ten with her parents' approval. Showing a vocation for austerities, she fasted and performed rituals. In the convent, she learned to "assist at fasts and abstinences as well as to eat fungi and cedar seeds and to stop eating grains" ("cutting off grains" means fasting to the extreme). Moved by her discipline, dieties visited her. During a famine, a high god called the Supreme Thearch summoned Wang Fajin to his Jade Capital in heaven. His summons described her accomplishments in bodily terms: "Because you have cherished your natural endowments, your transcendent bones will return. Your heart and essence are clear and sincere." On arrival, the god gave her an elixir drug in the form of "auroral broth in a jade cup." The Supreme Thearch then proclaimed that he had sent the famine to punish people for despising the fruits of the earth. When Wang Fajin pleaded on the people's behalf, he awarded her a great public rite of repentance and thanksgiving. She in turn transmitted the ritual to Daoist clergy for the benefit of all humankind.

In 752, during the reign of the Daoist emperor Xuanzong, she reached the end of her earthly career. "Cloud cranes welcomed Fajin and she ascended to heaven." Her departure was accompanied by Manchurian cranes, vehicles of the immortals

and symbols of longevity. Ascent to heaven in broad daylight was the highest form
of celestial transformation. Only two Tang holy women in the "Records of the
Assembled Transcendents of the Fortified Walled City" depart in this fashion. (The
other is Bian Dongxuan, considered below.) Wang Fajin overcame death: her asceticism and transmission of saving rites resulted in bodily ascent.[8]

### Ms. Wang: An Invalid and Ascetic Who Left an Empty Husk

Du Guangting's next subject, Ms. Wang, "embraced sickness and retreated into
chronic invalidism" right after marriage. Although she bore several daughters during the next decade, her symptoms allowed her to refuse sexual relations and other
domestic obligations most of the time. After ten years, Daoist Master Wu Yun
(d. 788) "gave her interdicted water and had her swallow a talismanic letter. After
passing one night, she improved." Ms. Wang thereupon began a rigorous physical
regimen including fasting and meditation, lasting the rest of her life. "She con-
templated in stillness, dwelling alone in a quiet room. Her goal and hope was to
fly to the chronograms [stars]. Accordingly, she cut off the five grains and swal-
lowed *qi* [breath, vital essence] so that her spirits became harmonious and her body
light. Sometimes there was a rare fragrance or strange clouds drew near and illuminated her."

In a deathbed speech to her daughters, Ms. Wang attributed her former illness
to common acts and emotions of household life. About to enter her final meditation, she tells her daughters, "Now my heart is still clouded and obstructed, my organs still dark and not yet in communication with the Way. I must visualize the *yin*
landscape within, wash my heart, and transform my organs. After these twenty
years, I will obtain a cicada's skin." Before entering that final trance, Wang leaves
instructions concerning the disposal of her body. She orders her uncoffined corpse
exposed in the woods with just a cedar screen for ceremonial respect. When she
dies that night, her children follow her orders and expose her corpse in a reclining
position in the woods. Twenty years later, attracted to the site by thunder and lightning, her whole household "rushed ahead to look. When they arrived there and
lifted out the corpse, her body was as light as an empty husk. Her flesh, nails and
hair were all complete. But on the right side of her rib cage a scar more than a
foot long had split open." The evidence of her remains verifies that Ms. Wang has
achieved *shijie*, "liberation by means of the corpse."[9] As evidence of sainthood, this
form of transcendence is surpassed only by ascent to heaven in broad daylight. In
cases of liberation by means of the corpse, the adept appears to die, leaving behind a body. But that body is just a hollow shell like the skin shed by a cicada; really the adept has already ascended secretly. The "empty husk" may bear physical
signs of the adept's escape, like the scar through which Ms. Wang made her exit.
The physical rigors of Daoist asceticism transformed her body during her lifetime
and freed her afterward.[10]

### *Hua Gu: A Shrine-Restoring Hermit Who Escaped Her Coffin*

The following account in Du's record concerns Hua Gu (d. 721), who "at the age of eighty had a youthful face and the appearance of a baby, whose Daoist practice was lofty and pure." A wandering hermit, she traveled around locating and restoring holy sites connected to the Shanqing Daoist divinity known as Lady Wei Hua-cun. Hua Gu went where she was guided by spirits or dreams, caring little for her own comfort or safety.

Like Ms. Wang, Hua Gu achieved liberation by means of the corpse. Also like Ms. Wang, Hua Gu's departure was accompanied by signs of divinity, such as prediction and bodily escape. Hua Gu's corpse is uncorrupted, even fragrant. Foretelling her own death,

> she said to her disciples, "My transcendent journey is becoming urgent. I cannot stay here any longer. After my body is transformed, do not nail my coffin shut, but just cover it with crimson netted gauze." The next day she came to an end without even being sick. Her flesh and muscles were fragrant and pure, her form and breath warm and genial. A strange fragrance filled the courtyards and halls. Her disciples followed her orders and did not nail her coffin shut, simply covering it with crimson netted gauze. Suddenly they all heard lightning and thunder strike. There was a hole about as big as a hen's egg in the silk gauze, and in the coffin were only her shroud and some wooden slips. In the ceiling of the room was a hole big enough for a person to pass through. At the base of her coffin they made an offering of a gourd which after several days sprouted creepers and set two fruits like peaches. Each time the anniversary of her death came around, wind and clouds would grow thick and suddenly enter right inside the room.

Physical manifestations of Hua Gu's departure, such as the openings in the gauze and the roof of the room containing her coffin, play important roles in legitimizing her as a holy person and in the observances of her cult. Like Ms. Wang's scar, the holes prove that something escaped. The peaches that grew from offerings at the foot of her coffin signify her immortality.[11]

### *Xu Xiangu: A Daoist Spellbinder Who Conquered Buddhist Monks*

Next Du takes up Xu Xiangu of the Sui dynasty (589–618) who lived on into the Tang dynasty. Gifted in spells, Xu achieved longevity. "After several hundred years, her appearance was still that of a twenty-four- or twenty-five-year-old." Xu Xiangu learned Daoist arts together with her husband—our one case of a married couple with joined religious vocations—but left the household life after his death. She petrified some Buddhist monks who wanted to knife and rape her.

> Once she was suddenly set upon by several rows of Buddhist monks, using insulting expressions and insinuating words. The maiden abruptly and unceremoniously cursed them. Roused to anger, the flock of monks was about to stab her with their knives. As the tone of their words became increasingly urgent, the maiden laughed as she

said: "I am a woman who can reject the household life. Amidst clouds and water I do not shun serpents and dragons or tigers and wolves. Why should I be afraid of you rats?" Then she undressed and lay down, swiftly snuffing out her candle. The flock of monks was happy, thinking they would get their way. But the maiden had devised a plan to emerge safely from the mountains the next day. For that single night, all the various monks became stiff, standing like corpses or sitting as if restrained by being tied up. Their mouths were stopped so they could not speak. After the maiden had departed several *li* [the next day], the monks returned to their former selves.

Buddhist monks, main rivals to the Daoist clergy for the hearts and donations of Tang people and rulers, are demonized in this story. The author shows Xu Xiangu's heroism and the monks' villainy through physical actions and changes. The monks' magical stiffness is fitting punishment for their sexual advances. Her Daoist arts enabled her to reverse the aging process and conquer powerful aggressors who outnumbered her. Xu's victory over the Buddhists must be her most memorable practice for Du Guangting: he does not describe her departure.[12]

### Gou Xiangu: Ascetic and Victorious Defender of the Faith

After Xu Xiangu, Du Guangting narrates the life of Gou Xiangu, another adept who looked young in old age. "At over eighty years of age, her countenance and color were extremely youthful." Like Hua Gu, she restored a shrine associated with Lady Wei Huacun. Like Xu Xiangu, she repelled violent and evil-intentioned Buddhist monks with her magical powers. Her austerities in a mountain hermitage were rewarded by visits from deities who encouraged and protected her. Her familiar was a blue bird, the messenger of the Queen Mother of the West. The Queen Mother, the highest goddess of Shangqing Daoism, was a special patron of women in the faith.

One evening, over ten Buddhist monks came to Lady Wei's transcendent altar. [The altar] was a huge slab of stone some ten feet in circumference. Underneath, it seemed to float on another projecting stone. If a single person pushed it with his hand, it would tremble and move, but if many people did so, it would stand there like a mountain peak. That night, the group of monks entered her apartment, carrying fire and grasping swords with the intention of harming Xiangu. The maiden was on her bed, but the monks did not see her. There was a rumbling noise: mountains quaked and valleys split open. One would have said the altar had already toppled off, but in the end [those monks] could not budge it. At dawn one of them reached a distant village. The other nine monks had separated and scattered and were gnawed to death by tigers. The single monk who had not joined the evil deed during the altar-pushing episode had escaped being harmed by the tiger. The Lady's transcendent altar remained upright and undamaged. The maiden was also uninjured.

Once again, a solitary Daoist holy woman overcomes a gang of Buddhist monks who mean to kill her and demolish a shrine. The nine participating monks pay with their lives for their assault when they are eaten by tigers. (The tiger is a companion and alter ego of the Queen Mother of the West.) In the stories of Gou and Xu, female Daoists represent physical virtue and heroism in contrast to the libidinous and cowardly Buddhist monks. The Daoist women's bodies remain intact while the men's bodies are violated.

Gou Xiangu's reputation for physical austerities earned her disciples, including Confucian officials. Speaking to one of these male disciples, Prime Minister Zheng Tian, she predicted difficult times to come for the Tang dynasty and announced that she would be leaving soon. "Then one morning she departed."[13]

### Bian Dongxuan: An Ascetic Who Took Elixir Drugs and Ascended to Heaven

The ultimate practitioner of fasting and ingesting elixir drugs is Bian Dongxuan (d. 713). According to Du Guangting, Bian is one of only two female adepts of the Tang who ascend to heaven in broad daylight. (The other is Wang Fajin, discussed above.) Bian is an exemplary model of the Shangqing adept on the ascetic path to individual liberation. She is Du Guangting's stellar representative of his own lineage. Bian's acts of austerity wrote her religion on her body.

Both intelligent and compassionate, Bian Dongxuan saved and fed hungry creatures from childhood on. "When she was fifteen, she revealed to her father and mother that she wanted to enter the Way and refine her body by cutting off grains and nourishing her vital essence." When her parents refused to let her become a nun, she refused to marry and remained at home to serve them. "After several years, she mourned her father and mother. Broken down and emaciated, she would not eat. Her fasting almost reached the point of extinguishing her life force." After the mourning period ended, she entered a convent. When she had some money after taking care of her ritual needs, Bian "would frequently purchase and store such things as the five grains. People questioned her about it: 'Since you have not eaten these past several years, why store up rice and wheat? Could it possibly be that during those eternal nights and freezing dawns you think of hunger and thirst?' " But she was feeding starving animals again. As a result, rats never bothered her convent.

Bian Dongxuan fearlessly pursued immortality by the path of elixir drugs, sometimes alarming her sisters. "It was also her nature to love to ingest special morsels. Whenever someone handed over cinnabar [elixir] drugs or bestowed pills or powders upon her, she was always sure to burn incense, make offerings, and pray in the Audience Hall of the Revered of Heaven. Only afterwards would she ingest the drugs. Often made to suffer by some drug, she would vomit it up, her retching and diarrhea bringing her to the point of exhaustion and distress. But she never felt resentful or sighed in complaint. After her symptoms were over, she would swallow drugs again as usual. Those sharing the same Way worried about her."

Finally a heavenly messenger disguised as an old man brought her an elixir he claimed she had earned by austerities and hidden good works. "He opened his bag and showed her some two or three dippers of drug pellets that were blue-black in color and the size of paulownia seeds. He ordered her to feel around inside his bag for them herself. Following her own whim, Dongxuan grasped three pellets from his drug bag. The old gent said: 'If you ingest this cinnabar elixir, it will transform your intestines and exchange your blood. After three days you will ascend to heaven.' . . . Then again he brought out a little bit of a drug that had the appearance of peach sap and a fragrance also like that of peaches. The old gent himself drew water from the well and blended it with this peach sap, then ordered her to swallow the pill." He told her: "After you take these two drugs, you will no longer need to transform your intestines and exchange your blood. Then dwelling suitably in a pavilion on top of a platform, you will join realized ones and meet transcendents, never again to live in stinking and turbid rooms. After seven days you will ascend to heaven." When her anxious sisters asked Dongxuan what had happened, she told them.

Bian Dongxuan then predicted her own departure, notifying people of the time and place. "The masses brought about a great fast meeting. On the fifteenth day of the seventh month, from the hours of seven to nine A.M., heavenly music filled the void. Dense and impenetrable purple clouds wound around the storied buildings of the belvedere. The masses of the people saw Dongxuan ascend, with standards and pennants (of her heavenly honor guard) spread out and arrayed. She departed straight to the south. By noontime, the clouds had just scattered." She overcomes death and decomposition. Predicting her own departure, she ascends before a huge audience, accompanied by fragrant, auspicious clouds.[14]

### Huang Guanfu: A Chaste Suicide Who Turned Out to Be a Banished Immortal

Huang Guanfu (d. 665) also showed devotion to the Way and fasted from childhood. "Sometimes she ate cedar leaves and drank water, but she did not eat the five grains." When her parents wanted her to marry, she preserved her celibacy by committing suicide. "She threw herself into a river. After a good long time passed and she did not emerge, her father and mother dredged the river and obtained a wooden statue, like those carved of the Heavenly Honored Ones [great Daoist gods] in the olden days. Its gilding and painted colors were already mottled. Its form and appearance were no different from their daughter." Setting this image up beside the road, Huang Guanfu's parents returned home. Later she appeared in the form of a transcendent to her mother. Explaining that her sojourn on earth was punishment for a small transgression she had committed in heaven, she warns her family of an approaching plague. This story brings together several elements from traditional Chinese lore: a teenage girl's suicide, committed to avoid marriage and followed by a cult centered on an image set up on the site of her death, a banished immortal, a filial daughter, and a plague savior. The elements all join in the physical image of the girl's body in her statue.[15]

### Shen Gu: Marvelous Craftswoman Transformed into Feathered Transcendent

Shen Gu (b. 791), the Divine Maiden, was an informal title of Lu Meiniang. She was unusual from birth: Du Guangting tells us "she was born with long green eyebrows." She was a miraculously skilled craftswoman who could embroider detailed scenes of the Daoist heavens in a piece of cloth a yard wide that was so fine it weighed less than three ounces but so strong it would never tear. She was sent as tribute to the imperial court of Shunzong in 805 when she was fourteen. She fasted: "every day she ate only two or three spoonsful of sesame flavored rice." Under the reign of Shunzong's successor, Xianzong, in about 813, she was finally allowed to take holy orders. "For a long time she had been unwilling to dwell in the palace annex, so [Xianzong] released her, making her a female Daoist Master, sending her to the south seas, and giving her the cognomen 'Fancy Free.' For a long time she did not eat. Divine people regularly descended to meet her. One morning she was transformed into a feathered transcendent. When they lifted her coffin to begin her burial, it felt light. So they removed its cover, finding only her old shoes. From time to time people see her riding over the sea on a purple cloud." The physical evidence of her empty coffin indicates that Shen Gu, after a life of asceticism, achieved liberation by means of the corpse.[16]

### Wang Fengxian: A Visionary and Ascetic Nun

Wang Fengxian (ca. 835–85), from a poor household of weavers, was visited from puberty onward by female transcendents bearing divine foods. When her worried parents interrogated her about her strange visitors, she dissembled. She traveled to the heavens and practiced flying in the courtyard of her family compound. "In addition, she never drank or ate. Day by day she grew increasingly odd. One day towards evening her mother saw her throwing herself to the ground from the tips of bamboo plants growing in the corner of their courtyard [learning how to fly]. Growing more and more depressed and anxious, her mother begged Wang to tell her why she did this. So she told her mother and father about the things she had encountered. Finally, before she had finished discussing the whole matter, various [transcendent] girls [suddenly appeared and] cut Fengxian's hair, exposing her eyebrows in front and leaving just enough hair hanging down in back to reach the tops of her shoulders. From this time on, for several years, her hair simply did not grow longer." Fengxian's abrupt haircut resolved any disputes with her parents about marriage versus the convent: the divine bob signified her ordination.[17]

Continuing to refuse normal food, Wang Fengxian grew ever more beautiful. "She did not eat for a year or more. Her flesh and muscles were rich and lustrous, as clean as ice or snow. With her cicada-shaped head and rounded [lit., "maggot-

"DAOIST HOLY WOMEN OF TANG CHINA*" *263*

shaped"] neck, she seemed made of luminous matter with bright pupils. Her appearance was like that of a heavenly person." She spent her life teaching the masses, ministering to female religious, and practicing austerities. She lectured on the Dao and disputed with learned men. When an official wanted to bring her to the imperial palace to swell the emperor's seraglio, she hid in a temple until he gave up.

In her thirties and forties she continued her service and her Daoist self-cultivation. "Subsequently her ascetic practices and nurturing the breaths were not restrained or restricted to those of the rear courtyard [women's quarters]." Her austerities made her young. "[W]hen anyone saw her, she looked like a girl of eighteen or nineteen. Her face and appearance were different from those of ordinary people. She wore a garment with huge sleeves, made of damask and embroidery with patterns of clouds and auroral mists. What she held were transcendent flowers and nunimous grasses." Chanting Daoist scriptures, teaching Daoist secrets of longevity and transcendence, she reaped the fruits of her own practice. "Consequently, whenever she went about she could ramble at leisure or rush in a hurry, but she never experienced fatigue."

Wang Fengxian traveled to the court of the Heavenly Honored One in the heavens high above the Milky Way; that god predicted that she would return to heaven when she was fifty. He had his attendants "take a single cup of jade [elixir] broth and give it to her to drink. When she finished, he warned her: 'As for the produce of the hundred grains or the fruits of the grasses and trees, eating them kills people in their youth. If you want longevity, you should cut them off.' From this time on, she did not eat for twenty years."

In about 885 Wang Fengxian retreated to a mountain cottage. "After a year she was transformed without ever getting sick. She was forty-eight years old. There were cloud cranes and strange auspicious tokens of jade. . . . In addition she had not eaten for thirty years. She had a youth's complexion and snowy flesh as if she had remained a virgin. If not through the work of gold and cinnabar elixirs and jade fluid, how could she have reached this point? Also her spirits frequently wandered to the borders of heaven, and she could sit upright for a whole day. . . . People in this world do not recognize that all her accomplishments are on account of sitting in forgetfulness [meditation]." After her departure she became the companion of two high Daoist goddesses. Her physical practices led to bodily transformations during her life on earth and to celestial office afterward.[18]

*Xue Xuantong: A Married Woman Who Gained Liberation through Austerities*

Du Guangting's final entry in his "Records of the Assembled Transcendents of the Fortified Walled City" tells the story of Xue Xuantong (d. 882). Married for twenty years to an official, she told him she wanted to live chastely and "used illness as a pretext for dwelling alone." Thirteen years of study followed, during which she read and reread the "Yellow Courtyard Classic," a scripture concerning the Daoist body, longevity, and visualization.[19] In 874 Xuantong was visited by two goddesses who gave her a register enabling her to call upon great Daoist deities for instruction. They told her to prepare for a descent of Lady Wei Huacun. That goddess soon arrived and taught Xue Xuantong to contact deities and perform visualizations.

"Giving [Xuantong] one grain of nine-fold elixir, [Lady Wei] ordered: 'Swallow it after eight years. Then I will certainly send jade girls and a whirlwind chariot to welcome you to Marchmount Song [holy mountain of the center].' They said farewell, then scattered and departed. From this time on, Xuantong darkened her heart and stilled her spirits. She never ate. Realized transcendents descended to invite her, while radiant phosphors lit up empty space, numinous winds and strange fragrances arose, and harmonious music of cloud harps played in her room." Her husband was doubtful and suspicious.

In 881, as she fled with her household by boat during a rebellion, her party encountered what they thought was a host of rebels. Xuantong recognized them as a divine army coming to see her home and told them her time had not yet come. The following year

> Xuantong washed her hair and face, then took the tidbit of elixir that the Primal Ruler of the Purple Void [Lady Wei Huacun] had given her. Two transcendent women secretly descended to her room, urging her to proceed to Marchmount Song. On the fourteenth day of that month, she manifested symptoms and passed away in a single evening at her private residence. Thirty-six wingspans of transcendent cranes gathered on top of her room. Xuantong's form and substance were light and warm; her appearance was like that of a living person. The center of her forehead looked misty, and there was a dot of radiant light which after a good long time transformed into purple vapor. When her body was washed, her dark hair had increased in thickness and grown several feet in length.
>
> On the night of the fifteenth day, clouds of variegated colors filled her room, and suddenly people heard the sounds of thunder and lightning shaking and crashing. Her coffin lid flew up inside the courtyard; her corpse had disappeared, leaving behind just her empty burial garments and quilt. Strange fragrances arose. The cloud cranes stayed ten days before departing.

After years of asceticism and study, Xue Xuantong achieved liberation by means of the corpse. Fulfilling a prediction of her immortality, she took a magic elixir and departed. She left behind no corpse, just clothes and a mysterious fragrance.[20]

The tales told by Du Guangting are full of details about physical practices and corporeal manifestations. He dwells on how the physical discipline of his subjects' asceticism results in positive changes that are visible in their external appearance. As we shall see below, these life stories are a rich source of material on Tang notions of body, gender, discipline, and liberation. But first let us read poetry of Daoist women of the Tang to hear an echo of their voices.

BODY AND PRACTICE IN TANG POETRY: WRITING NUNS

Du Guangting's work, however abundant in information and understanding, is the work of a male authority. A Daoist Master and court official, he represented both civil and religious power. Sympathetic though he might be, Du could not speak with the voice of his subjects. One source rich in women's voices is poetry.[21] Poems by Daoist holy women of the Tang dynasty are preserved in the *Complete Tang Poetry*. They appear in a section near the end of the book that includes works by Buddhist and Daoist nuns, ghosts, and talking animals. The unifying concept behind this classification is creatures normally without voices: women are not supposed to write, the dead are not supposed to speak to the living, and animals are not supposed to possess language. But women did write, ordering the world around them in so doing, just as they did with their bodily practices. The Qing dynasty editors of the collection save poems by several Daoist nuns, among the most famous of whom are Li Ye and Yu Xuanji. Whereas Du Guangting traces the course of an adept's career, the two female poets illuminate moments of personal experience along her path and open her practice to our view.

Li Ye (d. 756 or 784?), also called Li Jilan, was a Daoist nun of the south as much admired for her calligraphy and musicianship as for her skill in writing and conversation. One story has it that when she was five or six, her father carried her to the courtyard of their family compound, where she impressed his guests with her spontaneous composition on a rose. At the time her father said it would be a great waste of talent if she were to marry. She became a Daoist nun. In 756, after her talents gained her widespread recognition, she was summoned to the capital. She arrived there at the height of the An Lushan rebellion, then abruptly disappeared. According to another source, she resurfaced, only to be executed for treason in 784 after she composed a poem to a rebel. One critic wrote of her: "For men there are a hundred courses, for women only the four virtues. Jilan was not like this. Her form and capacities were heroic. From Ban Zhao on down, there has hardly been her equal."[22]

One poem by Li Ye bears the title "Lying Sick in Bed Beside the Lake, I Delight in Lu Hongjian's Arrival":

> Formerly, you departed during the month of accumulated frost;
> Now you come at the time of bitter mists.
> When we meet again, I'm still lying in bed sick;
> We want to talk but tears stream down first.
> I urge you to drink Mr. Tao [Qian's] wine;
> In response, you chant Visitor Xie [Lingyun's] poetry.
> Suddenly I'm completely drunk;
> Aside from this, what else is there to do?[23]

Li Ye's friend is the reclusive Lu Yu (d. 800), author of the "Classic of Tea." He had left during the coldest weeks of winter and returns in the fall to find the poet still in her sickbed. She offers him wine, emulating the earlier poet and recluse Tao

Qian (365–427). In return, he chants the works of the great Buddhist nature poet, his ancestor Xie Lingyun (385–443). Sickness is a theme in Du's biographies of Ms. Wang and of Xue Xuantong; ill health can provide a pretext for avoiding sexual relations or a way to wisdom through physical suffering. Like many Daoists and literati before them, Li and her friend find release and joy in drunkenness. Li's poem assumes literacy, independence, and friendship with men, appealing aspects of a nun's life that were not the norm for a Tang householding woman.

Shangqing Daoist writers, including Du Guangting, harbor a deep suspicion of marriage as an obstacle to religious life. Despite Du's reference to the honorable estate of "one yin and one yang"[24] among paths to immortality, most of his subjects refused to marry or tried to live a celibate life together with their spouses. They rejected sexual intercourse and the processes of birth and child raising. Li Ye's riddling poem of paradoxes, "The Eight Extremes," presents a humorous but dim view of the vocation of marriage:

> Nearest yet farthest: east and west.
> Deepest yet shallowest: a clear and flowing stream
> Highest yet brightest: sun and moon
> Most intimate yet most distant: husband and wife.[25]

The Daoist priestess Yu Xuanji (844–68), the best-known woman poet of the Tang dynasty, is remembered more for her short, violent life, her friendships with eminent literati, and her love affairs than for her religious practice or thought. Yet many of her poems concern Daoist people, teachings, and acts. The first of a pair of poems entitled "Sadness" uses her richly emotional tone to express Daoist notions:

> Falling leaves flutter and swirl, joining the evening rain;
> Alone strumming scarlet strings, I break into a pure song.
> Releasing my feelings, I stop resenting heartless mates;
> Nourishing my nature, I toss off as empty the waves of the bitter sea.
> Sounds of leaders' chariots outside my gate,
> Daoist documents and scrolls pile up beside my pillow.
> This cotton-clad lay person turns out to be a sojourner from the cloudy empyrean,
> From time to time passing the green waters and blue mountains [of old].[26]

Chanting Daoist prayers, nourishing her inborn nature, and stacking books beside her bed, Yu Xuanji tries to console herself over her loneliness and view the bitter sufferings of this world as empty. She observes her own transformation through Daoist work from a lovelorn courtesan to a freely wandering transcendent. In the last couplet she compares herself to a banished immortal, disguised as a commoner, returning to enjoy the transient beauty of the landscape. She may be poor, marginal, and ignored, but she knows she's a goddess. Du's biographies do not discuss romantic disappointment as a motivation for turning to the Dao. But he depicts several of his subjects engaged, like Yu Xuanji, in Daoist ritual song, nurturing the vital essence, and reading canonical texts.

Yu Xuanji composes her own interpretation of the well-known poetic theme of visiting a Daoist recluse. Several Tang poets describe their visits to male Daoist or Buddhist hermits in their secluded mountain dwellings. Yu makes a spring outing to see a female friend with the elevated title of Refined Master Zhao. Refined Master (*lianshi*) is an honorific bestowed on women religious, the highest title granted in a Daoist cloistered community. Its bearers have no administrative duties but bring prestige to a temple by their practice and charisma. Yu's friend is nowhere to be seen, but her presence is everywhere, prompting the poet to write:

> *I Visit Refined Master Zhao without Meeting Her*
> Where are you and your transcendent companions?
> Your green-clothed servant is alone in the household.
> In a warm pot: remains of your steeped herbs,
> In the adjoining courtyard: boiling tea.
> Painted walls dim in the lamps' radiance;
> Shadows from the banners' poles slant.
> Anxiously I turn my head back again and again,
> At numerous branches of blossoms outside your walls.[27]

Master Zhao has just left—her medicine pot is still warm, her tea is ready, and her servant is waiting. Yu Xuanji drinks tea alone, appreciates the murals and prayer flags, then leaves at sunset with a backward glance to spring flowers outside the cloister. Here the poet stretches a conventional topic to let us glimpse a moment in the shared women's culture that developed among female Daoist practitioners. Finding her host gone, the visitor enjoys herself in a beautiful and sacred spot among familiar comforts of herbs and tea. She admires her friend's relaxed, contemplative life.

Yu Xuanji addresses a second poem to a Refined Master, perhaps the same person, expressing admiration and awe. Yu identifies with her subject, longing to emulate her independence and ease. The parentheses in the translation below each represent one missing character.

> *I Send the Refined Master a Poem I Wrote about Her*
> Auroral clouds of many colors, cut to make your robes;
> Burgeoning incense emerges from embroidered screens.
> White lotus flowers and leaves ( );
> Mountains and waterways spread out ( ) and disperse.
> Stopping in your steps, you listen to bush warblers chatter;
> You open cages, releasing cranes to fly away.
> In the High Audience Hall, you awaken from a spring sleep,
> In evening rain just now full and driving.[28]

Yu Xuanji's images convey a powerful physicality. The opening line sees the master through her clothes.[29] Yu imagines her trailing robes of multicolored dawn clouds, like celestial goddesses of Shangqing Daoism. After the person, Yu pictures her room, with ceremonial incense smoke billowing through decorated screens. The next couplet describes her garden and the landscape stretching beyond. The third couplet has the Refined Master casually listening to the songs of chattering birds (a common trope for the chatter of young girls, perhaps her acolytes). Then she frees cranes, those auspicious symbols of longevity and mounts of the gods, who escape back to the heavens. In the sanctum of her convent, she dozes and awakens to driving rain. The High Audience Hall of the seventh line recalls the story of the goddess and the shamanistic king of Chu told in the "*Fu* [Prose Poem] on the High Audience Hall" by Song Yu. There the meeting of immortal woman and mortal man is figured in clouds and rain, signifying both sexual and divine union. Images from poems in this tradition are important to Shangqing Daoism. They supply, in a language at once erotic and mystical, ways of imagining the meeting of Daoist adept and divine teacher. This same tradition inspires Yu Xuanji, who frequently alludes to its stories. The last couplet of her hymn of praise compares sexual and religious ecstasy. Images of sexual intercourse represent the joy an adept such as the Refined Master feels in divine union achieved through meditation on the Dao.[30]

Extant poems written by the women themselves prove a source of great value. In spite of the fact that their editors favor conventional topics and notorious priestesses, the works are a mine of information. Unfortunately, there is little overlap between Du's subjects and women authors collected in the *Complete Tang Poetry* anthology. We can regret the words that must have been lost, but in the meantime we can use what remains.[31]

Poetry by and about women Daoists fills out the emotional and social context for Du Guangting's subjects. Poetry complements the biographies and canonical texts, filling in knowledge they omit. Poets are less constrained than the Daoist Master Du Guangting by requirements of religious propriety and orthodoxy. They are more likely to consider feelings, inner motivations, and women's relationships with each other. To understand the religious context of the women adepts' lives and practice, we must turn to works in the Daoist canon on yoga, ritual, and meditation.

### BODY AND PRACTICE IN DAOIST CANONICAL TEXTS

Several types of texts in the Daoist canon dating to the Tang dynasty and earlier periods describe religious practice. One category includes the general category of Daoist *yangqi* ("nourishing the breath or vital essence") practices. Such practices operate upon the body with the intention of bringing about health, longevity, and ultimately physical immortality. They include respiration techniques, Daoist yoga, sexual abstinence, and rejection of various foods, including meat and the five grains.

A second category of canonical text describes ritual. Rites are generally intended to bring the devout into harmony with society, deities, and the Dao. A third group of texts describes visualization and meditation. These instruct the adept in forms of meditation and visualization intended to lead to well-being in this world and immortality in the next. All of these forms of practice may be done by a man or woman living the householder's life. Extreme forms of any of them will take the adept out of the body of society.[32]

### GENDER DISTINCTIONS IN OUR SOURCES

What difference does it make to Du Guangting that his subjects in the "Records of the Assembled Transcendents of the Fortified Walled City" are women rather than men? Gender distinctions must have some significance to him: he collects his female subjects' lives in a separate book, notes that their divine offices have titles parallel to but distinct from those of male transcendents, and identifies a special Way for women. On the other hand, he takes pains to point out that when it comes to holy office, there is no distinction between male and female. He also asserts that the Dao is one. Engaging in the same practices as men, Tang dynasty women expect to achieve the same individual immortality. Du's subjects are special among women. Their choices are not recommended as models for Everywoman; he singles them out as examples of perfection beyond the reach of the ordinary man or woman. They represent the ultimate liberation made possible by the teachings of his school. That even women obtain freedom from mortality may be less a sign of equality before the Dao than evidence of the miraculous efficacy of the Shangqing methods. A holy woman's presence during an emperor's reign is seen as an auspicious omen and token of the continuing Mandate of Heaven even in terrible times.[33]

The Qing dynasty editors of the *Complete Tang Poetry* anthology segregate Daoist women poets, placing them together with ghosts and animals. They saved little of the women's total output, and what they did save must have been highly selected to conform to their own values. The topics chosen by women religious often resemble those of contemporary men, and Tang poetic language is highly conventional. Even with these limitations, the poetry that remains provides us with unique insights into the voices, emotional lives, relationships, physical experiences, and practices of individual Daoist holy women. Surviving poetic works balance the biographical narratives and canonical manuals on practice to provide a full picture of the women's acts and culture.

Most medieval texts collected in the Daoist canon make no gender distinction in discussing practice; I believe that this is due less to religious egalitarianism than to the texts' assumption that Everyman is male. After the Song dynasty, when gender separation in the family and society became more strict, special texts on Daoist ritual and meditation for women were created.[34]

Women Daoists of the Tang performed the same practices and had the same goals as men; but differences in context give their practice different meanings. As

people who did not have the right to make decisions about where and with whom
they would live, medieval Chinese women faced greater obstacles in choosing a
religious vocation outside the household life than men did. The principal obstacles to practice for women included filial piety and loyalty: for women, both required childbearing. Marriage and motherhood created identity and place for
women. And, as we have seen in the chapter by Du and Mann, wifely fidelity could
even bring communal recognition and imperial rewards. It was hard for a woman
even to imagine leaving the family to pursue a religious vocation. Xu Xiangu, one
of Du's subjects, compared leaving home to facing wild beasts: "I am a woman who
has left the household life. . . . I do not fear serpents and dragons or tigers and
wolves."[35]

The life course of women in religion seems different from that of men: the
women's biographies show more continuity of faith and behavior, less radical con-
versions and fewer crises. Their main crisis occurs when they must choose marriage
and family or the convent. Fasting and sexual abstinence also have special meanings for women. Where men can reject power and money, women renounce what
they have control over: food, sexuality, and reproduction.[36]

Du Guangting's ten subjects and others like them are special in having gained
admittance to the club at all. Once a woman passes the threshold and enters the
Way, gender distinctions, like class distinctions, are no longer as significant. Everyone is on the same path. But women emphasize food and reproductive abstinence
more than men do, and understand a different meaning for the same acts. I will
return to the question of gender and practice. Let us next turn to the body, the location where practice takes place, and then to the physical practices of our women
adepts.

### DAOIST NOTIONS OF THE BODY

What did Tang Daoists mean by "body"? Daoist definitions begin with the general medieval Chinese notion of the body as a location and are given importance
by the Daoist goal of individual physical immortality. First of all, a medieval Chinese person did not divide body and self. Today in the West we assume a notion of
the relationship between body and self that is at least dualistic: a heritage of Greek,
Christian, and Enlightenment doctrines. I would argue that we divide the post-
modern person into many more than two parts, into several fragments that include
physical body, rational thought, emotions, subconscious, and so on. A fractured self
is so much an assumption in Western culture that the notion is built into our languages; it is hard to even articulate anything different. But medieval China was
something very different. The terms commonly translated as "body" (*shen*) and
"self" (*ji*) are used synonymously in many texts.[37] This self, imagined as a location,
is considered the center of individual thought and action. This is a general Chinese notion, found in Confucian classics that were part of the education of any
Tang literatus, such as the *Great Learning*,[38] which the Daoists share with everybody

else. Contrast this to the Western idea that the soul is prisoner of the body, a cliché from the time of Saint Augustine onward, or that the body is prisoner of the soul, articulated in modern times by Michel Foucault.[39] For medieval Chinese, the body is honored. As a center, the body is the location of practice, presenting the adept with opportunities for transcendence. Without a body there is no identity, no self to become transcendent.

The body is also the location of Chinese cultural constructions of gender. Women's bodies are associated with sexuality, reproduction, and motherhood, which find their proper order within the structures of marriage and the family. Women and men occupy separate spheres, with women controlling the domestic economy and private life. Women are also identified with beauty, sensuality, and luxury. Full participation in women's family and domestic role can become a sign of humanity, weakness, society, impurity, and mortality for Daoists; renunciation, a sign of transcendence, discipline, purpose, selection, purity, and immortality.

In addition to its centrality and gendered nature, the body is the location of Chinese cultural constructions of health and balance. A healthy body is maintained by balanced nutrition and a harmonious sex life.[40] Eating, especially eating the five grains, and sexual intercourse become signs of unenlightened humanity for the Daoists, implying purposelessness, impurity, and mortality; their control is a sign of transcendence, discipline, purity, and immortality.

To the Daoists, the human body is a microcosm, full of gods.[41] The deities who preside over the macrocosm have their counterparts inside the adept, body gods on whom he or she can call for assistance in the processes that lead to perfection. The great gods are available inside our own bodies. Daoists also view the human body as the site where transformations leading to immortality take place, alternately figured as an alchemist's crucible, metallurgist's furnace, or potter's kiln.[42] These metaphors reveal the respect owed the human body as a transcendent factory—a location where a process of production occurs. Clearly, you need a body to become immortal.

Related to the notion of the body as an oven for baking immortality is the Daoist idea of the body enclosing a womb, which in turn contains and nourishes an immortal embryo. Daoists believe that each human being is born harboring an immortal embryo, pregnant with the potential for immortality. Daoist religious practices are all intended to strengthen this embryo so that it can ascend to heaven at the end of earthly life.[43] Male and female Daoists alike must nurture this potential to achieve individual immortality. Appropriation of the image of pregnancy does not imply that the actual process of childbearing was granted any special prestige in medieval Daoism. On the contrary, giving birth was regarded as an obstacle to religious goals.

Daoist notions of the body as crucible and womb do not seem so startling in women's practice as in men's. Pregnancy, birth, and breast feeding are part of a woman's normal life cycle in society. In Daoist practice for women, body metaphors associated with these processes represent continuity with and a reinterpretation of the social norm rather than a dramatic reversal. As we shall see, women do the same thing in a different way, or reverse the meaning of what they are doing. In contrast, for men, images of pregnancy and nurturing are startling inversions that suggest the power of their religious intent and the extent of their sacrifice.[44]

### WOMEN DAOISTS' PHYSICAL PRACTICES DURING THE TANG

Daoists believe that discipline leads not to bondage but to liberation from mortality. Here we are concerned with physical discipline of women's bodies. Women's Daoist practices are arranged in a hierarchy; the adept progresses through a succession of levels, each characterized by certain religious practices, to reach the final goal of immortality. As we can tell from Du Guangting's biographies, Tang poetry, and Daoist canonical texts, the subject moves along an orderly path that begins with reverence and good works, then progresses to physical disciplines, physical results, and finally physical liberation. The steps of this path can be expressed as a series of correspondences that invert or reverse contemporary norms. Each step or set of correspondences involves medieval Chinese social expressions of universal human needs of family, nutrition, and sexuality—understood, renounced, and transcended in a specific way. Each act takes the practitioner out of the body of family and society and transforms her physical body. In each, the Daoist adept performs a physical practice that appears contrary to the healthy or social norm ("common sense") in order to pursue the higher goal of perfection.

I have identified eight sets of correspondences. They are fasting while feeding others, fasting while ingesting elixirs, abstaining from sexual intercourse while experiencing divine union, abstaining from sexual intercourse while pregnant with an immortal embryo, refusing to bear children while being filial, practicing extreme asceticism while becoming youthful and healthy, replacing mortality with immortality, and, finally, ascending to heaven instead of being buried in the earth. A woman adept might go through them one by one, in order, as she progressed along her religious path from good works to transformation. Below I discuss them in both chronological and hierarchical sequence.

The first four steps involve controlling her appetites for food and sex, areas of her life over which she has power. She replaces eating and intercourse with religious practices. First, the adept fasts while feeding others. Fasting does not just mean avoiding meat or spicy foods; the adept often "cuts off the five grains," or abstains from eating a normal diet. Doing this, she cuts herself off from a large part of family and social life. The holy women often fast to the point of emaciation or even starvation. Refusing to be a mother or wife, she extends both the maternal role of sacrificing her body to feed her children and the wifely duty of preparing meals for her household to the task of nurturing others. Her religious vocation takes her outside the domestic sphere, where she turns the familiar services of mother and wife to good works. This is described in biographies as *yin* (hidden) virtue. Second, our adept fasts, ingesting only elixir drugs. She rejects normal foods for divine ones.

Third, she practices sexual abstinence while enjoying blissful relations with divine teachers or mystical union with the Dao. Fourth, she is celibate, yet pregnant with an immortal embryo. Refusing to marry or living chastely with her husband, she nevertheless enjoys divine union with a heavenly teacher and conceives an embryo. The images are continuous from the ordinary household life of medieval women, but the object, purpose, and consequences are inverted.

Fifth, her apparently unfilial and disloyal behavior in refusing to marry and to bear male heirs to carry on her husband's lineage and serve the Tang emperor is in fact a higher form of filial piety and loyalty, because she brings about, through her religious practice, divine blessings for her family and state. Reality is the reverse of appearances: what looks at first glance like improper behavior turns out to be perfect filial piety and loyalty. Du Guangting's biographies contain examples of women who save their families and benefit the state.

Sixth, her fasting, elixir ingestion, and celibacy allow her to achieve effective meditation and visualization, which in turn lead to supreme health, beauty, perfection, and finally transcendence. Her sacrifices benefit not only family and society but also herself. Her apparent suicide by self-starvation and elixir poisoning leads to transformation of her body; death becomes eternal life.

With the seventh step, the cumulative result of all these inversions is the big reward: mortality is replaced by immortality. Suffering, decay, and death give way to transcendence and perfection. The stink of putrefaction is transformed to a fragrant "odor of sanctity."[45] Instead of a fleshly body, the adept obtains an immortal one, as permanent as jade or gold. Instead of being heavy, her body is light— ready for flight. Her transformation is swift, painless, and pure. Many specific physical manifestations of the reversal of normal processes of aging are mentioned in Du Guangting's biographies and in Tang poetry as special signs of the holiness of the subjects. Examples include fragrance, radiance, hair growing, youthful appearance in old age. The holy women also predict their time of departing. In short, they control and defeat death.

Finally, in the end, they go up instead of down. Instead of descending to tombs beneath the earth to rot, they ascend to the Daoist heavens to dwell there forever as members of the celestial imperium. Two of Master Du's subjects climb to heaven in broad daylight in front of a large audience. Others ascend secretly. They may appear to die but their corpses are mere husks; their perfected selves have flown up to heaven. All their physical practices lead in the end to conquering death and replacing it with eternal life.

## CONCLUSION

The Dao finally transcends and harmonizes all oppositions and distinctions: what matters the most is the distinction between practicing and not practicing, not the hierarchies between male and female, or between upper and lower classes. As Du writes, "[T]he Way is one, although its practice shows distinctions."[46] But for us humans on the ground, distinctions can be important. For women in medieval Chinese society, who were rarely able to make choices about the direction of their lives, getting to practice at all was difficult. Once they are on the Way, there are distinctions in practice and in how practice is understood for men and for women. For all Daoists, the body, identified with the self, is the center of practice. For all Daoists, discipline leads to liberation. But for women of the Tang dynasty, whose bodies are identified with motherhood and sexuality, practice meant disciplining the body. In particular, practice meant restraining physical appetites for food and sex as well as the social needs for family and offspring. In their quest for liberation, women tended to discipline and find religious significance in food and reproduction, aspects of life over which they had control. In contrast, men tended to discipline wealth and power. In the context of Tang society, with its limited opportunities for women, the holy women considered here created their own path, which resonates across the centuries with issues that face women today: how to make choices, formulate goals, create meaningful relationships, and face suffering and death with hope for liberation.

## NOTES

This chapter is part of a longer study on Tang Daoist holy women. I would like to thank Charlotte Furth, JaHyun Kim Haboush, Dorothy Ko, Livia Kohn, Susan Mann, Hal Roth, Audrey Spiro, Christena Turner, Ann Waltner, Yamada Toshiaki, and Ye Wa for their comments.

1. A very different way of perceiving the whole body and its parts from what we understand today in the West is vividly presented in Barbara Duden, *The Woman Beneath the Skin: A Doctor's Patients in Eighteenth-Century Germany* (Cambridge, Mass.: Harvard University Press, 1991). The process by which the body is dismembered and agonizingly separated from the internal self to produce the modern person is described in Francis Barker, *The Tremulous Private Body: Essays on Subjection* (New York: Methuen, 1984). A statement of the argument that gender is a performance rather than a state appears in Judith Butler, *Gender Trouble: Feminism and the Subversion of Identity* (New York: Routledge, 1990). The argument that even our interpretations of the physical manifestations of what we call biological sex are cultural constructions appears in Thomas Laqueur, *Making Sex: Body and Gender from the Greeks to Freud* (Cambridge, Mass.: Harvard University Press, 1990). One exploration of the ways in which we might link self and body in various cultures in future research is found in Nancy Scheper-Hughes and Margaret M. Locke, "The Mindful Body: A Prolegemonon to Future Work in Medical Anthropology," *Medical Anthropology Quarterly* 1, no. 1 (1987): 6–41. Discipline of the body as a means to liberation finds its classic study in Peter Brown, *The Body and Society: Men, Women, and Sexual Renunciation in Early Christianity* (New York: Columbia University Press, 1988). On the body in China, see Angela Zito and Tani Barlow, eds., *Body, Subject, and Power in China* (Chicago: University of Chicago Press, 1994).

2. On Confucianism during the Tang dynasty, see David McMullen, *State and Scholars in Tang China* (Cambridge: Cambridge University Press, 1988). For a history of the Daoist religion, see Stephen R. Bokenkamp, *Early Daoist Scriptures* (Berkeley: University of California Press, 1997). On making saints in the Daoist tradition, see Suzanne Cahill, "Smell Good and

Get a Job," in *Presence and Presentation*, ed. Sherry Mou (New York: St. Martin's, 1999). To compare Catholic canonization, see Kenneth L. Woodward, *Making Saints* (New York: Simon and Schuster, 1990).

3. On body as self in early China, see Roger T. Ames, "The Meaning of the Body in Classical Chinese Philosophy," in *Self as Body in Asian Theory and Practice*, ed. Thomas P. Kasulis, Roger T. Ames, and Wimal Dissanayake (Albany: State University of New York Press, 1993).

4. Phrases like "longevity greater than that of metal or stone" are frequently inscribed on bronze mirrors of the late Han dynasty. One example is a second- to third-century bronze mirror (9.240) in the Freer Gallery of Art in Washington, D.C.

5. The work of Ann Waltner on the Ming holy woman Tan Yangzi provides an example of historical scholarship that situates the saint in the cultural and religious context of her times. See Ann Waltner, *The World of a Late Ming Visionary: T'an-yang-tze and Her Followers* (Berkeley: University of California Press, forthcoming).

6. The most important text for this study is Du Guangting, *Yongcheng jixian lu*, "Records of the Assembled Transcendents of the Fortified Walled City," in *Yunji qiqian*, "Seven Slips from a Bookbag of Clouds," HY 1026, *zh.* 114. The text is found in the *Daozang*, "Treasure House of the Way," or Daoist Canon, Zhengtong edition (Taipei: Yiwen, 1976, vol. 38), pp. 30323–47. (Hereafter this text is cited as DG, followed by page number.) Daoist texts are referred to here by the letters HY, followed by the number assigned to the text in Weng Dujian, *Daozang zimu yinde*, "Combined Indexes to the Authors and Titles of Books in Two Collections of Taoist Literature" (Peking: Harvard-Yenching Institute, 1935), vol. 25. Tang poems cited are found in the *Quan Tang shi* (Complete Tang poetry [anthology]) (Beijing: Zhonghua shuju, 1979) (hereafter *QTS*, followed by page number).

7. On the *Gaoseng zhuan*, see Arthur F. Wright, "Biography and Hagiography: Hui-chiao's *Lives of Eminent Monks*" [1954], in *Studies in Chinese Buddhism*, ed. Robert M. Somers (New Haven: Yale University Press, 1990). On the *Biqiuni zhuan*, see Kathryn Ann Tsai, *Lives of the Nuns: Biographies of Chinese Buddhist Nuns from the Fourth to Sixth Centuries* (Honolulu: University of Hawaii Press, 1994). The *Lienü zhuan*, a tradition of biographies of illustrious women, begins with a work of that name by Liu Xiang of the Han dynasty. On *Lienü* texts, see Marina Sung, "The Chinese Lieh-nü Tradition," in *Women in China: Current Directions in Historical Scholarship*, ed. Richard W. Guisso and Stanley Johanesson (Youngstown, N.Y.: Philo Press, 1981); and Lisa Raphals, *Sharing the Light: Representations of Women and Virtue in Early China* (Albany: State University of New York Press, 1998). For tales of Daoist transcendents, see the *Liexian zhuan*, "Biographies of Arrayed Transcendents," HY 294; and Robert Ford Campany, *To Live as Long as Heaven and Earth: A Translation and Study of Ge Hong's Traditions of the Divine Transcendents* (Berkeley: University of California Press, 2002).

8. DG, pp. 30334–35.

9. On "liberation by means of the corpse," see Isabelle Robinet, "Metamorphosis and Deliverance from the Corpse in Taoism," *History of Religions* 19 (1979): 37–70.

10. DG, pp. 30335–36.

11. Ibid., pp. 30336–37. On Hua Gu, see Russell Kirkland, "Huang Ling-wei," *Journal of Chinese Religion* 19 (1991): 47–72.

12. DG, pp. 30337.

13. Ibid., pp. 30337–38. This biography appears in Edward Shafer, "Three Divine Women of South China," *Chinese Literature: Essays, Articles, and Reviews* 1 (1979): 31–42. The story of the monks is repeated in Du Guangting, *Daojiao lingyan ji, Yunji chichian*, HY 1026,

*zh.* 117–22. Minister Zheng Tian has a biography in Liu Xu et al., *Jiu Tang shu* (The Old Book of Tang) (Beijing: Zhonghua, 1975), *zh.* 178.

14. DG, pp. 30340–42. This biography is translated in Suzanne E. Cahill, "Pien Tung-hsuan: A Taoist Woman Saint of the T'ang Dynasty," in *Women in World Religions: Biographies,* ed. Arvind Sharma (New York: State University of New York Press, 2000). Other biographies of Bian appear in Li Fang et al., *Taiping guangji* (Broad records of the Era of Great Peace) (Beijing: Renmin wenxue, 1969), 63:2a–b; and in the *Lishi zhenxian tidao tongjian* (A comprehensive mirror of the perfected and transcendents who have embodied the Dao throughout successive ages), by Zhao Daoyi of the Yuan, HY 297, vol. 8, 6534.

15. DG, pp. 30342–43.

16. Ibid., p. 30344. This biography is translated in Schafer, "Three Divine Women of South China." Du Guangting based his account on Su O's *Duyang zabian.* The *Taiping guangji,* 36:413, preserved another version. The *Complete Tang Poetry* preserves three of her poems, *QTS,* p. 9756.

17. Daoist nuns, like Catholic and Buddhist nuns, traditionally cut their hair when they entered holy orders. On Taoist ordination for women, see Charles D. Benn, *The Cavern-Mystery Transmission* (Honolulu: University of Hawaii Press, 1989).

18. DG, pp. 30344–46. This biography is translated by Suzanne Cahill, "Biography of the Daoist Saint Wang Fengxian by Du Guangting (850–933)," in *Under Confucian Eyes: Writings on Gender in Chinese History,* ed. Susan Mann and Yu-Yin Cheng (Berkeley: University of California Press, 2001).

19. "Yellow Courtyard Classic," *Huangting jing,* in "Seven Slips form a Bookbag of Clouds," *Yunji qiqian,* HY 1026, *zh.* 17.

20. DG, pp. 30346–47.

21. On uncovering a female voice in the conventional and heavily selected poetry of Tang and late imperial China, see Maureen Robertson, "Voicing the Feminine: Constructions of the Gendered Subject in Lyruic Poetry by Women of Medieval and Late Imperial China," *Late Imperial China* 13, no. 1 (1992): 63–110; and Susanne Cahill, "Resenting the Silk Robes That Hide Their Poems: Female Voices in the Poetry of Li Ye, Lu Meiniang, and Yu Xuanji," forthcoming in *Tang yanjiu* (Tang Studies), Peking University, Beijing.

22. A short biography of Li Ye and five poems appear in the *Tangshi jishi* (Record of affairs or circumstances concerning Tang poetry), by Ji Yugong of the Song dynasty (Hong Kong: Zhongguo shuju, 1972), vol. 2, pp. 1123–24. She has sixteen poems in *QTS,* pp. 9057–60.

23. *QTS,* p. 9057.

24. DG, p. 30324.

25. *QTS,* p. 9059.

26. Ibid., pp. 9050–51. The earliest extant biography of Yu Xuanji is found in the "Little Tablets [by the Fellow] from Three Rivers," *Sanshui xiaotu,* by Huangfu Mei, completed in about 910, in Wang Guoyuan, *Tangren xiaoshuo* (Tang peoples' fiction) (Hong Kong: Zhonghua shu ju, 1958), pp. 293–95. A short biography and some poems appear in the *Tangshi jishi,* vol. 2, pp. 1125–26. The *Complete Tang Poetry* preserves fifty of her poems, plus fragments (*QTS,* pp. 9047–56).

27. *QTS,* p. 9052. Visiting a recluse who was not there is a conventional topic in Tang poetry. Several Tang poets (such as Wang Wei, *QTS,* p. 974) also wrote in praise of Refined Masters. For a study that provides methods for investigating women's culture, see Dorothy Ko, *Teachers of the Inner Chambers: Women and Culture in Seventeenth-Century China* (Stanford: Stanford University Press, 1994).

28. *QTS*, pp. 9047–48.

29. On clothing depicted in art purposely providing information about the subject, see Ann Hollander, *Seeing through Clothes* (Berkeley: University of California Press, 1975).

30. Song Yu's *Gaotang fu* appears in Xiao Tong, *Wen Xuan* (Selections of refined literature) (Shanghai: Shangwu, 1973), vol. 1, pp. 393–400. Yu Xuanji's language resembles descriptions of celestial goddesses in the Shangqing Daoist scripture entitled *Zhengao*, "Declarations of the Perfected," HY 1010.

31. On another source, poems by Tang men concerning Daoist women, see Suzanne E. Cahill, *Transcendence and Divine Passion: The Queen Mother of the West in Medieval China* (Stanford: Stanford University Press, 1993), chaps. 4 and 6.

32. Daoist practices for nourishing the vital essence (*yangqi*), have been studied by Henri Maspero. Several of his articles appear in *Taoism and Chinese Religion*, trans. Frank Kierman (Amherst: University of Massachusetts Press, 1981). On ritual texts, see John Lagerway, *Taoist Ritual in Chinese Society and History* (New York: Macmillan, 1987). On meditation texts, see Livia Kohn, *Seven Steps to the Tao: Sima Chengzhen's "Zuowan lun,"* Monumenta Serica Monographs (Nettetal: Steyler Verlag, 1987); and Isabelle Robinet, *Taoist Meditation: The Mao-shan Tradition of Great Purity*, trans. Julian F. Pas and Norman J. Giradot (Albany: State University of New York Press, 1993).

33. On separate titles for female transcendents, see DG, p. 30333; on the Way of female transcendence, see DG, p. 30333. On the Way as one, see DG, p. 30324; on the granting of celestial office based on virtue and talent rather than distinctions of male and female, see DG, p. 30333. On the holy woman as living omen, see DG, p. 30347.

34. On separate texts and practices for women, see Douglas Wile, *Art of the Bedchamber: The Chinese Sexual Yoga Classics including Women's Solo Meditations Texts* (Albany: State University of New York Press, 1992).

35. DG, biography of Xu Xiangu, p. 30337.

36. On the importance of food in women's religious practice, see Rudolph Bell, *Holy Anorexia* (Chicago: University of Chicago Press, 1995); and Caroline Walker Bynum, *Holy Feast and Holy Fast: The Religious Significance of Food to Medieval Women* (Berkeley: University of California Press, 1987).

37. For example, three versions of one original meditation text (HY 220, 435, 221) use *shen* and *ji* interchangeably.

38. A well-known passage in the *Daxue*, "Great Learning," on rectifying one's heart, one's family, and finally the state, makes the individual, in particular his heart, the center of thought and ethical action. It appears in James Legge, trans., *The Chinese Classics* (Taipei: Wenshi zhe chubanshe, 1972; reprint of 1892 edition), vol. 1, pp. 357–59.

39. See Saint Augustine, *The Confessions of Saint Augustine*, trans. Edward B. Pusey (New York: Collier, 1961); and Michel Foucault, *Discipline and Punish: The Birth of the Prison*, trans. Alan Sheridan (New York: Vintage, 1989).

40. See Charlotte Furth, "Rethinking Van Gulik: Sexuality and Reproduction in Traditional Chinese Medicine," in *Engendering China: Women, Culture and the State*, ed. Christina Gilmartin, Gail Hershatter, Lisa Rofel, and Tyrene White (Cambridge, Mass.: Harvard University Press, 1994).

41. On body gods, see Kristofer Schipper, *The Taoist Body*, trans. Karen C. Duval (Berkeley: University of California Press, 1993).

42. The image of the body as crucible or kiln goes back to the *Zhuangzi* and is frequently used in Taoist religious texts concerning inner alchemy (*neidan*).

43. On the stages of a Daoist holy woman's career, see Suzanne E. Cahill, "Practice Makes Perfect: Paths to Transcendence for Women in Medieval China," *Taoist Resources* 2, no. 2 (1990): 23–42.

44. On the continuities in women's physical practices contrasted to the abrupt inversions typical for men, see Caroline Walker Bynum, *Fragmentation and Redemption* (New York: Zone Books, 1992). Bynum argues that Victor Turner's descriptions of religious austerities as creating a liminal state pertains more to men than to women. Men can humble themselves by imitating women, but women cannot do the same by imitating men. Women, already marginal, use their identification with the body, suffering, and birth to forge religious practices for themselves that identify them with the means of their salvation.

45. On the importance of smells in the West before the time of Pasteur and their relation to body, health, society, and sanctity, see Alan Corbin, *The Fragrant and the Foul* (Cambridge, Mass.: Harvard University Press, 1986). A fragrant body was a potent sign of holiness.

46. DG, p. 30323.

# CHAPTER ELEVEN

# Versions and Subversions

## Patriarchy and Polygamy in Korean Narratives

### JaHyun Kim Haboush

In Korea, the patriarchal system that evolved during the Chosŏn dynasty (1392–1910) was closely linked to the Confucianization of society as a whole. Though certain elements of patriarchy were in place before the Chosŏn, the patriarchal family structure combined with strict patrilineality was implemented under the Chosŏn state, which subscribed to a Confucian social vision. Thus patriarchy was equated with Confucianism, which has been seen as a force with adverse effects on women. It has been established that as the native structure was incorporated into Confucian patriarchy, women, at least upper-class yangban women, lost much of their social space, were deprived of legal and property rights, and were increasingly confined to the inner quarters behind the walls of their husband's homes and that these changes were more or less in place by the mid-seventeenth century.[1] According to this view, the normative behavior of women and their gender roles were scripted and determined by male authorities and male-dominated institutions.

One notes, however, a very curious and seemingly contradictory phenomenon concerning this very group of women. Just as they were losing social privileges, they began to write in quantity and thereby to actively participate in written discourse. This was made possible by the invention of the Korean script, the *han'gŭl*, in the mid-fifteenth century. Unlike classical Chinese, which was for the most part inaccessible to women, *han'gŭl* script was easy to master and was viewed as a suitable medium for women. Women avidly availed themselves of this new medium, and for the first time in Korean history, they emerged as writing subjects who projected their own visions and perspectives. It is well known that they were major contributors to vernacular Korean writing during the middle and late Chosŏn. One observes that there was a parallel phenomenon in China. Dorothy Ko has shown that there was a similar loss of legal and economic standing among Chinese upper-class women from Song to Ming times but that this was accompanied by increased lit-

eracy among women and a more active role in cultural life.[2] In the case of Korean
women, the loss of their social and economic privileges seems to have been greater
while their role in written culture was more pronounced because of the separate-
ness of their medium.

With this new Korean script and women's participation in it, Korea's written
culture became far more complex and pluralistic. It is also logical to assume that
as they wrote, women played a more active part in the process of constructing gender, especially female gender. Of the four elements Joan Scott speaks of in the social construction of gender—symbolic representations, normative concepts, social
institutions, and subjective identity[3]—at least three would most likely be directly
affected by women's participation in written culture. After the invention of the
*han'gŭl* script, it would seem logical to see Korean women of this period, writing as
they did, as participating in the process of scripting and shaping their gender roles,
however unconsciously, rather than as passive and silent objects, as is often assumed.

Women did not write in a vacuum. They wrote in the context of the larger literary tradition in which male discourse was dominant. As a feminist critic points
out, a female text is "bitextual" in that it refers to both men's and women's literary
traditions.[4] Their writing should be seen as engaged in a continuous and elaborate process of adjusting and responding to social forces and defending women's
space. In other words, while a female text scripts its own concept of gender and
womanhood, it does so through acts of "revision, appropriation and subversion"
of male symbols of power.[5] In this sense, the gendered nature of a woman's text is
embodied in the cultural repertory prevalent at the time. Hence if we wish to use
a woman's text to "recover, articulate, and elaborate positive expressions of women's
points of view,"[6] we must find a reading strategy that will enable us to see the cultural and temporal constituents of its gendered construction. It is necessary not
only to identify the male symbols of power but also to examine the way in which
the text revises, appropriates, and subverts them.

This chapter is largely concerned with an interpretive strategy that permits a
gendered reading of a vernacular Korean narrative, a story that seems to date to
the eighteenth century, and its establishment as a female text. I am fully aware of
the danger of relying exclusively on a subjective reading of the text. Terry Eagleton points out that the text should be seen as the product of "complex historical
articulations" of various structures and proposes specific critical categories to analyze its production. What is interesting is that while Eagleton stresses the examination of the mode of production as an essential constituent of an analysis of the
text, he also emphasizes the text's internalization of the material conditions of its
production: "every literary text intimates by its very conventions the way it is to be
consumed, encodes within itself its own ideology of how, by whom and for whom
it was produced."[7] I consider to the extent possible the literary mode of the production of the texts involved. More specifically, I examine the points at which gender and culture intersect. I discuss the male symbols of power that this text appropriates and the way in which it revises and subverts them. I would also like to

raise what I consider a central question in the gender-culture matrix. If women constructed the female view of gender by revising, appropriating, and subverting the male symbols of power, what is the relationship of women to the hegemonic ideology? Not surprisingly, the male symbols of power that this text uses to affirm a woman's moral agency are fundamental to Confucianism. We will ponder the implications of this question toward the end of the chapter, for it prompts us to reevaluate the relationship between Confucian ideology and gender construction.

## WOMEN'S WRITING AND PROBLEMS
## OF ANDROCENTRIC READING

In the 1980s American feminist scholars celebrated a shift in emphasis in feminist scholarship from male texts to female texts and from woman as reader to woman as writer. Elaine Showalter announced the birth of gynocriticism: "It is no longer the ideological dilemma of reconciling revisionary pluralisms but the essential question of difference. How can we constitute women as a distinct literary group? What is the *difference* of women's writing?"[8] Patrocinio P. Schweickart spoke of the "recovery and cultivation of women's culture" this shift will bring.[9] Her enthusiasm for women's writing is accompanied by a sober realization of how difficult it is to accurately read women's writing as gendered text.

The problem is not only that a text is produced in layers of cultural and gendered complexity. The meaning of the text, produced in the process of reading, is also embedded in similar social structures. Stanley Fish observes that while the meaning of a text depends on the interpretive strategy one employs, the choice of strategy is determined by concepts of acceptability within the community in which the reading is located.[10] As Schweickart notes, because the interpretive community has been male dominated, the choice of strategy available has also been androcentric, and this "androcentricity is deeply etched in the strategies and modes of thought that have been introjected by all readers, women as well as men."[11] How does one free oneself from this entrenched androcentricity? Some critics pronounce that it is impossible to do so. Catherine MacKinnon, for instance, maintains this view and says that one feminist task is to point out its impossibility.[12]

The problem of a reading strategy for Korean women's texts produced before the modern era presents its own set of possibilities and difficulties. On the one hand, as the world of women's writing and reading existed quite separately from men's, one imagines that there might have been interpretive strategies that were particular to this world. If there existed a critical apparatus with which to discuss women's writing, however, it has not been transmitted. The critical negligence of vernacular writing is attributable mainly to the diglossic of written culture (vernacular Korean did not diminish either the prestige or the vitality of classical Chinese) and to the gender and class divide that tended to separate practitioners. Writing in vernacular Korean, termed *ŏnmun* (writings for the ignorant), as opposed to classical Chinese, termed *chinsŏ* (truth writing), was seen as unworthy of attention.

Nor did premodern women's writing fare particularly well in the modern era. Although nationalists have reclaimed vernacular writing as Korea's own, more authentic and superior to writings in "borrowed" and "foreign" classical Chinese, the genres that were singled out have been in the main those that are seen as uniquely native. The *p'ansori*, or one-person opera, is one of the more conspicuous examples in this category.[13] Moreover, in the nationalistic and ideological ethos of postcolonial Korea, it was the masses who were seen as embodying the Korean spirit and were credited with having carried on with writing in Korean script, as opposed to the elite, who, cosmopolitan and lacking in national soul, wrote in Chinese.[14] The special role women played in vernacular writing and the genres they developed were largely overlooked or relegated to a marginal subcategory.

The most conspicuous blind spot, however, is the modern view of premodern women as helpless victims devoid of agency who could write only to express their victimhood. Just as the May Fourth reformers rendered premodern Chinese women as suffering victims in need of rescue,[15] Korean thinkers of the early modern era portrayed traditional Korean women as an oppressed lot without autonomy or agency. This view of women-as-victims, a pronounced feature of literary discourse in the colonial period, was revived in the people's movement (*minjung*) of the 1970s and 1980s. Although the revisionist historiography of the movement located the source of the democracy in the masses and its beginning in the peasant "revolution" of 1894,[16] it was male peasants who were transformed from oppressed objects into empowered subjects participating in the nation's destiny.

In such an environment, women became the sole embodiment of the oppressed victim.[17] Indeed, in modern nationalistic discourses women became the symbol of *han*, unrequited sorrow, and represented the *han* of individual Koreans as well as the collective *han* of all oppressed Korean people. Women's writings were viewed as a pure crystallization of *han*.[18] It has been noted that in the discourse of nationalism women's subordination to patriotic causes is taken for granted and that women are expected to devote themselves to the national movement at the expense of their individual fulfillment or independence.[19] The same is true for the image of women in Korea. If women as the bearers of *han* offered an emotional fulcrum for the dissident movement of the 1970s and 1980s, it did little in the way of establishing women as free agents. In the politically charged literary culture of this period, there was no space for imagining women as writing subjects who actively negotiated with their environments.

## THE TRUE HISTORY OF QUEEN INHYŎN AND AN INTERPRETIVE STRATEGY

The central text I discuss in this chapter is *The True History of Queen Inhyŏn* (Inhyŏn wanghu chŏn), one of the best known "women's" narratives written in Korean.[20] Though the authorship of the work is unknown, it is commonly believed to have been written by one of the ladies-in-waiting of Queen Inhyŏn.[21] Its time of composition is disputed also, though it is usually placed in the early eighteenth century, not long after Queen Inhyŏn's (1667–1701) death.[22] The work is a nonfiction hagiography of Queen Inhyŏn. It is written in what is arguably the most inclusive and popular genre, *chŏn*, which encompasses works ranging from biographies included in the official historiography to fictional narratives written in the form of life stories of a subject. Its main events center on a colorful love triangle, one of the most celebrated stories of the Yi court. In 1681 King Sukchong (1661–1720) married Inhyŏn. The royal couple were twenty and fourteen years old respectively. They lived together happily for eight years but for the fact that she could not produce an heir. Meanwhile, Lady Chang, a lowly concubine, gave birth to a son. Enamored of Lady Chang and delighted to have an heir, Sukchong dethroned Inhyŏn and enthroned Lady Chang in 1689. In 1694, however, the king changed his mind, restored Inhyŏn to the queenship, and demoted Lady Chang to the position of secondary consort. In 1701 Inhyŏn died after an illness. Her death was thought to have been caused by black magic practiced by Lady Chang. On discovery of this, Sukchong grew enraged and put Lady Chang to death.

*The True History of Queen Inhyŏn*, a popular narrative, portrays Queen Inhyŏn as the embodiment of ideal Confucian womanhood. In the modern era, she has most often been seen as a saintly woman who willingly suffered in self-abnegation for the public good. A survey of recent scholarship on *The True History* affirms this. One scholar says that Queen Inhyŏn is a woman who "submits herself to any suffering without complaint."[23] A woman scholar describes her as "extraordinary in that, despite a fervent desire universally shared by every woman that she be loved by her husband and that that love last a long time, she represses her emotion to further the greater public good."[24] I feel that this reading of Inhyŏn of *The True History* is of modern vintage and that it has nothing to do with the way in which the text was read in premodern times.

The modern reading is the result of androcentric interpretation, codified since the establishment of literature departments in the universities at the beginning of the twentieth century. The previously separate world of women's writing and reading was merged into an open field of literature and literary criticism, both of which have been dominated by men. To this day, a curiously imbalanced situation remains; there are few prominent women literary critics in Korea, despite the fact that many important writers are women. This imbalance, coupled with the prevalent modern assumption that all traditional women were victims, contributes to the one-sided image of Queen Inhyŏn. Indeed, men and women today contend that the queen's virtue lies in the self-sacrifice she makes to shore up order in the realm, an order that was, ironically, defined by patriarchy.

Was this how women before the modern era read this text? If *The True History* is a female text, it would project a gendered view of women and their lives. Unlike many works that have been transmitted in both Korean and classical Chinese editions, indicating a readership of both genders, the extant editions of *The True History* are all in Korean,[25] suggesting a predominantly female readership. Under the circumstances it is not far-fetched to assume that texts such as *The True History* were sites of female discourse on strategies of survival as a fully dignified person within the strictures of patriarchy and that the popularity of *The True History* was rooted in these very features.

Schweickart's proposals of a multistep process to reach a dialectical reading of a female text seems quite applicable to reading *The True History*. She postulates that a feminist reader first extricate herself from the androcentric mode of reasoning by her awareness of her role as reader and then succeed in establishing a "mediation between her perspective and that of the writer."[26] In addition, it is imperative to confront the bitextuality of a female text. That is, the reader has to identify the male symbols of power and to analyze the ways in which the female text revises, appropriates, and subverts these symbols. Both the symbols and the way in which they are used in the text are embedded in the cultural matrix specific to the time of its production.

That the Queen Inhyŏn of *The True History* represents a female conception of the ideal woman, distinct from those associated with either male or modern readings, becomes evident when the text is read and compared to its contemporaneous male texts. I will read *The True History* and the pertinent portion of the *Sukchong sillok* (Veritable records of King Sukchong) followed by *Madame Sa's Conquest of the South* (Sassi Namjŏng ki). Rather than discuss the three texts at once, I foreground *The True History* by reading it separately with each of the male texts.

These two additional texts are chosen because the three texts deal with the same event, they were written in roughly the same period, and, most important, they represent different linguistic and narrative traditions. Each narrative is constructed within its own tradition of "the relation among the points of view on those events belonging to characters in the story, the teller of the story, and the audience to whom the story is told" and are distinct from one another in these elements. David Carr suggests that analysis of these points raises the narrative to a social level by detaching the subject and the teller of the story from the individual and that this process will enable us to move the discussion beyond individual subjectivity without completely discarding the idea of subjectivity itself.[27] My strategy of reading *The True History* with *Sillok* and *Madame Sa's Conquest of the South* one at a time is based on a belief that depending on which text the female text is intertextualized with, different constitutive elements that are employed to contest symbols of male power will come into focus. By deconstructing the two different ways in which the same text can be read, one hopes to gain insight into the multilayered elements with which the text is structured and the complex modes in which it subverts the male view.

## OFFICIAL HISTORIOGRAPHY AND PRIVATE BIOGRAPHY: PUBLIC AND PRIVATE

The *Sukchong sillok*, an official historiography (*chŏngsa*),[28] and *The True History of Queen Inhyŏn*, an unofficial biography, are representative works respectively of discourse in classical Chinese that was canonical, public, and male and of discourse in Korean vernacular writing that was noncanonical, private, and female. Each is written in accordance with the demands and conventions of its genre. The *Sillok* was written to be consulted by future governments, although it was also hoped that it would edify future generations. The official histories' claims to the highest authority were based on assertions of objectivity and impartiality.[29] Official histories were compiled by a committee and narrated in a third-person impersonal tone.[30]

The *Sillok* of the Chosŏn dynasty consists of the collected *Silloks* of separate reigns. Each was compiled after the death of the king in question and was written under strictly regulated procedures.[31] The format of the *Sillok* highlights its claim of objectivity. The *Sillok* is not a narrative in the strict sense of the word in that it neither employs emplotment nor synthesizes disparate heterogeneous factors in life to transform events into a meaningful story.[32] Rather it consists of daily entries of events and information that were thought to be of particular importance to the court and the nation. While the *Sillok* takes the form of annals[33]—and indeed it is often rendered into English as the *Annals*—this is deceptive in that its temporality is not contemporaneous with the events described but is that of retrospection. In terms of format it is similar to a modern daily newspaper. It consists of diachronically and synchronically multifocal parallel discussion. Still, just as certain events dominate newspapers for days, so do certain events take center stage in the *Sillok* for days until their eventual resolution. In this way, this seemingly non-narrative seamless text is not free of its own narrative intentionality. Moreover, unlike newspapers, which record events as they unfold, the *Sillok* presents each event with a coherent view wrought of the historical hindsight of the compilers.

*The True History*, in contrast, is a straightforward narrative. It is classified as palace literature, and it lies between fiction and nonfiction. It too attempts to strike an objective tone in the third person in the manner of the *Sillok*. Its intended audience having been women,[34] however, this was done not so much to claim status as the most impartial of public records but to establish the moral superiority of its protagonist.

Both the *Sillok* and *The True History* are posited on the assumption that one's worth is determined by one's morality and that individual morality bears a direct relation to the public order. They both subscribe to Mencius's theory of human nature—that it is originally and morally good and that goodness is attainable by nurturing one's inborn moral potential[35]—but they part ways in how they apply it to women. The Mencian notion, as presented in the Confucian classic bearing the same name, was not gendered, but later scholars developed supplementary theories to gender human nature, rendering women less well endowed than men both in inborn nature and in their ability to nurture it. This provided a theoretical basis for extremely wide ranging possibilities in assessing women's nature. Chosŏn Koreans certainly had no difficulty assembling a repertoire of competing ideas and images with which to construct their own gendered visions. Thus, while it is not surprising that the *Sillok* and *The True History* display gendered interpretations diametrically opposed to each other, their respective views can be located as different points on a spectrum of discourses on women. Given the prevalence of male texts at the time and their tendency toward ambivalence and reservation concerning women, the condescending views of women in the *Sillok* seem to fall within the perimeter of commonly held views, whereas the uncompromised view that *The True History* adopts seems to have been a deliberate construction.

In addition, both texts employ the binary of public and private as a mode of evaluating the moral quality of the persons in question, albeit their interpretations of the binary differ. The structure of this binary is sufficiently complex to allow different viewpoints. During the Chosŏn period, the Neo-Confucian moral view was very influential at least in the official hegemonic discourse, and the superiority of the public over the private was never contested. The private and the public were two poles ranging from the most narrow and personal to the widest and most public concerns, from self to humanity, with family and state as intermediate points along the line.[36]

In this graded hierarchy, what was considered public was what benefited the wider sphere, and activities associated with each sphere were viewed with correspondingly graded values.[37] When this binary of public and private is applied to spheres of activity, its function might overlap with a related binary, that of the public and the domestic. Despite some convergence, however, these two sets of binaries are distinct. Claude Lévi-Strauss notes that the public/domestic construct has been widely used to organize human society and explain gender differentiation; it may in fact be a universal construct.[38] The construction of the public and the private—what constitutes the public and the private as well as the relationship between the two—is far more culture- and time-specific.[39] Jean Bethke Elshtain points out that in the Western tradition, images of public and private have been "tied to views of moral agency."[40] Similarly, in Korea the binary of public and private was essentially a signifier of moral quality. Even when it was used to refer merely to spheres of activity, the implicit moral component still rendered the public superior to the private. When the binary was used as a determinant of individual behavior, the moral nature of the construction becomes even more apparent. In these instances, "public" implies "public-mindedness" whereas "private" means "self-seeking."

How was gender construction related to the binary of public and private? Because men are identified with the public sphere and women with the domestic sphere, there is a tendency to infer that public and private would naturally coincide with this division. This is not necessarily the case. Elshtain portrays not only a much more complex picture of the history of Western social thought, but also maintains that one's views of women have had a crucial role on one's conception of public and private.[41] Korea also displayed complex views on this matter. Because of the different social spaces men and women occupied, each gender had different conceptions of private and public. For instance, a woman could view her husband's family as "public" while her husband might regard holding office as "public." More crucially, when the binary of public and private is used as a determinant of individual action, there is no intrinsic reason why a woman should not be more moral and hence more "public" than a man. It is this theoretical flexibility of public and private as well as an interpretation of the Mencian notion of human nature that *The True History* appropriates to confer moral superiority on its female protagonist.

Since the *Sillok* purports to be a record of the public activities of the court, Queen Inhyŏn is mentioned only in relation to her public functions. The royal wedding was considered a public matter, and Sukchong's wedding to Inhyŏn is duly recorded. Except for occasional references to birthday celebrations and her participation in mourning Sukchong's mother, the next time Inhyŏn is discussed at length is on a certain occasion in the fourth month of 1689. Saying that the queen is jealous of Lady Chang, Sukchong expresses a wish to depose her.[42] Beginning on this occasion and for eleven days, until the day Queen Inhyŏn leaves the palace, the *Sillok* records mounting bureaucratic opposition to this royal wish. The matter is treated entirely as a confrontation in the public sphere between the king and his officials.

They all agreed that the marriage of the king, as the father-ruler, represented the patriarchal order and concerned the entire country. The king and his officials disagreed, however, over how order in the patriarchy should be maintained when the king found his queen remiss. The official position was that the royal marriage had public and personal components and that the king should respect the distinction between them. The king and the queen were parents to the nation and hence the deposal of the queen would disrupt public order. Their relationship as man and wife belonged to the private sphere, however, and problems in this sphere should be solved appropriately and should not impinge on the public sphere. They did not dispute the king's description of the queen as unvirtuous. Rather they resorted to a discourse of alterity, insisting that all women were irrational, perverse, and lacking in judgment and virtue. A responsible husband, they added, should endeavor to improve his wife's virtue.[43] In other words, Queen Inhyŏn's lack of virtue was intrinsic to her gender and thus she could not be deposed for that. They also maintained that matters concerning a wife's behavior certainly belonged to the domestic sphere and that Sukchong was wrong to make this matter a public concern. Thus the first stage of the royal-bureaucratic confrontation concerned the proper boundaries between public and private as spheres of activity.

Their confrontation moved on to the next stage. This time the public and the private were used as determinants of behavior. The bureaucratic protest took two forms—a collective strike[44] and a joint memorial to the throne signed by eighty-six former and present minor officials. It was the memorial that proved incendiary. Declaring the memorial a criminal act of sedition (*moban taeyŏk*), Sukchong decided to conduct a personal interrogation of several men responsible for it.[45]

The *Sukchong sillok* presents the interrogation as an unequal contest of power and morality. The king had power on his side and the officials had morality on theirs. The officials' claim to superior morality was based on their belief that faithfulness to principle takes precedence over blind obedience to ruler and that, as autonomous moral beings, they should discern and adhere to principle. Even under torture they maintained that the king, by proposing to depose the mother of the nation, deviated from his public duty and that they, as loyal subjects, had a duty to exhort him against it. The king, on the other hand, attempted to exact his officials' agreement by equating ministerial loyalty with personal submission to the ruler. At one point, enraged at the outspoken Pak T'aebo, Sukchong exclaimed: "Do you wish to establish your integrity by defending a woman and betraying your ruler?"[46] By prioritizing officials' loyalty to his own private person above their duty to principle, the king is portrayed as having lost his moral status.[47]

The king nevertheless had his way. This was made possible by a change of power that Sukchong instituted, replacing a bureaucracy dominated by the Sŏin faction with a bureaucracy of the Namin faction.[48] Sukchong demoted Inhyŏn and made her a commoner. On that day, Inhyŏn, the subject of the furor, finally appears in the *Sillok*. It records: "The queen, in a plain palanquin, left the palace by Yogŭm Gate and returned to the residence of her natal family. The officials of the court who had been dismissed as well as scholars and students followed the palanquin into the streets, loudly wailing."[49] Although Inhyŏn makes an appearance in this departure scene, she remains silent and concealed by the palanquin while officials are seen and heard in public.

In this text, the queen has only a symbolic value; it is immaterial what kind of person she is. True, her departure signifies the disruption of public order, but being a woman, she belongs to the domestic sphere. It is the male officials who protect public order. The disruption of public order is clearly indicated by their ejection from the court to the open streets and by their wails. At the same time, their very existence—even in exile—and their wailing are signs of hope that order will eventually be restored. That the *Sukchong sillok* was compiled by the Sŏin faction whose political fortunes paralleled Queen Inhyŏn's explains its sympathy for these officials. But even without this editorial bias, an assumption about the central role of male officials as guardians of public order who can right all wrongs is deeply embedded in the official historiography.

In *The True History of Queen Inhyŏn*, however, the silent and barely visible Inhyŏn of the *Sillok* becomes the focus of the narrative, and she replaces the officials as the locus of moral order. *The True History* is structured as a variation of a prototypical hero tale: a young man, slandered by a stepparent, leaves the court; disorder ensues, after which the hero, having suffered trials and attained manhood, returns home and restores order. By rearranging the roles of the main characters, the narrative subtly subverts accepted gender roles. The protagonist becomes a stepmother, and it is she who is slandered while it is Sukchong who matures and gains manhood during the separation. All the same, her departure from the palace, the center of the civilized sphere, signals that the moral order is in eclipse. It is her return that effects the restoration of order. Her return procession from her family residence to the palace, greeted enthusiastically by a huge throng on the street, is literally portrayed as a procession of light, dispelling darkness and disorder along the way. This subversion of gender roles is achieved through revising and appropriating the binary of public and private.

In *The True History,* the dramatic center of the narrative involves the conflict between Queen Inhyŏn as a moral being and as an emotional being. Whereas official Pak T'aebo's confrontation with the king is a contest of moral principle, Inhyŏn has to deal with her husband's rejection and all the emotional ramifications it entails. The text resolves the problem by allowing Inhyŏn to equate moral autonomy with emotional autonomy. She achieves this autonomy by realizing that one's life consists of internal and external worlds, that the two do not necessarily coincide, and that although one has control over one's internal world, what happens to the external world is beyond one's control. Throughout the narrative, Queen Inhyŏn's moral and emotional autonomy is made to transcend the vicissitudes of her social station. Of particular interest are the instances in which the discrepancy between her social position and her interior state is greatest. When she is cast out of the palace, she is extremely shabbily treated. There is a marvelous scene when she is leaving the palace: "One of the court ladies, instructed by Lady Chang, accosted the departing queen and demanded that she open her wardrobe for inspection. The queen complied with a smile, and her clear and innocent eyes caused the woman to withdraw abashedly."[50]

Inhyŏn is fully committed to fulfilling the demands of her moral imperatives, but she does so with no expectation of rewards. She merely wishes to adhere to her proper moral path. In this sense, she displays more independence than such male officials as Pak T'aebo in the *Sillok.* Though Inhyŏn shares with Pak a commitment to exercising moral autonomy, she is different from him in that when she realizes that her husband prefers Lady Chang, she neither attempts to change his mind nor, during her years of banishment, shows any sign that she wishes to be vindicated in history. In so doing, she embodies the ideal of public-spiritedness: she endeavors to live for principle for its own sake rather than for any tangible personal gain.

Inhyŏn's indifference to rewards becomes her source of power. Because she seeks nothing, nothing can disturb her inner calm. When her husband rejects and expels her, reducing her to utter powerlessness, she is unperturbed because of her knowledge that she is without blame.[51] When her husband, repentant, wishes her to return, she remains serene in her awareness that external events have a way of following their own logic. In Queen Inhyŏn's emotional autonomy, one is reminded of Charlotte Brontë's heroine, Jane Eyre. In discussing *Jane Eyre,* Nancy Armstrong and Leonard Tennenhouse point out that Jane Eyre dominates by placing herself in a position of powerlessness. Because she abstains from partaking of any form of social power, she attains power.[52] Similarly, Queen Inhyŏn attains power because she expects nothing.

*The True History* takes pains to show that Inhyŏn's cool composure is not cold-heartedness and that her emotional autonomy does not mean disengagement. The narrative includes several anecdotes designed to portray her as loving and kind. When she receives mushrooms from her family, she bursts into tears. They remind her of her mother-in-law and grandmother-in-law who used to enjoy those same mushrooms.[53] She is affectionate to her stepson. She takes in an eight-year-old niece and teaches her about books, sewing, and embroidery. She cries as she parts from her niece to return to the palace.[54] She also takes pity on a stray dog and lets it stay at her residence.[55] What is stressed here is not just her kindheartedness but her recognition of the presence of others. In discussing four Western women autobiographers from the fourteenth to seventeenth centuries, Mary Mason writes that the discovery of female identity acknowledges the presence of another consciousness and that women's life-writing is an "evolution and delineation of an identity by way of alterity." In Inhyŏn, we see that alterity, or a sense of self built on the inclusion of the other, coexists with emotional autonomy.[56]

Although she is portrayed as perfect, Inhyŏn's perfection displays two opposing ideologies. On the one hand, she is the supreme realization of Confucian ideals based on the Mencian theory of the goodness of human nature. Thus while goodness is seen as enhancing rather than denying or repressing nature, the ultimate test for achieving it rests on whether emotion, a tricky component in this theory, is consonant with morality. Inhyŏn represents a state in which emotion and morality cohere. She is not only good but also perfectly in tune with her emotions. This was the highest state of moral perfection envisioned but was thought to be rarely achieved. In achieving this state, Inhyŏn becomes the supreme ideal.

The idealization of Inhyŏn culminates when she is made the moral force that restores public order. *The True History* completes this process by revising the concept of the public and private spheres. Rather than see the two spheres as separate ones that divide gender as the *Sillok* does, *The True History* sees them as interconnected moral spheres. Thus the moral person, regardless of gender, should assume his or her appointed place. In this case, it is Inhyŏn who occupies the moral center. *The True History* does not challenge the structure of patriarchy. The king remains the father-ruler, the center of the political order, and Inhyŏn supports this order through her moral influence.

On the other hand, Inhyŏn subtly subverts the Confucian patriarchy, not only because she is presented as more moral and perfect than the king, but also because of the way in which her perfection is presented. Confucian patriarchy is a hierarchical order in which everyone is expected to live according to a finely tuned graded system of values and priorities. An intelligent and virtuous person is someone who knows exactly how to prioritize the demands placed on the self. Queen Inhyŏn, however, deviates from this model. She does not prioritize. She is perfectly good and loving to everyone equally, and she achieves this because of her complete disinterest in reward or reciprocity. In her very perfection, she evokes an alternative to Confucian patriarchy. Indeed, her serenity seems to evoke a Buddhist ideal of detachment and compassion.

There are several reasons why I believe that *The True History* is a female text. First, it establishes the moral superiority of its female protagonist through the appropriation of the symbols of male power. It blithely ignores the ambivalence toward women routinely present in male texts. True, many male texts also recognize that women possessed rational minds and are capable of developing them. In fact, the instructional and didactic texts for women both of male and female authorship are premised on this assumption. Song Siyŏl, a famous scholar of the Zhu Xi School of Neo-Confucianism and a leader of the Sŏin faction whom King Sukchong put to death in 1689 just before he expelled Queen Inhyŏn, wrote an instructional manual for his daughter on the occasion of her marriage. He advises her to respect and follow her husband's wishes whenever possible, but he repeatedly urges her to use her mind. He says: "If you happen to meet events of great consequence, be as firm and precise as a sharp knife in executing your decision. Do not listen to others but rely on your own judgment"; "It is best not to demean yourself. The ancients did not demean themselves when they met great predicament. Why should one demean oneself over small matters? Seeking something from others when there is no need, accepting food under undesirable circumstances, or, urged by someone else, doing something against your will, all can be construed as demeaning. Please take it to your heart to live courageously and with principle."[57]

Song Siyŏl's admonitions could well have been applied to Queen Inhyŏn. There is no denying, however, that in male texts women's rationality is seldom presented as equal to men's, as Martina Deuchler shows in her chapter in this volume. We have already encountered an extreme manifestation of this view in the discourse of alterity in the *Sillok*. *The True History*, on the contrary, does not acknowledge inferiority based on gender. It pushes the theoretical limit of the Mencian notion of the perfectibility of human nature and reinterprets the notion of public and private. In this way, it confers moral perfection on Inhyŏn, far superior to that of any male.

Second, *The True History* presents emotional autonomy as the most important quality of the queen and construes it as stemming from her moral autonomy. The text does not attribute to Inhyŏn, as androcentric readings have commonly done, self-abnegation that leads her to submit to suffering without complaint. Rather it is her consciousness of her independent moral self that enables her to accept ordeal with equanimity and to maintain her own correctness of behavior unaffected by changes in her social station. Unlike women in the male discourse of alterity, she is not portrayed as "emotional" in the dichotomy, emotion versus reason. Nor does Inhyŏn, as androcentric readings have assumed, attain moral rectitude through the repression or negation of emotion. Indeed, Inhyŏn is strongly self-possessed, exercises autonomy of emotion instead of repressing it, and takes control of her destiny from the options available to her. She is distinctly an ideal constructed by and for women. The dignified image of a woman who exercises completely rational judgment must have had a tremendous appeal to women readers. In Inhyŏn, the subjectivity of women that is only hinted at in instructional texts is fully realized.

The corollary of the unequivocal praise reserved for Inhyŏn is a profound aesthetic revulsion for Lady Chang, Queen Inhyŏn's rival and arguably the most famous femme fatale of Chosŏn court ladies. Undoubtedly this is to a certain extent a class-biased hostility. Presumably written for upper-class ladies, *The True History* is pervaded by a sense of suspicion of the lowly upstart who did not stay in her place and "usurped" Inhyŏn's place. Thus when it is discovered that Lady Chang has practiced black magic that is believed to have caused Queen Inhyŏn's death, *The True History* applauds her execution and gleefully describes her gruesome end.[58] This contrasts with the *Sillok*, which treats Lady Chang exclusively as the mother of the heir apparent and thus opposes her execution on his behalf.[59] *The True History*'s verdict on her is much more severe than the view that because Lady Chang has committed evil she must be punished. It is deeply contemptuous of her, viewing her as unaware of her moral self and manipulative of and dependent on her man. But her unawareness does not end with herself. She encroaches on other people's space and wreaks havoc on the whole system. The most intense denunciation of her one encounters in the chorus of outraged women's voices is that to gain favor with men, she hurt other women and thus betrayed her own sex.

Third, *The True History*'s admiration for Queen Inhyŏn is intermingled with a sympathy for the lot of women and an exposure of the powerlessness of women who lived under male dominance. Inhyŏn's independence in her interior space is stressed because of her powerlessness over the exterior space. Her moral and emotional autonomy was the only defense available to her in dealing with the unpredictability she faced. True, life is intrinsically unpredictable, but women must contend with the unreliability of men's hearts and depend on their good auspices. *The True History* certainly does not present Inhyŏn's fate as a desirable one. As virtuous and accomplished as she is, she has to face her husband's rejection. After her trial is over and she has everything to live for, she falls victim to evil forces and dies prematurely.

Fourth, in *The True History*, Inhyŏn, who has been so dignified and serene in life, is given power in death to seek justice for her wrongful death. After her premature death, Inhyŏn appears to her husband in a dream and informs him that her death was caused by Lady Chang's malicious practice of black magic. She then requests that he avenge her and restore peace to the palace by eliminating the evil presence. Sukchong accomplishes this for her.[60] This version differs from the account presented in the *Sillok*, which attributes the discovery of Lady Chang's practice of black magic to someone else.[61] In allowing Inhyŏn the ability to seek justice for her death, *The True History* seems to embody women's desires to be compensated for the powerlessness they had to endure in their lifetimes. Thus Inhyŏn becomes an emblem of consolation and encouragement to other women who lived similarly under male dominance and who had to seek solutions in solitude to the difficulties posed by the unpredictabilities of men, women, and life (see Figures 11.1 and 11.2).

Figure 11.1. *Fortune-Telling* by Kim Hongdo. Courtesy of the National Museum of Korea, Seoul.

## FICTION AND NONFICTION: COSMIC AND PERSONAL

*Madame Sa's Conquest of the South* is a vernacular Korean novel written by Kim Man-jung (1637–92) sometime between 1689 and his death in 1692 in his place of banishment.[62] Kim was one of the prominent Sŏin officials who were banished when the faction lost power with the expulsion of Queen Inhyŏn. It is believed that Kim wrote it as a roman à clef to satirize and criticize Sukchong's expulsion of Queen Inhyŏn.[63] Judging by the number of extant editions in both Korean and Chinese translation, *Madame Sa's Conquest of the South*, like Kim's other novel, *Nine-Cloud Dream* (Kuun mong), was widely read by both men and women.[64] *Conquest of the South* is one of those works of vernacular fiction that proves that the relationship between

Figure 11.2. *Family Greeting an Acquaintance* by Kim Hongdo. Courtesy of the National Museum of Korea, Seoul.

the written culture in vernacular Korean and that in classical Chinese was far more complex than the simplistic notion that they were divided by gender. Written by a ranking Confucian scholar-official, it presumably represents a male perspective on patriarchy and polygamy in that period. It appears that *Conquest of the South* exerted a great deal of influence on the structure and conceptions of works in the genre known as "family novels" (*kamun sosŏl*) that came later.[65]

Even if we accept the traditional view that *Conquest of the South* is based on true events in the Sukchong court, it is written in accordance with the conventions of vernacular fiction. Thus, except for the broad outlines of the plot, this novel is set in a very different world from the Korean royal court, in fact in China during the Ming dynasty as were many Korean novels of the period. *Conquest of the South* is the tale of an ordinary scholar family. It tells of Yu Yŏnsu, a young Confucian scholar-official, and his wife, Sa Chŏngok, who must undergo trials as a consequence of the machinations of Madame Kyo, Yu's duplicitous concubine.

The title, *Madame Sa's Conquest of the South*, refers to the perilous journey Madame Sa is forced to undertake when she is expelled from her husband's home. This also refers to the period when the patriarchy of the Yu family is in peril. One is reminded of the time Queen Inhyŏn spent in seclusion at her natal home during her banishment. Despite similarities in the way the two women are expelled—a concubine's slanders and a husband's change of heart—the ways in which each confronts her situation and is restored to her previous position are vastly different from one another. I argue that these differences establish that one is a male text and the other a female text; the two are distinguished from each other in the ways they assign different concepts of womanhood to their protagonists.

*Conquest of the South* is constructed on the binary of the inner-domestic and outer-public spheres (see Figures 11.3 and 11.4). The central notion of the novel is that women belong to the inner-domestic sphere. Once married, women become members of their husbands' families, and their worth is judged by whether they successfully carry out their roles within this patriarchal family. Cast out, they become worthless and lose their raison d'être. Only when they are restored to their husbands' families do they repossess their worth. Madame Sa is the embodiment of this concept. Thus her goodness is manifested by her undying devotion to her husband and her loyalty to the Yu family during her exile. When her husband expels her from the Yu family premises, for instance, she goes to the grave site of her parents-in-law. When her brother arrives to take her to her parents, she refuses to leave the spot, saying, "If I were to return to my natal family now, my connection to the Yu family will be severed for good. Though my husband has discarded me, since I have committed no sin against my father-in-law, I wish to spend the rest of my life beneath his grave."[66] She leaves only when she is apprised that evil people sent by Madame Kyo are on their way to capture her.

Madame Sa is described as peerlessly beautiful, virtuous, and accomplished, just as Queen Inhyŏn of *The True History* is, but she does not display the inner strength of Inhyŏn. As she is a woman of an ordinary scholar class, she is not afforded the same degree of dignity as the queen. Even beyond this, the author egregiously deprives her of self-possession and autonomy in his characterization. Unlike Inhyŏn, Madame Sa assumes that once a woman is placed in an untenable position by being cast out by her husband's family, she will naturally be in great distress and sorrow. Thus Madame Sa's goodness is repeatedly equated to the depth of her distress. When she is accused of infidelities, she is so stricken by it that she cannot rise from her bed. During the time she spends at the grave site of the Yu family, she "grieves her pathetic fate and nothing but sighs and tears fill her days." During her flight from the enemies sent by Madame Kyo, at several moments of extreme danger when she feels that there is no way out, she despairs, weeps, and attempts to kill herself.[67]

Nor is Madame Sa, a creature of the inner-domestic sphere, seen as being able to negotiate with the rigors of the outside world. The main attribute of her predica-

Figure 11.3. *Mat-Making* by Kim Hongdo. Courtesy of the National Museum of Korea, Seoul.

ment during her journey is that she is a woman cast into the outside world. This world appears as completely alien territory to her, riddled with all sorts of danger. Some of the perils she experiences are wrought by Madame Kyo's schemes, but these merely accentuate her displacement. On one occasion when she has to flee by boat, for instance, she exclaims: "As a woman of the inner quarter, I am drifting in the wide sea perched in a leaf of a boat. Where am I heading? . . . I have been expelled by my husband's family but continue to live in shame. Now I am supposed to go to Changsa. How sad is my lot! I would rather throw myself into the blue waves of the sea and follow the spirit of [the loyal Chinese minister] Qu Yuan." On another, she even writes a farewell inscription on a piece of wood: "On such and such day and year, Sa Chŏngok, having been expelled from her husband's fam-

Figure 11.4. *Washing Clothes* by Kim Hongdo. Courtesy of the National Museum of Korea, Seoul.

ily, drowns herself on this spot."[68] On each occasion, she is rescued from her attempt at self-annihilation by supernatural forces.

Unlike the *Sillok* and *The True History*, which pay scant attention to any realm of action but the real world, *Conquest of the South* is set in an eclectic cosmos of popular religions in which the world of the living is connected with those of spirits and deities. Patriarchy is projected onto this cosmic order, and disturbances in the patriarchal family and state are repaired by an array of spirits and deities that inhabit the cosmos. For example, the spirits of Madame Sa's parents-in-law appear to her in a dream to warn of the dangers she faces and to instruct her to be ready with a boat to save a person in six years' time. She obeys and the person she saves turns out to be her husband who has also fallen victim to Madame Kyo's machinations.

The spirits of virtuous women of myth and ancient history also appear in her dreams to comfort her and to prevent her from drowning herself. Finally, a Buddhist nun, Myohye, directed by the Bodhisattva Kwanŭm (C: Guanyin; J: Kannon), appears and offers guidance when Madame Sa faces extreme danger.[69]

This contrasts sharply with the Inhyŏn of *The True History*. There, Inhyŏn is the agent of her own moral destiny, transcending her role as a member of her husband's family. While she is alive, she fulfills her destiny with the enlightened detachment and kindness not unlike that of the Bodhisattva Kwanŭm. Thus while Madame Sa is depicted as a passive recipient of the protection of Kwanŭm, Inhyŏn is imagined as the goddess of mercy herself. Moreover, in *Conquest of the South*, though Kwanŭm bestows favors on Madame Sa and plays a crucial role at several junctures of her life,[70] Kwanŭm is thrust into a supplementary role as defender of the Confucian patriarchy. I have already mentioned that, in her evenhanded kindness, the Inhyŏn of *The True History* subverts the Confucian patriarchy of graded hierarchy. Read against *Conquest of the South*, the Bodhisattva-like Inhyŏn, in her universal and uniform kindness, evokes a world of antihierarchical, almost utopian values and beliefs.

CONCLUSION

When we read *The True History of Queen Inhyŏn* first with the *Sillok* and then with *Madame Sa's Conquest of the South*, different constitutive elements of the text become vivid. Quite frequently the same elements take on different meanings when read with different texts. In this way, one is able to see complex layers of assumptions and appropriations that intertextualize *The True History* with the male texts. When one reads them as gendered texts next to one another, it becomes all too apparent that to interpret Queen Inhyŏn in *The True History* as an emblem of submissive and self-negating womanhood is to submit to an androcentric reading.

Distinct conceptions of women separate *The True History* from the two male texts. The two male texts project patriarchy onto either the national political order or the cosmic order and define a woman's role solely in relation to the patriarchy. *The True History*, in contrast, is informed by the notion that women are autonomous moral beings with distinct moral destinies and that a woman's worth depends on the extent to which she fulfills this destiny. Another crucial difference is that whereas the male texts identify women's roles strictly from an ethical or structural perspective, *The True History* imagines women's emotional trajectories. It simultaneously exposes the precariousness of women's positions, living as they did under male dominance with no power of their own, and offers a strategy of how to survive and to avoid being devastated. This female understanding of womanhood stressing moral and emotional autonomy must have been one of the competing elements affecting the construction of the female gender.

In conclusion, I would like to evaluate two issues concerning Confucianism and women. The first is the way in which Confucianism is presented in these texts and whether one can detect the gendered use of it. As expected, the *Sillok*, the official male text, is embedded in a total and complete Confucian worldview. *Madame Sa's Conquest of the South*, an unofficial male text, embraces an eclectic cosmos that includes popular religious worlds but in which spirits and deities are made to support Confucian patriarchy. *The True History of Queen Inhyŏn*, an unofficial female text, uses basic Confucian concepts to construct a world in which women are conferred with subjectivity and autonomy, but it also evokes competing images from Buddhism to subtly subvert the Confucian patriarchal order.

The next question is how to conceptualize Confucian ideology in relation to women. The introduction of Confucian discourses in Korea and Japan often ushered in policies and practices disadvantageous to women, as chapters in this book have amply demonstrated. This does not mean, however, that we can draw the facile conclusion that Confucianism is an ideology that oppresses women. Post-Althusserian developments in the theory of ideology have dispelled the old notion that an ideology is immutable. In particular, the question of causality is now cast in a more complicated light. For example, Paul Hirst maintains that to pose "questions of causality is to assume a social totality in which particular instances are governed by their place in the whole."[71] Hirst challenges Althusser's thesis that ideology is relatively autonomous.[72] In the same vein, Parveen Adams elaborates on the danger of the theory of ideology: "[T]he complicated and contradictory ways in which sexual difference is generated in various discursive and social practices is always reduced to an effect of that always existent sexual division."[73] In other words, it is difficult to assert that a certain ideology "causes" a certain gendered division or hierarchy. Instead, we must examine the discursive and social processes that produced such distinctions in time- and culture-specific situations.

The same is true in the case of "Confucian ideology" in Korea, and in China and Japan for that matter. The reductionism associated with attributions of causality must be avoided. Throughout this book, we have stressed that in Confucian discourses there existed a certain theoretical flexibility that lent itself to the construction of woman-centered ideas and images, and often women availed themselves of these possibilities to construct alternative visions of womanhood. It is the execution of these possibilities that makes *The True History* a female text. Given the complexity of discursive and social practices, it should come as no surprise that Confucianism, while constricting the lives of premodern East Asian women, was also to a limited extent an empowering force.

NOTES

1. Martina Deuchler, *The Confucian Transformation of Korea* (Cambridge, Mass.: Harvard University Press, 1993); Also see JaHyun Kim Haboush, "The Confucianization of Korean Society," in *The East Asian Region: Confucian Traditions and Modern Dynamism*, ed. Gilbert Rozman (Princeton: Princeton University Press, 1991).

2. Dorothy Ko, *Teachers of the Inner Chambers* (Stanford: Stanford University Press, 1994), pp. 10–23.

3. Joan Wallach Scott, *Gender and the Politics of History* (New York: Columbia University Press, 1988), pp. 42–43.

4. Naomi Schor, "Dreaming Dissymmetry: Barthes, Foucault, and Sexual Difference," in *Men in Feminism*, ed. Alice Jardine and Paul Smith (London: Methuen, 1987), p. 110.

5. Elaine Showalter, "Introduction: The Rise of Gender," in *Speaking of Gender*, ed. Elaine Showalter (New York: Routledge, 1989), pp. 4–5. Quotation is from Elizabeth Abel, introduction to *Writing and Sexual Difference* (Chicago: University of Chicago Press, 1982), p. 2.

6. Patrocinio P. Schweickart, "Reading Ourselves: Toward a Feminist Theory of Reading," in *Speaking of Gender*, ed. Elaine Showalter (New York: Routledge, 1989), pp. 34–35. Quoted with slight changes.

7. Terry Eagleton, *Criticism and Ideology* (London: Verso, 1976), p. 48. Quoted in Michèle Barrett, "Ideology and the Cultural Production of Gender," in *Feminist Criticism and Social Change*, ed. Judith Newton and Deborah Rosenfelt (New York: Methuen, 1985), pp. 76–77.

8. Elaine Showalter, "Feminist Criticism in the Wilderness," *Critical Inquiry* 8 (1981): 182–85. Also, Showalter, "Introduction," pp. 1–13.

9. Schweickart, "Reading Ourselves," p. 35.

10. Stanley E. Fish, *Is There a Text in This Class? The Authority of Interpretive Communities* (Cambridge, Mass.: Harvard University Press, 1980).

11. Schweickart, "Reading Ourselves," p. 34.

12. MacKinnon says that "feminism affirms women's point of view by revealing, criticizing and examining its impossibility." Catherine A. MacKinnon, "Feminism, Marxism, Method, and the State: Toward Feminist Jurispridence," *Signs* 8 (1981): 637.

13. Male and female singers can take any roles interchangeably unrestricted by gender differences. In other words, male singers can sing females roles and vice versa. Chŏng Pyŏnguk, *Han'guk ŭi p'ansori* (Seoul: Chipmundang, 1981), pp. 69–70, 171–224. In recent years, *p'ansori* has been viewed as the representative genre of indigenous and folk art. Chŏng, *Han'guk ŭi p'ansori*, pp. 87–93. See also Marshall Pihl, *The Korean Singer of Tales* (Cambridge, Mass.: Council on East Asian Studies, Harvard University, 1994), pp. 58–68.

14. This was first suggested by Sin Ch'aeho in the early years of the last century. Sin Ch'aeho, *Chosŏn sanggosa*, in *Tanje Sin cha'eho chŏnjip* (Seoul: Hyŏngsŏl ch'ulp'ansa), vol. 1, pp. 40–46; Michael Robinson, "National Identity and the Thought of Sin Ch'aeho: *Sadae juŭi* and *chuch'e* in History and Politics," *Journal of Korean Studies* 5 (1984): 121–42.

15. Ko, *Teachers of the Inner Chambers*, pp. 1–5.

16. An Pyŏngok, "Tonghak nongmin chŏnjaeng yŏn'gu hyŏnhwang kwa munjejŏm," *Yŏksa munje hoebo* 5 (1987): 10–12; Kim Chonggyu, *Han'guk kŭnhyŏndaesa ŭi ideollogi* (Seoul: Nonjang, 1988). For the discourse on Tonghak in recent social movements, see Nancy Abelmann, *Echoes of the Past, Epics of Dissent: A South Korean Social Movement* (Berkeley: University of California Press, 1996), pp. 27–35.

17. You-me Park, "'And They Would Start Again': Women and Struggle in Korean Nationalist Literature," *Positions* 3, no. 2 (1995): 393–414, esp. pp. 398–492.

18. For instance, see various articles on Pak Kyŏngni's *Toji* (Land), which interpret the novel as the literary embodiment of *han*. *Toji pipy'ŏngjip: Han, saengmyong, taeja taebi* (Seoul: Sul, 1995), pp. 107–234.

19. Sabina Sawhney, "Mother India through the Ages: The Dilemma of Conflicting Subjectivities," in *Narratives of Nostalgia, Gender, and Nationalism*, ed. Jean Pickering and Suzanne Kehde (New York: New York University Press, 1997); see also Loretta Stec, "Female Sacri-

fice: Gender and Nostalgic Nationalism in Rebecca West's *Black Lamb and Grey Falcon*," in *Narratives of Nostalgia*.

20. The text I consulted is a commonly available standard edition by Uryŭ munhwasa, first published in 1971. *Inhyŏn wangho chŏn* will be abbreviated *IWC*.

21. Cho Yunje, *Han'guk munhaksa* (Seoul: Tongguk mnhwasa, 1949), pp. 263–64; Yi Pyŏnggi and Paek Ch'ŏl, *Kungmunhak chŏnsa* (Seoul: Sin'gu munhwasa, 1957), pp. 166–67; Chang Tŏksun, *Han'guk munhaksa* (Seoul: Tonghwa munhwasa, 1975), pp. 234–36.

22. Pak Yosun concludes that it was composed soon after Queen Inhyŏn's death but departs from the commonly held view by saying that there is not enough evidence to conclude it was composed by one of Queen Inhyŏn's ladies-in-waiting. She offers no theoretical or evidential grounds for questioning this. Pak Yosun, "Inhyŏn wanghu chŏn," in *Han'guk kojŏn munhak sinjaryo yŏn'gu* (Ch'ungju: Hannam taehakkyo ch'ulp'anbu, 1992), p. 543.

23. Cho Tongil, *Han'guk munhak t'ongsa* (Seoul: Chisik sanŏpsa, 1989), vol. 3, p. 394.

24. Chŏng ŭnim, *Kungjŏng munhak yŏn'gu* (Seoul: Solt'o, 1993), p. 105.

25. For a discussion of different editions, see Pak Yosun, "*Inhyŏn wanghu chŏn*," in *Kojŏn sosŏl yŏn'gu*, ed. Hwagyŏng kojŏn munhak yŏn'guhoe (Seoul: Ilchisa, 1993). See also Pak Yosun, "Inhyŏn wanghu chŏn: T'ukhi mibalp'yo ibon ŭl chungsim ŭro," in *Han'guk kojŏn munhak sinjaryo yŏn'gu*.

26. Schweickart, "Reading Ourselves," p. 38.

27. David Carr, *Time, Narrative, and History* (Bloomington: Indiana University Press, 1986), p. 5.

28. The official historiography was referred to as the "standard or legitimate histories."

29. This was not just in Confucian East Asia but also in classical Europe. Pei-Yi Wu, *The Confucian's Progress* (Princeton: Princeton University Press, 1990), pp. 6–8.

30. This practice was already in place in China. See Lien-sheng Yang, "The Organization of Chinese Official Historiography: Principles and Methods of the Standard Histories from the T'ang through the Ming Dynasty," in *Historians of China and Japan*, ed. W. G. Beasley and E. G. Pulleyblank (London: Oxford University Press, 1961).

31. See G. M. McCune, "The Yi Dynasty Annals of Korea," *Transactions of the Korea Branch of the Royal Asiatic Society* 18 (1929): 57–82. The compilation of the *Sukchong sillok* began in 1720 soon after Sukchong's death and was completed in 1727.

32. Paul Ricoeur, for instance, takes emplotment as an important function of narrative. Paul Ricoeur, *Time and Narrative*, trans. Kathleen McLaughlin and David Pellauer (Chicago: University of Chicago Press, 1984), pp. 65–66.

33. For a discussion of this form, see Hayden White, "The Value of Narrativity in the Representation of Reality," in *The Content of the Form* (Baltimore: Johns Hopkins University Press, 1987).

34. Judging by the existence of many different editions, *The True History* must have been quite popular.

35. A. C. Graham, "The Background of the Mencian Theory of Human Nature," *Tsing Hua Journal of Chinese Studies* 6, no. 2 (1967): 234.

36. This is specified in *Da xue/Taehak* (Great learning).

37. In this scheme, public service was given a superior moral value because it was assumed to benefit the widest sector. When government was seen as so corrupt that one could not serve the public well by holding office, for instance, public service was no longer thought superior to living in retirement. Some argued that taking an office under the circumstances

was morally suspect, born of a selfish desire for private gain. Living in retirement was truer to the ideal of "public-spiritedness." This concept existed from a very early era in Confucian East Asia. But as a social phenomenon, a large group of scholars explicitly choosing to shun office seems to come later. Peterson discusses this as a phenomenon of the late Ming in China. See Willard Peterson, *Bitter Gourd* (New Haven: Yale University Press, 1979). In Korea, this seems to begin late in the seventeenth century.

38. Claude Lévi-Strauss, *The Elementary Structures of Kinship* (Boston: Beacon Press, 1969). See also Michelle Zimbalist Rosaldo, "Women, Culture, and Society: A Theoretical Overview," in *Woman, Culture, and Society*, ed. Michelle Zimbalist Rosaldo and Louise Lamphere (Stanford: Stanford University Press, 1974).

39. Linda J. Nicholson, *Gender and History* (New York: Columbia University Press, 1986), pp. 78–81.

40. Jean Bethke Elshtain, *Public Man, Private Woman: Women in Social and Political Thought* (Princeton: Princeton University Press, 1981), p. 4.

41. Ibid., p. 5.

42. *Sukchong sillok* (hereafter *SS*), 20:48a–48b.

43. *SS*, 20:49a–52a.

44. The Ministers of the Left and the Right led a strike by the entire bureaucracy. *SS*, 20:53b–54b.

45. *SS*, 20:55a.

46. Ibid., 56b–60a.

47. Several days later, on his way to his place of exile, Pak died of wounds incurred during torture, earning a reputation as one of the most righteous officials of history. After Queen Inhyŏn was restored, Pak was honored posthumously. *SS*, 21:5a.

48. The prime minister called off the strike. *SS*, 20:61a.

49. *SS*, 21:2a.

50. *IWC*, p. 205.

51. She clearly states that she is completely without blame (*paegok muha*). *IWC*, p. 45.

52. Nancy Armstrong and Leonard Tennenhouse, "Introduction: Representing Violence, or 'How the West Was Won,'" in *The Violence of Representation: Literature and the History of Violence*, ed. Nancy Armstrong and Leonard Tennenhouse (London: Routledge, 1989), p. 8. Rey Chow likens Jane Eyre to a self-righteous Maoist. Rey Chow, *Writing Diaspora* (Bloomington: Indiana University Press, 1993), pp. 11–12.

53. *IWC*, pp. 45–46.

54. Ibid., p. 56.

55. Ibid., pp. 46–47.

56. Mary G. Mason, "The Other Voice: Autobiographies of Women Writers," in *Autobiography: Essays Theoretical and Critical*, ed. James Olney (Princeton: Princeton University Press, 1980).

57. Song Siyŏl, *Kyenyŏsŏ*, in *Kugŏ kungmunhak ch'ongnim* (Seoul: Taejehak, 1985), pp. 38–39.

58. The enraged Sukchong has lethal poison forced down her throat. *IWC*, pp. 84–95.

59. *SS*, 35B:12a–38a.

60. *IWC*, p. 82–98.

61. The *Sillok* says that it was Lady Ch'oe, the mother of another royal prince, who secretly brought the matter to royal attention. Lady Ch'oe was the mother of King Yŏngjo, a half brother of King Kyŏngjong and another of Sukchong's sons. King Kyŏngjong was

Lady Chang's son. Lady Ch'oe is said to have informed Sukchong because of her wish to repay Queen Inhyŏn's kindness. *SS*, 35B:12a.

62. Chŏng ŭnim wrote an article comparing *Sassi Namjŏng ki* and *Inhyŏn wanghu chŏn*. Gender is not one of the considerations in this article. Chŏng ŭnim, "Sassi Namjŏng ki wa Inhyŏn wanghu chŏn ŭi pigyo yŏn'gu," in *Kungjŏng munhak yŏn'gu*, pp. 163–89.

63. See Pak Sŏngŭi, *Kuun mong Sassi Namjŏng ki* (Seoul: Chŏngŭmsa, 1986), p. 269. This is the standard edition; page references are to this edition, abbreviated *Sassi*.

64. There are a number of Korean and Chinese editions of *Sassi Namjŏng ki*. It is believed that Kim Manjung wrote it in Korean but that it was translated into Chinese soon thereafter. There are a number of studies concerning different editions of the novel. See Yu K'waeje, "*Sassi Namjŏng ki*," in *Kojŏn sosŏl yŏn'gu* (Seoul: Ilchija, 1993), pp. 616–20.

65. For a discussion of the evolution of the family novel, see Chang Hyohyŏn, "Chang-p'yŏn kamun sosŏl ŭi sŏngnip kwa chonjae yangt'ae," in *Han'guk kamun sosŏl yŏn'gu nonch'ong*, ed. Yi Subong (Seoul: Kyŏngin munhwasa, 1992), pp. 208–34.

66. *Sassi*, pp. 168–69. The translation is mine.

67. Ibid., pp. 152, 168.

68. Ibid., pp. 177–78, 184.

69. Ibid., pp. 173–75, 227–29, 187–91.

70. Madame Sa's relationship to the Bodhisattva Kwanŭm is presented in an interesting light. Madame Sa declares herself ignorant of Buddhism but admires Kwanŭm. Earlier, before her marriage, she writes a poem in praise of Kwanŭm on the margins of a portrait of the bodhisattva. Myohye, the Buddhist nun, asks her to compose this piece at the request of the elder Mr. Yu, Madame Sa's future father-in-law who wishes to test the young woman's virtue. Subsequently he becomes convinced of it. Myohye acts as a mediator to bring about Sa Chŏngok's marriage to the Yu family on this occasion. Then when Madame Sa is in need, it is Kwanŭm who, through Myohye, her living disciple, protects and provides a haven for Madame Sa for several years until she is returned to her husband.

71. Paul Q. Hirst, *On Law and Ideology* (London: Macmillan, 1979), p. 18; quoted in Barrett, "Ideology," p. 67.

72. Ibid.

73. Parveen Adams, "A Note on the Distinction between Sexual Division and Sexual Difference," *M/F* 3 (1979): 52.

# GLOSSARY

| | | | |
|---|---|---|---|
| An Kyŏn | 安堅 | ch'ilch'ul | 七出 |
| Andong | 安東 | chinsŏ | 眞書 |
| *Andong Chang-ssi silgi* | 安東張氏實記 | Chiŭn | 知思 |
| | | ch'ŏ | 妻 |
| bafeng zhi qi | 八風之氣 | chōdō | 朝堂 |
| bakufu | 幕府 | chŏl chaeyong | 節財用 |
| Ban Zhao | 班昭 | ch'ŏlbu | 哲婦 |
| bei | 悲 | Chŏng Ch'ŏl | 鄭澈 |
| Bian Dongxuan | 邊洞玄 | chŏng puin | 貞夫人 |
| *Biqiuni zhuan* | 比丘尼傳 | Chŏng Yagyong | 丁若鏞 |
| bunke | 分家 | chŏngmun | 旌門 |
| bushi | 武士 | chŏngmyŏng | 正名 |
| "Buxu tanban" | 不須檀板 | chŏngnyŏl | 貞烈 |
| | | chŏngp'yo | 旌表 |
| | | chŏngsa | 正史 |
| Cai Yan | 蔡琰 | Chosŏn | 朝鮮 |
| chaku | 嫡 | chū | 忠 |
| chakusai | 嫡妻 | chuanqi | 傳奇 |
| chakushi | 嫡子 | chūgi | 忠義 |
| changyou | 倡優 | chūkō | 忠孝 |
| che | 悌 | Chungjong | 中宗 |
| cheng yu yue | 成于樂 | *Chungyong* | 中庸 |
| ch'ï ga | 治家 | *Chunqiu* | 春秋 |

| | | | |
|---|---|---|---|
| Dahe zhi dao | 大和之道 | Gou Xiangu | 緱仙姑 |
| daijin | 大臣 | "Guazhi'er" | 卦枝兒 |
| daijin-zenshi | 大臣禪師 | *Gujin lienü zhuan* | 古今列女傳 |
| Daijōkan | 太政官 | "Guo Chuihong" | 過垂虹 |
| daijōtennō | 太上天皇 | guofeng | 國風 |
| daikan | 代官 | | |
| *Dainihonshi* | 大日本史 | hachi gyaku | 八虐 |
| dairi | 內裏 | han | 恨 |
| Daji | 妲己 | Han | 漢 |
| dan | 淡 | Han E | 韓娥 |
| Dao (Tao) | 道 | hangmun | 學問 |
| *Daozang* | 道藏 | han'gŭl | 한글 |
| daraniju | 陀羅尼呪 | *Hanjung mallok* | 閑中漫錄 |
| *Daxue* | 大學 | *Hanjungnok* | 恨中錄 |
| "Dazaogan" | 打棗桿 | hansa | 寒士 |
| Diaochan | 貂嬋 | hansi | 漢詩 |
| Dong Zhongshu | 董仲舒 | *Hanzhou zhi* | 漢州志 |
| Du Guangting | 杜光庭 | He Liangjun | 何良俊 |
| | | hitsugi | 日嗣 |
| Fan Ye | 范曄 | Hŏ Kyun | 許筠 |
| fangzhong yue | 房中樂 | Hŏ Nansŏrhŏn | 許蘭雪軒 |
| *Fengsu tongyi* | 風俗通義 | Hong Ikhan | 洪翼漢 |
| fu | 賦 | Hongmungwan | 弘文館 |
| fuhen jōten | 不変常典 | Hōō | 法王 |
| furigana | 振り仮名 | Hu Wenyu | 呼文如 |
| fūzoku yoroshi | 風俗宜 | Hua Gu | 花姑 |
| | | Huang Guanfu | 黃觀福 |
| gaiten | 外典 | Huang Lingwei | 黃靈微 |
| *Gaoseng zhuan* | 高僧傳 | Huangfu Fang | 皇甫汸 |
| gegu | 割股 | "Hujia shibapai" | 胡笳十八拍 |
| gizetsu | 義絕 | *Hunmin chŏngŭm* | 訓民正音 |
| gong | 宮 | hwa | 化 |
| gong ganzhi | 貢甘旨 | hwarang | 花郎 |
| gongshi | 貢士 | Hwawang | 花王 |
| Gongsun nizi | 公孫尼子 | Hwawang kye | 花王戒 |
| gorin | 五倫 | hyakumantō | 百万塔 |
| *Gosechi* | 五節 | *Hyakunin isshū* | 百人一首 |

| | | | |
|---|---|---|---|
| Hyegyŏng (Lady) | 惠慶 | *Jinpingmei* | 金瓶梅 |
| *Hyogyŏng* | 孝經 | jinshi | 進士 |
| hyŏn | 賢 | jiuchou | 九疇 |
| hyŏnbu | 賢婦 | jokun | 女訓 |
| hyŏnch'ŏp | 賢妾 | joshi yō ōraimono | 女子用往來物 |
| hyŏnin | 賢人 | ju | 儒 |
| | | jue | 角 |
| i | 理 | juren | 舉人 |
| ichizoku mutsumaji | 一族睦 | | |
| ie | 家 | kabŏp | 家法 |
| ie no osa | 家長 | kachi | 徒 |
| ihyo | 移孝 | kado | 家道 |
| illyun | 人倫 | Kaesŏng | 開城 |
| Im Yunjidang | 任允摯堂 | *Kaifūsō* | 懷風藻 |
| in | 仁 | kambun | 漢文 |
| Inhyŏn (wanghu) | 仁賢王后 | kami | 神 |
| *Inhyŏn wanghu chŏn* | 인현왕후전 | kamun sosŏl | 家門小說 |
| Injong | 仁宗 | kana | 仮名 |
| Iryŏn | 一然 | kanai mutsumagi | 家內睦 |
| iyashiki | 斯下しき | *Kankoku kōgiroku* | 官刻孝義錄 |
| | | kannagara | 惟神 |
| ji (extreme) | 極 | kantsū | 姦通 |
| ji (self) | 己 | kasa | 歌辭 |
| *Jiaonü yigui* | 教女遺規 | katami | 形見 |
| jiating | 家庭 | keppaku | 潔白 |
| jiazu | 家族 | ki | 氣 |
| "Jibinxian" | 集賓賢 | Kichijōten | 吉祥天 |
| jie | 節 | Kim Manjung | 金萬重 |
| jiefu | 節婦 | Kim Pusik | 金富軾 |
| jiejiao fu | 接脚夫 | Kim Yusin | 金庾信 |
| jielie | 節烈 | kitoku | 奇特 |
| jiexiao | 節孝 | kō | 皇 |
| jiexiao ci | 節孝祠 | kō | 公 |
| Jin | 金 | kōgi | 孝義 |
| "Jinghetang bixun zixu" | 敬和堂筆訓自序 | kōgō | 皇后 |
| | | kōgōgū | 皇后宮 |
| | | Koguryŏ | 高句麗 |

| | | | |
|---|---|---|---|
| *Kojiki* | 古事記 | lülü | 律呂 |
| *Kokinshū* | 古今集 | *Lüshi chunqiu* | 呂氏春秋 |
| kōkō | 孝行 | | |
| kōkōmono | 孝行者 | Maech'ang | 梅窓 |
| kokubunji | 国分寺 | man'yōgana | 萬葉仮名 |
| kokugaku | 国学 | *Man'yōshū* | 萬葉集 |
| kokugakusha | 国学者 | Mazu | 媽祖 |
| Koryŏ | 高麗 | Ming | 明 |
| *Koryŏsa* | 高麗史 | ming juan | 命圈 |
| koseki | 戸籍 | *Ming shilu* | 明實錄 |
| koshu | 戸主 | *Mingjian* | 明鑑 |
| koto | 琴 | *Mingshi* | 明史 |
| "Ku fu wen" | 哭夫文 | minjung | 民衆 |
| "Ku qiqi" | 哭七七 | misok | 美俗 |
| kubunden | 口分田 | misoka otoko | みそか男 |
| Kugyō bunin | 公卿補任 | moban taeyŏk | 謀反大逆 |
| Kurōdodokoro | 蔵人所 | Momotarō | 桃太郎 |
| kusong | 口誦 | Mulan | 木蘭 |
| *Kuun mong* | 九雲夢 | munan | 問安 |
| Kwanŭm | 觀音 | Myoch'ŏng | 妙清 |
| kyōdai mutsumaji | 兄弟睦 | myŏng | 命 |
| kyubŏm | 閨範 | | |
| | | *Naehun* | 內訓 |
| *Langui baolu* | 蘭閨寶錄 | naejo | 內助 |
| li | 禮 | naengbo | 冷譜 |
| Li Jilan | 李季蘭 | naishi | 內待 |
| Li Ye | 李冶 | nakatsugi | 中継ぎ |
| lianshi | 鍊師 | Namin | 南人 |
| lie | 列 (烈) | namjon yŏbi | 男尊女卑 |
| *Liechao shiji xiaozhuan* | 列朝詩集小傳 | nangbu | 浪婦 |
| Lienü | 列 (烈) 女 | nanxi | 南戲 |
| *Lienü zhuan* | 列女傳 | neidan | 內丹 |
| *Liezi* | 列子 | *Neixun* | 內訓 |
| Lingbao | 靈寶 | *Nihon shoki* | 日本書紀 |
| Liu Xiang | 劉向 | nin | 仁 |
| Lu Hongjian | 陸鴻漸 | nōgyō shussei | 農業出精 |
| Lu Meiniang | 盧眉娘 | *Nü lunyu* | 女論語 |

| | | | |
|---|---|---|---|
| *Nü sishu* | 女四書 | qin | 琴 |
| *Nü xiaojing* | 女孝經 | qing xun | 情殉 |
| *Nüfan jielu* | 女範捷錄 | *Qingshi gao* | 清史稿 |
| *Nüjiao* | 女教 | Qiuzi | 龜茲 |
| *Nüjie* | 女誡 | Qu Yuan | 屈原 |
| nusumibito | 盜人 | *Quan Tang shi* | 全唐詩 |
| nüyue | 女樂 | | |
| "Nüyue jiming" | 女曰雞鳴 | ren | 仁 |
| *Nüze* | 女則 | renyu | 人欲 |
| | | ritsu | 律 |
| ŏnhaeng ilch'i | 言行一致 | ritsuryō | 律令 |
| ŏnmun | 諺文 | ryō | 令 |
| *Onna daigaku* | 女大学 | | |
| *Onna Imagawa* | 女今川 | sadae chuŭi | 事大主義 |
| *Onna kōkyō* | 女教経 | sadang | 祠堂 |
| *Onna Shisho* | 女四書 | *Samgang haengsilto* | 三綱行實圖 |
| onna shorui | 女書類 | *Samguk sagi* | 三國史記 |
| *Onna teikin* | 女庭訓 | *Samguk yusa* | 三國遺史 |
| onyō | 陰陽 | *Samiin kok* | 思美人曲 |
| ōraimono | 往来物 | samjong | 三從 |
| oryun | 五倫 | sancong | 三從 |
| ōtoshiyori | おう年寄 | sangang | 三綱 |
| | | sanjū | 三從 |
| Paekche | 白濟 | sankō | 三綱 |
| p'ansori | 판소리 | *Sassi Namjŏng ki* | 사싸남정기 |
| po chongmul | 保宗物 | se | 畝 |
| pong chesa | 奉祭祀 | Sejong | 世宗 |
| pon'gi | 本記 | shamisen | 三味線 |
| ponsŏng | 本性 | shang (sad) | 傷 |
| pudo | 婦道 | shang (one of five tones) | 商 |
| pudŏk | 婦德 | Shangqing | 上清 |
| pyŏn i pijŏng | 變而非正 | Shao | 詔 |
| P'yŏngyang | 平壤 | she | 社 |
| | | shen | 身 |
| qi (bizarre) | 奇 | Shen Gu | 神姑 |
| qi (breath, vital essence) | 氣 | sheng | 聲 |
| Qian Qianyi | 錢謙益 | shichi shutsu | 七出 |

| | | | |
|---|---|---|---|
| shidafu | 士大夫 | sŏnhaeng | 善行 |
| *Shiji* | 史記 | su | 守 |
| shijie | 尸解 | suk | 淑 |
| shijuku | 私塾 | Sukchong | 肅宗 |
| *Shikyō ruijū* | 私教類從 | *Sukchong sillok* | 肅宗實錄 |
| shingaku | 心学 | suyue | 俗樂 |
| shishen | 士紳 | | |
| shiten'ō | 四天王 | *Taehak* | 大學 |
| shitoku | 四德 | taeŭi | 大義 |
| shōsōzu | 小僧都 | taichang si | 太常寺 |
| shōya | 庄屋 | taigukon | 対偶婚 |
| shuka | 主家 | tan | 反 |
| shukon | 主婚 | Tang | 唐 |
| "Shuluo shanpoyang" | 数落山坡羊 | tankon | 単婚 |
| Shusun Tong | 叔孫通 | tei | 帝 |
| sihoe | 詩會 | teisetsu | 貞節 |
| sijo | 詩調 | tennō | 天皇 |
| Silla | 新羅 | tenshi | 天子 |
| *Sillok* | 實錄 | terakoya | 寺子屋 |
| Sima Qian | 司馬遷 | tianli | 天理 |
| Sin Ch'aeho | 申采浩 | Tōkaidō | 東海道 |
| Sin Saimdang | 申師任堂 | "Tuoxi" | 攛兮 |
| *Sinjǔng tongguk yǒji sǔngnam* | 新增東國輿地勝覽 | ŭi | 義 |
| *sirhak* | 實學 | ŭmsa | 淫祀 |
| sōgōsho | 僧綱所 | utsushi'e | 写し絵 |
| *Sohak* | 小學 | | |
| Sohye (wanghu) | 昭惠王后 | waka | 和歌 |
| Sŏin | 西人 | wakan | 和漢 |
| *Sok samgang haengsilto* | 續三綱行實圖 | wakatō | 若党 |
| Sŏl Ch'ong | 薛聰 | Wang Fajin | 王法進 |
| sŏn | 善 | Wang Fengxian | 王奉仙 |
| Song | 嵩 | Wang Xiang | 王相 |
| Song | 宋 | Wang Zhaojun | 王昭君 |
| Song Siyŏl | 宋時烈 | wanwu | 萬物 |
| sŏngin | 聖人 | Wanyan Yun Zhu | 完顏惲珠 |
| Sŏngjong | 成宗 | | |

| | | | |
|---|---|---|---|
| watakushi | 私 | "Yimian pipa qiang-shang gua" | 一面琵琶牆上掛 |
| Wei Huacun | 魏華存 | | |
| wen | 文 | yin (musical note) | 音 |
| Wu Yun | 吳筠 | yin (female force) | 陰 |
| "Wugeng diao" | 五更調 | yin (hidden) | 隱 |
| wusheng | 五聲 | "Yinniusi" | 銀紐絲 |
| | | *Yi-ssi kamch'ŏn-gi* | 李氏感天記 |
| xianshu | 賢淑 | *Yŏbŏm* | 女範 |
| xiao | 孝 | *Yŏbŏm ch'ŏmnok* | 女範捷錄 |
| xiao jie | 孝節 | *Yŏgye* | 女誡 |
| xiao xing | 孝行 | *Yŏlbujŏn* | 列婦傳 |
| "Xiaohong dichang wo chuixiao" | 小紅低唱我吹簫 | *Yŏlburon* | 列婦論 |
| | | yŏllyŏ | 列女 |
| *Xiaojing* | 孝經 | *Yŏllyŏjŏn* | 列女傳 |
| xiaonü | 孝女 | yong | 庸 |
| *Xiaoxue* | 小學 | *Yongcheng jixian lu* | 墉城集仙錄 |
| Xijun | 細君 | *Yŏngjo* | 英祖 |
| Xu Wei | 徐渭 | *Yŏnonŏ* | 女論語 |
| Xu Xiangu | 徐仙姑 | yŏsa | 女史 |
| Xuanzong | 玄宗 | *Yŏsasŏ ŏnhae* | 女四書諺解 |
| Xue Xuantong | 薛玄同 | yu | 羽 |
| | | Yu Xuanji | 魚玄機 |
| *Yamato zokkun* | 大和俗訓 | Yuan Cai | 袁采 |
| yang | 陽 | *Yuan shi* | 元史 |
| yangqi | 養氣 | "Yubaodu" | 玉抱肚 |
| *Yanshi jiaxun* | 顏氏家訓 | yue | 樂 |
| yayue | 雅樂 | "Yueben bian" | 樂本篇 |
| ye | 禮 | Yuefu | 樂府 |
| Yejong | 睿宗 | *Yueji* | 樂記 |
| yi | 義 | "Yueli pian" | 樂禮篇 |
| Yi Chagyŏm | 李資謙 | *Yuelü quanshu* | 樂律全書 |
| Yi Ik | 李瀷 | *Yueshu* | 樂書 |
| Yi Saek | 李穡 | "Yuezi wanwan zhao jizhou" | 月子彎彎照几州 |
| Yi Sangjŏng | 李象靖 | | |
| Yi T'oegye | 李退溪 | Yun Chŭng | 尹拯 |
| Yi Tŏksu | 李德壽 | Yun Zhu | 惲珠 |
| Yi Yulgok | 李栗谷 | *Yunjidang yu'go* | 允摯堂遺稿 |

| | | | |
|---|---|---|---|
| zao | 躁 | zhong | 忠 |
| Zhang Honghong | 張紅紅 | *Zhongyong* | 中庸 |
| "Zhaonan" | 召南 | *Zhouguan* | 周官 |
| zheng | 正 | "Zhounan" | 周南 |
| Zheng Tian | 鄭畋 | Zhu Wuxia | 朱無瑕 |
| Zheng Yi | 鄭綺 | Zhu Xi | 朱熹 |
| *Zhengshi guifan* | 鄭氏規範 | Zhu Zaiyu | 朱載堉 |
| zhenlie | 貞烈 | zhunei | 主內 |
| zhennü | 貞女 | Zhuo wenjun | 卓文君 |
| zhenren | 眞人 | zongfa | 宗法 |
| zhi (moral conviction) | 志 | *Zuozhuan* | 左傳 |
| zhi (one of five tones) | 徵 | | |

## WOMEN AND GENDER IN CHINA

Bray, Francesca. *Technology and Gender: Fabrics of Power in Late Imperial China.* Berkeley: University of California Press, 1997.

Cahill, Suzanne E. *Transcendence and Divine Passion: The Queen Mother of the West in Medieval China.* Stanford: Stanford University Press, 1993.

Chang, Kang-I Sun, and Haun Saussy, eds. *Women Writers of Traditional China: An Anthology of Poetry and Criticism.* Stanford: Stanford University Press, 1999.

Deng Xiaonan. "Women in Turfan." *Journal of Asian Studies* 58.1 (1999): 85–103.

Ebrey, Patricia Buckley. "Conceptions of the Family in the Sung Dynasty." *Journal of Asian Studies* 43.2 (1984): 219–45.

———. *The Inner Quarters: Marriage and the Lives of Chinese Women in the Sung Period.* Berkeley: University of California Press, 1993.

———. "Women, Marriage and the Family." In *Heritage of China*, ed. Paul Ropp. Berkeley: University of California Press, 1990.

Furth, Charlotte. *A Flourishing Yin: Gender in China's Medical History, 960–1665.* Berkeley: University of California Press, 1999.

Ko, Dorothy. *Teachers of the Inner Chambers: Women and Culture in Seventeenth-Century China.* Stanford: Stanford University Press, 1994.

Mann, Susan. *Precious Records: Women in China's Long Eighteenth Century.* Stanford: Stanford University Press, 1997.

Paul, Diana. *Women in Buddhism.* Berkeley: University of California Press, 1985.

Raphals, Lisa. *Sharing the Light: Representations of Women and Virtue in Early China.* Albany: State University of New York Press, 1998.

Sommer, Matthew H. *Sex, Law, and Society in Late Imperial China.* Stanford: Stanford University Press, 2000.

Tsai, Kathryn Ann. *Lives of the Nuns: Biographies of Chinese Buddhist Nuns from the Fourth to Sixth Centuries.* Honolulu: University of Hawaii Press, 1994.

Zito, Angela. *Of Body and Brush: Grand Sacrifice as Text / Performance in Eighteenth-Century China.* Chicago: University of Chicago Press, 1997.

Zito, Angela, and Tani E. Barlow, eds. *Body, Subject, and Power in China.* Chicago: University of Chicago Press, 1994.


## WOMEN AND GENDER IN KOREA

Deuchler, Martina. *The Confucian Transformation of Korea.* Harvard-Yenching Monograph No. 36. Cambridge, Mass.: Council on East Asian Studies, Harvard University, 1992.

———. " 'Heaven Does Not Discriminate': A Study of Secondary Sons in Chosŏn Korea." *Journal of Korean Studies* 6 (1988–1989): 121–63.

Grayson, James. "Some Structural Patterns of the Royal Families of Ancient Korea." *Korea Journal* 16.6 (1976): 27–32.

Haboush, JaHyun Kim. "Filial Emotions and Filial Values: Changing Patterns in the Discourse of Filiality in Late Chosŏn Korea." *Harvard Journal of Asiatic Studies* 55.1 (June 1995): 129–77.

———. *The Memoirs of Lady Hyegyŏng: The Autobiographical Writings of a Crown Princess of Eighteenth-Century Korea.* Berkeley: University of California Press, 1996.

Phil, Marshall. *The Korean Singer of Tales.* Harvard-Yenching Institute Monograph. Cambridge, Mass.: Council on East Asian Studies, Harvard University, 1994.

Rutt, Richard, and Chong-Un Kim, eds. *Virtuous Women: Three Classic Korean Novels.* Seoul: Royal Asiatic Society, Korea Branch, 1974.

Walraven, Boudewijn. "Muga: The Songs of Korean Shamanism." Ph.D. dissertation, Leiden University, the Netherlands, 1985.

———. "Popular Religion in a Confucianized Society." In *Culture and the State in Late Chosŏn Korea,* ed. JaHyun Kim Haboush and Martina Deuchler. Harvard East Asian Monograph. Cambridge, Mass.: Asia Center, Harvard University, 1999.


## WOMEN AND GENDER IN JAPAN

Bargen, Doris. *A Woman's Weapon: Spirit Possession in the "Tale of Genji."* Honolulu: University of Hawaii Press, 1997.

Bernstein, Gail Lee, ed. *Recreating Japanese Women, 1600–1945.* Berkeley: University of California Press, 1991.

Brazell, Karen, trans. *Confessions of Lady Nijō.* Stanford: Stanford University Press, 1980.

Edwards, Walter. "In Pursuit of Himiko." *Monumenta Nipponica* 51.1 (1996): 53–80.

Ellwood, Robert. "Patriarchal Revolution." *Journal of Feminist Studies in Religion* 2.2 (1986): 23–37.

———. "The *Saigū.*" *History of Religions* 7 (1967): 35–60.

———. "Sujin Religious Revolution." *Japanese Journal of Religious Studies* 17.2–3 (1990): 199–217.

Faure, Bernard. *The Red Thread: Buddhist Approaches to Sexuality.* Princeton: Princeton University Press, 1998.

Field, Norma. *Splendor of Longing.* Princeton: Princeton University Press, 1987.

Goodwin, Janet R. "Shadows of Transgression: Heian and Kamakura Constructions of Prostitution." *Monumenta Nipponica* 55.3 (2000): 327–68.

Hurst, G. Cameron. "Heian Kinship." In *Insei: Abdicated Sovereigns in the Politics of Late Heian Japan, 1086–1185.* New York: Columbia University Press, 1976.

Marra, Michele. "Buddhist Myth-making of Defilement." *Journal of Asian Studies* 52.1 (1993): 49–65.

Matsumae, T. "The Heavenly Rock-Grotto Myth." *Asian Folklore Studies* 39.2 (1980): 9–22.

———. "Origin and Growth of Worship of Amaterasu." *Asian Folklore Studies* 37.1 (1978): 1–11.

McCullough, William H. "Japanese Marriage Institutions in the Heian Period." *Harvard Journal of Asiatic Studies* 27 (1967): 103–67.

Mulhern, Chieko. *Japanese Women Writers, a Bio-critical Sourcebook.* Westport, Conn.: Greenwood Press, 1994.

Mulhern, Chieko, ed. *Heroic with Grace: Legendary Women of Japan.* Armonk, N.Y.: M. E. Sharpe, 1991.

Nakamura, L. "The Significance of Amaterasu." In *Book of the Goddess, Past and Present: An Introduction to Her Religion,* ed. Carl Olsen. New York: Crossroad, 1983.

Nickerson, Peter. "Matrilocality." *Monumenta Nipponica* 48.4 (1994): 429–67.

Nishimura, H. "The Family, Communal Ties, and Women." In *Historical Studies in Japan, 1983–87,* vol. 7, ed. National Committee of Japan Historians. Tokyo: Yamakawa shuppan, 1988.

Pflugfelder, G. "Strange Fates." *Monumenta Nipponica* 47.3 (1992): 347–68.

Tonomura, Hitomi. "Long Black Hair and Red Trousers: Gendering the Flesh in Medieval Japan." *American Historical Review* 99.1 (1994): 129–54.

———. "Re-envisioning Women in the Post-Kamakura Age." In *The Origins of Japan's Medieval World,* ed. Jeffrey P. Mass. Stanford: Stanford University Press, 1997.

———. "Women and Inheritance in Japan's Early Warrior Society." *Comparative Studies in Society and History* 32.3 (1990): 592–623.

Tonomura, Hitomi, Anne Walthall, and Haruko Wakita, eds. *Women and Class in Japanese History.* Ann Arbor: Center for Japanese Studies, University of Michigan, 1999.

Wakita, Haruko. "Marriage and Property in Premodern Japan." *Journal of Japanese Studies* 10.1 (1984): 73–99.

Walthall, Anne. *The Weak Body of a Useless Woman: Matsuo Taseko and the Meiji Restoration.* Chicago: University of Chicago Press, 1998.

Yamakawa, Kikue. *Women of the Mito Domain: Recollections of Samurai Family Life.* Trans. Kate Wildman Nakai. Stanford: Stanford University Press, 2000.

*Suzanne E. Cahill* received her Ph.D. in Oriental languages from the University of California, Berkeley. She teaches Chinese history, Asian religions, and women's studies as an adjunct associate professor at the University of California, San Diego. She has published on women's poetry, religious practice, and art in medieval China. She is the author of *Transcendence and Divine Passion: The Queen Mother of the West in Medieval China* (Stanford University Press, 1993). Currently she is working on Tang dynasty Daoist women and Tang material culture.

*Martina Deuchler* is Professor Emerita of Korean History at the School of Oriental and African Studies of the University of London. She studied Chinese at the University of Leiden and received her Ph.D. in history from Harvard University. She has worked on the social and intellectual history of Chosŏn Korea. Her publications include *Confucian Gentlemen and Barbarian Envoys* (University of Washington Press, 1977) and *The Confucian Transformation of Korea: A Study of Society and Ideology* (Council on East Asian Studies, Harvard University, 1992). In addition, she coedited *Culture and the State in Late Chosŏn Korea* (Asia Center, Harvard University, 1999).

*Fangqin Du* is Director and a founder of the Women's Studies Center at Tianjin Normal University, China, where she is a professor at its Research Institute in Rare Books. She received graduate training in the linguistics of ancient Chinese at Henan University and is a specialist in the history of women and gender in ancient China. Her many books in Chinese include *The Evolution of Concepts of Women* (1988), *Selected Works of the Peasant Woman Poet He Shuangqing* (1993), and *Trajectories of Gender in Chinese History and Culture* (1998).

*JaHyun Kim Haboush* is King Sejong Professor of Korean Studies at Columbia University, where she received her Ph.D. in East Asian languages and cultures. Her recent research has concentrated on the problems of premodern national identity and the dual linguistic culture of Korea. Her publications include *A Heritage of Kings: One Man's Monarchy in the Confucian World* (Columbia University Press, 1988) and *The Memoirs of Lady Hyegyŏng: The Autobiographical Writings of a Crown Princess of Eighteenth-Century Korea* (University of California Press, 1996). Also, she coedited *Culture and the State in Late Chosŏn Korea* (Asia Center, Harvard University, 1999).

*Dorothy Ko*, a native of Hong Kong, received her Ph.D. in East Asian history from Stanford University. She is the author of *Teachers of the Inner Chambers: Women and Culture in Seventeenth-Century China* (Stanford University Press, 1994) and *Every Step a Lotus: Shoes for Bound Feet* (University of California Press, 2002). Her current research focuses on clothing, bodies, and civility in premodern East Asia. She is Professor of History at Barnard College, Columbia University.

*Joseph S. C. Lam* is Associate Professor of Music at the University of Michigan. He is the author of *State Sacrifices and Music in Ming China: Orthodoxy, Creativity, and Expressiveness* (SUNY Press, 1998) and many articles on Chinese and Asian American musics and cultures. Currently, he is working on a monograph on Southern Song Chinese state sacrificial music and music historiography.

*Hai-soon Lee* is Professor of Korean and Comparative Literature at Ewha Woman's University, Seoul, Korea. She studied Korean and comparative literature at Seoul National University and the University of Illinois and received her Ph.D. from National Taiwan Normal University. She has published extensively in Korean, including *Comparative Literature: Theory and Practice* (1981) and *Literature of Korean Envoys to Japan* (1996). She was recently elected president of the Society of Korean Classical Women's Literature.

*Susan Mann* is Professor of History at the University of California, Davis. She received her Ph.D. in Asian languages from Stanford University in 1972. Her recent research has focused on family and gender relations in the history of the Qing dynasty. She is most recently the author of *Precious Records: Women in China's Long Eighteenth Century* (Stanford University Press, 1997) and coeditor (with Yu-Yin Cheng) of *Under Confucian Eyes: Writings on Gender in Chinese History* (University of California Press, 2001).

*Joan R. Piggott* is the Gordon L. Macdonald Professor of Pre-1600 Japanese History at the University of Southern California, where she directs the newly established Project for Japanese Premodern Historical Studies and the Kambun Workshops. Her publications include *The Emergence of Japanese Kingship* (Stanford University Press, 1997) as well as the forthcoming *Capital and Countryside in Japan, 300–1180* and *Regent Fujiwara Tadahira: The Year 939 in His Journal, "Teishinkoki."*

*Hiroko Sekiguchi* received her B.A. from Tokyo University. Having taught high school and raised a family, she obtained an M.A. degree from Tokyo Metropolitan University and a Ph.D. degree from Tokyo University. As an independent scholar, she devoted thirty-five years to the research of the ancient legal, family, and marriage systems in Japan. Her two-volume book, *A Study of the History of Marriage in Ancient Japan*, was published in Japanese in 1993. A recent book, also in Japanese, is *A Study of the Otomezuka Lore: Tragedy of a Beauty Who Had Multiple Husbands* (1996).

*Noriko Sugano* is Professor at Teikyō University, Japan. A specialist in the economic and social histories of early modern Japan, she received her M.A. degree from the Tokyo Metropolitan University in 1964. She is the author of *Village and Reform: Studies in Rural and Women's History* (1992) and *Filial Exemplars in Edo Japan* (1999), both published in Japanese. She has also published on the topics of women's work, child rearing, and the relationship between patriarchy and commoner families.

*Martha C. Tocco* is an independent scholar living in Los Angeles, California. She received her Ph.D. in Japanese history from Stanford University in 1995.

*Jian Zang* is Associate Research Fellow at the Institute for Ancient History at Beijing University, where she also serves as Lecturer in History. Having worked in the fields and factories in Inner Mongolia during the Cultural Revolution, she returned to obtain a B.A. degree in history from Beijing University in 1975. Her research ranges from medieval history to gender equality and from development to bibliography. She has published more than twenty research articles on women's history and girl's education in China and is the chief editor of a major reference work in Chinese, *Annotated Bibliography of Works on Chinese Women in the Recent Century* (1993).

# INDEX

Indexer: Margie Towery
Compositor: Impressions Book and Journal Services, Inc.
Text: 10/12 Baskerville
Display: Baskerville
Printer and Binder: Edwards Brothers